Russia's invasion of Ukraine is one of the most important conflicts of the twenty-first century. With the start of military hostilities in 2014 also came an onslaught of propaganda, to both convince and confuse audiences worldwide about the war's historical and ideological underpinnings. Based on extensive research drawing on tens of thousands of news articles and hundreds of pages of legal documents and internal correspondence, this book offers the first comprehensive analysis of the role of propaganda, ideology, and identity in the Russian–Ukrainian war. It argues that, despite Russia's efforts to set up a media machine at home and abroad with eight years of propaganda legitimising Russia's presence in eastern Ukraine, Russia failed to vocalise a convincing alternative to Ukrainian nationhood. Instead, Russian propaganda backfired: Ukraine is now more united than ever before.

Jon Roozenbeek is an award-winning researcher whose work straddles psychology, area studies, and computer science. He studies the psychology of misinformation and group identity in times of conflict. Roozenbeek holds a PhD in Slavonic Studies from the University of Cambridge and is the author of *The Psychology of Misinformation* (Cambridge University Press, 2024) with Sander van der Linden.

Contemporary Social Issues Series

General Editor: Brian D. Christens, *Vanderbilt University*

Contemporary Social Issues is the official book series of the Society for the Psychological Study of Social Issues (SPSSI). Since its founding in 1936, SPSSI has addressed the social issues of the times. Central to these efforts has been the Lewinian tradition of action-oriented research, in which psychological theories and methods guide research and action addressed to important societal problems. Grounded in their authors' programmes of research, works in this series focus on social issues facing individuals, groups, communities, and/or society at large, with each volume written to speak to scholars, students, practitioners, and policymakers.

Other Books in the Series

Propaganda and Ideology in the Russian–Ukrainian War

Jon Roozenbeek

University of Cambridge

CAMBRIDGE
UNIVERSITY PRESS

CAMBRIDGE
UNIVERSITY PRESS

Shaftesbury Road, Cambridge CB2 8EA, United Kingdom

One Liberty Plaza, 20th Floor, New York, NY 10006, USA

477 Williamstown Road, Port Melbourne, VIC 3207, Australia

314–321, 3rd Floor, Plot 3, Splendor Forum, Jasola District Centre, New Delhi – 110025, India

103 Penang Road, #05-06/07, Visioncrest Commercial, Singapore 238467

Cambridge University Press is part of Cambridge University Press & Assessment, a department of the University of Cambridge.

We share the University's mission to contribute to society through the pursuit of education, learning and research at the highest international levels of excellence.

www.cambridge.org
Information on this title: www.cambridge.org/9781009244015

DOI: 10.1017/9781009244039

First published 2024

A catalogue record for this publication is available from the British Library.

Library of Congress Cataloging-in-Publication Data
Names: Roozenbeek, Jon, 1990- author.
TITLE: Propaganda and ideology in the Russian-Ukrainian war / Jon Roozenbeek, University of Cambridge.
DESCRIPTION: Cambridge, United Kingdom ; New York, NY : Cambridge University Press, 2024. | Series: Contemporary social issues series | Includes bibliographical references and index.
IDENTIFIERS: LCCN 2024005655 (print) | LCCN 2024005656 (ebook) | ISBN 9781009244015 (hardback) | ISBN 9781009244008 (paperback) | ISBN 9781009244008 (epub)
SUBJECTS: LCSH: Russo-Ukrainian War, 2014—Propaganda. | Russo-Ukrainian War, 2014- | Propaganda, Russian. | Propaganda, Anti-Ukrainian–Russia (Federation) | Hybrid warfare–Russia (Federation) | Russia (Federation)–Foreign relations–21st century. | Russia (Federation)–Foreign relations–Ukraine. | Ukraine–Foreign relations–Russia (Federation) | National characteristics, Ukrainian.
CLASSIFICATION: LCC DK5529.P76 R66 2024 (print) | LCC DK5529.P76 (ebook) | DDC 303.3750947–dc23/eng/20240206
LC record available at https://lccn.loc.gov/2024005655
LC ebook record available at https://lccn.loc.gov/2024005656

ISBN 978-1-009-24401-5 Hardback
ISBN 978-1-009-24400-8 Paperback

CONTENTS

FIGURES

MAPS

TABLES

ACKNOWLEDGEMENTS

I have many people to thank for helping me write this book. First of all, I would like to thank my doctoral supervisor, Rory Finnin, who has supported me ever since I emailed him on a whim with my PhD proposal in 2015. Second, as part of the research that went into this book I have spent substantial amounts of time in Kramatorsk, Donetsk oblast. Many people, but especially Tetiana Ivanova-Zhadan, helped make my stay there extremely comfortable, and I am forever indebted to them for all their help. The same goes for Oleksiy Matsuka and the wonderful people at the Donbas Media Forum. Third, I am grateful to the Section of Slavonic Studies and the Department of Psychology at the University of Cambridge, and particularly Sander van der Linden, for their hospitality and for hosting my research activities for such a long time. The same goes for the members of the Cambridge Social Decision-Making Lab and the MMLL Grad Centre. I also wish to express my thanks to Janka Romero, Rowan Groat, Neema Jayasinghe, Emily Watton, Laura Simmons, and Brian Christens of Cambridge University Press, who have been of great help commissioning, editing, and revising this book. I am also thankful to Hiroaki Kuromiya and Harald Wydra, who read the PhD dissertation on which this book is based in great detail and gave me many helpful comments. My dear friend Adrià Salvador Palau also provided a lot of incredibly useful and detailed suggestions, as did Andrii Smytsniuk. Finally, I wish to thank Yara Kyrychenko, whose doctoral research I've had the privilege of supervising. Her brilliant work has helped me better understand the dynamics of identity and ideology in wartime Ukraine.

NOTE ON TRANSLITERATION

This book uses sources that were originally written in Ukrainian and Russian. To display relevant terms in Latin script, I use a simplified version of the US Library of Congress transliteration system for modern Russian and Ukrainian (without ligatures for purposes of readability). Places in parts of Ukraine often have both a Russian and a Ukrainian name. I use the Russian transliteration when referring to places, proper names, or organisations in the Donetsk and Luhansk oblasts, as Russian is the dominant spoken language here, and the Russian version of names are the most commonly used (e.g., the newspaper *Makeevskii Rabochii*). For places located outside Donetsk and Luhansk oblasts (e.g., Kyiv and not Kiev, Kharkiv and not Kharkov), I use the Ukrainian transliteration, as well as for Ukrainian proper names (e.g., Volodymyr Zelensky). The only exceptions are the name of the city of Luhansk, which is written as 'Luhansk' and not 'Lugansk', and Donbas, which is written as such and not 'Donbass'. Finally, to avoid confusion, some proper names (e.g., Boris Yeltsin, Viktor Yushchenko, Viktor Yanukovych) are spelled in the way that they appear most commonly in popular media.

ABBREVIATIONS

ATO   anti-terrorist operation
DNR   Donetsk People's Republic (*Donetskaia Narodnaia Respublika*)
LNR   Luhansk People's Republic (*Luganskaia Narodnaia Respublika*)
ORDLO Separate Raions of Donetsk and Luhansk Oblasts (*okremi raiony Donetskoï ta Luhanskoï oblastei*)
OSCE   Organization for Security and Co-operation in Europe
SBU   Security Service of Ukraine (*Sluzhba Bezpeky Ukraïny*)
VSU   Armed Forces of Ukraine (*vooruzhennye sily Ukrainy* [Ru.])
ZSU   Armed Forces of Ukraine (*zbroini syly Ukraïny* [Ukr.])

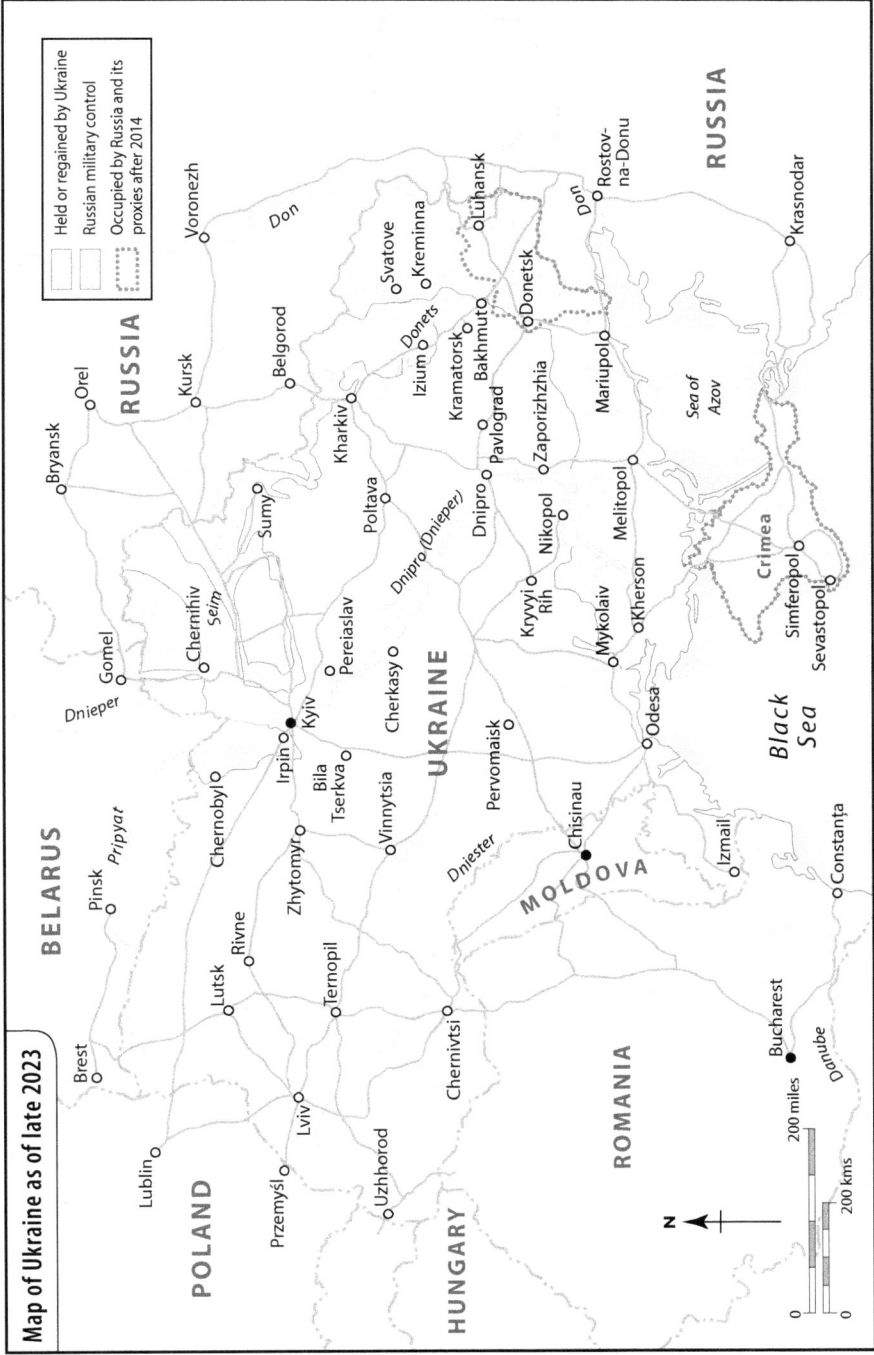

Map of Ukraine as of late 2023

Legend:
- Held or regained by Ukraine
- Russian military control
- Occupied by Russia and its proxies after 2014

POLAND

BELARUS

RUSSIA

HUNGARY

ROMANIA

MOLDOVA

UKRAINE

RUSSIA

Black Sea

Sea of Azov

Crimea

Brest
Lublin
Przemyśl
Lviv
Uzhhorod
Lutsk
Rivne
Ternopil
Chernivtsi
Pinsk
Gomel
Chernobyl
Zhytomyr
Vinnytsia
Bila Tserkva
Irpin
Kyiv
Chernihiv
Pereiaslav
Cherkasy
Pervomaisk
Chisinau
Izmail
Constanța
Bucharest
Odesa
Mykolaiv
Kherson
Kryvyi Rih
Nikopol
Melitopol
Simferopol
Sevastopol
Zaporizhzhia
Pavlograd
Dnipro
Poltava
Sumy
Bryansk
Orel
Kursk
Belgorod
Kharkiv
Izium
Kramatorsk
Bakhmuto
Donetsk
Luhansk
Svatove
Kreminna
Voronezh
Mariupol
Rostov-na-Donu
Krasnodar

Pripyat
Dnieper
Seim
Dnipro (Dnieper)
Dniester
Danube
Don
Donets
Don

200 miles
200 kms
N

MAP 0.1 Map of Ukraine as of late 2023 (www.dvdmaps.co.uk/).

Map of Donbas as of late 2023

Occupied by Russia and its proxies after 2014

Occupied by Russia after February 24th, 2022

Kharkiv

UKRAINE

Svatove

Kreminna

Lyman

Severodonetsk

Donets

Sloviansk

Lysychansk

Stantsiia Luhanska

Kramatorsk

Bakhmut

Stakhanov

Luhansk

Konstantynivka

Alchevsk

Donets

Krasnoarmiisk

Gorlovka

Debaltsevo

LNR

Krasnodon

Enakievo

Antratsyt

Rovenki

Avdiivka

Krasnyi Luch

Shakthersk

Sverdlovsk

Makeevka

Khartsyzk

Donetsk

Ilovaisk

Torez

Amvrosiivka

DNR

RUSSIA

Vuhledar

Volnovakha

Telmanovo

Taganrog

Rostov-na-Donu

Zaporizhzhia

N

Azov

Mariupol

0   40 miles

0   40 kms

Sea of Azov

DNR refers to Donetsk People's Republic and LNR to Luhansk People's Republic.

MAP 0.2 Map of Donbas as of late 2023 (www.dvdmaps.co.uk/).

Introduction

In the early hours of February 24, 2022, Russian president Vladimir Putin ordered his armies to 'demilitarise and denazify' Ukraine, and Europe was changed. Within minutes, Russian missiles struck most major Ukrainian cities, and scores of military units began pouring in from Crimea in the south, Donetsk in the east, and Belarus in the north. Their goal was to encircle Kyiv, Ukraine's capital located in the country's north, and overthrow the government. Ukrainian president Volodymyr Zelensky, who had addressed the Russian people that same night in his native Russian pleading with them to oppose the invasion, declared martial law and ordered the Ukrainian Armed Forces to fire at will.

This 'special operation' did not go as Putin expected. Russia sent its elite paratrooper division, the VDV (*vozdushno-desantnye voiska*), to take over Hostomel airport ten kilometres north of Kyiv and establish air superiority. The plan was to provide a forward operating base for the planned assault on Kyiv, which failed almost completely. The VDV managed to briefly capture Hostomel on February 24, but were met with fierce resistance from the inexperienced Ukrainian soldiers and volunteers stationed there. Recognising the airport's strategic importance, Ukrainian general Valery Zaluzhnyi ordered a large-scale counterattack by both ground troops and the Air Force. By evening, his forces had pushed back the VDV and re-established control of Hostomel. Failing to adapt to a changing situation, Russia's plans for a lightning war quickly became unrealistic. With large numbers of military vehicles bogged down in a forty-mile traffic jam, frustrated Russian forces resorted to cruelty. Images of civilians tortured to death in Bucha and Irpin, two towns north of Kyiv briefly occupied by Russia, shocked the world. Ukraine, meanwhile, proved adept at military strategy and made effective use of Western weaponry.

Russia's assault on Kyiv was a disaster. By April, Russian troops had withdrawn entirely from northern Ukraine, and redirected their attention towards the east and south. The goal of the invasion became the 'liberation of

Donbas' rather than the 'demilitarisation and denazification' of all of Ukraine (BBC News, 2022b). Donbas refers to the Donets Basin, the catchment area of the Donets River, which flows through southwest Russia and eastern Ukraine. The Ukrainian part of Donbas consists mainly of the *oblasts*, or provinces, of Donetsk and Luhansk. The region has a long and storied history, being a former part of the Russian Empire as well as independent Ukraine. Its (waning) preference for the Russian language over Ukrainian, however, shouldn't prompt the assumption that the people of Donbas are Ukrainian in name only. The matter of Donbas identity is one of the questions at the heart of this book.

Nonetheless, Russia's eastern and southern offensives were, at least in a military sense, more successful than its botched assault on Kyiv. Large parts of Kharkiv, Donetsk, Luhansk, Zaporizhzhia, and Kherson oblasts fell under Russian occupation, and the key cities of Kherson and Mariupol were captured, the latter after a months-long, bloody battle. In September 2022, Russian authorities organised 'referendums' in the occupied parts of these four oblasts, to formalise their incorporation into the Russian Federation. Between 87 and 99 per cent of referendum participants supposedly voted in favour of this proposition (Minzagov, 2022). Russia announced the 'annexation' of these territories shortly after, although there was confusion over whether it claimed to have incorporated all four oblasts in their entirety, or merely the parts that it actually controlled.

Meanwhile, fighting continued unabated. Ukraine staged a successful counteroffensive, retaking large parts of Kharkiv oblast and the strategically important southern city of Kherson during the autumn of 2022. After a lull during the winter of 2022–2023, Ukraine renewed its efforts to retake its territories in the spring. This second counteroffensive yielded diminishing returns, with limited territorial gains on both the Russian and the Ukrainian side. Although both Russia and Ukraine have been on the initiative at various moments throughout 2023 and 2024, major momentum shifts have become increasingly rare.

The outcome of the war is as yet unclear, and can range from all-out victory for Ukraine and the collapse of Russia to a prolonged territorial stalemate or a limited, Pyrrhic Russian victory (Plokhy, 2023). But whatever happens, it's clear that Russia has failed to achieve its initial objectives, namely, to seize Kyiv, oust Zelensky, and install a puppet government. More than two years into the war, it's increasingly unlikely that this will pan out even if Russia's fortunes reverse.

But Russia's invasion isn't a failure only in the military sense. In this book, I examine the impotence of the propaganda campaign that preceded it. Despite enormous efforts to set up a sprawling media machine at home and abroad, and eight years of propaganda aimed at legitimising Russia's presence in eastern Ukraine, Russia never managed to vocalise a convincing alternative to Ukrainian identity and nationhood. Instead, Russia's efforts backfired: Ukraine is now more united than ever before. Russian-speaking Ukrainians, at times sceptical of Ukrainian nationalism and western Ukrainians' desire for integration with the EU, are now almost unanimously siding with Zelensky against Russia. If ever there was a chance to lure Donbas and southern Ukraine into the Russian fold, it is now gone forever, not only because of Russia's military aggression but also thanks to its inability to understand, or take seriously, Ukrainian and Donbas identity.

To understand why, we must go back to the start of the Russian-Ukrainian War, eight years before the 2022 full-scale invasion. On February 21, 2014, months of pro-European demonstrations on Kyiv's Maidan Nezalezhnosti (Independence Square) resulted in the flight of Ukraine's then-president Viktor Yanukovych from office. This event, locally referred to as the 'revolution of dignity' but known in the West as the Euromaidan Revolution, led to fundamental changes in Ukraine's political, societal and geographical make-up. Soon after Yanukovych's cabinet was deposed by parliament and a new, pro-Western government was sworn in, groups of masked men in unmarked uniforms began to appear in strategic locations throughout Crimea, a peninsula in the country's south. These armed men captured local administration buildings and army bases, and took over the Crimean parliament building and installed a new, pro-Russian local government. After a 'referendum' was held on March 16, the new Crimean parliament issued a declaration of independence from Ukraine. Russia formally annexed Crimea two days later, in contravention of international law (Grant, 2015). Crimea became de facto if not de jure Russian territory, despite widespread international condemnation and unresolved legal disputes.

Around the same time, pro-Russian and anti-Euromaidan demonstrations began to pop up throughout southern and eastern Ukraine. Donbas became a hotbed of protest, with demonstrations escalating into violent clashes between (local and non-local) protesters, law enforcement, and pro-Ukrainian activist groups. In Donetsk, the capital of Donetsk oblast, pro-Russian activists occupied the city's Regional State Administration building between March 1 and March 6, until they were removed by the Ukrainian security services. One month later, on April 6, some 1,000–2,000 people gathered in front of the same building once again, this time demanding a status referendum similar to the one held in Crimea and threatening to capture the regional government by 'people's mandate' (BBC News, 2014a). When their demands were not met, the protesters again occupied the building. Inside, a meeting was held in which the attendants voted to declare independence from Ukraine and to proclaim the 'Donetsk People's Republic' (*Donetskaia Narodnaia Respublika*; DNR). In the weeks that followed, armed groups took over various administration buildings and infrastructure in other towns and cities in Donetsk oblast. Then-acting

Ukrainian president Oleksandr Turchynov launched a large-scale 'anti-terrorist operation' (ATO) against the DNR. Russia sent equipment and military personnel across the border to support the insurgency (Bellingcat, 2018). The Russian–Ukrainian War started right here, and not, as is sometimes assumed, in 2022 (Hauter, 2021, 2023).

Also on April 6, pro-Russian protesters in Luhansk, the capital of Luhansk oblast (which borders Donetsk as well as Russia), seized the office of the local Security Service of Ukraine (*Sluzhba Bezpeky Ukraïny*; SBU). Security forces were quickly able to recapture the building, but around 2,000 protesters gathered outside for a 'people's assembly' to demand federalisation or outright independence. Clashes continued, and on April 27, the protesters, now in control of various regional administration offices, proclaimed the 'Luhansk People's Republic' (*Luganskaia Narodnaia Respublika*; LNR) and announced that they would fight alongside the DNR (RFE/RL, 2014).

A violent confrontation with the Ukrainian army followed. For much of 2014 and part of 2015, swaths of territory in the Luhansk and Donetsk oblasts changed hands multiple times between ATO forces and the insurgents, who shared the same enemy but not always the same goals. Conflicts between rivalling militias within the DNR and LNR would erupt with regularity, and power in the region was divided between various armed groups (Mitrokhin, 2015). Although it's not correct to refer to the conflict as a 'civil war' due to Russia's direct involvement, the new DNR and LNR authorities remained in control of parts of Donbas between 2014 and 2022, and sought to build legitimacy and popular support for their unrecognised breakaway from Ukraine.

A core component of these efforts was the mass media. Right from the start of their insurgency, the DNR and LNR set up a large and well-funded propaganda machine of TV channels, websites, and newspapers. Their purpose was to bring their story to the masses, both internally (i.e., the people living in DNR and LNR territory) and externally (mainly Ukrainians living in Donbas, but also Russians and even Western audiences). This provided a huge opportunity to promote the DNR's and LNR's ideology, and to try to build support for the idea that Donbas doesn't belong with Ukraine.

In this book, I argue that this opportunity was never seized. In a series of diatribes, including a much-publicised interview with the American conservative activist Tucker Carlson in February 2024, Vladimir Putin has argued that the root causes of his war can be found in the histories and identities of the Russian and Ukrainian peoples, but the data presented here shows that this is false. Despite a vast reservoir of ideological and historical referents to draw from, neither the DNR/LNR nor Russia cared much for ideology or history at all, and to their peril. All attempts to build a collective identity (an 'ingroup') were short-lived, vocalised rarely and inconsistently on the pages of local newspapers and websites. Meanwhile, the outgroup, or the 'they' that opposes the 'we', was subject to a highly detailed and rich discursive construction. Internally (addressing the local population), this outgroup-focused discourse hearkened back to past conflicts, primarily World War II, and projected a sense of guilt on the part of Ukraine towards Donbas. Externally (addressing audiences outside the DNR and LNR, primarily Russian-speaking Ukrainians), this discourse ignored history altogether, and instead projected a sense of shame rather than guilt, seeking to discredit the Ukrainian government without reference to a shared connection that was lost.

The result of this propaganda campaign was that many Russians came to view Ukraine and Ukrainians in a much more negative light, to the point where many continue to feel that the 2022 invasion was a justified course of action against an illegitimate, 'fascist' regime. In occupied Donbas, few were convinced by the ideological propositions of the DNR and LNR, although the idea of unification with Russia became somewhat more popular. In Kyiv-controlled Donbas and everywhere else in Ukraine, however, the events of Euromaidan and the war that followed served as a catalyst for Ukrainian identity, building on developments set in motion by the Orange Revolution of 2004, Ukraine's independence from the Soviet Union in 1991, and the preceding centuries of Ukrainian nation building. Instead of directing their discontent at Kyiv, Russian-speaking Ukrainians settled into a civic yet explicitly nationalist Ukrainian identity.

SCOPE AND CHAPTER OUTLINE

Based on extensive research drawing on tens of thousands of news articles and hundreds of pages of legal documents and internal correspondence, this book offers the first comprehensive analysis of the role of propaganda, ideology, and identity in wartime Ukraine. It's helpful to first explain what I mean by these terms. Propaganda refers to 'the more or less systematic effort to manipulate other people's beliefs, attitudes, or actions by means of symbols', which includes all forms of media output (B. L. Smith, 2023). By ideology I here specifically mean *political* ideology, or 'a set of ideas, beliefs, values, and opinions, exhibiting a recurring pattern, that competes deliberately as well as unintentionally over providing plans of action for public policy making in an attempt to justify, explain, contest, or change the social and political arrangements and processes of a political community' (Freeden, 2001). And finally, this book focuses on *group* identity in the tradition of social identity theory, which relates to how people see themselves in relation to their membership of social groups, both 'ingroups', or groups that an individual experiences kinship with, and 'outgroups', groups with which an individual does not identify (Tajfel, 1982).

This book is based in large part on research I conducted between 2016 and 2020 as part of my PhD dissertation (Roozenbeek, 2020b), which served as a preprint for this publication. It is made up of six chapters. Chapter 1 provides a backdrop to the current conflict, detailing Russian–Ukrainian relations and the emergence of Ukrainian identity from the ninth century until today. Chapter 2 looks at political developments inside the DNR and LNR between 2014 and 2022, focusing especially on the role of ideological projects. Chapter 3 examines the development of the DNR and LNR media landscapes, and how the authorities took control over local media to set up a powerful propaganda machine.

Chapters 4–6 are empirical, drawing on large volumes of data obtained from local DNR and LNR newspapers and websites to identify the most prevalent narratives aimed at local and external audiences. To do so, I make use of a variety of automated content analysis methods, primarily topic modelling. For an explanation of how these methodologies work, I refer to Appendix A at the back of this book. Chapter 4 explores the content of twenty-six DNR and LNR newspapers, to see what stories and narratives residents inside the DNR/LNR were subjected to during the period of occupation. Chapter 5 looks at DNR and LNR internet media, and the differences between media content that is exclusively aimed at locals (i.e., local newspapers) and content that is also intended for external consumption (news sites). Finally, Chapter 6 explores the consequences of this years-long propaganda campaign in terms of how it affected people's attitudes and sense of collective identity in Russia, Donbas, and the rest of Ukraine. I examine the content of two local newspapers from Kramatorsk, a city that was under DNR occupation for a brief period in 2014, as well as social media and survey data from Ukraine collected between 2016 and 2022. My focus is thus on media discourse produced by Russia and its proxies; I do not discuss media content production by Ukrainian media, or the efforts by the Ukrainian government to persuade and inform audiences domestically and abroad. For this, I refer to work by other scholars such as Olga Onuch (2018), Taras Fedirko (2020, 2021), Volodymyr Kulyk (2006), Dariya Orlova (2016), and Marta Dyczok (2016).

The empirical nature of this book, which relies in large part on data collected over the course of seven years of research, prohibits me from providing all information necessary to replicate my analyses in written form. I have therefore created an online appendix on the Open Science Foundation's public repository: https://osf.io/3846a/. Here, readers can find my original data sets (primarily the contents of DNR and LNR newspapers and news sites and summaries of legal documents), analysis scripts (written in Python) and resulting topic models, data scraping permissions, and additional background information that I could not include in this book or the appendices. I will refer to this online appendix in footnotes where relevant.

Finally, it is difficult if not impossible to write about historical events as they are unfolding. By the time you read this, some information (for example, about territorial control) is likely to be outdated. Nonetheless, I have done my best to ensure that this book provides as comprehensive an analysis as possible of the Russian–Ukrainian War, and the role (or lack thereof) that propaganda and ideology have played in Europe's foremost theatre of conflict.

1

A History of Russian–Ukrainian Relations

INTRODUCTION

INTRODUCTION

This chapter covers Russian–Ukrainian relations from the ninth century onwards. I discuss three different time periods: pre-Soviet times (ninth century CE until about 1921), the Soviet era (1921–1991), and the period between the fall of the Soviet Union and Ukrainian independence in 1991 and the Euromaidan revolution of 2014. The purpose of this chapter is to explain the historical ties between the two countries and to illustrate how their shared and separate histories serve as a backdrop to the ongoing Russian–Ukrainian War. Of course, it is not possible to cover 1,200 years of history in sufficient detail in a single chapter. I therefore refer to works by Serhii Plokhy, Paul Robert Magosci, Andrew Wilson, Anne Applebaum, Volodymyr Kulyk, Olga Onuch, and Timothy Snyder, whose excellent research on Ukraine's storied history I've relied on a great deal for this chapter.

BEFORE THE SOVIET UNION

The ongoing debate about Ukrainian identity that is at the centre of this book starts at Ukraine's (and Russia's) very conception, with the rise of Kyivan Rus' in the late ninth century (Magosci, 2010, chapter 5; Wilson, 2022). These lands were Christianised in 988, when Prince Volodymyr I abolished paganism and required all citizens of Kyivan Rus' to be baptised. At its peak under Iaroslav the Wise in the eleventh century, this amalgam of political entities stretched from the mouth of the river Dnipro in southern Ukraine to present-day Karelia in north-western Russia, near the border with Finland. Opinions about the origins of Kyivan Rus' diverge (Plokhy, 2015, p. 41), with some scholars (the Normanists) arguing that it has its roots in Scandinavia, most likely the Swedish coastal district of Uppland. Under this theory, the name Rus' is said to come from *ruotsi*, the Finnish name for Sweden (or from Roslagen, the name of a Swedish coastal region). On the other hand, the Anti-

Normanists argue that the name Rus' came from a tribe that lived in the Ros' River valley south of Kyiv, a tributary to the Dnipro River. The former theory is more commonly held in the West, whereas the latter was popular among Soviet historians. A third theory came from Serhii Shelukhyn, who argued that the origins of Kyivan Rus' were Celtic, with the Hunnic invasions provoking migrations of Celtic tribes from France into eastern Europe in the fifth century CE. According to this theory, the name Rus' comes from Rutheni, the name of the tribe that migrated to the lands that later became Ukraine (Magosci, 2010, chapter 5).

Whatever the case, Kyivan Rus' was a powerful state, with its own legal code (the *Rus'ka Pravda*) and religion, until it fell apart into smaller fiefdoms during the twelfth century (Wilson, 2022). One of these was the Principality of Vladimir-Suzdal, which with time became a powerful entity in its own right, despite coming under lengthy Mongol suzerainty in the 1230s. In 1263, at the age of two, Prince Daniil inherited the then-minor Principality of Moscow (also known as the Grand Duchy of Moscow or Muscovy) from his father, Prince Aleksandr Nevsky of Vladimir-Suzdal. Daniil officially took seat as the Prince of Moscow around 1282. The principality gradually expanded throughout the fourteenth, fifteenth, and sixteenth centuries, eventually becoming the Tsardom of Russia under Ivan IV (Ivan the Terrible) in 1547.

The lands that would become Ukraine, meanwhile, came to be ruled by various external powers throughout the fourteenth and fifteenth centuries, including the Grand Duchy of Lithuania, the Crimean Khanate, and the Mongolian Golden Horde. After the Union of Lublin of 1569, much of Ukraine came under the control of the newly formed Polish-Lithuanian Commonwealth, more specifically, the Crown of the Kingdom of Poland. Serhii Plokhy (2015, p. 64) argues that the Union would 'initiate the formation of the territory of modern Ukraine and its intellectual appropriation by the local elites'. The Union was met with much resistance, especially from groups of ethnically, religiously, and politically diverse people known as Cossacks. Cossacks built their lives around fortified settlements known as *Sich*, and consisted of Orthodox refugees from the Polish-Lithuanian Commonwealth, Muscovites, Jews, Muslims, and others. The Cossacks had long been known as raiders with a fluid attitude towards geopolitics, joining the Polish army in its attempts to take Moscow in 1610 and 1618 (Applebaum, 2017, p. 4). Not much later, Bohdan Khmelnytskyi, a famous Cossack Hetman (commander), led a series of successful military campaigns *against* the Polish crown throughout right-bank (western) Ukraine, eventually capturing Kyiv in December 1648. Over the next few years, Khmelnytskyi and his troops conducted a series of military campaigns with the goal of creating their own state (Plokhy, 2015, p. 100). In 1649, near the town of Zboriv, Khmelnytskyi's forces (aided by regiments of Crimean Tatars) dealt a decisive blow to the new Polish king, John II Casimir. In the subsequent negotiations,

Khmelnytskyi managed to secure permission to rule over the Kyiv, Bratslav, and Chernihiv palatinates of the Polish-Lithuanian Commonwealth. These territories formed a new state, known as the Cossack Hetmanate. According to Plokhy (2015, p. 101), Hetmanate lands overlapped with steppe lands that Polish and French cartographers of the time had referred to as 'Ukraine', which means 'borderland'.

Being unable to declare independence outright (after having struggled for decades to achieve more political autonomy; see Plokhy, 2015, pp. 82–84), and seeking protection against a powerful and unpopular enemy in Poland, Khmelnytskyi first pursued an alliance with the Ottomans (especially the Crimean Tatars). This uneasy friendship came apart after several disastrous military defeats to Poland in 1651 and 1653. Khmelnytskyi then decided to pledge allegiance to Aleksei Romanov, the Tsar of Muscovy, which became known as the Pereiaslav Agreement of 1654 (Wilson, 2022). Plokhy (2015, p. 105) writes that the agreement was understood differently by both sides, which would come to have important consequences for Russian–Ukrainian relations for centuries to come: Khmelnytskyi saw the agreement as he and his Cossacks pledging loyalty and military service in exchange for protection, whereas the Tsar saw the Cossacks as his new subjects, and Ukraine as his new territory. After Khmelnytskyi's death in 1657, the Hetmanate began to disintegrate. His successors failed to prevent infighting, and soon Ottoman forces began to besiege several important Ukrainian cities. The Hetmanate soon all but ceased to exist, apart from several stretches of territory on the left bank (eastern side) of the Dnipro River.

Under Hetman Ivan Mazepa, some (though not all) of the remaining Cossacks formed an alliance with King Charles XII of Sweden.[1] They staged a final revolt against Muscovy and Tsar Peter I (Peter the Great) in 1708, after learning that the latter intended to relieve Mazepa of his duties. The revolt ended with the defeat of the Swedish army at the Battle of Poltava (1709). This spelled doom for Mazepa's vision for an independent Ukraine, and the 'idea of Ukraine as a separate polity, fatherland, and indeed nation did not disappear entirely but shifted out of the centre of Ukrainian discourse for more than a century' (Plokhy, 2015, p. 119). Large swaths of what is today known as Ukraine came under the tutelage of the Russian Empire. With this tutelage came a period of Russification, with Ukrainian lands often being referred to in Moscow and Saint-Petersburg as 'Little Russia' (Malorossiia). In the late eighteenth century, the term 'Novorossiia' also began to be used as an administrative term for the regions of present-day Ukraine that were incorporated into the

---

[1] Many of the Zaporizhian Cossacks were sceptical of Mazepa's alliance with Sweden and refused to join him in battle. They elected Ivan Skoropadskyi as Hetman on 11 November 1708. Skoropadskyi sought to improve relations with Peter I after Mazepa's defeat.

Russian Empire under Catherine the Great (who ruled between 1762 and 1796); this included Crimea and cities such as Dnipro and Odesa, but not Kharkiv. The Novorossiia Governate was formed in 1764 in anticipation of the Russo-Turkish War (1768–1774), and expanded in 1775 with the Russian annexation of the (Cossack) Zaporizhian Sich. Malorossiia and especially Novorossia later became the subject of mythmaking and identity building in Donbas, which will be discussed in more detail in Chapter 2 (Laruelle, 2015; O'Loughlin et al., 2017; Suslov, 2017). Around the same time, some Ukrainian and Cossack elites were granted noble status within the Russian Empire, which led to a decline in the use of the Ukrainian language, particularly among elites, with Ukrainian cultural and linguistic preservation mainly taking place through folk songs and storytelling (Wilson, 1997). The westernmost part of present-day Ukraine came under Austro-Hungarian rule.

Ukrainian nationalism reawakened gradually during the nineteenth century. Authors such as Lesia Ukrainka, Ivan Kotliarevskyi, and especially Taras Shevchenko helped legitimise Ukrainian as a literary language (Finnin, 2011), and offered a sense of identity beyond what the Russian Empire could provide. Political efforts to establish an independent (or at least more autonomous) Ukraine also began to appear. The 1848 Austro-Hungarian revolutionary unrests led to the founding of the first Ukrainian political organisation, the Supreme Ruthenian Council (Magosci, 2010, p. 435). The Council issued a manifesto proclaiming Ukrainians to be distinct from both Poles and Russians, and soon the first Ukrainian-language newspaper, *Zoria Halytska*, was for sale in kiosks around Lviv. These developments were most visible in Galicia (which comprises parts of south-eastern Poland and the present-day Ukranian oblasts of Ivano-Frankivsk and Lviv, under Austrian rule at the time), which became a hub for the development of a Ukrainian press, scholarship, and national identification. In the minds of Ukrainian political activists, most notably the historian Mykhailo Hrushevskyi, Ukrainian identity reached beyond the Austro-Hungarian borders, but in the Russian Empire identity-building efforts were met with substantial resistance. In 1876, Tsar Aleksandr II banned the use of Ukrainian in theatres and outlawed Ukrainian books and publications. These efforts had their consequences: by 1917, only about 20 per cent of people in Kyiv spoke Ukrainian (Applebaum, 2017, p. 9). Despite this, in 1900, the first political party in Russia-ruled Ukraine began to explicitly strive for Ukrainian independence (Plokhy, 2015, p. 192). Mykola Mikhnovskyi, a lawyer from Kharkiv, wrote a programme for Ukrainian national liberation and developed a legal and historical argument denouncing the 1654 Pereiaslav Agreement as illegitimate.

The nineteenth century was also a period of rapid development for Donbas. The discovery of coal and the subsequent exploitation of mining and heavy industry made the region an important source of wealth for the Russian Empire (Applebaum, 2017, p. 9). The resulting influx of miners and workers from all over the Empire contributed to the region's Russification, with most industrialists being Russian (with some exceptions such as the Welshman John Hughes, who founded Donetsk, then known as Yuzivka in his honour). Hiroaki Kuromiya has argued that Donbas has long been a haven for fugitives, outcasts, anarchists, and others seeking to escape authority (Kuromiya, 1998). Donbas is, in Kuromiya's view, the literal and symbolic 'last frontier of Europe' (Kuromiya, 2008): the region is the least amenable to Western cultural and democratic values due to the long history of violence, political repression, and purges that have plagued Donbas since it first became inhabited in the mid-seventeenth century. Before the 1917 revolution, Donbas was also the locus for large-scale anti-Jewish pogroms and other forms of violent repression.

The failed revolution of 1905 against the Russian Tsar reawakened hopes of liberalisation for the Russian Empire's subjugated peoples, including Ukrainians. The Russian Imperial Academy of Sciences published a memorandum advocating for lifting the ban on Ukrainian-language publications in February 1905, an important step towards recognition of Ukrainian as a language rather than a dialect (Plokhy, 2015, pp. 193–194). These hopes proved to be short-lived. So many Ukrainian nationalists came to loathe the Tsar's return to a violent repression of Ukrainian culture that they began to reassess the relative benefits of remaining under Austro-Hungarian rule (Plokhy, 2015, p. 197). Magosci (2010, p. 481) even mentions that representatives of Ukrainian political parties in Galicia jointly declared during a meeting in 1912 that 'with a view to the welfare and future of the Ukrainian people on both sides of the border, in case of war between Austria and Russia, the entire Ukrainian community will unanimously and resolutely stand on the side of Austria against the Russian Empire, as the greatest enemy of Ukraine'.

The outbreak of World War I in 1914 initially worked out poorly for Ukrainian nationalists (Plokhy, 2015, pp. 202–205). The Russian government made use of the opportunity to further crack down on Ukrainian organisations and to shut down Ukrainian-language publications. The Russian imperial army also managed to conquer Ukrainian territories that fell under Austrian control, including Lviv and the Carpathian mountain passes in the west. This occupation lasted until May 1915, enough time for the occupying authorities to replace Ukrainian with Russian as the language used in schools, alongside other Russification efforts. A joint German-Austrian offensive pushed back the Russian armies in the summer of 1915, recapturing most of Galicia and neighbouring Bukovina. A short-lived Russian counteroffensive led by general Aleksei Brusilov in mid-1916 proved to be the last of the Russian Empire's military successes on Ukrainian territory.

The February Revolution of 1917 happened after months of workers' strikes and mutiny by members of the military, mainly in Petrograd (present-day St Petersburg). Tsar Nicholas II was persuaded by the Russian Duma (parliament) to abdicate, and a Provisional Government was installed, led by Aleksandr Kerensky. Ukrainian activists, initially caught off-guard by these events, quickly created a coordinating body known as the Central Rada, electing Mykhailo Hrushevskyi as its head and declaring autonomy (though not outright independence) from Russia in June 1917. This act became known as the 'First Universal' of the Central Rada. One month later, on July 16, the Rada and Kerensky's Provisional Government signed the Second Universal, in which the latter further acknowledged Ukraine's right to autonomy.

The Rada's programme of nationalism combined with socialism found support from workers, the peasantry, and soldiers (who wanted the war to end as quickly as possible). It also managed to forge alliances with key interest groups in Ukraine, including Jewish and left-wing activist groups (Applebaum, 2017, p. 13). However, the Rada proved inept at governance, failing to establish a reliable army as well as a functioning state apparatus (Applebaum, 2017, p. 15; Plokhy, 2015, p. 207). Local Bolshevik Soviets (councils), who supported neither the Rada nor Kerensky, began to gain more support as time went on, with especially people in the countryside becoming frustrated with the Rada's inability to make good on its promises of land and peace. The October Revolution of 1917 saw the Bolsheviks seize power from the Provisional Government in Moscow and St Petersburg, which sparked the Russian Civil War (1917–1923). In response to these events, the Rada pro-claimed the Ukrainian People's Republic in November 2017 (the Third Universal), which was to be nominally part of Russia but would have wide-ranging autonomy.

The Bolsheviks quickly attempted to remove the Rada from power in Kyiv, but initially failed to do so. They then made for Kharkiv, where they proclaimed the Ukrainian People's Republic of Soviets on December 25, 1917. Shortly after, Bolshevik troops marched on Kyiv again, and this time the Rada found itself unable to defend its territory. On January 22, 1918, the Rada issued the Fourth (and final) Universal, this time attempting to break away from Russia entirely. However, with Russian troops advancing on Kyiv and other major cities, the Rada was forced to abandon Kyiv on February 9. It called in the help of the Austrian and German armies, which was granted, and soon the Bolsheviks were in retreat again (Plokhy, 2015, p. 210).

In an attempt to retain control over important territories, the Bolsheviks created (mostly on paper) several short-lived 'people's republics' in southern and eastern Ukraine, such as the Odesa People's Republic and the Donetsk-Kryvyi Rih Soviet Republic (Semiryad & Voskoboinikov, 2019). A coalition of Ukrainian, German, and Austrian forces subsequently managed to conquer almost all of present-day Ukraine, including Crimea (which the Rada had never claimed as part of its territory). In March 1918, the Bolshevik govern-ment signed the Treaty of Brest-Litovsk with the Central Powers, thus ending World War I for Russia and most of Ukraine. As part of the Treaty, the

Bolsheviks recognised Ukraine as a de facto independent state. However, the Germans did not trust the Rada to be able to deliver the large amounts of grain needed to support the German war effort, and they installed Pavlo Skoropadskyi, a descendant of the Cossack Hetman Ivan Skoropadskyi, as the new leader of the Ukrainian government. Skoropadskyi proved to be widely unpopular, resulting in revolts by both workers and peasants. Germany's surrender on November 11, 1918, marked the end of World War I and Skoropadskyi's government, and the Rada retook power.

By early 1919, the Bolsheviks were again marching on Kyiv and the Rada, whose armed forces by that point were little more than a loosely coordinated band of warlords (Plokhy, 2015, pp. 217–219). At the same time, Polish forces under general Józef Haller von Hallenburg invaded Galicia in western Ukraine, succeeding in driving the Ukrainian armies eastward. Political divisions between the more conservative western Ukrainian leadership and the socialist-leaning Rada led to infighting, until a major typhoid epidemic all but wiped out most Ukrainian troops in November 1919 (Magosci, 2010, p. 533). With the feasibility of Ukrainian independence quickly fading, control over Ukrainian territories was contested between the Bolsheviks, the White Army (a loose coalition of Russian anti-Bolshevik forces), and the Polish armies. Vladimir Lenin, head of the Bolshevik government and a long-time sceptic of nationalism for fear of it sowing division among the working class (Applebaum, 2017, p. 21), realised that the Bolsheviks had underestimated Ukrainian national sentiments. When they returned to Ukraine in late 1919 and early 1920, they did so under the banner of the Ukrainian Socialist Soviet Republic (Ukrainian SSR), professing to abandon Russification and allowing for the promotion of Ukrainian culture. This strategy worked: Bolshevik forces slowly managed to conquer important Ukrainian territories, although there remained plenty of resistance from both the Polish armies and independent forces such as Nestor Makhno's anarchist Black Army (Darch, 2020). Anne Applebaum (2017, p. 33) observes that Lenin's strategy existed in name only: over the course of 1919, the Bolsheviks banned Ukrainian newspapers, stopped the use of Ukrainian in schools, and arrested activists on suspicion of 'separatism'.

In March 1921, the drawn-out civil war came to an end, at least for Ukraine. Representatives of the Russian Federation, the Ukrainian Socialist Soviet Republic, and Poland signed the Treaty of Riga, in which the signing parties agreed on the Polish–Soviet border (Plokhy, 2015, p. 226). Most of present-day Ukraine was ceded to the Soviet Union, including Kyiv, but major cities in the west (such as Lviv and Ternopil) became part of the Second Polish Republic. Ukraine found itself divided between four countries: Poland (which controlled Galicia and Volhynia), Romania (which had controlled Bukovina since 1918), Czechoslovakia (which controlled Transcarpathia), and the Soviet Union. Plokhy (2015, pp. 226–227) blames the failure of the Ukrainian national idea on a combination of factors: the presence of powerful and militarily aggressive neighbours vying for control over Ukraine's fertile land, the immaturity of its national movement, and its inability to form a united front against its opponents (partly due to a preponderance of regionalism over nationalism in some parts of especially western Ukraine).

THE SOVIET ERA

By the time the Russian Civil War officially ended in 1923, the Bolsheviks had established firm control over Russia, most of present-day Ukraine, and various other territories that became known as Soviet Republics. They almost immediately began implementing land reforms, confiscating large estates and encouraging peasants to join collective farms (Applebaum, 2017, pp. 34–36). Ukraine was seen as an important region for the new Soviet government, not only because of the economic importance of the Donbas coal industry but also because of its 'black earth', a highly fertile type of soil only found in the Dnipro Basin. In Ukraine – unlike in Russia – the practice of peasants sharing land communally was uncommon, and so communist efforts to set up farm collectives were often met with derision. Nonetheless, the Bolsheviks divided the Ukrainian peasantry into three different categories: *bedniaki* (poor peasants), *seredniaki* (middle peasants), and *kulaki* (rich peasants, or Kulaks). They then recruited from among the *bedniaki* some of the worst performing peasants and rewarded them with land confiscated from their well-to-do neighbours, and power. These collaborators were responsible for identifying 'grain surpluses', which were to be sent to Russia to feed the growing numbers of factory workers. These mandatory grain collections, and the pitting of Kulaks and *bedniaki* against each other, generated 'overwhelming anger and resentment [against the Bolshevik government], neither of which ever really went away' (Applebaum, 2017, p. 36).

In the early 1920s, the Soviet Union faced a set of near-insurmountable economic hurdles resulting from years of war. In response, Lenin implemented the New Economic Policy (NEP), which allowed for a certain degree of market-isation and private ownership, and a policy of *korenizatsiia*, or 'indigenisation', which aimed to foster a local communist bureaucracy in each Soviet Republic by allowing for a degree of mixing between national cultural symbolism and Soviet doctrine. Within Ukraine, Ukrainisation (*Ukrainizatsiia*) became a massive movement. In 1923, the Soviet Ukrainian government issued a decree requiring all public officials to learn Ukrainian (Liber, 1982, p. 676). Large-scale literacy programmes were set up, and newly literate ethnic Ukrainians flocked from the countryside to the cities. The percentage of Ukrainian-language schools rose from 50.7 per cent in 1923 to 88.1 per cent in 1932

(Pauly, 2014, p. 4). The Ukrainian publishing industry experienced a revival: the percentage of Ukrainian-language books published during this time rose from 16.3 per cent in 1923 to 60.9 per cent in 1928 (Liber, 1982, pp. 679–681). Ukrainian literature thrived as well, with the generation of authors and poets of the 1920s and early 1930s becoming known as the "Red" (and later, as Stalin's repressions worsened, "Executed") Renaissance (Hryn, 2005).

Lenin died from a stroke in January 1924 and was succeeded by Joseph Stalin. Having been seen as an underdog for the position of Lenin's successor (with Lenin himself strongly preferring Red Army commander Lev Trotsky), Stalin's road to power was a bloody one. After successfully dispatching several key rivals, including Trotsky, he also did away with the NEP and indigenisation, opting instead for rapid socialist industrialisation and collectivisation (Plokhy, 2015, pp. 246–248).

As the second largest of the Soviet Republics, Stalin regarded Ukraine as a key target for industrialisation and investment. The first Soviet Five-Year Plan (1928–1933) went relatively well for Ukraine, which received 20 per cent of all state investments. This changed in 1932, when the Kremlin redirected investments towards the Ural and Siberia. Land collectivisation was increased significantly all throughout the Soviet Union in 1929, but hit hardest in the grain-producing areas of the country, including Ukraine. By 1930, some reports indicated that up to 70 per cent of all arable land had been collectivised. This led to substantial resistance, with Ukrainian Soviet authorities registering more than 1,700 peasant uprisings in March 1930 alone (Plokhy, 2015, p. 249). In the subsequent crackdown, tens of thousands of (alleged) Kulak families were deported from Ukraine to remote parts of the Soviet Union.

Accusations of sabotage became common. Stalin and his aides had become suspicious that Ukrainian peasants were deliberately hiding grain, in an attempt to thwart collectivisation and starve workers in the cities. Authorities began to demand greater and greater grain quotas, which, combined with below-average harvest yields (Snyder, 2010, p. 33), led to widespread famine. This famine became known as the Holodomor.[2] Ukraine was hit extremely hard: grain procurements became farcically harsh (Applebaum, 2017, p. 172), resulting in the death from starvation of millions. Attempts to bring this problem to the attention of the Central Committee in Moscow (and Stalin individually) failed. Even though the leadership in both Moscow and Kharkiv (the capital of Soviet Ukraine until 1934) fully understood that Ukraine could not produce enough grain to feed even itself, little was done in 1932, already a famine year, to avert certain catastrophic famine the year after. Stalin, having been made aware of what he believed to be alarming reports from Ukraine about its political situation, along with alleged grain theft by starving peasants, withdrew what

---

[2] Most likely from *holodom moryty*, 'to inflict death by hunger'.

little food aid had been sent to help the starving, and demanded that the Ukrainian Communist Party continue confiscating farm equipment from 'underperforming' collectives. Stalin saw a connection between the perceived problems with grain requisitions and the perceived threat of Ukrainian nationalism. He fired several members of the Ukrainian Communist Party leadership and assigned his close aide Lazar Kaganovich to the task of 'quickly transforming Ukraine into a true fortress of the USSR', noting that 'without [these political and ideological measures] ... we could lose Ukraine' (Applebaum, 2017, p. 188). In the long run, Stalin reasoned, the death of a few hundred thousand wouldn't matter too much (Snyder, 2010, p. 35). A compounding problem was that decision-makers knew of Stalin's involvement, and couldn't feasibly criticise his collectivisation policy which lay at the root of the problem, or even provide aid, which would be seen as a tacit admission of the failure of Stalin's policies (Applebaum, 2017, p. 176).

More famines struck Ukraine throughout the 1930s and 1940s, although none as bad as in 1932–1933. However, Adolf Hitler's rise to power in 1933 meant yet another challenge. In August 1939, Germany and the Soviet Union signed the Molotov-Ribbentrop Pact, which contained a 'Secret Protocol' defining the borders of Germany's and the Soviet Union's respective spheres of influence in Eastern and Northern Europe. Not long after, both countries invaded Poland and several other nations (Snyder, 2010, p. 128), marking the start of World War II. Stalin moved his troops westward, enlarging the Belorussian and Ukrainian Soviet Republics on their western borders, against the stipulations of the Molotov-Ribbentrop Pact.

Hitler invaded the Soviet Union on June 22, 1941, a surprise attack that baffled Stalin. This invasion, known as Operation Barbarossa, killed more than 10 million soldiers, and a similar number of civilians. Hitler's vision of *Lebensraum* ('living space') included a *Drang nach Osten*, an eastward drive, of Germanic peoples. In practice, this meant displacing Ukrainians and other Slavs, whom Hitler considered to be subhuman, to make room for Germans (Plokhy, 2015, p. 260). He saw Ukraine as a 'geopolitical asset, and its people as instruments who tilled the soil, tools that could be exchanged with others or discarded' (Snyder, 2010, pp. 161–163). Ukraine was a key factor in Hitler's war plans, who intended for it to serve as the Third Reich's breadbasket. By November 1941, almost all of Soviet Ukraine was under German control (Magosci, 2010, p. 667). German planners decided to use Ukraine's collective farms as a weapon, known as the Hunger Plan: Ukraine's fertile land would be used to feed German soldiers and starve Soviet citizens, especially in the cities. This plan, however, proved to be logistically difficult, and was further complicated by the fact that Operation Barbarossa did not turn out to bring the anticipated 'lightning victory' over the Soviet Union. It instead became a drawn-out battle, particularly at Stalingrad, where the Soviet Army eventually managed to drive back the German troops after years of fighting and millions of deaths.

Nazi-occupied Ukraine was incorporated into an administrative unit known as the Generalgouvernement. Many Ukranians welcomed the German occupation of 1941 (Plokhy, 2015, p. 265). Unlike the Soviets, the Nazis allowed for Ukrainian cultural and religious expressions, and new Ukrainian-language schools were set up (Magosci, 2010, pp. 664–665). Many also fondly remembered the Austrian period from before World War I, comparing it favourably to Soviet occupation. The Germans, for their part, saw promoting nationalism in Soviet Republics as a way to undermine Stalin. The Organisation of Ukrainian Nationalists (OUN), a radical-nationalist political party, was one of the entities put in charge of the Generalgouvernement by the German occupiers. At this time, its leadership was split in two, between the conservative Andrii Melnyk and the radical-revolutionary Stepan Bandera. The latter had made a deal with the German military intelligence to form several Ukrainian battalions, which were to be deployed against the Soviet armies. But Bandera, who shared the Nazis' anti-Semitic views (Marples, 2006), had other plans: after entering Lviv in June 1941, the OUN declared Ukrainian independence. Bandera was arrested and spent most of the war in the Sachsenhausen concentration camp (Plokhy, 2015, p. 267). After the Battle of Kursk in July 1943, the German armies were forced into a retreat from Soviet territories. Locals came to meet the advancing Red Army as liberators, but Soviet officials doubted their sincerity (Plokhy, 2015, pp. 274–275). This doubt, stemming from suspicions about Ukrainians' loyalty towards the Soviet system and ideology, would last until well after the Soviet Union came apart in 1991. Even after World War II ended in 1945, organisations such as the Ukrainian Insurgent Army continued to pose a challenge for Soviet rule until well into the 1950s (Plokhy, 2015, pp. 295–296). Bandera, in exile in Germany, was killed by a KGB agent in 1959.

Stalin died after suffering a stroke in March 1953 and was succeeded by Nikita Khrushchev, whose roots lay in Donbas. In 1954, as part of the festivities celebrating the anniversary of the 1654 Pereiaslav Agreement, the Crimean Peninsula was transferred from the jurisdiction of the Russian Federation to the Ukrainian SSR (Plokhy, 2015, p. 298). This came ten years after the Crimean Tatars' deportation to far-flung parts of the Soviet Union, after Stalin had accused them of collaborating with the Germans. The event was propagandised as being symbolic of the eternal friendship between Russia and Ukraine, but the transfer was primarily practical in nature: Crimea is cut off from the Russian mainland by the Kerch Strait, and infrastructure, waterways, and communication lines all ran through Ukraine. Ukraine, according to Khrushchev, was also in a better position to help Crimea economically, which had been ravaged after years of war.

The periods under Khrushchev (1953–1964) and Leonid Brezhnev (1964–1982) were otherwise relatively calm, and the reigns of Brezhnev's successors Iuri Andropov and Konstantin Chernenko were short-lived. Soviet industrial and agricultural output dropped steadily, and the country became increasingly dependent on the export of oil and other natural resources. Mikhail Gorbachev, who became General Secretary of the Communist Party of the Soviet Union in March 1985, attempted to jump-start Soviet society with a series of reforms (*perestroika*), which included partial liberalisation and marketisation as well as efforts to democratise and liberalise the Soviet media landscape.

Before Gorbachev's reforms could take effect, Ukraine was hit by the worst ecological disaster in European history. On the night of April 26, 1986, reactor four of the Chernobyl Nuclear Power Plant exploded after a scheduled safety test went awry (Plokhy, 2019). Radioactive fallout was measured everywhere between Belarus and Sweden, and parts of northern Ukraine and southern Belarus remain uninhabitable even today. Approximately thirty-one people died in the immediate aftermath, and thousands more perished from radiation-related illnesses in the years and decades hence. The disaster sharply increased tensions between Kyiv and Moscow, as the radiation affected everyone from peasants to party bosses (Plokhy, 2015, pp. 311–315). Ukrainian writers and activists, emboldened by Gorbachev's stated policy of openness (*glasnost*), were at the forefront of Ukraine's new democratic opposition. In July 1990, the Ukrainian parliament declared Ukraine to be a sovereign (but not yet independent) country. The October 1990 Revolution on Granite (*Revoliutsiia na Hraniti*) was a series of student protests against the Soviet authorities, and constituted the first major political event that took place on Maidan Nezalezhnosti in Kyiv (Onuch, 2017).

By this time, the writing was on the wall for the Soviet Union. In August 1991, a desperate attempt was made by the Soviet secret service (the KGB) to overthrow Gorbachev, which was thwarted by the newly elected Russian president Boris Yeltsin. In the coup attempt's immediate aftermath, the Supreme Soviet of the Ukrainian SSR voted to declare independence. This declaration was put to a referendum held on December 1, 1991. Ukrainians voted overwhelmingly in favour of independence: Crimea voted to join Ukraine by a margin of 54 to 46 per cent. In both Donetsk and Luhansk, this margin was approximately 84 to 16 per cent. All other oblasts reported even higher margins, demonstrating an overwhelming desire of Ukrainians to move ahead without Moscow. Without Ukraine and Russia there was no Soviet Union (Plokhy, 2014), and the country officially ceased to exist on December 26, 1991.

Ukrainian identity was more polarised and divided in the early 1990s than it is today. Scholars such as Volodymyr Kulyk (2001, 2011, 2016), Olga Onuch (2014, 2017; Onuch & Hale, 2018), and Lowell Barrington (2021, 2022b, 2022a) have identified factors such as (native) language and ethnicity as important factors in Ukrainians' self-identification at the time. However, there are nuances to be considered here: some Ukrainians took 'native' language to mean the language they grew up speaking or spoke every day, whereas others understood it to refer to something more akin to ancestral language (i.e., the language spoken by the ethnic group they identified most strongly with). A common theme among commentators was that Ukraine was supposedly divided between a Soviet-nostalgic, Russian-speaking east and a pro-European west (Pirie, 1996; Zhurzhenko, 2014). For example, in the 1994 presidential elections, the pro-Russian Leonid Kuchma won in all oblasts east and south of the Dnipro River, whereas his rival, the more pro-Western Leonid Kravchuk, won in all oblasts to the river's west (Arel, 2018). However, this view is too simplistic (Kulyk, 2001) and ignores the complex mix of ethnic, regional, national, and linguistic identities present in Ukraine at the time (Pirie, 1996).[3]

AFTER THE SOVIET UNION

The breakup of the Soviet Union was less violent than it could have been, but it was not peaceful. Figure 1.1 shows a timeline of geopolitical events relevant to Russian–Ukrainian relations between 1990 and the present day.

A common theme throughout this period was Russia's support for 'independence' movements in countries formerly in its orbit. Even before the formal dissolution of the USSR, the War of Transnistria led to the breakaway of the Pridnestrovian Moldavian Republic (PMR) from the Moldavian Soviet Socialist Republic. The Soviet Union and later Russia supported the PMR, usually referred to as Transnistria, with funding and military equipment. Transnistria continues to claim independence from Moldova proper to this day. In 1992, ongoing tensions and skirmishes between Georgia and Abkhazia, a Georgian province on the Black Sea, erupted into a full-scale war that killed thousands and displaced hundreds of thousands. Further hostilities occurred in 1998, 2006, and especially 2008, when the Russo-Georgian War spilled over into Abkhazia. Today, Abkhazia is de facto independent, although it's not recognised as such by the international community (the main exception being Russia).

Also in 1992, tensions between the newly independent Azerbaijan and Armenia came to a head over the province of Nagorno-Karabakh, resulting in a war that lasted until 1994. Ethnic Armenians declared the Republic of

---

[3] For instance, Kulyk (2001, p. 206) notes that 'ethnic identification is by no means limited to exclusive categories; instead, it consists of varying degrees of affiliation with two or more groups, as well as weak connections to any one group. According to a nationwide survey conducted in 1993 and 1994, as many as a quarter of all respondents declared themselves to be both Ukrainians and Russians. This share is much larger in eastern and southern Ukraine, first of all in the Donbas, where dual or marginal ethnic identification has been facilitated by a very high rate of intermarriage and urbanization.'

2021–22 Rus-Ukr. tensions

2022 - Full-scale invasion

2017–20 NATO expansion (Montenegro, North Macedonia)

2019 Zelensky elected

2014 Euromaidan Revolution, Crimea annexation

2014 - Donbas War

2009 Energy crisis

2009 NATO expansion (Albania, Croatia)

2008 Russian–Georgian war

2004 Orange Revolution

2004 NATO expansion (Baltics, Romania, etc.)

1999 NATO expansion (Poland, Czechia, Hungary)

1999 NATO bombings of Yugoslavia

1997 NATO-Russian 'Founding Act'

1994 Budapest Memorandum

1991–94 Abkhazia & Nagorno-Karabakh wars

1990–92 Transnistria war

1991 Soviet Union dissolution

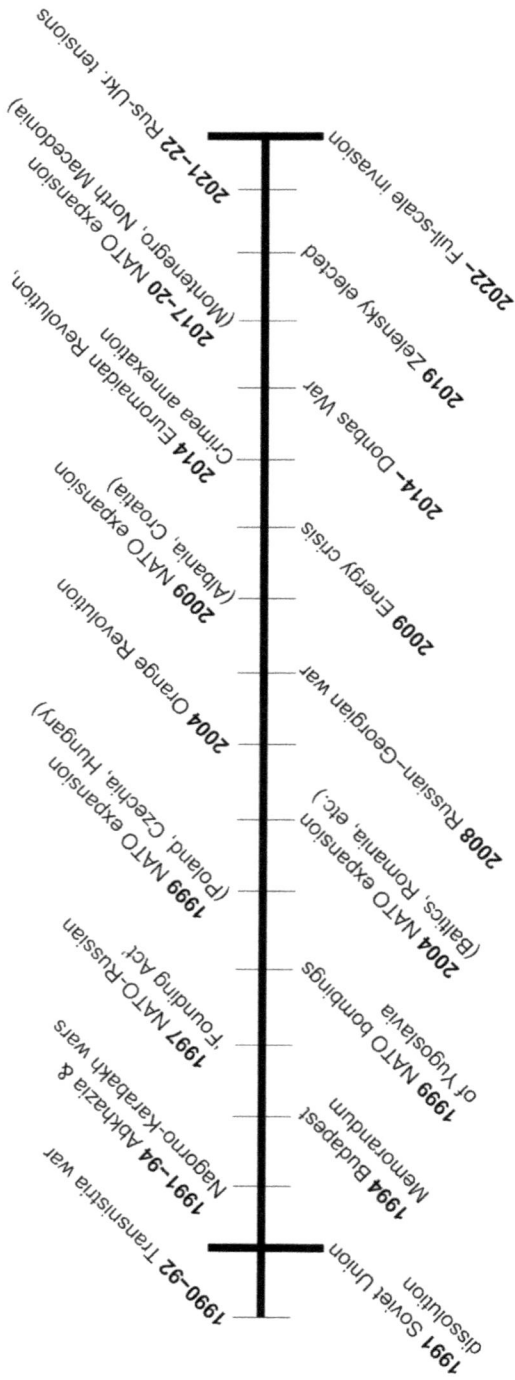

FIGURE 1.1 Timeline of relevant events between the break-up of the Soviet Union and the present day.

Artsakh, nominally an independent state but heavily reliant on Armenia. Tensions were not resolved, however, and after several years of skirmishes, Armenia and Azerbaijan went back to war in 2020. This war ended with a partial Azeri victory, and Nagorno-Karabakh came under blockade. In September 2023, Azerbaijan launched another invasion into the enclave, resulting in many Armenians fleeing the territory and the eventual dissolution of the unrecognised republic. Russia's two wars in Chechnya (1994–1996 and 1999–2009) also cost large numbers of lives, although Chechnya never managed to achieve independence from Russia, either de facto or de jure. At present, the Chechen Republic is run by Ramzan Kadyrov, a former independence advocate who switched sides to Russia during the Second Chechen War.

Relations between Russia and Ukraine were initially mostly peaceful, although the two countries quarrelled over who should assume command over the Black Sea Fleet (stationed in Crimea) in 1992. In 1994, Russia, the United Kingdom, and the United States signed the Budapest Memorandum, which would guarantee the sovereignty and existing borders of Ukraine, Belarus, and Kazakhstan, in exchange for these countries giving up their nuclear arsenals (United Nations, 1994). However, Russian–Western relations began to sour in the mid- to late 1990s. A serious point of disagreement was NATO's military intervention in the Federal Republic of Yugoslavia in early 1999, to put a halt to the ethnic cleansing of Albanians in Kosovo. Although NATO failed to obtain approval from the UN Security Council (Russia and China voted against intervention), NATO forces nonetheless carried out an aerial bombing campaign over Yugoslavia. This campaign lasted for two months, until an agreement was reached to withdraw Yugoslav troops from Kosovo. Yeltsin expressed strong disapproval of the campaign at the time, saying that 'morally, we are above America' (*Guardian*, 1999).[4] Despite this, Yeltsin felt in no position to intervene himself; Russia's military was weak, and the country was reliant on the West to help boost its economy.

There were also other disagreements, particularly over NATO's eastward expansion. To address Russia's concerns about Western powers' increasing influence in Eastern Europe,[5] NATO and Russia signed the 'Founding Act' of 1997, in which potential future NATO expansion as well as its preconditions were discussed. The Act notes that 'NATO and Russia do not consider each

---

[4] Yevgeny Primakov, prime minister of Russia at the time, was on his way to Washington, DC, to meet with NATO leadership when he learned of the start of the bombing campaign. He immediately ordered his plane to turn around and fly back to Moscow, a move popularly known as 'Primakov's Loop'. This move is seen by some as symbolic for the turnaround in Western-Russian relations.

[5] In a meeting with Gorbachev on February 9, 1990, US Secretary of State James Baker is said to have told the Soviet leader that NATO would expand 'not one inch eastward' (Savranskaya & Blanton, 2017).

AT ISSUE IS THE RATHER EXPLICIT ASPIRATION OF THESE
COUNTRIES, AS WELL AS OF A NUMBER OF OTHER STATES OF
CENTRAL AND EASTERN EUROPE, TO GET CLOSER TO NATO AND TO
ACHIEVE INTEGRATION, IN ONE FORM OR ANOTHER, INTO THE
ALLIANCE. NATURALLY, WE EXPRESSED OUR APPRECIATION OF THE
SOVEREIGN RIGHT OF ANY STATE TO CHOOSE HOW IT ENSURES ITS
OWN SECURITY, INCLUDING BY PARTICIPATION IN POLITICO-
MILITARY ALLIANCES. WE ARE ALSO SYMPATHETIC TO THE BY NO
MEANS NOSTALGIC SENTIMENTS OF THE EAST EUROPEANS TOWARD
PAST "COOPERATION" WITHIN THE FRAMEWORK OF THE WARSAW PACT.
OVERALL, THE IMPRESSION IS THAT THEY DO HAVE GROUNDS FOR A
CERTAIN AMOUNT OF APPREHENSION ABOUT THEIR SECURITY.

AT THE SAME TIME, I CANNOT HELP BUT EXPRESS OUR UNEASINESS
AS WELL OVER THE FACT THAT THE DISCUSSION OF HOW NATO
MIGHT EVOLVE IS CENTERING WITH INCREASING FREQUENCY ON THE
SCENARIO OF QUANTITATIVE EXPANSION OF THE ALLIANCE BY
ADDING EAST EUROPEAN COUNTRIES.

I ALSO WANT TO CALL ATTENTION TO THE FACT THAT THE SPIRIT
OF THE TREATY ON THE FINAL SETTLEMENT WITH RESPECT TO
GERMANY, SIGNED IN SEPTEMBER, 1990, ESPECIALLY ITS
PROVISIONS THAT PROHIBIT THE DEPLOYMENT OF FOREIGN TROOPS
WITHIN THE EASTERN LANDS OF THE FEDERAL REPUBLIC OF
GERMANY, PRECLUDES THE OPTION OF EXPANDING THE NATO ZONE
INTO THE EAST.

FIGURE 1.2 Excerpts from a 1993 letter from Boris Yeltsin to US president Bill Clinton on NATO expansion (US Department of State, 2006).

other as adversaries. They share the goal of overcoming the vestiges of earlier confrontation and competition and of strengthening mutual trust and cooperation' (NATO, 1997). The Czech Republic, Poland, and Hungary became NATO members in 1999, the first countries to join the military alliance since the newly unified Germany in 1991.[6] This irked Yeltsin. In a letter to US president Bill Clinton dated September 15, 1993, he acknowledged the right of former Warsaw Pact countries to join military alliances of their choosing, but also expressed his 'uneasiness' with NATO expansion and argued that it violated the 'spirit' of the 1990 agreement between the Soviet Union and Western countries on the conditions of the 1989 reunification of Germany (see Figure 1.2). NATO underwent further expansion with the ascension of Bulgaria, Estonia, Latvia, Lithuania, Romania, Slovakia, and Slovenia in 2004; Albania and Croatia in 2009; Montenegro in 2017; and North Macedonia in 2020.[7]

Vladimir Putin, a former secret service agent from St Petersburg, became president of Russia in early 2000 after Yeltsin unexpectedly resigned from his post. US–Russian relations initially thawed somewhat, with Putin being

---

[6] West Germany had been a NATO member since 1955.
[7] Finland and Sweden also joined the coalition in 2023 and 2024, respectively.

among the first world leaders to call US president George W. Bush after the 9/11 attacks, promising him that Russia would be on America's side in Bush's 'War on Terror' (McFaul, 2001). This initial rapprochement would not last, with NATO expansion being Putin's chief object of frustration. In a speech at the Munich Security Conference in 2007, he expressed his anger at NATO in front of a crowd of high-level diplomats and government leaders, framing the alliance as a threat to Russian national security: 'I think it's obvious that NATO expansion has no relation with the modernisation of the Alliance itself or with ensuring security in Europe. On the contrary, it represents a serious provocation that reduces the level of mutual trust' (Eckel, 2021). Putin reiterated this frustration and sense of betrayal by NATO in a speech given shortly after Russia's annexation of Crimea in March 2014: 'They have lied to us many times, made decisions behind our backs, placed us before an accomplished fact. This happened with NATO's expansion to the east, as well as the deployment of military infrastructure at our borders' (Kendall, 2014). In 2008, Georgia and Ukraine became NATO candidate countries, which prompted the 2008 Russo–Georgian War, seen by many as a warning to former Soviet states to halt any attempts to leave Russia's sphere of influence (Asmus, 2009).

The legitimacy of these sentiments has been a long-running topic of debate (Anderson, 2023; Gati, 1999; Goldgeier & Itzkowitz Shifrinson, 2023; Sarotte, 2022). On the one hand, US Secretary of State James Baker's 'not one inch eastward' promise to Gorbachev in 1990 seems to imply that there was at one point a shared sentiment among both Russian and NATO officials that the alliance would forestall expansion for the foreseeable future. Russia's frustrations about NATO's bombing of Yugoslavia may also be somewhat legitimate, considering Russia's well-documented, vehement disapproval at the time (and the fact that the campaign went ahead despite Russia and China vetoing it in the UN Security Council). On the other hand, US and NATO officials argued that no assurances regarding expansion were ever part of a written agreement (with the 1997 Founding Act even mentioning some conditions *for* expansion) and that verbal communications with Gorbachev had little relevance for the Russian Federation, as the Soviet Union no longer existed (Sarotte, 2022).

What's often left out of these discussions is the perspective of the nations seeking NATO membership and Western rapprochement. It's easy to forget in the midst of Russian–American sabre-rattling that support for NATO membership in Poland, for example, was between 60 and 70 per cent in 1999 (Statista, 2023);[8] this was somewhat lower but still substantial (around 50–55 per cent) in the Czech Republic, with about 20 per cent of the

---

[8] Polish support for NATO rose to over 90 per cent after the 2022 Russian invasion of Ukraine.

population opposed (Mareš & Šmídová, 2000). In a referendum held in 1997, 85.3 per cent of Hungarians voted to join the alliance (Perlez, 1997). Aside from ensuring popular support, new member states also rapidly undertook the economic, military, and political reforms that NATO (and European Union) membership required. This was in large part informed by negative memories among many Eastern Europeans of the Soviet Union and its legacy, along with a continuing fear of Russian imperialism and territorial ambitions (Kostadinova, 2000). So, rather than NATO one-sidedly asking countries to join the Alliance, the relationship ran to a significant extent in the opposite direction: most Eastern European countries saw NATO membership as an opportunity to leave the Russian orbit, and were willing to meet any require- ments necessary to achieve this. When faced with such realities, one could argue that it would be unreasonable for NATO to refuse good-faith requests for expansion on the off-chance that Russia, which at the time was not considered an adversary, might one day experience a nationalist revival and use NATO expansion as a justification for military overreach.

Russian–Ukrainian relations came under significant pressure in 2004, when the results of the Ukrainian presidential elections were marred with accusations of corruption and voter fraud. Ukrainians widely believed the results of the run-off election to have been rigged by the authorities to favour the official winner, the pro-Russian Viktor Yanukovych. His challenger, the pro-Western Viktor Yushchenko, contested the election results, believing it was he who had received the most votes (Wilson, 2005). Yushchenko had also been the victim of an assassination attempt by way of dioxin poisoning, which disfigured him. The case remains unsolved, although Yushchenko himself suspected some Ukrainian officials with strong Russian ties. Maidan Nezalezhnosti in Kyiv once again became the centre of protest, with activists staging sit-ins, general strikes, and civil disobedience. The revolution was successful: the Ukrainian Supreme Court overturned the results of the run- off election, and ordered a revote, which was won by Yushchenko. The events became known as the Orange Revolution, part of a series of 'Colour Revolutions' in Ukraine, Georgia, and Kyrgyzstan in the early 2000s (Mitchell, 2012). In 2009, it became clear how much Russian–Ukrainian relations had deteriorated as a result of Yushchenko's pro-Western course when the two countries failed to agree on a deal over the supply of natural gas. As a result, gas supplies passing through Ukraine were heavily disrupted throughout much of Europe. This lasted until Ukraine and Gazprom (a Russian state-owned energy company) resolved their differences after the 2010 Ukrainian presidential elections.

These elections were won by Viktor Yanukovych, who beat Yushchenko, fairly this time according to most observers. Yanukovych ran a much more pro-Russian course than his predecessor. One important event during his presidency was the arrest, trial, and imprisonment of Yulia Tymoshenko, the former prime minister under Yushchenko. Tymoshenko had been accused of abuse of power and embezzlement. Her trial received a great deal of international attention, with the European Union warning the Yanukovych government that its treatment of Tymoshenko could have consequences for the ongoing negotiations over EU–Ukrainian economic cooperation (Interfax-Ukraine, 2011).

In November 2013, after these negotiations had concluded, Yanukovych unexpectedly withdrew from the EU–Ukraine Association Agreement, provoking widespread protests. For the third time in twenty-five years, activists took to Kyiv's Maidan Nezalezhnosti. The square once again became the centre of widespread demonstrations ('Euromaidan'),[9] and the Yanukovych government's response became increasingly erratic. Several journalists and activists were killed in early 2014, and many more were injured when Berkut (riot police) officers repeatedly attempted to sweep the square and clear it of protesters. These rising tensions eventually came to a head between February 18 and 20, when snipers shot dozens people to death near Maidan Nezalezhnosti and injured many more (Gatehouse, 2014). Overall, 108 protesters perished in the clashes.

On February 21, Yanukovych and the Ukrainian parliamentary opposition signed an agreement aimed at finding a way out of the crisis, agreeing to instate a temporary unity government, introduce several constitutional reforms, and call early elections (Wilson, 2022). That same evening, riot police abandoned Kyiv, and Yanukovych himself fled to Russia, where he remains to this day. The opposition parties voted to officially remove Yanukovych from office and put in place an interim government led by Oleksandr Turchynov. These events were soon followed by the annexation of Crimea and the start of the Donbas War,[10] which are discussed in more detail in Chapter 2. In May 2014, Ukraine held presidential elections, which were won by the candy magnate Petro Poroshenko. The next elections, which were held in 2019, saw Poroshenko challenged by Volodymyr Zelensky, an actor who had previously played the role of president in a comedic TV series and who ran on a platform of anti-corruption and brokering a solution to the Donbas War. Zelensky won the run-off with about 73 per cent of the vote.

Scholars have argued that the events of Euromaidan served as a catalyst that accelerated Ukrainian identity formation, speeding up developments set in motion before 1991 (Kulyk, 2016; Onuch, 2014; Zhurzhenko, 2014). Evidence suggests that the Euromaidan revolution provoked a shift away from ethno-nationalist and towards a civic national identity (Barrington, 2021; Kulyk, 2016; Onuch et al., 2018); in other words, Ukrainian identity

[9] In Ukraine, these events are known as the *Revoliutsiia Hidnosti*, or Revolution of Dignity.
[10] By 'Donbas War' I mean the early stages of the Russian–Ukrainian War (until the full-scale invasion of 2022), and specifically the part that took place in Donbas.

increasingly came to be based on shared *values* rather than shared characteristics (such as ethnicity or language). Words such as 'Russian' and 'Ukrainian'
became increasingly poor designators of distinct identities. Rather, more
Ukrainians, especially in the predominantly Russian-speaking areas of the
country, came to describe Ukraine as their 'homeland' (Pop-Eleches &
Robertson, 2018), accompanied by a noticeable 'shedding' of 'Russian-ness'
(Kulyk, 2018).

CONCLUSION

This chapter has provided a brief history of Russian–Ukrainian relations,
starting from the ninth century with the founding of Kyivan Rus' and ending
with the 2014 Euromaidan Revolution. I have covered Ukraine's storied
history of alternating periods of independence and subjugation, not only by
Russia but also by other nations such as Poland, Austria-Hungary, and
Germany. From the heyday of Rus' to the Cossack Hetmanate, the lands that
form present-day Ukraine have been inhabited by independent-minded
peoples for centuries. Ukrainian identity began to take on a national character
in the 1800s, when writers and activists set up a sprawling network of political
movements pursuing an independent Ukraine. The Soviet era – or the
occupation of Ukraine by the Soviet Union, as many Ukrainians see it today –
was marked by periods of intense suffering: the famines of the 1930s and the
slaughters of World War II, during which millions of Ukrainians died as a
result of both war and policy. After the Soviet Union came undone in 1991,
relations between Russia and independent Ukraine gradually soured after the
2004 Orange Revolution and especially the 2014 Euromaidan Revolution.
Over the course of this period, a shift away from ethno-nationalism and
towards a civic national identity took place in the country, with especially
Russian-speaking Ukrainians 'shedding' parts of their 'Russian-ness'. I have
not discussed how Russian-Ukrainian relations developed after 2014, as I will
touch on these matters in the following chapters. In the next chapter, I discuss
the aftermath of the latter, especially the outbreak of the Donbas War and the
emergence of the Donetsk and Luhansk 'People's Republics'.

2

The Politics of the Donbas 'Republics'

INTRODUCTION

This chapter examines ideological projects in the Donetsk and Luhansk 'People's Republics' (DNR and LNR), from the outbreak of the Russian–Ukrainian War in early 2014 until after the start of the full-scale invasion in February 2022. I will pay special attention to ideological and political developments such as the ouster of the head of the LNR, Igor Plotnitskii, by way of a coup d'état, and of the head of the DNR, Aleksandr Zakharchenko, by way of a car bomb. The goal of this chapter is to give a comprehensive overview of how the leadership of the two 'Republics' have sought to find numerous different historical, ideological, and identity-based justifications for their declaration of 'independence' from Ukraine. As we will see, neither the DNR nor the LNR should be considered projects that are ideological in nature. Instead, the ideological underpinnings of both statelets have always been fractured, erratic, and ad-hoc.

IDEOLOGY IN THE DNR AND LNR

In both 'People's Republics', political and ideological projects were established in tandem with the escalation of military engagements in March–April 2014. The first rumblings of such projects were heard in Donetsk in early April, when disgraced Party of Regions MP and former presidential candidate Oleg Tsariov announced the founding of a new 'Federal Republic of Novorossiia' (Interfax-Ukraine, 2014; Prestupnosti.net, 2014a). This announcement constituted Tsariov's first attempt to make a name for himself as a member of Donbas' new political elite. His declaration lacked detail, however, and turned out to be premature due to the unstable military situation at the time and the fact that it was still unclear which of the rivalling militias would eventually come out on top (Babiak, 2014).

A month later, on May 11 and 12, 'referendums' on self-rule were held in Donetsk and Luhansk, an important step in the centralisation of power. The question on the ballot was the same in both regions: 'Do you support the Act of state independence of the Donetsk/Luhansk People's Republic?'[1] From the start, the organisation of these 'referenda' was marred with controversy. The use of the word 'independence' led to confusion, as the Russian word that was used on the ballot (*samostoiatelnost* instead of *nezavisimost*) can mean both full independence and something akin to autonomy or self-dependency. A journalist for *Vice News* who was on the ground reported conflicting stories from local residents as to whether they thought they were voting for independence or self-rule within Ukraine (Salem, 2014). The votes themselves were not monitored by internationally recognised election observers, despite the DNR's and LNR's attempts to contact representatives of the Organization for Security and Co-operation in Europe (OSCE) for this purpose. Their democratic legitimacy was contested by the Ukrainian government, journalists, and international observers. A German journalist working for *Bild*, who was in Donetsk during the referendum, recorded one man casting his vote eight times in different voting stations, as well as instances of people from places outside the DNR, such as Luhansk and Dnipro, voting in Donetsk (Ronzheimer, 2014). The *Economist* (2014) called the referenda 'fake, the product of an extraordinary information war'.

The DNR and LNR authorities reported overwhelming margins in favour of independence/self-rule: 89.07 per cent in Donetsk (with a self-reported 74.87 per cent turnout) and 96.2 per cent in Luhansk (turnout 75 per cent). Oleksandr Turchynov, the acting president of Ukraine, mentioned far lower turnouts (32 and 24 per cent in Donetsk and Luhansk, respectively; see Peremitin, 2014). Regardless of these controversies, the results appeared to provide the acting DNR and LNR authorities with the leverage needed to refuse to participate in the Ukrainian presidential elections, to be held later that month. According to the *Guardian*, Denis Pushilin, a former candy salesman and purveyor of Ponzi schemes and then-chairman of the Supreme Council of the DNR, put out the following statement:

All [Ukrainian] military troops on our territory after the official announcement of referendum results will be considered illegal and declared occupiers.... It is necessary [for the DNR] to form state bodies and military authorities as soon as possible.

(Walker et al., 2014)

Oleg Tsariov, having moved from Donetsk to Luhansk, expressed satisfaction with the results when addressing a group of World War II veterans at a polling station there:

Having looked at the results of the referendum, we see the way people are going, how they vote. We ask them who they vote for, and we have preliminary results.... The

---

[1] In Russian: 'поддерживаете ли Вы Акт о государственной самостоятельности [Донецкой/Луганской] Народной Республики'? (Wikimedia, 2014b, 2014a).

people support independence, they support the sovereignty of Luhansk and Donetsk, not from the people of Ukraine, but from its fascist authorities.

(Lugansk 24, 2014)

A political leadership structure was set up to reflect the referendum results as interpreted by the local authorities. Aleksandr Borodai, a Russian citizen and former advisor to prime minister of the 'Republic of Crimea' Sergei Aksionov, became the DNR's first prime minister (BBC News, 2014b). Pavel Gubarev, a Ukrainian-born former member of a neo-Nazi paramilitary group, was appointed as 'People's Governor', although he was forced to play second fiddle to Borodai. Igor Girkin (best known by his nom de guerre Strelkov), a Russian nationalist and war veteran who had fought alongside Borodai in Transnistria in the 1990s, became minister of defence. Aleksandr Zakharchenko, the head of the Donetsk branch of the Kharkiv-based social-political movement Oplot ('Stronghold') and leader of a local militia by the same name, became the DNR's military commander.[2] And Denis Pushilin became chairman of the Supreme Council (*verkhovnyi sovet*), the legislature of the DNR. It was later renamed to People's Council (*narodnyi sovet*) (Taylor, 2014). Pushilin soon resigned from his position and was replaced by Andrei Purgin. He took over again in September 2015.

A brief but fierce battle for control broke out among the DNR's various factions, which was won decisively by Zakharchenko. In August, Girkin/Strelkov was relieved of his duties as defence minister. He was blamed for mismanaging the Battle of Sloviansk, which had resulted in the Ukrainian army recapturing the city, and for ceding other important territory to the Ukrainian army (C. Miller, 2014). He was succeeded by Vladimir Kononov. Borodai, meanwhile, resigned as prime minister, handing over his post to Zakharchenko. His resignation came amidst mounting criticism that Moscow was directing events in eastern Ukraine and that the demonstrations were less than organic. In Borodai's words, it was time to make sure Donbas was no longer run by a Russian citizen: 'I am a Muscovite. Donbas should be led by a genuine Donetsk native' (C. Miller, 2014). His resignation, however, did little to persuade most observers that Russia and its armed forces were disengaging from the conflict (Gibbons-Neff, 2015), nor did affirmations that Russian troops captured in Donbas by the Ukrainian army had crossed the border 'by accident' (BBC News, 2014c).

In Luhansk, the process of establishing political leadership was somewhat more tumultuous. Valerii Bolotov, who now led the South-eastern Army (*Armiia Iugo-Vostoka*) militia (ITAR-TASS, 2014d), became the first 'People's Governor' of the LNR on April 21. Infighting continued, however, and on May 13 an attempt was made to end his life, injuring him (ITAR-

---

[2] Denis Pushilin initially appointed Igor Kakidzhanov as the DNR's military commander in April, but he was replaced by Zakharchenko in May (ITAR-TASS, 2014b).

TASS, 2014c). Gennadii Tsypkalov was named as interim head of the LNR the same day, until Bolotov, still recovering, took over again a few days later on May 17. The Council of Ministers (*sovet ministrov*) of the LNR was established on May 18, 2014 (ITAR-TASS, 2014d), with Vasilii Nikitin as its head. Aleksandr Kariakin became chairman of the People's Council. Two days later, on May 21, the Republican Assembly of the LNR appointed Igor Plotnitskii as minister of defence (Rosbalt, 2014). The rest of the cabinet was named in the next session on May 27 (Yadocent, 2014). Plotnitskii called for a reorganisation of the Council of Ministers. On November 17, he issued a decree declaring the formation of the new Council, which was then officially instated on November 26 (Glava Luganskoi Narodnoi Respubliki, 2014). Aleksandr Chumachenko was appointed as minister of transport, communications, information, and mass communication.

Nikitin's term as head of the Council of Ministers ended quickly as tensions within the uncomfortable alliance between various competing factions came to a head. On July 3, Bolotov issued a decree forcing Nikitin to resign and the Council of Ministers to disband (Forbes, 2014; Vzgliad, 2014). The stated reason for this was the passing of the law 'On the System of Executive Bodies of State Power of the Luhansk People's Republic' and the termination of the law 'On the Cabinet of Ministers of the Luhansk People's Republic' (Narodnyi Sovet Luganskoi Narodnoi Respubliki, 2014b), a move that effectively nullified the existing political structure. Marat Bashirov, a confidant of Bolotov's, became interim prime minister.

Even Bolotov, however, was not impervious to infighting. On August 14, he resigned as head of the LNR, stating that his injuries sustained from the assassination attempt in May were preventing him from fulfilling his duties. He was replaced by Plotnitskii (Kanashevich & Ul'ianova, 2014). Bashirov resigned soon after as prime minister. He was initially succeeded by Plotnitskii, who briefly held both posts. Gennadii Tsypkalov took over as prime minister on August 26. Tsypkalov held onto his post until his resignation on December 26, 2015, after being forced out. He was found hanged in his room on September 24, 2016, after having been arrested on suspicion of planning a coup d'état (Bulanov, 2016).

The 'referendums' and the subsequent centralisation of power cleared the way for attempts to establish the ideological foundations of the DNR and LNR. Most of this activity originated with Tsariov in Luhansk and especially with Gubarev in Donetsk. On May 22, the founding congress took place of Gubarev's new political party (officially a 'social-political movement' [*obshchestvenno-politicheskoe dvizhenie*]), *Partiia Novorossiia*. At the conference, Gubarev laid out the party's political and ideological objectives, and proclaimed the founding of the 'Federal State of Novorossiia' (V Makeevke; VMakeevke.com, 2014). *Partiia Novorossiia*'s programme went into some detail about its historical and cultural foundations:

The creation of the State of Novorossiia (*gosudarstvo Novorossii*) is not only the withdrawal of all southeastern Russian lands of Ukraine from subjugation to the authorities in Kyiv, not only the liberation from the yoke of a fascist junta, but also the construction of a new, truly fair, scientifically and technologically developed state, all of whose resources not only in words, but also in reality, belong to the people and are fully used for their benefit.

(Novorossia, 2014)

Gubarev envisioned a modern state with an economy focused on science and technological innovation. Culturally, 'Novorossiia' was to be part of Greater Russia and the Russian World,[3] with Russian as its state language and Orthodox Christianity as its religious norm. Religious discrimination would not be allowed, 'with the exception of aggressive totalitarian sects alien to the Russian cultural and civilisational milieu that destroy the foundations of social life and social harmony'.

Also in attendance at the conference was Aleksandr Dugin, a controversial far-right Russian academic and public intellectual known for his anti-Western and anti-Ukrainian viewpoints and his work on political organisation. Dugin published his views on the ideological foundations of 'Novorossiia' on Gubarev's website:

It is important that, among all the regions inhabited mainly by people who reject Kyiv–Galician identity, so far only Donetsk and Luhansk have gone all the way to Independence.[4] This is the land of the Don Army, dominated by a population of Cossacks with a special ethno-social structure and a very warlike and freedom-loving frame of mind. In fact, the DNR and LNR are a new iteration of the Don Cossack Republic (*donskaia kazachia respublika*),[5] which is a special part of the Russian World (*russkii mir*), very close to the Rostov and Krasnodar regions of Russia, and significantly different from other regions of central and eastern Russia.

(Dugin, 2014)

Dugin went into detail about the 'Cossack identity' of the people of Donbas. He rejected the notion that the DNR and LNR ought to simply become part of the Russian Federation, and instead insisted that 'Novorossiia' form a special zone of Russian–Cossack freemen (*volnitsa*). The end goal was not 'entry into the Russian Federation', but rather the restoration of the old Russian Empire. Dugin also argued that, while parts of what was to be 'Novorossiia' had been 'liberated', 12 million people in Donbas continued to suffer under the yoke of 'neo-Nazi cartels', who 'reject the course taken by the

---

[3] The 'Russian World' (*russkii mir*), a term dating back to the eleventh century, describes the totality of Russian civilisational space, including cultural values, political organisation, and religious identity (Laruelle, 2015).

[4] Dugin uses the word *nezavisimost* here, which means independence; *samostoiatelnost* refers more to autonomy or self-rule. Capitalisation in original.

[5] Dugin here mentions the Don Cossacks, who have a long history of joining Russian rulers in battle against the Ottomans, Mongols, and Napoleon. Although the Don Cossacks did control parts of Donbas, historically these lands fell under Zaporizhian (Ukrainian) Cossack control.

Banderite[6] Right Sector, pro-American liberals, and murderous Jewish oligarchs'. Finally, Dugin expressed the conviction that the 'beautiful, delightful little-Russian language' (by which he meant Ukrainian) should not become a victim of the DNR's and LNR's battle with 'Ukrainian Nazism'; the language, he said, is not guilty by itself, and its rich and beautiful history deserved to be part of the 'Novorossiian' space.

During the first months of their existence, the DNR and LNR leadership was united in a desire to bring the two territories closer together under the banner of 'Novorossiia'. Two days after the *Partiia Novorossiia* congress, the first DNR prime minister DNR Aleksandr Borodai and then-chairman of the LNR People's Council Aleksandr Kariakin signed a document (behind closed doors) confirming the establishment of the 'Confederation of Novorossiia' (URA-Inform, 2014). On June 26, the DNR and LNR announced the passing of a 'constitutional act' establishing a 'Union of People's Republics' (*Soiuz Narodnykh Respublik*; SNR). The SNR constituted the formalisation of the aforementioned Confederation:

We, the representatives of the Donetsk People's Republic and the Luhansk People's Republic, relying on the common historical destinies of the people living in the territories of our states and guided by its desire for unity, proceeding from universally recognised principles of equal rights and self-determination, being convinced that a union of our states will allow us to unite our efforts in the interest of ensuring our security and economic and social development, confirming our desire to live in peace and harmony with other states, hereby acknowledge this Constitutional Act establishing the Union of People's Republics.

(Vechernii Donetsk, 2014)

DEATH IN THE SKIES

Oleg Tsariov was appointed speaker of the SNR joint parliament, and the ideological project of 'Novorossiia' appeared well on its way to becoming a reality. Soon, however, the Donbas conflict would make headlines worldwide in a way that substantially limited the DNR's and LNR's ability to continue their state-building efforts below the radar (Abibok, 2019). On July 17, 2014, Malaysian Airlines flight 17, en route from Amsterdam to Kuala Lumpur, was shot down over the village of Hrabove in DNR-controlled territory. All 15 crew members and 283 passengers, 196 of whom were Dutch, were killed instantly. The DNR insurgents initially assumed they had shot down a Ukrainian military cargo plane. Igor Girkin, writing under his pseudonym Strelkov, wrote a post on his Vkontakte page around twenty minutes after the crash in which he claimed responsibility for the plane's demise:

---

[6] After Stepan Bandera (see Chapter 1).

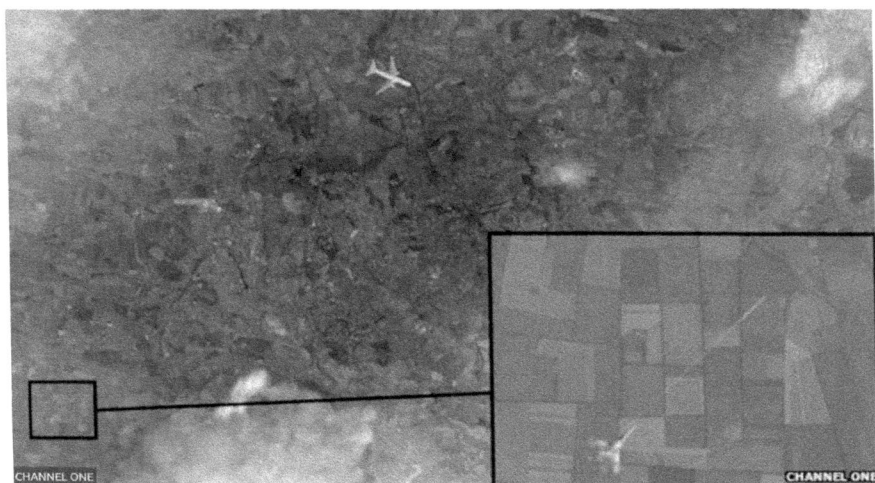

FIGURE 2.1 A still image shown on a Russian state television channel (Channel One) supposedly showing a fighter jet firing a missile at flight MH17. The image is photoshopped (Rudin, 2016).

> An An-26 airplane was just shot down in the Torez region. It came down somewhere behind the 'Progress' mine. We already warned you not to fly through 'our skies'. Here is video confirmation of the latest 'birdfall' (*ptichkopad*). The bird came down behind a slagheap, residential areas were not affected. Peaceful people were not hurt.
>
> (Strelkov, 2014)

DNR insurgents sent to the crash site soon found out that the plane was civilian and not military. A few weeks after the crash, an audio recording was released by the Ukrainian Security Service of militants arriving at the scene of the crash expecting to see the remains of an Antonov cargo jet, but instead finding foreign passports, children's teddy bears, and suitcases packed for vacation (Demirjian, 2014). As soon as it became clear that civilians had been killed, Strelkov deleted his Vkontakte post and DNR officials began issuing denials that they had shot down an airplane (Luhn, 2014). Theories began to circulate in DNR, LNR, and pro-Russian media blaming Ukraine for the crash. One popular conspiracy theory alleged that MH17 was shot down by a Ukrainian fighter plane because it looked similar to Vladimir Putin's government jet (StopFake, 2017). See Figure 2.1 for an example of how this conspiracy theory was broadcase on Russian state media.

Two official investigations by the Dutch Safety Board and the Netherlands-led Joint Investigation Team (JIT) determined that the plane had been hit by a BUK TELAR surface-to-air missile launched from a field that was in DNR insurgents' hands at the time (Landelijk Parket, 2018). The MH17 disaster highlighted the extent of Russia's involvement in the Donbas conflict. Based on video evidence, intercepted phone conversations, and satellite data, investigations by the JIT, the Dutch Safety Board, and investigative journalism website Bellingcat concluded that the missile launch system belonged to the Russian army's 53rd Anti-Aircraft Missile Brigade, stationed in Kursk (Joint Investigation Team, 2018; Romein, 2016). The launch system was escorted out of the area and back into Russia shortly after the disaster. In 2018, the governments of the Netherlands and Australia held Russia accountable for its role in providing the launch system, and would pursue legal avenues to indict those responsible in a court of law (Government of the Netherlands, 2018). In November 2022, a court in The Hague sentenced (in absentia) Russian citizens Igor Girkin (Strelkov) and Sergei Dubinskii and the Ukrainian Leonid Kharchenko to life in prison for their role in the downing of MH17. Another Russian, Oleg Pulatov, was cleared of all charges (NOS, 2022).

The downing of flight MH17 put the Donbas conflict at the centre of global attention, prompting concerted efforts to bring about a ceasefire. These efforts culminated in the signing of the first Minsk Protocol in September 2014. It was signed by representatives of the so-called Trilateral Contact Group on Ukraine (consisting of Ukraine, the Russian Federation, and the OSCE), as well as Plotnitskii and Zakharchenko, who represented the LNR and DNR, respectively (OSCE, 2014b). The protocol contained twelve points, the most important of which were an agreement to an immediate ceasefire and a decentralisation of power in Donetsk and Luhansk oblasts, resulting (in theory) in increased autonomy for the two regions.

The protocol was an almost immediate failure. The ceasefire was violated instantly, leading to the signing of a memorandum clarifying the original protocol and the creation of a thirty-kilometre (nineteen-mile) buffer zone between the two warring parties (OSCE, 2014c). A few days later, new clashes broke out at the Donetsk airport, which had been captured by Ukrainian forces in May. The battle continued well into the new year, with both sides suffering heavy casualties until the airport was finally overrun and captured by DNR and Russian forces in January 2015 (Walker & Grytsenko, 2015).

THE END OF IDEOLOGY?

Internally, the simmering tensions between various factions in both the DNR and LNR were beginning to boil over. In Donetsk, Gubarev's star began to wane as other figures expanded their influence. On October 13, 2014, the car he was driving in was shot at by unknown assailants and crashed into a pillar. Gubarev escaped with relatively minor injuries (BBC News, 2014d). This happened while the DNR and LNR authorities were planning to hold simultaneous elections on November 2. It soon became clear that Gubarev's *Partiia*

Novorossiia, despite its hopeful beginnings, was out of the loop. The party was banned from participating in elections 'failing to meet requirements', along with the local Communist party and the block *Edinyi Donbass*. Only so-called social movements (*obshchestvennye dvizheniia*) were allowed to take part, provided they had the proper credentials to do so (Artem'ev et al., 2014).

The only two such entities standing in the DNR elections were *Svobodnyi Donbass*, led by Ievgenii Orlov and Iurii Sivokonenko, and *Donetskaia Respublika*, led by Zakharchenko. Unlike *Partiia Novorossiia*, the latter was not an entirely new entity in the region. According to Taras Kuzio, *Donetskaia Respublika* was 'a successor to the International Movement of Donbas founded in 1989 by Andrei Purgin, Dmitrii Kornilov, and Sergei Baryshnikov.... [I]t was launched a year after the 2004 Orange Revolution and, similar to the Soviet-era Inter-Movement, with support from Russian intelligence. [*Donetskaia Respublika*] and other Russian nationalist groups were provided with paramilitary training in summer camps organised by Aleksandr Dugin.... [It] was banned by the Ukrainian authorities in 2007–2008' (Kuzio, 2017, p. 10). Its main purpose was originally to obtain a special status within Ukraine for Donetsk oblast and other parts of Donbas. Until 2014, it was a movement operating in the margins of society. Its rallies were attended by at most thirty to fifty people at a time (Politrada, 2019).

With Pavel Gubarev's fall from grace, *Donetskaia Respublika* became the dominant political force in the DNR. Sivokonenko, Zakharchenko's only competitor for the position of head of the DNR, put up no resistance, and was quoted by the *New York Times* as saying that he 'didn't ask people to vote for [him], because [he doesn't] have any differences in principle with Zakharchenko' (Kramer, 2014). Zakharchenko won handily with 78.93 per cent of the vote, defeating Sivokonenko and independent candidate Aleksandr Kofman, who was later given the post of foreign minister (Ukraïns'ka Pravda, 2014c). *Donetskaia Respublika* obtained 68 out of 100 parliamentary seats, and *Svobodnyi Donbass* 32 (DNR Today, 2014).

Parliamentary and leadership elections were also held in Luhansk. Here, the social movement 'Peace for the Luhansk Region' (*Mir Luganshchine*), led by Plotnitskii, won 69.46 per cent of the votes and obtained thirty-five out of fifty seats in the LNR's People's Council. Its main rival, the 'Luhansk Economic Union' (*Luganskii Ekonomicheskii Soiuz*), led by Oleg Akimov, got 21.17 per cent of the electorate behind it, and with that the remaining fifteen People's Council seats. The third social movement vying for seats, the 'People's Union' (*Narodnyi Soiuz*), received approximately 3 per cent of the votes, failing to meet the electoral threshold. Voter turnout, incidentally, was registered at 99.99 per cent (Lugansk-Online, 2014).

The elections, together with the DNR's takeover of the Donetsk airport and the fierce battle for control over the strategic railway town of Debaltsevo a few months later, had spelled disaster for the first Minsk protocol (OSCE,

2014e). At the initiative of French president François Hollande and German chancellor Angela Merkel, a new attempt to broker a ceasefire was made in early February 2015. Marathon talks between Hollande, Merkel, Poroshenko, Putin, Plotnitskii, and Zakharchenko, under the auspices of the OSCE, led to the signing of the Minsk-II agreements (OSCE, 2015b). As heavy fighting was still ongoing during the negotiations, the agreements were criticised as fragile and unrealistic (Foxall, 2015). Minsk-II contained mostly the same provisions as the original Minsk protocol (including a call for an immediate ceasefire, withdrawing heavy weaponry and artillery, and the creation of a fifty-kilometre buffer zone). The new agreement also contained a provision on constitutional reform in Ukraine that would acknowledge the special status of parts of Donetsk and Luhansk oblasts (*Financial Times*, 2015).

The future of the DNR and LNR as ideological projects, meanwhile, became more and more uncertain. After the disappearance of Gubarev's *Partiia Novorossiia* from the political stage, the unification of the DNR and LNR (as well as potentially other parts of Ukraine) under the 'Novorossiia' banner became increasingly unpopular. On May 18, 2015, DNR foreign minister Aleksandr Kofman announced that the 'Confederation of Novorossiia' would cease to exist 'for the time being' (Sindelar, 2015). This was confirmed by the speaker of the parliament of the Union of People's Republics (SNR), Oleg Tsariov, on the same day. Tsariov's official explanation was that the confederation was not in line with the new Minsk agreements, which did not contain provisions allowing for the independence of eastern Ukrainian territories. The LNR and DNR, however, continued to refer to themselves as independent (O'Loughlin et al., 2017; Sindelar, 2015). In July 2016, one final attempt was made to revive the 'Novorossiia' project. Valerii Bolotov, former head of the LNR, announced a surprise return to LNR politics on Facebook by stating he was asked by Novorossiian deputies to become speaker of the now-defunct Novorossiian parliament (Lesiv, 2016). Bolotov's proposal was quickly shot down by almost everyone involved, with Igor Girkin, the former DNR defence minister, saying that the Novorossiia project had been a 'colossal failure for the Kremlin' (Dialog UA, 2016).

RESUSCITATION ATTEMPTS

The disappearance of the idea of 'Novorossiia' from official discourse did not mean the end of DNR/LNR ideological projects altogether. In February 2015, the DNR legislature adopted a memorandum declaring the DNR to be the 'legal successor' to the Donetsk-Kryvyi Rih Soviet Republic (DKR),[7] a self-declared Soviet Republic that existed between February 12 and March 20,

---

[7] In Russian: Донецко-Криворожская советская республика; Krivoi Rog is the Russian name of Kryvyi Rih.

1918 (see Chapter 1). The capital of the DKR was first Kharkiv and then Luhansk, until it was officially abolished at the second All-Ukrainian Congress of Soviets and incorporated into the new Ukrainian Soviet Socialist Republic after Vladimir Lenin expressed his disapproval of its existence, fearing that it might weaken Ukraine.[8] The memorandum read as the following:

> On February 12th, 1918, the Donetsk-Kryvyi Rih Republic (DKR) was created at the fourth Congress of Soviets of the Donetsk-Kryvyi Rih basin, on the basis of ideas of agricultural and economic integration.... The Donetsk-Kryvyi Rih Republic never officially ceased to exist, despite the German occupation, military operations, and other social cataclysms. Its ideas have lived on in the hearts and souls of millions of people.
>
> The 'International Movement of Donbas' was created in the late 1980s under the leadership of Dmitrii Kornilov,[9] which first raised the black-blue-red flag of the DKR in 1991. In March 1994, the people of Donbas spoke out in favour of a federalised structure of the state [of Ukraine]. Federalist tendencies were expressed at the Severodonetsk Congress in 2004, where it was decided to hold a referendum in the Donetsk and Luhansk oblasts on the issue of gaining the status of independent republics. Similar attempts to reorganise the state were declared criminal by the authorities in Kyiv. Popular protests resulted in the creation of the political movement *Donetskaia Respublika*. The people of Donbas finally confirmed their choice in the 2014 referendum.
>
> (Narodnyi Sovet Donetskoi Narodnoi Respubliki, 2015)

Then-Chairman of the DNR People's Council Andrei Purgin asserted that the memorandum was a 'political document about the historical continuity (*preemstvennost*) between the DKR and DNR. We feel part of this historical construct, which was first proclaimed in 1917' (Russkaia Vesna, 2015). And while the project originated in Donetsk, the LNR leadership also expressed agreement with the memorandum. Daria Mazaeva, coordinator of the Donetsk-based 'Novorossiia' press centre, stated that the move marked the beginning of a movement towards a unification of the DNR and LNR (Dergachev & Kartsev, 2015). Observers such as the Russian political scientist Aleksei Makarkin remarked that the move constituted a significant step in the search for a local identity, which the DNR and LNR leadership deemed particularly important in light of the Minsk-II negotiations.

Influential local figures, most notably the brothers Dmitrii and Vladimir Kornilov, emphasised the historical significance of the Donetsk-Kryvyi Rih Republic. Its symbols, they claimed, continued to hold relevance in the modern

---

[8] This action followed the signing of the Treaty of Brest-Litovsk between Germany and the other Central Powers in World War I and the new Bolshevik government of Russia. The Treaty stipulated, among other things, that Russia would cede large swaths of territory in Eastern Europe and Central Asia. See Chapter 1.

[9] Vladimir Kornilov, Dmitrii's brother, is a self-declared 'political analyst and historian' who has written about the Donetsk-Kryvyi Rih Soviet Republic (Edwards, 2014).

FIGURE 2.2 The flag of the Donetsk People's Republic (black/blue/red). The coat of arms in the centre says *Donetskaia Rus'*, a curious turn of phrase of unclear origin that combines Donetsk with (Kyivan) Rus' (see Chapter 1) (adapted from Wikimedia, 2014).

era (Edwards, 2014). For example, as the memorandum cited above suggests, the official DNR flag (see Figure 2.2) was claimed to be based on the DKR flag from 1918. And indeed, Andrew Wilson argues that the foundation of the DKR showed the 'determination of the local population to have no truck with Ukrainian nationalism' at the time (Wilson, 1995, p. 280); employing its historical symbolism could therefore be seen as a way for the DNR and LNR authorities to build legitimacy and contribute to the formation of a local identity.

Other observers, however, were not convinced that the Donetsk-Kryvyi Rih Republic constituted a legitimate historical legacy for the DNR and LNR. For example, Valerii Solovei, a history professor and political analyst at Moscow State University, said the following:

Some legal artifices (*zatsepki*), even extremely dubious and ridiculous ones, are necessary to justify [the DNR's and LNR's] position in the [Minsk] negotiations. And, of course, this move is at the same time a hint at possible territorial expansion. Historical continuity has merit only when it is backed by resources. And their main resource is the position of Russia. In this case, the key issue is the financial and economic conditions of these republics.

(Dergachev & Kartsev, 2015)

Others pointed out that there was no evidence that the DKR flag looked anything like the present-day DNR flag; rather, the black/blue/red banner appears to be that of the aforementioned International Movement of Donbas, which was first presented during a public demonstration in 1991 (Butko, 2017; Edwards, 2014).

The Donetsk-Kryvyi Rih Republic memorandum proved the last serious bilateral attempt at unification. After a period of relative calm, the animosity between the LNR and DNR leaders Plotnitskii and Zakharchenko again began to escalate. On January 23, 2016, a man named Zorian Shkiriak wrote a post on Facebook claiming that Plotnitskii and Zakharchenko had ordered each other's assassination (Shkiriak, 2016). Shkiriak worked at the Ukrainian ministry of internal affairs at the time and professed to cite 'sources close to both terrorist leaders', claiming that each man was willing to shell out one million US dollars for the other's killing (Lenta.ru, 2016). The main reason for this escalation appears to have been a conflict over railway management and the export of industrial products. In January 2017, Zakharchenko reiterated that the reunification of the DNR and LNR was an 'impossibility' (Lenta. ru, 2017a).

This isn't to say that Zakharchenko and Plotnitskii had nothing in common, ideologically speaking. For instance, both men appear to have harboured similar views about Jews and LGBTQ+ people. During a press conference in February 2015, Zakharchenko described the leadership in Kyiv as 'miserable representatives of the great Jewish people' (Haaretz, 2015). On a separate occasion, Zakharchenko remarked that he 'respected' Ukraine's far-right Pravyi Sektor movement for 'beating up the gays in Kyiv' (Korrespondent, 2015). Not to be outdone, Plotnitskii gave a lecture at a Russian university a few months later, where he said: 'I'd like to ask the historians . . . or maybe the philologists, can't choose really, why was it called "Euromaidan"? Where did the name come from? From the area [Maidan Nezalezhnosti in Kyiv]? Or perhaps from the people? Those same people who now make up the majority of leaders of what was once our Ukraine?' (Sokol, 2015). What he means here is that Euromaidan sounds similar to *Evreimaidan*, *Evrei* being Russian for 'Jew'. During the same lecture, Plotnitskii also referred to then-president of Ukraine Petro Poroshenko as 'Valtzman', as some conspiracy theorists believe that Poroshenko is secretly Jewish and changed his name from Valtzman to hide this fact.

In 2016, the political situation in the DNR and LNR became more and more volatile. Igor Plotnitskii narrowly survived an assassination attempt in August, after an explosive that had been planted under his car went off near a set of traffic lights, injuring him and several others (BBC News, 2016b). In September, *Luganskii Telegraf*, a Luhansk-based news site and newspaper, reported of a 'conspiracy plot' aimed at overthrowing Plotnitskii's government and staging a coup d'état (Luganskii Telegraf, 2016). LNR officials refused to either confirm or deny the report. The grapevine blamed Zakharchenko for instigating the attempted coup, although neither he nor anyone else from the DNR was officially accused. Several other high-profile leaders of the region's armed militias were, however, assassinated. In October 2016, Arsen Pavlov (known under his nom de guerre Motorola), the Russian-born commander of the pro-DNR *Sparta* battalion, was killed in a bomb blast in a lift in his apartment block (BBC News, 2016c). A few months later, in February 2017, Mikhail Tolstykh (nom de guerre Givi), commander of the *Somali* battalion,[10] was killed in his office when it was struck by a rocket (BBC News, 2017b). And in Luhansk, Oleg Anashchenko, the LNR defence minister, was killed in a car bomb attack (BBC News, 2017a). The deaths of Motorola and Givi proved especially beneficial to Zakharchenko, whose grip on power was now stronger than ever. The deaths also made reconciliation attempts between the DNR and LNR more feasible. In the same month as Givi's and Anashchenko's deaths, Zakharchenko and Plotnitskii announced the start of a social programme providing aid to Donbas residents living in areas under Ukrainian control, stating that the people of Donbas are 'one people' and that 'no one will be left to the fascists' (Gordeev, 2017; Telekanal Iunion, 2017).

Throughout it all, ideological projects stayed on the political agenda. The DNR and to a lesser extent the LNR tried to gain support and recognition from the international community. In 2016, DNR representatives opened an 'honorary consulate' in Ostrava in the Czech Republic (Telekanal 'Oplot TV', 2016). A judge disbanded the mission in 2018. Similar (unsuccessful) diplomatic missions popped up in Austria and Greece (Euromaidan Press, 2016; Gazeta.ru, 2017). The LNR tried to do the same in Sicily (Von Twickel, 2018) and made headlines in the United States when the retired American mixed martial artist Jeff Monson, who had previously fought in the Ultimate Fighting Championship (UFC) promotion, announced that he had become an LNR 'citizen': 'Look, I support your fight for your own autonomy, for your own freedom, for your own ability to make decisions for yourself' (A. Smith, 2016).

Internally, the DNR's and LNR's search for a collective identity was far from over. In August 2016, officials working at the LNR ministry of information exchanged emails containing three documents that outlined the LNR's ideological foundations: the 'Declaration of the Right to Self-Determination', the 'Declaration of Sovereignty', and the 'Statement on the Ideological Principles of the LNR'.[11]

---

[10] The *Somali* battalion (*Batal'on 'Somali'*) was one of the military units fighting under the DNR banner. Tolstykh stated that the battalion got its name because its members were as 'fearless as Somalis' (Kim, 2014).
[11] My English translation of these three documents can be found in the online appendix. Link: https://osf.io/3846a/, in the 'Background Information' folder.

The 'Declaration of the Right to Self-Determination' sets out the reasons why the LNR had the right to secede from Ukraine: the 'criminal, anti-constitutional, anti-state coup of February 2014' and the 'destruction of Ukraine's statehood', which was started by the 'robber baron oligarchs relying on financial, diplomatic, moral, and military support from international capital', as well as an unwillingness to reconcile with the Ukrainian government's 'neo-fascist ideology', all of which left Donbas with no choice but to break away.

The 'Declaration of Sovereignty' of the LNR is comparable in scope to the 'Declaration of the Right to Self-Determination'. It also mentions the 2014 'coup d'état' in Kyiv and the country's subsequent descent into neo-fascism as prime motivations for secession. It adds that Ukraine's 'Russian-speaking population, constituting more than half of the citizens of Ukraine, has not even had its own official language, which in the modern world is an absolutely unprecedented and scandalous fact. These citizens are subject to linguistic and cultural genocide by the state.' In addition, the document claims that the transfer of south-eastern Ukraine and Crimea to the Ukrainian Soviet Republic in 1954 was illegitimate and based on 'purely political considerations'.

The 'Statement on Ideological Principles' goes into more specific detail about the ideological foundations of the LNR. It states that 'the traditions of Donbas regionalism have deep roots. Since ancient times, our homeland has been an industrial and mining centre, being the oldest metalworking centre in Europe. In ancient times, the area of Azov and Podontsoviia became an important corridor for trade routes from Asia to Europe.' With respect to the development of the LNR after 2014, the document states that 'by adopting the name People's Republic, the revolutionary leadership voluntarily committed itself to building a system based on popular law. Any other way leads either to a return to oligarchic anarchy, or to a slide into a nationalist, anti-Russian, anti-people Ukrainian swamp.' It calls the 'purposeful formation of collectivist thinking, the idea of serving one's homeland – the Donbas' as one of the LNR's main challenges. Finally, the statement situates the LNR firmly within the so-called Russian World (*Russkii Mir*): 'in the Soviet past, the attitude towards a person was never defined by their nationality, for all Russian-speaking people were considered a priori "our own"'.

All three documents also mention the Donetsk-Kryvyi Rih Republic as a historical precedent for the DNR's and LNR's right to self-determination. 'Novorossiia', however, is not mentioned, nor is there any trace of an ambitious ideological framework to achieve a 'greater Russia' as espoused by Gubarev and Dugin in 2014. Instead, the main justification for wanting to break away from Ukraine appears to be the (perceived) ideological shift that Ukraine underwent during and after the Euromaidan revolution, and an apparent disdain for its new and allegedly 'fasist' government and its Western allies. I return to these themes in Chapters 4–6.

In Donetsk, the question of ideology resurfaced with a start in July 2017, when Aleksandr Zakharchenko announced the founding of the 'new state of Malorossiia', or 'Little Russia' (Obshchestvennoe TV Donbassa, 2017b). This term has a long and charged history (see Chapter 1). In Tsarist times, it referred to the territories of the Russian Empire that later became present-day Ukraine (BBC News, 2017c). 'Malorossiia' was first used in the fourteenth century by the last prince of Galicia, Iurii II Boreslav, and for a long time was used alongside a host of other terms (such as Rus' and Ukraine) to denote the lands at the edge of Muscovy, and later of the Cossack Hetmanate and Russian Empire (Kohut, 1986, p. 564). After the Pereiaslav Agreement of 1654 between Bohdan Khmelnytskyi's Cossacks and the Tsar of Muscovy, 'Malorossiia' became the most commonly used term to describe the Cossack Hetmanate (Kohut, 1986, p. 565). Over the course of the next few centuries, 'Malorossiia' became a source of self-identification for local elites, and a prototype for national consciousness, not only for local Cossacks but also for Ukrainians seeking to set themselves apart from Russia and Russians (Kotenko et al., 2011). Gradually, however, Ukrainian (as opposed to 'Little Russian') identity gained the upper hand in large parts of what is now Ukraine due to the destruction of Cossack Hetmanate legal practices and political structures, paired with the rise of Ukrainian national consciousness through humour, music, poetry, and literature (Kohut, 1986, p. 573). Moscow, fearing the rise of nationalism in both Poland and Ukraine, promoted the concept of a 'triune' Russian national identity, with Belorussians, Little Russians, and Greater Russians all cut from the same cloth (Edwards, 2017). After the revolutions of 1917 and the civil war, the Bolshevik government instated a policy of *korenizatsiia* ('indigenisation') that (in the Ukrainian SSR) was aimed at promoting Ukrainian language and culture, and Malorossiian identity fell out of use despite multiple attempts to revive it (Kotenko et al., 2011).

In his announcement, Zakharchenko claimed that 'representatives of Donbas', as well as of seventeen Ukrainian oblasts[12] (not including Crimea, likely because Zakharchenko considered it to be Russian territory), signed a document declaring the Ukrainian state null and void, replacing it with the state of 'Malorossiia'. This new state would have Donetsk as its capital and Kyiv as a centre of 'historical and cultural importance' (Edwards, 2017). Donbas, Zakharchenko claimed, would not reunite with Ukraine; instead, it was Ukraine that would be reuniting with Donbas (Novosti Donetskoi Respubliki, 2017a). Zakharchenko also presented the new Malorossiian flag; see Figure 2.3.

---

[12] Zakharchenko claimed to have support from people from the oblasts of Kharkiv, Dnipro, Zaporizhzhia, Kherson, Mykolaiv, Odessa, Sumy, Poltava, Chernihiv, Kirovohrad, Kyiv (both the city and the oblast), Cherkasy, Rivne, Volyn, Ternopil, Ivano-Frankivsk, and Lviv.

FIGURE 2.3 Flag of 'Malorossiia' (red and white), as presented by Zakharchenko (Edwards, 2017). The symbol in the top left is the coat of arms of the Cossack Hetmanate (see Chapter 1) (adapted from Wikimedia, 2017).

Zakharchenko argued that Ukraine had proven itself to be a 'failed state', incapable of providing its citizens with 'a prosperous present and future'. He also announced the creation of an organisational committee, tasked with drafting a constitution for the newly minted state. This committee was to consist of three people: Zakharchenko himself, Zakharchenko's right-hand man, vice prime minister of the DNR Aleksandr Timofeev (nickname Tashkent), and one Viacheslav Gubin, who declared himself to be a 'representative of Kharkiv Oblast' (Vatnik, 2017). What exactly the three men meant by 'representative' was not immediately clear.

Key figures both inside and outside the DNR responded to Zakharchenko's announcement with confusion. Initially, nobody knew how to react: Zakharchenko held his press conference at around 8 am local time on July 18, 2017. Two hours later, by 10 am, both the Luhansk Press Centre (*Luganskii Informatsionnyi Tsentr*) and the English-language, Donetsk-based *DONi News Agency* were yet to make mention of it. When reactions finally did come, they were mostly derisive. The announcement of the founding of 'Malorossiia' appears to have taken the Kremlin by surprise. The Russian news outlet *RBK* reported that two sources close to Vladimir Putin claimed that the development was 'unexpected' (Dergachev, 2017; UNIAN, 2017b).

Aleksei Chesnakov, an 'expert' close to Vladislav Surkov, a high-level Kremlin official said to be in charge of Russia's involvement in eastern Ukraine, told the *ITAR-TASS* press agency that the project was not taken seriously even within the DNR and that it should be seen as more of a literary project than a political one (Gordo & Gal'skaia, 2017). 'In a month's time', he said, 'everyone will have forgotten about Malorossiia.' Then-chairman of the People's Council of the DNR Denis Pushilin issued a carefully worded response later in the day. Even he had been surprised by Zakharchenko's announcement:

The formation of the state of Malorossiia could be an interesting initiative. However, in my opinion, it would have been more correct to submit such questions in advance for discussion in parliament and by way of a national referendum. The issue is debatable, and we must learn the opinion of society. As for the legal aspects [to this case], no formal legislation was passed and the DNR and LNR parliaments are not undertaking political activities in this direction. When such tasks are set by our leadership, we are ready to discuss them. However, at the moment this is only an idea, which is still perceived very ambiguously in both the LNR and the DNR, and in the Russian Federation.

(Pushilin, 2017)

The reaction from the LNR was more blunt. Vladislav Deinego, the LNR foreign minister, said that the LNR leadership had 'learned about this through the media. No one discussed this project with us [beforehand]' (Novosti Donetskoi Respubliki, 2017b). Zakharchenko had overplayed his hand, overestimating local elites' and the Kremlin's willingness to go along with his idea. A few weeks later, he backed away from the 'Malorossiia' project, stating that the 'overturning of Ukraine evoked much interest within society', but that the name 'Malorossiia' was receiving little support (Lenta.ru, 2017b). The ultranationalist Russian writer Zakhar Prilepin, an early proponent of the DNR and LNR who had been involved with the 'Malorossiia' project from the start, stated in an interview that the idea behind 'Malorossiia' had been to surprise Moscow, Washington, and Kyiv, and that the end goal was a 'unified state with Russia and Belarus' (Kots, 2017). But in the end, despite well-known figures like Pavel Gubarev openly identifying with a 'Malorossiian' identity (Kuromiya, 2016), the project was abandoned.

COUPS AND ASSASSINATIONS

In Luhansk, internal tensions between influential political figures came to a head at the end of 2017. On November 9, Plotnitskii forced his interior minister Igor Kornet, with whom he had had several political altercations before, to give back his lavish house in Luhansk to its supposed lawful owner, in a rather humiliating display that was broadcast on live TV.[13] Eleven days

---

[13] The original video used to be on YouTube, but has since been removed (C. Miller, 2017).

later, Plotnitskii fired Kornet, officially for the latter's illegal seizure of private property. An unhappy Kornet publicly contested his firing, and it turned out that Plotnitskii had underestimated Kornet's popularity: a contingent of soldiers loyal to Kornet prevented Plotnitskii from appointing a successor for the position of interior minister.

The next day, on November 21, troops arrived in Luhansk, wearing no insignia except for white ribbons. While many initially suspected these troops to be Russian special forces, rumours soon started to swell of DNR forces being involved. For example, some observers noted the similarities between known DNR military vehicles and vehicles spotted in the LNR (Necro Mancer, 2017). The OSCE Special Monitoring Mission also observed a large convoy of military vehicles near Debaltsevo, in DNR territory, on its way to Luhansk (OSCE, 2017b).

These rumours were confirmed one day later, when the DNR ministry of state security came out stating that the DNR had carried out a 'security operation' inside the LNR, with cooperation from the LNR interior ministry (MGBPLNR, 2017b). Kornet gave a press conference in which he claimed that an 'intelligence operation' had penetrated the high ranks of the LNR leadership and that his ministry had detained 'about ten' agents involved in this plot. Kornet accused this mysterious cabal of giving Plotnitskii 'distorted information'. Plotnitskii also gave a press conference on the same day to react to the situation. When asked about what was going on, he denied that anything was the matter. He called Kornet names, stating among other things that 'this small man has acquired big ambitions' (Luxmoore, 2017).

Plotnitskii's grip on power was slipping. His former allies began to put out reports to discredit him. The LNR's ministry of state security reported that the former LNR prime minister Gennadii Tsypkalov had not actually hanged himself, but that he had 'died from torture' and that the medical examiner's reports were falsified by one Kachenko (MGBPLNR, 2017a). The implication was that Plotnitskii had been involved. Stories also came out alleging that the failed 2016 coup attempt was secretly organised by Plotnitskii himself to get rid of his opponents (Von Twickel, 2017).

Plotnitskii's position had become untenable, and on November 22, he fled to Moscow. In the wake of this shake-up, Ukrainian forces tried to make use of the instability and take back several LNR-controlled towns. Heavy fighting broke out in the village of Krymske. Plotnitskii's website was taken offline.[14] Two days later, the head of the LNR ministry of state security, Leonid Pasechnik, announced that Plotnitskii had resigned voluntarily for health reasons. Plotnitskii was allowed to remain a representative of the LNR in the Minsk negotiations, being one of its signatories. Pasechnik became the

---

[14] www.glava-lnr.su. A cached version of this website can be found at http://web.archive.org/web/*/www.glava-lnr.su.

new head of the LNR, a position that he holds to this day. Kornet continued to serve as interior minister (Luganskii Informatsionnyi Tsentr, 2017f). Plotnitskii, meanwhile, was arrested in St Petersburg in February 2018 and charged with embezzlement and abuse of power. What became of him after this is unknown (Krutov, 2018).

The involvement of DNR troops in the LNR coup could have been a precursor to increasing hostilities between the two sides, but this wasn't the case. On November 30, Igor Kornet made a public announcement that the LNR security service had foiled an assassination attempt on Aleksandr Zakharchenko's life. He claimed that the same people had been involved in the killing of Oleg Anashchenko, the former LNR defence minister (Novosti Donbassa, 2017b). Whether there really was a plot to kill Zakharchenko was unclear, but Kornet's announcement did manage to bring down the mounting tensions.

Eventually, however, Zakharchenko's knack for surviving assassination attempts caught up with him. On August 31, 2018, Zakharchenko, together with his right-hand man Aleksandr Timofeev and their security detail, entered the 'Separ' café in Donetsk to have a meal. Seconds later, an explosion, caused by a device planted in a car outside, killed Zakharchenko and wounded Timofeev (BBC Russian, 2018a). It was unclear who was behind the assassination; Vladimir Putin accused the Ukrainian security service, and DNR security officials soon arrested what they called 'Ukrainian saboteurs'. The Ukrainian government blamed infighting rebels and their 'Russian sponsors' (BBC News, 2018; BBC Russian, 2018b). In anonymous channels on private messaging apps such as Telegram, which for many DNR and LNR residents served as a source of information for lack of opposition media, rumours circulated of Moscow's involvement in the assassination. Yulia Abibok argues that Zakharchenko's attempts to put together private militias that took orders from him and not Moscow had angered Vladislav Surkov and others within the Russian government, potentially providing a reason for getting rid of him (Abibok, 2019). The case remains unsolved. Zakharchenko was succeeded by Dmitrii Trapeznikov, who held the post for about a week. Denis Pushilin, who had been at the top of DNR politics since its conception in 2014, was then elected as head of the DNR, a post that he still holds as of this writing (Meduza, 2018).

It is fair to say that, from the perspective of ideology, not much happened in either the LNR or the DNR after Pasechnik and Pushilin took over. Both men knew how to keep a low profile and not ruffle the Kremlin's feathers too much. If anything, the two statelets became more explicit about their ties to Russia in the lead-up to the 2022 full-scale invasion. In February 2020, Pushilin appointed Vladimir Pashkov, a Russian official who had previously been deputy governor of Irkutsk oblast, as a deputy to DNR prime minister Aleksandr Ananchenko and the 'acting chairman of the government'

(Antoniuk, 2020).[15] Both the DNR and LNR stripped Ukrainian of its status as an official language and forbade its use in schools in early 2020 (Coynash, 2020a, 2020b). In January 2021, at a conference in Donetsk, Pushilin presented his 'Russian Donbas doctrine', which he had been working on since 2020, consisting of seven steps to be taken by the DNR and LNR in the 'near future', the most important of which being 'establishing [DNR/LNR] control over all territories of the former Donetsk and Luhansk oblasts'. The purpose of the doctrine, according to Pushilin, was 'to express in a document our inner feelings, the impulse that rallied us when we rebelled against injustice, the lies, the persecution of everything Russian, in order to return to our historical roots' (Novosti Donbassa, 2021). The doctrine, however, stopped short of calling for a formal unification with Russia, and instead called for a 'deepening of economic integration' and an 'intensification of socio-cultural, scientific, educational and other' links with the Russian Federation.

This hesitance to openly express a desire to join Russia changed just before the full-scale invasion in February 2022, when the Russian Duma voted to officially recognise the independence of the DNR and LNR. In September 2022, more than half a year later, Russia announced that the Ukrainian oblasts that they claimed control over (Donetsk, Luhansk, Zaporizhzhia, and Kherson) would hold referendums on whether to be incorporated by the Russian Federation. The referendums were widely condemned as illegitimate as well as ridiculed for apparently including parts of these oblasts that were under Ukrainian government control. Nonetheless, the LNR and DNR were reported to have voted 98.4 per cent and 99.2 per cent in favour of Russian annexation, respectively (Euronews, 2022). In the face of such overwhelming popular support, Vladimir Putin announced the annexation of the four oblasts on September 30. One hundred forty-three members of the UN General Assembly voted to condemn this action, with 5 states voting against condemnation and 35 abstaining (BBC News, 2022c). After this, numerous reports emerged about a Russian campaign to 'Russify' the annexed territories. For example, the Parliamentary Assembly of the Council of Europe (2023) condemned the 'Russification' of Ukrainian children and their forced transfer to Russia, calling it 'evidence of genocide'. Many residents of the occupied territories were also encouraged or forced to obtain Russian passports, and the hryvnia was replaced by the rouble as the main currency (C. Miller et al., 2022). School curricula were changed to reflect pro-Russian views, and governance structures in the occupied territories were staffed by individuals from Russia proper trusted by the Kremlin (Domańska et al., 2023).

---

[15] 'De facto' because Ananchenko had 'quietly disappeared' a while before that and was no longer active, according to one observer (Kazanskii, 2020).

CONCLUSION

This chapter has discussed the DNR's and LNR's development from unorganised but well-armed militias into statelets with a considerable degree of political organisation. I've focused mostly on how the leadership of these statelets leveraged history and ideology to justify and legitimise their existence as separate entities from Ukraine. Although several attempts were made to arrive at a consistent ideological framework, all of them were soon abandoned. Their leadership likely harboured views compatible with far-right ideologies including strong views on Jewish and LGBTQ+ people, but this doesn't appear to have translated into a clearly defined set of ideological policies. Eventually, both the DNR and LNR settled into a comfortable non-ideological status, strongly tied to but never united with Russia, with neither their past nor future clearly vocalised.

An explanation for why this was the case can be found by looking at why two republics sprang up instead of one, a matter that has never been publicly addressed by any DNR or LNR official (Abibok, 2019). Throughout 2014, power in the DNR and LNR was divided between various loosely organised armed groups (the aforementioned *Armiia Iugo-Vostoka*, the *Somali* battalion, the LNR 'People's Militia', etc.). The DNR and LNR, in the words of Nikolai Mitrokhin (2015, 2017), should therefore be seen as a 'conglomerate of local principalities' at this time, consisting of people of various walks of life and political persuasions: true believers in the 'Novorossiia' project (the only true ideologues, whose influence waned after the MH17 disaster), small-time criminals looking to make a buck, former military personnel, people down on their luck, or simply political or financial opportunists. Especially in Luhansk, conflicts and tensions between rivalling field commanders would regularly escalate into violence. Slowly but surely, two dominant forces rose to the top (first Zakharchenko and Plotnitskii, and later Pushilin and Pasechnik) who managed to push their real and imagined rivals away from the centre of power and gain the approval of influential figures in Moscow. After this initial centralising phase, some have blamed Plotnitskii (and not so much Zakharchenko) for stymying further unification attempts between the DNR and LNR (Abibok, 2019). Moscow, meanwhile, was comfortable with the DNR's and LNR's non-status and to keep them in a state of suspended animation until the full-scale invasion of 2022. The next chapter will discuss how these political developments were reflected in the DNR's and LNR's media landscapes.

3

Building a Propaganda Machine

INTRODUCTION

This chapter traces the development of the media landscape in Donbas after the start of the DNR/LNR insurgencies in 2014. I focus on the DNR and LNR authorities' efforts to first break down and then rebuild local media, as well as what happened to local journalists who decided not to cooperate. These efforts consisted of two phases: one of destruction and one of reconstruction. The destruction phase involved tearing down the existing media structure and pressuring journalists into either leaving Donbas or cooperating with the new authorities. The reconstruction phase involved setting up new media channels or repurpose existing ones, as well as implementing new legislation to impose censorship and promote certain desired narratives.

PHASE 1: TAKING OVER

Gaining control over the media was a priority for the DNR and LNR authorities, as witnessed by the large number of incidents of repression, violence, and hostile takeovers of media outlets.[1] The war turned Donbas into an extremely dangerous place to be a journalist. Deaths, arrests, kidnappings, disappearances, physical attacks and injuries, threats of violence or retaliation, attacks on editorial offices or printing houses, and the forced suspension of publications and broadcasts became common.

Seven journalists lost their lives in DNR- and LNR-controlled territory between 2014 and 2017, most as a result of military hostilities. In May 2014, the Italian photographer Andrea Rocchelli and his translator Andrii Mironov died during a mortar shelling in the village of Andriivka (Andreevka), near Sloviansk (Seneghini, 2014). One month later, Igor

---

[1] A detailed timeline of reported incidents between 2014 and 2022 can be found in Appendix C.

Korneliuk, a correspondent working for the Russian channel *VGTRK*, suffered lethal injuries during the shelling of the town of Mirnyi in Luhansk oblast. His colleague, the video engineer Anton Voloshin, also died (BBC Russian, 2014). A few days later, Anatolii Klian, a camera operator for the Russian *Channel 1*, died after coming under fire in the vicinity of a Ukrainian military unit in Donetsk oblast, where his crew was filming a reportage (OSCE Representative on Freedom of the Media, 2014b). In August, DNR militiamen reported that they had discovered the remains of Andrei Stenin, a Russian photojournalist for *Rossiia Segodnia, RIA Novosti, ITAR-TASS*, and other outlets. Stenin had been reported missing while working as an embedded reporter in the conflict zone (Institut Masovoï Informatsiï, 2014ds; OSCE, 2014a). In November, crime reporter Aleksandr Kuchinskii, editor-in-chief of *Kriminal Ekspress*, and his wife were found dead near Sloviansk. They were stabbed to death (Obozrevatel', 2014). Kuchinskii had long reported on criminal gang activity in his hometown of Donetsk (Prestupnosti.net, 2014b). And in February 2015, Serhii Nikolaev, a photojournalist for the Kyiv-based newspaper *Segodnia*, died in the hospital after being injured in a shelling near the village of Piski in Donetsk oblast (Hromadske, 2015; Institut Masovoï Informatsiï, 2015c).

For the most part, however, journalists were not systematically killed. Rather, the DNR and LNR authorities used intimidation tactics to induce compliance or pressure journalists into leaving the region. Many did. By mid-2016, the National Union of Journalists of Ukraine estimated that around 500 media workers had relocated from DNR- and LNR-controlled areas to other parts of Ukraine (Sabera, 2016). An unknown number of others stayed behind but quit their profession. This was achieved through intimidation, threats, kidnappings, arrests, and in some cases physical violence. In the early stages of the conflict, representatives of the DNR and LNR would regularly accost journalists covering anti-Kyiv or pro-DNR/LNR demonstrations and force them to turn off their cameras, destroy their equipment (Institut Masovoï Informatsiï, 2014aq; TSN Ukraina, 2014c), or physically assault them (Gaisford, 2014; Institut Masovoï Informatsiï, 2014az). In other cases, journalists would be detained, sometimes for up to two weeks (Mijatović, 2014a).

As the DNR and LNR authorities strengthened their grip on power, they wasted no time taking control of the region's mass media. Television channels were the first to be seized. The Luhansk-based local television channel *IRTA* first became an object of interest to the insurgents on March 10, 2014. Members of the *Luganskaia Gvardiia* militia went into *IRTA*'s office and intimidated and verbally threatened the journalists present. A video of the event shows the altercation (Telekanal LOT, 2014). Despite the threatening atmosphere, *IRTA* continued to broadcast. A second, unsuccessful attempt to take over the television station was made on April 29 (Rebrova, 2014). On May 30, Valerii Bolotov held a press conference in which he declared *IRTA* to be a 'vehicle of heavy propaganda for the Kyiv regime, which is shooting its own people and our fighters in the back' (Russnov.ru, 2014). *IRTA* was then taken off the air and replaced with the Russian TV channel *LifeNews*.

National television channels were also targeted. On May 1, the largest Ukrainian channels *Pershyi Natsionalnyi, 1+1,* and *Channel 5* were taken off the air by representatives of Bolotov's *Armiia Iugo-Vostoka*. Under pressure from them, the Luhansk Radio and Television Centre stopped broadcasting all Ukrainian channels and began showing Russian ones instead. Local news stations were also taken off the air, including *LKT, IRTA,* and *LOT* (PRportal, 2014).

While television channels were seized almost immediately, newspapers continued to publish more or less unrestricted for about a month. Around 600 newspapers were registered in and around Luhansk at the start of 2014. Of these, around 200 were being printed regularly. Some of these newspapers were seen as more or less independent, but many of them were considered to be little more than PR outlets for former president Viktor Yanukovych's Party of Regions, which prior to the 2014 revolution had been the largest political party in Donbas. Around mid-May, armed men in camouflage gear began to enter newspaper offices, demanding positive coverage of the LNR and the 'Novorossiia' project. Printing houses were suffering from power outages, and for a brief while almost no newspapers were printed and distributed throughout the area (Luganskii Telegraf, 2016). Only the Luhansk-based newspaper *XXI Vek* was allowed to keep publishing, using a gasoline generator as a power source. Other newspapers in the towns and cities under LNR control were shut down (PRportal, 2014). By the time the electricity was working again, many newspaper employees had fled the region.

A similar development took place in the DNR. Starting in April 2014, Ukrainian television channels were taken off the air and replaced with Russian channels until local television stations could be established. Often, this was done through coercion and violence. The authorities took control of television and broadcasting towers in the region, and used signal blockers to shut out Ukrainian television and radio signals. Print media in the DNR immediately became the subject of repression. On May 6, DNR officials made their way into the editorial office of *Torezskii Gorniak*, a small newspaper from the town of Torez. The officials began smashing equipment, warning journalists to change their editorial line. The journalists refused, and the officials left. On June 6, on a newly instated holiday called the 'Day of the Journalist', separatist officials came back to the *Torezskii Gorniak* office and burned it down (Horodetskii, 2014; Pro Gorod, 2014). Another small newspaper from Donetsk, simply named *Donbass*, suffered a similar fate.

According to its editor-in-chief Aleksandr Brizh, the paper was allowed to continue publishing for a short while after the DNR took over. On June 2, however, armed men walked into their office claiming to represent the DNR administration. Brizh and several of his associates, including *Donetsk Vechernyi* editor-in-chief Leonid Lapa (a newspaper operating from the same building), were removed from the offices and led to a cellar, where they were questioned. The interrogators told them that the staff had to either start working for 'them' or be shot in public. Brizh and his colleagues fled Donetsk and were forced to continue publishing from the nearby city of Mariupol (Ostrov, 2014d; Prigodich, 2015). Another high-profile case was that of Stanislav Aseev (also known under his pseudonym Stanislav Vasin), a Donetsk-based author and journalist who wrote about the DNR for *Ukrainska Pravda* and *Radio Liberty*. Aseev was taken captive by DNR operatives in June 2017 and accused of spying for Ukraine. He remained imprisoned for two years (Dmytruk, 2017; Radio Svoboda, 2017a).

Other local journalists were more eager to join the insurgency. Sergei Shvedko, editor-in-chief of a Novoazovsk-based newspaper named *Rodnoe Priazove*, had directed his newspaper to oppose the Euromaidan demonstrations in Kyiv and supported calls for independence referendums for Donbas. When Novoazovsk was retaken by the Ukrainian army in June of 2014, Shvedko decided to leave for the region of Kuban in southern Russia. When the town was eventually recaptured by the DNR, Shvedko returned and resumed his work (Korrespondent, 2012; Vlasenko, 2016).

PHASE 2: RECONSTRUCTION

After this initial phase in which existing media structures were broken down and replaced by outlets and people favourable to the new authorities, a key phase directed toward the development of a new media landscape began.[2] The DNR established a 'ministry of information and communications' in August 2014, with the goal of 'regulating the mass media and building a unified information space', according to its head, Elena Nikitina (ITAR-TASS, 2014e; Ministerstvo Informatsii Donetskoi Narodnoi Respubliki, 2018). Nikitina would remain the DNR's minister of information for three years (Donetskoe Agenstvo Novostei, 2018). She made it a priority to set up local television channels such as the *First Republican Channel* (*Pervyi*

---

[2] The online appendix to this book contains a spreadsheet that provides an overview of the DNR and LNR media landscape, including newspapers, websites, television channels, and radio stations. Some of the numbers in this section are based on the data from this supplement. This file also contains information on DNR and LNR social movements and political parties, and academic journals, as well as an overview of local media outlets that operate in opposition to the DNR and LNR authorities. Link: https://osf.io/3846a/. 'DNR and LNR Media Landscape Overview', in the 'Background Information' folder.

Respublikanskii), *TV Novorossiia*, and *Oplot TV*. Under the supervision of Janus Putkonen, a Finnish journalist who had relocated to Donetsk, the DNR authorities also set up *DONi Donbass News Agency TV*, an internet-cum-television channel, broadcasting partly in Russian and partly in English.[3] It also ran an English-language YouTube channel until it was banned for violating YouTube's terms and conditions with regards to 'spam, misleading practices or misleading content'.[4]

In total, twelve local television channels and eight radio stations were set up, focusing on the provision of news and, to a lesser extent, entertainment. Twenty-five news websites came online with news about the conflict and the DNR. The vast majority of these websites published in Russian, but in some cases an English-language page was available as well. One website (*DONi News*) catered to an international audience and published primarily in English, but also in Russian, Ukrainian, Italian, French, Finnish, and Swedish. Additionally, fifty-two newspapers were either set up or continued to publish under their old name after the DNR took over. But although the DNR ministry of information and other legislative bodies were quick to establish a legal framework that severely limited the media's capability to operate (see below), there was no formal structure for state-run news outlets for several years after the outbreak of the war. This changed in March 2017, when the DNR set up the 'Republican Media Holding' (*respublikanskii mediia kholding*), 'in order to ensure the implementation of state policy in the field of public and mass communications, the formation and promotion of a positive image of the DNR' (Sovet Ministrov Donetskoi Narodnoi Respubliki, 2017). Under the Holding came eighteen local media outlets, one for each city or major town in the DNR. Some of these were entirely new and some were long-running, well-known newspapers operating under new management. The authorities also tried to increase their control over media and journalists from outside the DNR.

After the Minsk agreements were signed in February 2015, the DNR ministry of information created a colour-coded list of local, Ukrainian as well as Western media outlets: 'neutral' media outlets were coloured yellow, orange was given to outlets that 'require monitoring by the Secret Service', and red was for 'bad' outlets whose journalists should be 'deported', should they ever try to report from DNR territory (Novosti Donbassa, 2017a). Valerii Gerlanets, editor-in-chief of *Vestnik DNR*, defended the existence of this list on DNR television, stating that it did not constitute actual censorship but a kind of 'internal' censorship, as journalists have to preserve the 'quality' of the

---

[3] The website (https://dninews.com/donitv) was available until mid-2017 but has since been taken offline.

[4] The link to the (deleted) channel can be found here: www.youtube.com/channel/UCw2reJns9WzoFmGDLgNTyUw.

publication that they work for (Obshchestvennoe TV Donbassa, 2017a). But some journalists working in the area derided the list as arbitrary and inaccurate. For example, Anna Nemtsova, a correspondent for *Newsweek* and the *Daily Beast*, reported being denied accreditation in the DNR for using the term 'separatist' to describe DNR militants (Atanasov, 2017).

In the LNR, the process of building a domestic media landscape only began in earnest in 2015. On February 7, Viacheslav Stoliarenko was appointed minister of information politics, print, and mass communication. His post was created as separate from Aleksandr Chumachenko's, who (rather confusingly) was minister of transport, communications, information, and mass communication. Chumachenko's remit related mostly to taking care of communications infrastructure. Stoliarenko's job would be to focus on media content. To add to the confusion, the ministry of transport, communications, information, and mass communication was split up into a ministry of transport and a ministry of communications in July 2015 (MSMKLNR, 2015). Mikhail Surzhenko, previously Chumachenko's deputy minister, was appointed minister of communications after this. One of his first actions was to announce the advent of an LNR-based mobile phone provider (RIA Novosti, 2015b).

Having taken control of the airwaves, printed press, and, to a lesser extent, the online media space, Stoliarenko's ministry began to develop a local broadcasting system. The State Television Company of the LNR (*Gosudarstvennaia Telekompaniia LNR*) began broadcasting on *LOT*'s former frequency, making use of technology and equipment that previously belonged to *LOT* and *IRTA*. The majority of its staff consisted of former local TV employees. In August 2014, the first local television programme was broadcast from Luhansk, with the help of *LifeNews* (Okkupatsiia.net, 2016). *Luhansk-24* became the main LNR-based TV channel for 'many citizens of Luhansk' (Institut Masovoï Informatsiï, 2014bn).

Stoliarenko also introduced an accreditation system for all media operating on LNR territory. The newspaper *XXI Vek* became the first printed outlet to receive an official seal of approval from the LNR ministry of information on July 8. On December 4, Stoliarenko claimed that seventy-three media outlets had been officially registered in the LNR: forty-two internet outlets, eighteen printed newspapers and magazines, four television channels, and four radio stations. By December 26, this had risen to ninety-two, including forty-two print outlets (Luganskii Informatsionnyi Tsentr, 2015i). Five of these outlets were privately run; the rest were managed either by the authorities in Luhansk or by local officials. While not mentioned explicitly in official documentation, 15 news sites also became accessible, some focusing on local residents and others on audiences in Russia or (non-occupied) Ukraine. As the LNR consisted of fourteen administrative units, fourteen 'state' newspapers were established under the auspices of local authorities

(Respubliki, 2016). These newspapers were distributed (nearly) for free to all residents of the LNR.

In 2016, the LNR authorities ordered local internet providers to block customer access to a list of websites (MSMKLNR, 2016). Most of the sites on the list were Ukrainian news sources such as *Argumenty*, *Hromadske*, and *Unian*. The DNR, however, did not follow the LNR's example. Investigations by the Digital Security Lab Ukraine revealed that DNR residents could access most if not all websites without restrictions, despite both territories having very similar legal frameworks regulating access to media content, more on which below (Digital Security Lab Ukraine, 2018, 2019).

The exact extent to which the Russian government was involved in the DNR's and LNR's media strategy has been a point of contention, but it's clear that it was substantial. In June 2016, Ukrainian activists published a large data dump of emails from 2015, sent to and from the LNR's ministry of information's email account (Bittner et al., 2016). These emails contained numerous exchanges between LNR officials and 'consultants' from Russia, most likely from within the Kremlin. The most important document that was uncovered in this leak was published by the German news outlets *ZDF* and *Die Zeit*. Entitled 'Strategy of Internal Information Politics in the Luhansk People's Republic' (*strategiia vnutrennei informatsionnoi politiki v Luganskoi Narodnoi Respublike*), this forty-one-page document constitutes an internal media strategy manual for LNR officials.[5] A similar document was not made public for the DNR, but it's likely that its media strategy was highly similar. The document describes not only the means of gaining control over information resources (through the 'unified presentation of information', a 'systematic approach', and an 'active position'), but also the leading thematic concepts and editorial lines that were to be promoted by LNR media. These include the following:

- *The development of the 'junta' image*: Ukraine has been taken over by a 'fascist junta' of unscrupulous murderers and thieves, aided by Western operatives, particularly from the United States.
- *'It's worse in Ukraine'*: Ukraine's economy is plummeting, and standards of living are dropping rapidly for all Ukrainian citizens. Russian speakers are persecuted, as are those who do not agree with Poroshenko's policies and members of the Russian Orthodox Church. This has caused all those capable of leaving to abandon the country for Europe, Russia, or even Moldova.

---

[5] My English translation of this document can be found in the online appendix. Link: https://osf .io/3846a/. 'LNR Media Strategy (2015)', in the 'Background Information' folder.

- *Ukraine is to blame for the LNR's misery*: Through blockades, artillery shelling, diplomatic pressure, and relentless information politics, Ukraine has set out to destroy the image and reputation of the LNR.
- *LNR patriotism*: Regional patriotism must be cultivated by promoting heroic stories of fallen citizens and 'warriors' of the LNR, by highlighting positive examples of sacrifice by common people and by encouraging 'pride' in the LNR's successes.
- *Russia is helping out*: Russia is a reliable ally of the DNR and LNR. Today's Russia is no longer the Russia of the 1990s, and it now stands on equal footing with the West. The image of a benevolent Russia is to be cultivated by emphasising the 'Russian World', Russia's humanitarian efforts, and the sacrifices (e.g., sanctions) that Russia makes on behalf of Donbas.
- *Putin as the DNR/LNR's 'saviour'*: Putin's popularity is to be used with great care, so as not to discredit him in the eyes of LNR residents. Without him, things would have been much worse, and he does not leave 'his people' hanging.
- *The Minsk negotiations are of the utmost importance*: LNR diplomates are participating in the Minsk negotiations to bring an end to the fighting. Ukraine is participating in form but not as an honest actor, and in reality wants to continue the war.
- *The Russian Orthodox Church supports the LNR*: The Russian Orthodox Church is popular in the LNR, and its support for the LNR 'People's Militia' should be highlighted. On top of that, the Church unifies the 'Russian World'.
- *An LNR ideology must be constructed and promoted*: Ideology is an important step in the construction of statehood. The LNR is pursuing 'cultural sovereignty' from Ukraine's 'Banderite' ideology, which has led to the outbreak of the war. The content of this ideology is to be determined by 'leading authors and scholars' in the LNR.

This document provides useful insights into what narratives the authorities and their Russian 'consultants' deemed worthy of attention. It doesn't say, however, in what proportion each narrative is to be administered, nor does it detail which of the above narratives is considered most important or to what extent topics not related to the above narratives (such as sports coverage) should be allowed. In addition, while it pays attention to the construction of a local ideology, the document does not delve deeply into details about what *kind* of ideology was to be promoted, only that it should involve the 'Russian World' in some way. Also notable is the strong emphasis on Ukraine and its new government; as we will see, the media strategy of the 'People's Republics' focused to a large extent on attempting to delegitimise and demonise Ukraine and its allies. Chapters 4 and 5 go into more detail about the extent to which these stipulations were followed by DNR and LNR media.

MEDIA LEGISLATION

In order to consolidate their position and formalise their fledgling propaganda machine, DNR and LNR lawmakers almost immediately set out to establish an extensive legal framework for domestic and international media. The DNR 'People's Council' passed the first media law on May 14, 2014, followed shortly after by the LNR on May 18. Between 2014 and 2017, the DNR and LNR authorities signed, respectively, thirty-four and twenty-four laws, decrees, statutes, and other legal documents to regulate the mass media. I discuss the content of each of these documents below. I retrieved these documents from the official website of the DNR,[6] which archives all legal documents; the official website of the People's Council of the LNR;[7] and the websites of the various ministries (of information, communications, etc.) that over time have been responsible for the regulation of the media and the flow of information in both territories.[8]

Donetsk People's Republic

The documents regulating the mass media adopted by the legislative and executive bodies of the Donetsk People's Republic between 2014 and 2018 paint a complex picture of an increasingly restrictive media landscape. Freedom of the press was officially guaranteed, both in the constitution and by law. Censorship was formally prohibited. Other freedoms and rights such as freedom of thought, information, and the press were also enshrined in law.[9] There thus existed a formal legislative framework that, in theory, allowed journalists to conduct their activities without fear of repercussions from the authorities.

The above rights and freedoms, however, were constrained in a number of ways. First, the propagation of information that promotes 'social, racial, national or religious hatred and enmity' or a 'cult of violence and cruelty', or otherwise 'demoralises society', was not allowed.[10] Numerous laws also

---

[6] www.dnr-online.ru; this is a news site as of this writing, but the older version (which contains all the relevant legislation) can be found at https://web.archive.org/web/20180220175545/https://dnr-online.ru/.

[7] www.nslnr.su, archived at https://web.archive.org/web/20180224085629/https://nslnr.su/.

[8] My English-language translation and summary of these documents can be found in the online appendix. References to the relevant legal documents are included in the footnotes. Link: https://osf.io/3846a/. 'Summary of Media Laws and Regulations in the DNR and LNR', in the 'Background Information' folder.

[9] Constitution, art. 22; Statute on the Accreditation of Journalists by the People's Council of the Donetsk People's Republic, arts. 1.2, 7; on state secrets, art. 7; on mass media, arts. 3, 57; on personal data, art. 6.8; on information and information technologies, art. 12.3; on penal code, art. 149.

[10] Constitution, art. 22.2; on the legalisation of the activities of media outlets and the rules for the production and dissemination of information in the Donetsk People's Republic, clause

forbade justifying and propagating 'terrorism'[11] and 'extremist activities'.[12] The spreading of 'fascist' ideologies was explicitly forbidden.[13]

Media outlets were banned from spreading information that is 'falsified', 'defaming', or 'misrepresenting ongoing affairs'.[14] In addition, the authorities prohibited criticism of the existence and legality of the DNR and its leadership,[15] 'collaborating with the enemy',[16] passing on information to 'unauthorised' persons not working in media,[17] propagandising 'non-traditional sexual relationships',[18] and spreading information about organisations or groups that were outlawed in the DNR.[19] Finally, there existed a ban on conducting 'electoral agitation'.[20]

Not only the production of, but also the access to certain types of information was restricted. The DNR's 'Law on Mass Media' stated that 'a restriction of access to information is established by the laws of the [DNR], in order to protect the foundations of the constitutional order, morality, health, rights and the legitimate interests of others, [and] to ensure the Republic's defence and security'.[21] The edict 'On the Approval of a List Containing the Official Information to Which Access Is Restricted', issued by the ministry of

---

VIII; on counteracting extremist activities, art. 1.1A; on mass media, art. 4.1; on the definition of authorised bodies in the field of granting military accreditation and approval of the rules for granting military accreditation to representatives of the media in the territory of the Donetsk People's Republic, arts. 7.1.4, 7.2.

[11] On counteracting terrorism, art. 2, 27; on counteracting extremist activities, art. 1; on mass media, art. 4.1; on personal data, art. 10.8; on information and information technologies, art. 12.1.

[12] On counteracting extremist activities; on mass media, art. 4.1; on information and information technologies, art. 12.1; on the protection of children from information harmful to their health and development, art. 5.2; on the establishment of an Interdepartmental Commission on suspending the publication of media and the approval of regulations on the Interdepartmental Commission on suspending the publication of media, art. 25.

[13] On counteracting extremist activities, art. 1B; on the protection of children from information harmful to their health and development, art. 5.2.

[14] On the legalisation of the activities of media outlets and the rules for the production and dissemination of information in the Donetsk People's Republic, clause XIX; Statute on the Accreditation of Journalists by the People's Council of the Donetsk People's Republic, art. 9; on information and information technologies, art. 12.2; on the definition of authorised bodies in the field of granting military accreditation and approval of the rules for granting military accreditation to representatives of the media in the territory of the Donetsk People's Republic, arts. 7.1.1, 7.1.2.

[15] Statute on the Accreditation of Journalists by the People's Council of the Donetsk People's Republic, arts. 9, 10.

[16] On the protection of children from information harmful to their health and development, art. 5.2.

[17] On the definition of authorised bodies in the field of granting military accreditation and approval of the rules for granting military accreditation to representatives of the media in the territory of the Donetsk People's Republic, art. 7.1.3.

[18] On the protection of children from information harmful to their health and development, art. 5.2.

[19] On mass media, art. 4.2.　　[20] Ibid., art. 59.

[21] On information and information technologies, art. 9.1.

information, reaffirmed these restrictions.[22] State and regulatory bodies were thus authorised to limit or prohibit the dissemination of certain types of information in order to prevent DNR residents from gaining access to it.

All journalists and media outlets had to undergo a registration procedure before they were allowed to operate inside the DNR. Until the moment they received their accreditation, they were not considered a media outlet and therefore not authorised to publish materials.[23] This registration procedure was updated regularly after first being instated on June 23, 2014, approximately two months and a half after the start of hostilities.

So-called special legal regimes could be imposed at the behest of the head of the DNR. In such cases, certain constitutional rights were further restricted, and additional limits were placed on the flow of information. Specifically, the 'Law on Special Regimes' stated that authorities may 'restrict the freedom of the press and other media through the introduction of preliminary censorship'.[24] No laws were passed that formally cemented a state of martial law, unlike in the LNR (see below). Nonetheless, through these 'special legal regimes', the authorities reserved the right to seize media outlets' property and suspend their activities without legal recourse.

Defamation was made a criminal rather than a civil offence.[25] The term (*kleveta* in Russian) was defined as follows: 'the dissemination of knowingly false information that discredits the honour and dignity of another person or undermines their reputation'. Punishment for a defamation conviction could range from a fine to compulsory labour, and was more severe if done in public or in the mass media. The vagueness embedded in the above definition left a degree of leeway for authorities to determine what does and what does not constitute defamation.

Finally, the authorities instated celebrations of and awards for journalists who operated within the guidelines. This was done by establishing a public holiday,

---

[22] On the approval of a list containing the official information to which access is restricted, the administrator of which is the Ministry of Information of the Donetsk People's Republic.

[23] On the legalisation of the activities of media outlets and the rules for the production and dissemination of information in the Donetsk People's Republic, Clauses IV, VII, XIV, XVI; Statute on the Accreditation of Journalists by the People's Council of the Donetsk People's Republic; on special legal regimes, art. 14; rules for obtaining accreditation for work in the territory of the DNR by representatives of the media and a new form of accreditation certificate; on the approval of the rules for the accreditation of journalists of mass media outlets registered in the Donetsk People's Republic, arts. 6.1, 9; on the establishment of rules of accreditation for foreign journalists and technical employees of foreign mass media outlets on the territory of the Donetsk People's Republic; on the definition of authorised bodies in the field of granting military accreditation and approval of the rules for granting military accreditation to representatives of the media in the territory of the Donetsk People's Republic.

[24] On Special Legal Regimes, art. 14.   [25] Penal Code of the DNR, art. 132.

with the purpose of promoting the professional creative activity of journalists in the territory of the DNR, promoting the establishment and realisation of the freedom of mass communications, strengthening the guarantees of citizens' right to promptly receive comprehensive and reliable information through electronic and printed media, forming a culture of honest and free journalism based on generally recognised principles of professional conduct and ethics, protecting journalists' rights and freedoms, their economic and professional creativity, their interests surrounding copyright and related rights, their honour, dignity and reputation to attract public attention, strengthening public confidence in printed and electronic media, and enhancing the social role of journalists and journalism.[26]

This holiday was celebrated on May 5 of each year.

Authorities in the DNR thus established numerous laws and regulations that constrained media freedom inside the territories under their control. While lip service was paid to the prohibition of censorship and the rights and freedoms of journalists and citizens to express themselves and freely disseminate and receive information, regulations were such that DNR authorities were legally allowed to crack down on dissent. This included not only the accreditation process (which was mandatory for all journalists and media outlets and runs through the central administration) but also the authorisation to shut down any media that criticise or challenge the legality, morality, war effort, cultural values, or leadership of the DNR (so-called opinion crimes).

Luhansk People's Republic

As in Donetsk, lawmakers in Luhansk were careful to pay lip service to freedom of speech, freedom of the press, governmental accountability, and freedom of creativity and thought.[27] Censorship was forbidden by the Constitution[28] as well as by the 'Law on Mass Media',[29] 'except in cases provided for by law'. In addition, the 'rights of journalists' were guaranteed (including the right to 'seek, receive and impart information; to obtain access to documents and materials; to make records; and to verify the reliability of information'[30]).

These official protections notwithstanding, LNR lawmakers imposed explicit limitations on press freedom from the start. The LNR's Constitution, first of all, forbade 'the activity of organisations propagating

---

[26] On the establishment of the working holiday 'Day of Workers in Media and Printing in the Donetsk People's Republic'.

[27] Constitution, art. 22; Law on Mass Media, arts. 3, 65, 67, 72; on state secrets, art. 7; on personal data, arts. 4.2, 6; on information, information technology, and the protection of information, arts. 5, 7, 12.3; on the procedure for reporting on the activities of public authorities in the state media, art. 4.

[28] Constitution, art. 22.　　　[29] Law on Mass Media, art. 3.

[30] Law on Mass Media, arts. 56, 77; on the procedure for reporting on the activities of public authorities in the state media, art. 4; penal code, art. 156.

violence, fascism, and nationalism'.[31] Similar prohibitions, mainly against 'extremism' and 'terrorism', were present in other legal documents as well.[32] These terms remained largely undefined, except in 'On the Foundations of Counteracting Terrorism', where terrorism was defined as 'an ideology of violence, as well as the practice of influencing decision-making by state authorities, local governments or international organisations related to the intimidation of the population and/or other forms of unlawful violent actions' (article 4). Enough leeway remained for authorities to use a relatively loose definition of terrorism that didn't necessarily include the use or planned use of violence. Another restriction on what type of information was allowed to be published can be found in the 'Law on the Committee of State Security of the LNR' (article 26), which stated that 'persons assisting the bodies of the State Security Committee are required … not to allow the deliberate provision of biased, incomplete, false or defamatory information'. Special attention was paid to 'electoral agitation':[33] journalists were subject to a 'prohibition on conducting electoral agitation, or agitation on issues surrounding referenda, while carrying out [their] professional activities'.

Aside from the above, there also existed restrictions on the access to information, similar to the DNR. First, the 'Law on Information, Information Technology and the Protection of Information' stated that 'restriction of access to information is established by the legislation of the [LNR] in order to protect the foundations of the constitutional order, morality, health, rights and the legitimate interests of others, and to ensure the country's defence and security'.[34]

Second, again as in Donetsk, journalists were allowed to operate and work inside the LNR only if they obtained an accreditation issued by the authorities. Article 9 of the 'Law on Mass Media' stated that 'the editorial staff of a mass medium can start carrying out its activities after its registration, except in cases of exemption from registration provided for by this law'.[35]

Special attention was paid to online media outlets. The 'Law on Information, Information Technology and the Protection of Information' stated that online media (including bloggers) were obliged to put their name, address, and email address on their website.[36] Online media outlets were required to notify state regulatory bodies of their existence[37] (the same went for bloggers[38]), and to store information on the 'reception, transmission, delivery and/or processing of

---

[31] Constitution, art. 9.4.
[32] Law on Mass Media, art. 4; on personal data, art. 10.8; on protecting children from information that is harmful to their health and development, art. 5; penal code, arts. 340, 341, 342, 344, 437; on the foundations of counteracting terrorism, art. 4.
[33] Law on Mass Media, art. 67.10.
[34] Law on information, information technology, and the protection of information, art. 9.1.
[35] This line was repeated in article 72, specifically within the context of television channels.
[36] Law information, information technology, and the protection of information, art. 10.2.
[37] Law on Mass Media, arts. 11.2 and 11.5.   [38] Ibid., art. 12.5.

[information from] internet users within the territory of the LNR for at least six months from the moment of the end of the implementation of such actions'. This did not apply to operators of state-owned media.[39]

The situation was slightly different for foreign media outlets and journalists. People and organisations that spoke 'disparagingly' of the LNR were denied accreditation,[40] implying that there was a verification system in place to check this. Restrictions placed on an individual journalist extended to the organisation for which they worked. If a journalist lost their accreditation (for whatever reason), the authorities were allowed to repeal their employer's accreditation for up to six months as well. Furthermore, the share of foreign ownership of media outlets was restricted to a maximum of 20 per cent.[41]

Ten days after the passing of the LNR constitution on May 18, 2014, the authorities issued a declaration imposing martial law in the regions under its control. Measures were taken to 'control the work of communication enterprises, printing enterprises, publishing houses, television and radio organisations, theatrical, concert and entertainment and other enterprises, cultural institutions and organisations'.[42] Authorities also reserved the right to confiscate any equipment that may be used for creating or disseminating information, including computers, video and audio equipment, et cetera.[43] Martial law was codified into law in 2015. From then on, the activities of opposition political parties and other organisations were suspended, rallies and demonstrations were restricted, and military censorship was imposed over postal items and messages transmitted through telecommunications systems.[44]

Censorship and media regulation were gradually extended into the online sphere. Starting in late 2015, the authorities moved to actively ban websites from operating inside the LNR.[45] By 2017, this list contained more than 350 websites of local, domestic as well as foreign origin, with new sites being added at regular intervals.

Defamation, as in the DNR, was a criminal rather than a civil offence.[46] The same definition of 'defamation' was used as in the DNR, namely, 'the dissemination of deliberately false information that discredits the honour and dignity of another person or undermines their reputation'. The penal codes of the DNR and LNR differed very little on this topic. In the LNR, defamation, broadly defined, carried a fine or compulsory labour. Punishment was heavier when the crime occurred through a mass medium or in a public display.

As in the DNR, the authorities promoted friendly journalists who complied with regulations and produced output that was amenable to the state

---

[39] Ibid., art. 11.7.   [40] Ibid., art. 17.   [41] Ibid. Law on Mass Media, art. 22.
[42] On the Declaration of Martial Law, art. 15.8.   [43] Ibid., art. 15.9.   [44] Ibid., art. 7.
[45] Law on the prohibition of the dissemination of information from information websites, which disseminate information that is against the law of the LNR; law on information, information technology, and the protection of information, art. 10, 11, 12.
[46] Penal code of the LNR, art. 139.

and its regulatory bodies. This development, however, started only in January 2017.[47] Particularly journalists whose 'professional achievements and active position contribute[d] to the development of the LNR' were rewarded.

Overall, while there were a few protections in place that can be said to formally guarantee the rights of journalists to operate within the LNR, media freedom, in practice, ceased to exist after 2014. The restrictions placed on journalists were such that the publication of material construed as going against the will of the authorities was prevented through a number of regulations and laws. Non-compliant media were relatively easy to outlaw, either by refusing accreditation or by outright banning them from operating inside LNR territory. The legal embedding of 'opinion crimes', censorship and arbitrary defamation laws further ensured a constricted media landscape.

Comparing the Two Republics

With few exceptions, the DNR and LNR put in place almost identical restrictions on the media and freedom of the press. In fact, many of the laws that were passed to regulate the media were in large part direct copies of legislation in the Russian Federation, including the 'Law on Mass Media', the 'Law on State Secrets', and the 'Law on Personal Data'. Both territories made reference to freedom of speech, thought, and the press. At least in strictly formal terms, journalists could refer to several legal documents affirming their right to operate. However, despite these formal guarantees, the DNR and LNR imposed similarly strict limits on media freedom. These limitations included 'opinion crimes', or prohibitions on disseminating information that justifies or propagates 'terrorism', 'extremist activities', or 'Nazism'. Both the DNR and the LNR employed rather loose definitions of these terms (especially of 'extremist activities'). Furthermore, the law forbade challenging or disparaging the republics' 'territorial integrity', national honour, and leadership, as well as the dissemination of 'false', 'biased', 'incomplete', or 'defamatory' information.

However, in terms of regulating the internet, the DNR was less openly restrictive than the LNR. Most importantly, the DNR did not have a list of blocked websites comparable in size to the list of more than 350 sites blocked by the LNR (MIPMKLNR, 2015), although it did have a registry with forbidden organisations according to the law 'On Counteracting Extremist Activities' (Donetskaia Narodnaia Respublika, 2016; Donetskaia Narodnaia Respublika – Glava Respubliki, 2016). Organisations on this list included Ukrainian nationalist organisations and political parties, pro-Ukrainian fighter battalions (Aidar and Azov, chiefly), and Islamic terrorist organisations such as Al-Qaida, the Taliban, Islamic State, and Jabhat Al-Nusra. The

---

[47] On the approval of the regulations on the contest for journalists of the LNR, 10-1-2017 and 13-6-2017.

DNR also published a list of 'extremist materials' banned by the High Court. These include individual pages of Vkontakte (a social network similar to Facebook) of political and social movements (such as the radical pro-Ukrainian group Pravyi Sektor), books on Ukrainian nationalism, audio files, images, and Islamic and certain Christian religious brochures (MIuDNR, 2017).

CONCLUSION

This chapter has detailed the DNR's and LNR's information policies and the breakdown and reconstruction of local media landscapes after their rise to power in 2014. The mass media were placed under the authorities' control almost immediately. This takeover was accompanied by a great deal of pressure, violence, arrests, and even deaths. Journalists considered undesirable were detained or beaten; editorial offices of unfriendly news outlets were ransacked, torched, or fired at; and journalists and editors were told to either start publishing material from a pro-DNR/LNR perspective or leave the region altogether.

Television was the new authorities' first priority: towers and studios were seized, Ukrainian television channels were taken off the air and replaced with Russian ones, and eventually new channels were set up, broadcasting pro-DNR/LNR news bulletins as well as entertainment programmes. Next came the newspapers. Most of the well-known and well-read publications either changed their name (along with their staff) or went out of print. Some managed to obtain accreditation from the authorities to keep publishing. In other cases, entirely new newspapers were created, replacing the old ones but making use of their offices and infrastructure. Dozens of internet outlets were also set up, publishing mostly in Russian but in some cases also in English and several other European languages.

After an initial phase of breaking down the existing media landscape, a period of building up a local, pro-DNR/LNR media space began. The DNR and LNR ministries of information, established in August 2014 and February 2015, respectively, promoted local media production and set limits to what was allowed to be published by implementing accreditation procedures and keeping track of journalists working in the region. This formalisation occurred through a system of laws, decrees, edicts, and other regulations passed by the DNR and LNR's People's Councils. Chapter 4 will detail how these laws were applied, by looking at the content that was produced by local DNR and LNR newspapers.

4

Newspaper Narratives in Occupied Ukraine

INTRODUCTION

This chapter examines newspaper discourse in the DNR and LNR. I analyse the content of twenty-six local newspapers between the start of the Euromaidan demonstrations in late 2013 and the end of 2017. The goal is to uncover the themes and narratives in DNR and LNR print media, and examine how these narratives relate back to ideology and identity building. Focusing on local newspapers allows for an examination of content created for the population residing in the territories under DNR and LNR control. Unlike much of the content available on news sites, social media, and even television, local newspaper coverage is almost exclusively tailored to local issues and concerns. Particularly in places like the DNR and LNR, where access to news sources is restricted and the media operate under strict control by the authorities (see Chapter 3), local news coverage tends to reach only local residents. Examining this content therefore gives insight into the narratives employed by the DNR and LNR authorities to construct a local identity in service of their continued existence as 'states', nominally independent from both Ukraine and Russia.[1]

METHOD OF ANALYSIS

The data set I use in this chapter consists of 42,423 articles published between 2014 and the end of 2017 in 26 local newspapers from both the Luhansk and Donetsk People's Republics. Twenty-one of these twenty-six newspapers were designated as 'official' media outlets by the authorities of the Donetsk People's

---

[1] In this chapter and the next, I cite numerous articles published by DNR and LNR media that are no longer active, or have altered their digital presence (for example, their website may have gone offline). It is therefore possible that some of the URLs found in the reference list no longer redirect to the correct article. To mitigate this, the full dataset of all articles cited here (among others) can be found in the 'Data' folder on the OSF page for this book: https://osf.io/3846a/.

Republic. Specifically, the *respublikanskii media kholding* (mentioned in Chapter 3) authorised these newspapers to represent the DNR authorities at the local level by attending and reporting on press conferences, publishing statements by DNR officials, et cetera, without being officially state-run. The advantage of examining these newspapers is that they offer insight into the kinds of narratives put forward at the direct behest of the authorities. Additionally, five newspapers were included that, at least in name, were not formally 'state'-run. While this doesn't mean that these outlets operated independently from the authorities (which would have been impossible due to the strict regulation of the media in both territories), they did have a significant local readership. Some newspapers were founded after the start of the conflict, sometime between November 2014 and mid-2016, as part of the DNR and LNR authorities' efforts to promote homegrown media. Other papers existed prior to the conflict and continued to operate under the same name, although in many cases the outlet's editorial staff and management underwent significant changes. Still others changed their name when, for instance, the paper's original staff left the region and continued to publish under the same name from Ukrainian-controlled territory. See Appendix B for more details about each outlet.

Using a method called topic modelling (see Appendix A), I extracted a total of 252 discussion topics from these twenty-six newspapers. I then grouped these topics together into twelve separate themes: local administration, local economy, education and children, sports, culture, home and garden, crime, war, humanitarian aid, ingroup and outgroup identity, Ukraine, and domestic and international politics. These themes were then compiled into three main narratives: 'business as usual', 'war and memory', and 'loss and guilt'. Figure 4.1 shows this process from corpus to narratives schematically.

I will use this framework to discuss these narratives qualitatively, specifically focusing on the role that ideology and group identity have played in DNR and LNR newspapers. Table 4.1 gives an overview of the relevant narratives and themes, and how many topics are associated with each of them (and in how many newspapers). I discuss these narratives separately below.

BUSINESS AS USUAL

'Business as usual' refers to themes that fall under the traditional function of local newspapers – namely, to chronicle local issues and events like sports, culture, the economy, and local politics (Hindman, 1996; Nielsen, 2015). How locally relevant events are discussed in newspapers is informative of how local identity is expressed (Montiel et al., 2014). Two key points are relevant here: how events relevant only to the local population are framed and discussed, and the proportion of such themes relative to others. Some 127 out of 252 topics in the data set (50.1 per cent; see Table 4.1) fall under this category. A reader of DNR and LNR newspapers would thus regularly

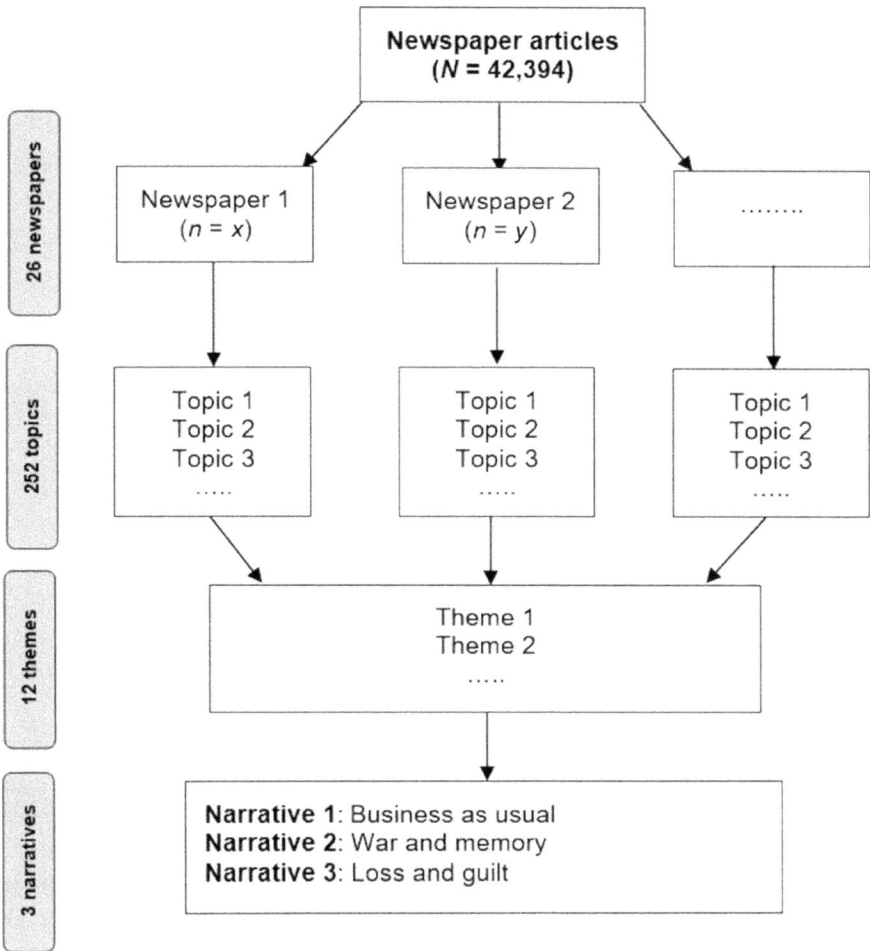

FIGURE 4.1 Schematic overview of the narrative analysis in DNR and LNR newspapers.

encounter articles about everyday topics that relate to mundane issues such as the weather or sports. This function runs counter to the idea of the DNR and LNR authorities using local newspapers almost exclusively for purposes of direct propaganda, with newspapers instead continuing to play a role as 'keystone media' (Nielsen, 2015), which inform people of local goings-on rather than serve as a vehicle for mass persuasion. As I will show below, these themes are not typically infused with identity discourse, lending support to the idea that the newspapers in the corpus continued to perform their roles as typical local newspapers, comparable to local newspapers outside active conflict zones. Nonetheless, articles that fall under one of the above themes are not entirely devoid of ideological discourse, so I will unpack them further.

TABLE 4.1 Overview of narratives and themes in DNR and LNR newspapers

Narrative	Theme	Number of topics	Number of newspapers
Business as usual		127 (50.4%)	
	Local administration	37	17
	Local economy	22	14
	Education and children	22	15
	Sports	17	13
	Culture	10	10
	Home and garden	10	7
	Crime	9	9
War and memory		25 (9.9%)	
	War	19	15
	Humanitarian aid	6	5
Loss and guilt		69 (27.4%)	
	Ingroup and outgroup identity	44	20
	Ukraine	19	17
	Domestic and international politics	6	4
Unclassified		31 (12.3%)	

Newspapers in the DNR and LNR dedicated a great deal of space to local football. Soon after taking over, the DNR and LNR authorities began to organise football competitions, despite the ongoing hostilities (Informatsionnyi Biulleten' Dokuchaevsk, 2015a). Luhansk was first. The Luhansk Football Union (*Luganskii Futbolnyi Soiuz*) was established in October 2014, and the LNR 'national' team played its first match against Abkhazia in March 2015. June of that year marked the start of the LNR football league, in which six teams took part. SK Zaria Stal won the competition, eighteen points ahead of its nearest competitor (Bessonova, 2015; Svetikov, 2015).

The DNR's 'national' football team was established somewhat later than the LNR's, in April 2015. It played its first 'official' match, also against Abkhazia, in May of that year. Its first football league was organised in 2016, with eight participating teams. Pobeda from Donetsk won the title, beating number two OD Donetskaia Respublika by eleven points (Bessonova, 2015; Futbol'nyi Soiuz Donetskoi Narodnoi Respubliki, 2019). Both the DNR and LNR also organised annual cup tournaments and 'international' matches against each other and other unrecognised entities such as Abkhazia and South Ossetia (a breakaway Georgian province in the Caucasus). Match reports in DNR and LNR newspapers were not typically merely descriptive (see, for example, Znamia Pobedy, 2015g); rather than merely reporting the match results, articles also included additional information about the event's political relevance:

On Sunday, November 8, the final match of the season was held between FC Oplot Donbassa and FC Vostok. FC Oplot Donbassa took home the victory with a score of 2-0. The following guests of honour came to support the team, which is a symbol of athleticism: the head of the Donetsk city administration, the president of FC Oplot Donbassa, Igor Martynov, members of the People's Council Anatolii Koval, Viktor Petrovich, Oleg Stepanov, Iurii Martynov and German Kadyrov, as well as the commander of the *Somali* battalion, lieutenant-colonel Mikhail Tolstykh (Givi).

(Golos Respubliki, 2015a)

Other sports tournaments were also organised, starting relatively soon after the outbreak of the conflict. Chess tournaments (Mitin, 2016), boxing (although there was a lack of proper equipment and available funding throughout 2016 and 2017, according to the head of the DNR boxing federation; see Donetskie Novosti, 2017a), ice hockey (Donetskie Novosti, 2017b), and volleyball matches were held in the DNR and LNR from 2015 (MKSMLNR, 2019). Sports federations were established or re-established soon after the start of the conflict. As Inna Bessonova (2015) argues, this was done to give structure to the comings and goings of everyday life. When all Ukrainian television channels were taken off the air in Donetsk in August 2014, a massive outcry prompted the authorities to quickly resume the broadcasting of sports channels *Futbol-1* and *Futbol-2*. The prominent role that the sports pages continued to play in DNR and LNR newspapers can be explained by their pacifying potential: being able to play and watch sports games as usual might, in the DNR and LNR authorities' reasoning, contribute to people's acceptance of the new status quo.

Quite a few articles covered local theatre performances, cultural festivals, song contests, folk music, and dance recitals (Informatsionnyi Biulleten' Dokuchaevsk, 2015b). These articles tend to be rather factual and don't go into much detail about the cultural or ideological significance of such events. A typical article would read as follows:

On March 13, the Donetsk State Academic Music and Drama Theatre welcomed guests from the Russian Federation: the Chernyshev family musical collective, the composer and singer Sergei Svetlov, and the documentary film director Aleksandr Belanov. The 'Russian Soul' duet (Mariia and Sofiia Chernysheva, plus their parents) have performed in thirty-five countries to promote Russian folk music. The girls previously performed in Luhansk, and during the Maslenitsa festivities came to entertain the people of our city with their creativity.

(Torezskii Gorniak, 2016)

It's relevant to note that while the dance ensemble is called 'Russian Soul' (*russkaia dusha*) and performs Russian folk music, the article itself does not elaborate on the cultural resonance that these concepts may possess within the DNR; identity and ideology were *mentioned* in articles about cultural events, but not explored in detail. The same can be said for the theme 'education and children'; one could imagine that newspapers would discuss, for example, curriculum reform or the importance of instilling the values and identity of the DNR/LNR into local children via the education system, but such articles are rare. Rather, topics of discussion centred around this theme include reading clubs (Znamia Pobedy, 2015d), summer camps for children (Novye Gorizonty, 2015), and scientific research (Znamia Pobedy, 2015b). Similarly, articles under the 'home and garden' theme include food recipes (Iasinovatskii Vestnik, 2015b), growing crops at home (Znamia Pobedy, 2015a), weather reports (XXI Vek, 2017a), animals (Snezhnianskie Novosti, 2015a), and outbreaks of common illnesses (Makeevskii Rabochii, 2015a). The theme of 'crime', meanwhile, covers topics such as 'terrorists' being apprehended for impersonating army officers and carrying heavy weaponry (Rodina, 2015a). Other common articles were weekly reports listing crime statistics and descriptions of instances of grand theft auto, theft, destruction of property, and drug offences (Rodina, 2015b). All of these are typical topics for local newspapers (Janowitz, 1967), and not directly relevant for identity building or the construction of political ideology.

Regarding discussions about local administration, pension payments were a contentious issue. DNR and LNR residents retained their right to a pension from the Ukrainian state, as Ukraine considers them to be Ukrainian citizens. But in order to receive payments, pensioners had to register as being internally displaced, as well as report in person to the authorities at least once every two months (Coynash, 2019). This caused difficulties, particularly in the winter months, as queues at checkpoints could be hours long. Some elderly people did not survive the journey (UNHCR, 2018). Pensions given out by the DNR and LNR authorities, meanwhile, were not very high due to lack of funding. Pensions were thus one of the rare topics over which criticism of the authorities was allowed:

Residents of house number 100 on '8th Congress of Soviets' Street and other nearby high rises were given the opportunity to ask questions about issues that concern them. The primary and perhaps the most relevant topic of conversation was the problem of controlling pricing in the commercial facilities in the city and in the district. The townspeople noted that with the current level of pension payments and salaries, many of them cannot afford to buy not only meat products, but also sugar.

(Novyi Luch, 2015)

Other reports were more factually oriented (without explicit or implicit criticism of the authorities) and related to topics such as the DNR and LNR authorities' approach to simplifying the tax code (Enakievskii Rabochii, 2016), the opening of new infrastructure projects (Kochegarka DNR, 2015), people dialling the emergency number for spurious reasons (Rodnoe Priazov'e, 2015), and the risks of going ice fishing in winter (Boevoe Znamia Donbassa, 2016). Again, references to ideology were mostly absent.

This was somewhat different, however, in articles about the local economy. Donbas has long been a region of heavy industry, particularly coal mining and metallurgy. DNR and LNR newspapers regularly reported on miners' productivity (Kazachii Vestnik, 2017a), modernising the mines and equipment (Znamia Pobedy, 2015c), mining disasters (Kazachii Vestnik, 2016b), and metallurgy (especially in Enakievo, home to a large metallurgy plant; Enakievskii Rabochii, 2015a). As Hiroaki Kuromiya (1998, 2008) notes, both the people and the rulers of Donbas have considered mining and the values associated with this harsh and often difficult profession to be an integral part of Donbas identity. This idea was reiterated in newspaper articles with some regularity:

Dear countrymen (*zemliaki*)! Esteemed residents of the Donetsk People's Republic! From my entire soul I congratulate you all on this holiday, which is dear to every family in our glorious, hard-working Donbas: the Day of the Miner! For our region, being a miner is not just a profession, it is the backbone of the Donetsk People's Republic. The world-famous Donbas character was forged in the mineshafts (*lavy*) of Donbas by such heroic miners as Nikita Izotov, Ivan Bridko, Aleksandr Kolchik and, of course, Aleksei Stakhanov. After being destroyed by the invaders during the Great Patriotic War, our native land quickly recovered, and in a short time, Donbas turned into a personification of industrial power.... All this was made possible largely thanks to the daily heroic work of the miners, who are famous for their courage, selfless devotion to their profession and unyielding character.

(Znamia Pobedy, 2015f)

WAR AND MEMORY

In DNR and LNR newspapers, the Donbas War was a prominent topic of discussion, from both a contemporary and a historical perspective. First and foremost, there was a hearkening back to World War II (known locally as the Great Patriotic War, *velikaia otechestvennaia voina*) and the role that Donbas played in it. When covering the ongoing conflict, writers would often compare the Donbas Republics' war against Ukraine with the Soviet Union's war against Nazi Germany, not only metaphorically but also geographically (Znamia Pobedy, 2015h). Another example is the commemoration of World War II through the march of the so-called immortal regiment (*bessmertnyi polk*). This tradition, which originated in the Siberian city of Tomsk in 2012, has gained popularity in Russia and some other places (including the DNR and LNR) as a celebration of World War II veterans (Novaia Niva, 2016a). In Makeevka (Makiivka), for example, the head of the local city administration Iurii Pokintelitsa said the following during an event commemorating World War II:

The work to perpetuate the memory of the Great Patriotic War in our city continues. The citizens of Makeevka remember their heroes.... On the eve of the 72nd anniversary of the liberation from the Nazi invaders, this holiday now takes on special meaning for us. Our boys are once again rising up to the defence of their native land! Dear veterans, thank you for the endeavour that you showed in your youth, and for the example you have set for the current generation. We will try not to let you down!

(Makeevskii Rabochii, 2015b)

Both the DNR and the LNR instated numerous annual holidays (Dikoe Pole, 2019; DNR-Online, 2019). Many of these were copies of Russian or former Soviet holidays, including Victory Day (May 9) and the Day of the Russian Language (an official UN holiday that was celebrated on June 6 in the DNR, but not in the LNR). Other official holidays were the Day of the Miner, various Orthodox-Christian holidays, and celebrations dedicated to professions such as the Day of the Journalist and the Day of the Builder. A closer look at articles about holiday celebrations reveals a similar pattern to what is observed in coverage about the conflict, a consistent connection between the Donbas War and World War II:

> Today, people gathered in the morning on Lenin Square to congratulate their defenders on the Holiday of the Airborne Forces (*prazdnik vozdushno-desantnykh voisk*).[2] There were many young people and children of all ages among those present, despite the fact that since the morning the echoes of heavy artillery shells were heard in the city.
>
> (Boevoe Znamia Donbassa, 2015)

Military feats were thus celebrated as Donbas achievements, as opposed to Soviet ones: while the heroism of the people of Donbas received ample attention, there was barely a mention of the (geo-)political context that World War II was embedded in. Soviet nostalgia, which has been on the rise in Russia (Levada Tsentr, 2018) and has played a significant role in Russian media (Nikolayenko, 2008), advertisements (Morris, 2005), and online communities (Kalinina & Menke, 2016), was largely absent on the pages of DNR and LNR newspapers. Rarely did these outlets evoke memories of the relative economic, political, or physical security from the Soviet past, nor did they hearken back to the glory days of heavy industry (cf. the pre-war era, when Donbas was responsible for more than 50 per cent of the total Soviet coal production; Danilin, 2002; S.L., 1951). What was continuously highlighted instead was the Soviets' military victory over Nazi Germany, which is particularly relevant in light of the DNR's and LNR's continued attempts to paint the Ukrainian government as pro-fascist.

LOSS AND GUILT

The third and in my view most important narrative is that of loss and guilt. DNR and LNR newspapers framed the prior relationship between the people of Donbas and post-Soviet Ukraine as uncomfortable but nonetheless peaceful, an arrangement between reluctant but willing participants. According to this framing, this peaceful relationship was brutally disrupted by Ukrainian

---

[2] The Day of the Airborne Forces has been celebrated annually on August 2 in Russia, Belarus, Kazakhstan, and some other territories, in some places since the 1930s.

'extremists' after the events of the Euromaidan revolution, leading to an armed conflict and excessive violence on the part of Ukraine. Articles circulating this narrative were key drivers of identity discourse in Donbas, and they mostly focused on the Ukrainian military and post-Maidan government, with relatively little emphasis on Ukrainian culture or society. The key frame that was repeated here is that of guilt: Ukraine and Ukrainians are 'guilty' (Klimova, 2015) of betraying Donbas by allowing themselves to be usurped by radical elements, leaving Donbas no choice but to leave Ukraine. I will discuss this narrative in two parts: (1) ingroup identity and (2) outgroup identity.

Ingroup Identity

Ingroup identity in DNR and LNR newspapers mainly ties back to various conceptions of Russia and Russian-ness. 'Novorossiia' is a term used historically to denote a region and later a province in the Russian Empire north of the Black Sea (see Chapter 2). The *Novorossiia* publication regularly employed the term 'Novorossiia' to refer to the DNR and LNR. 'Novorossiia' was often used as a frame of reference, equated to a vision of a 'Homeland' (*Rodina*). The following editorial from 2016 by a Donetsk-based author, which addresses former DNR and LNR combatants who left the conflict zone, brings many of these concepts together:

Guys (*rebiata*), if you really are patriots of your homeland (*Rodina*) and sincerely stand up for it, why do you keep writing your senseless blogs, sometimes frankly deceitful, and discredit the honour of your favourite cities, somewhere out there in a safe place, away from everything that's happening? Yes, you once took part in the Russian Spring (*Russkaia Vesna*), paid for it with your freedom, some with your health. But that was two years ago! Today, what are you really doing to help your homeland that is occupied by fascists? Why do you not join the ranks of the army of Novorossiia? Or come help us out here, behind the frontline, like the rest of the guys that we managed to free by exchanging prisoners of war? Why did you run away from Donbas after the prisoner exchange and, after recovering your health, did not return here? And, like the notorious thirty children of Lieutenant Schmidt,[3] you are engaged in self-promotion and shamefully extorting money from kind and trustful people! The war is not yet over. Our cities are under fascist occupation. Come to Donbas, help us whichever way you can, united in a single structure. After all, only in this case you will have the opportunity to really help your cities. The front, both military and political, is here.

(Novorossia, 2016c)

---

[3] The 'Children of Lieutenant Schmidt' (*deti leitenanta Shmidta*) is a Russian expression referring to a fraudulent enterprise or a person who swindles others out of money. The eponymous children are a set of characters from the novel *The Little Golden Calf* (*Zolotoi Telionok*) by Ilia Ilf and Evgenii Petrov, originally published in 1931. This group of swindlers pose as children of the famous Lieutenant Piotr Petrovich Schmidt, one of the leaders of the Sevastopol uprising during the Russian Revolution of 1905, to try to trick Soviet officials and other people into giving them money (Il'f & Petrov, 2016).

The armed forces of the DNR and LNR were not officially called the 'army of Novorossiia'. Importantly, *Novorossiia*, which was run by Pavel Gubarev (see Chapter 2), was the only newspaper that regularly used the term 'Novorossiia' to refer to local collective identity. In other newspapers, the term served no such purpose. It was instead used to describe, for example, a new strain of grape that was named Novorossiia (Enakievskii Rabochii, 2015b), or to refer to the newspaper (Novaia Zhizn', 2015) or the television channel *Novorossiia TV* (Rodina, 2015c); thus, with one exception, the term carried little to no significance in terms of signalling ingroup identity in the DNR and LNR. The trope was common enough to be mentioned from time to time in a variety of contexts, but the term 'Novorossiia' was decisively not at the core of DNR/LNR ideological discourse.

The concept of the so-called Russian World (*ruisskii mir*) was commonly used in *Novorossiia* as a way to link the DNR and LNR to the Russian political and especially cultural space:

At the heart of all the processes taking place in Novorossiia that have developed in this space over the past two decades, both before and after Maidan, lies the Russian Idea. To be Russian is the main motivation. To defend one's right to belong to the Russian World, to speak in Russian, to love and propagate Russian culture, to practice the Russian Orthodox faith, to enjoy the Russian nature, land and space, to communicate with the people around you. These are such simple, truly human desires, but how expensive they are to entertain.

(Novorossia, 2016b)

As with 'Novorossiia', the concept of 'Russian World' carried little to no ideological significance in other newspapers, and was instead mostly used in rather mundane ways. In the LNR, for example, 'Russkii Mir' was the name of a school programme designed to promote literacy (Xpress-Klub, 2016). The term was also used in a non-metaphorical sense within the context of the ongoing integration of the LNR with the Russian economic space (Xpress-Klub, 2017). 'Russkii Mir' was also the name of a Russian organisation that aims to popularise Russian culture and language in various parts of the world, including the DNR and LNR (Novaia Niva, 2016b). The notion of the 'Russian World' as a cultural or historical referent was almost entirely absent. This is notable considering the prevalence of the topic in rhetoric espoused by Vladimir Putin and other important political figures inside and outside the Russian Federation (O'Loughlin et al., 2016).

Language politics in the DNR and LNR were a contentious issue. The alleged repression of the use of Russian by the Ukrainian state has long been a grievance in Donbas (Sasse & Lackner, 2018). In DNR and LNR newspapers, this idea was given ample attention, for example, in an article by Aleksandr Zakharchenko decrying a decision by president Poroshenko to remove the Russian language from Ukrainian passports:

I cannot comment on the decision of the Ukrainian authorities, that is, the decision of the President of Ukraine, who signed this decree. I would like to comment on the attitude of Russians in Ukraine and even Ukrainians themselves with regards to this decree and to this policy. Let us remember why Donbas stood up (*podnialsia*) a year ago. The main reason for the protests was the banning of the Russian language.

(Snezhnianskie Novosti, 2015b)

The relation between the DNR and LNR and the broader Russian space posed complications for identity discourse in DNR and LNR newspapers. On the one hand, not much attention was paid to the idea of belonging to a Russian 'world', or of being part of the greater Russian Empire. On the other hand, the Russian language and culture were used to distinguish the DNR and the LNR from Ukraine. At the same time, however, the Ukrainian language was recognised as a 'state language' in both the DNR and the LNR (Narodnyi Sovet Donetskoi Narodnoi Respubliki, 2018; Narodnyi Sovet Luganskoi Narodnoi Respubliki, 2014a). And indeed, the status of Ukrainian was a common topic of discussion in DNR and LNR newspapers. On the one hand, the recognition of Ukrainian as a 'state language' was used to signal the lack of discrimination and freedom of people to express themselves without fear of reprisal (Znamia Pobedy, 2015i). On the other hand, Ukrainian was associated with the Ukrainian state, or more specifically with agents within the state promoting Ukrainian nationalism, and therefore treated with suspicion. The Russian language as a topic of discussion in DNR and LNR newspapers thus consists of three components: to promote the identification of the DNR and LNR with Russian and the 'Russian World' (rare), to promote the idea of the DNR and LNR as tolerant towards linguistic and other minorities, and to draw a contrast with Ukraine, which was portrayed as discriminatory towards Russian speakers.

Outgroup Identity

The outgroup in DNR and LNR newspapers refers first and foremost to Ukraine, and more specifically the 'Kyiv regime'. The narrative of guilt and loss at the hands of Ukraine becomes visible, first, in news outlets' coverage of the Donbas War. A common point of discussion was the damage done to buildings and people by the Ukrainian military, emphasising the horrors that Ukraine was inflicting on Donbas (Kazachii Vestnik, 2016a). For example, an article in *Golos Respubliki* noted the following:

On Tuesday November 17, Sergei Naumets, Minister of Construction and Housing and Public Utilities of the DNR, spoke about the second stage of the restoration of social facilities and housing that has been destroyed as a result of the hostilities . . .: 'As you know, 1,676 social facilities have been destroyed, 4,112 apartment buildings and 14,954 private housing units. 1,500 of these are beyond repair.'

(Golos Respubliki, 2015b)

The Minsk agreements (see Chapter 2) were also discussed. Particular attention was paid to portraying Ukraine as being in violation of the pact and actively using excessive force (XXI Vek, 2017b, 2017c). In an interview with

Novaia Niva, head of the DNR Aleksandr Zakharchenko was asked if he saw a way out of the conflict. In his answer, he focused on both Ukraine's military weakness and its lack of readiness to engage in ceasefire negotiations:

Do you remember that *they* attacked *us*? We were not the initiators of the conflict. And therefore it does not only depend on us when it ends. Unfortunately, Ukraine still hasn't lost hope of resolving this conflict by force. She does not want to learn from her mistakes. In recent days, a gap has appeared – a change in the opinion among the Western curators of Ukraine – but it is not yet possible to say whether this will lead to the end of the war by the end of the year. [What would be] a way out? There are still two options. Either Ukraine goes on the offensive to erase its mistakes, and loses, or Ukraine makes concessions and takes real steps towards a political settlement.

(Novaia Niva, 2016c)

Zakharchenko portrayed Ukraine as having initiated the conflict with Donbas, both by leaving Donbas no choice but to opt for separatism after the events on Euromaidan of February 2014 and by initiating military operations against the DNR and LNR. In addition, Ukraine was framed as guilty of excessive violence and being willing to destroy Donbas with reckless abandon, despite having coexisted relatively peacefully for about twenty-five years.

Second, a large number of articles discussed ongoing affairs in Ukraine – not only the state or the government, but also its people. Much ink was spilt revisiting the root causes of the conflict, focusing in particular on the role of the new Ukrainian authorities. The post-Maidan Ukrainian government was described as 'fascist' and 'neo-Nazi', having come to power after an unlawful 'coup d'état':

We cherish pleasant and joyful memories while trying to forget the moments of grief and sorrow, but things can happen that are impossible to get over or forget.... As soon as the Ukrainian people forgot about the horrors of the Great Patriotic War [World War II], brought upon our land by the Nazi invaders, neo-Nazism began to flourish in the country. What happened in Ukraine was a coup. Units of 'Pravyi Sektor' members (*pravoseki*) and similar elements marched through its cities. A new order came to power in the state that went under the name of Ukraine – one without the right to freedom, a native language, a culture, a history.... The organisers of this coup d'état in the capital probably did not expect that Donbas would refuse to tolerate this judicial chaos and the impunity espoused by the gangs of Euromaidanists (*evromaidanovtsy*). Through peaceful rallies and demonstrations, residents of the east tried to get through to the Kyiv regime and the international community, but instead of understanding and open dialogue, they received terror and political repression.

(Znamia Pobedy, 2015e)

A variety of terms were used to paint a vivid and detailed picture of the enemy: 'radical' forces in Ukraine, with the people's approval, took hold of power by force in collaboration with Western powers and NATO. The themes of shame and submission to the West appeared throughout both DNR and LNR newspapers. The illustrative article below sought to explain the downing of Malaysia Airlines flight MH17 in July 2014 by DNR insurgents (see Chapter 2):

In the skies of Donbas, junta[4] troops committed a terrible crime: the shooting down of a Malaysian Airlines Boeing 777 en route from Amsterdam to Kuala Lumpur, killing 298 innocent civilians from Europe and southeast Asia, among which at least three children. The authorities of neo-Nazi Ukraine immediately began to lob accusations at the militants (*opolchentsy*), throw around demands for letting NATO troops [into the country], accusing [us] of terrorism, et cetera.

(Novorossia, 2016a)

The quotes above are from editorials and news articles by DNR and LNR journalists. In other cases, however, the dissemination of these themes came directly from the top. Aleksandr Zakharchenko was quoted regularly in DNR newspapers, occasionally weighing in on the matter of identity and how the DNR came to be independent. When asked about the origins of the DNR, Zakharchenko skipped over the matter of Donbas identity and focused instead on Ukraine's history of ignoring and dismissing Donbas. The following quote is exemplary:

INTERVIEWER: How did the Donetsk People's Republic begin for you personally?

ZAKHARCHENKO: With a dream. I always dreamed of an independent, prosperous Donetsk state as part of the Russian World. I think many people in our region have dreamed of the same. Ukrainian politicians understood what the people wanted, and in their election programs and populist slogans constantly promised integration with the Russian Federation, recognition of the Russian language, and more self-government. They promised it but they always deceived [us]. The events of 2013–2014 served as a catalyst for the creation of the DNR. The coup d'état in Kyiv, the rise of radical nationalists to power, the repression of all those who disagreed, the Odesa-Khatyn [massacre].[5] All these events clearly showed that it was impossible to wait any longer, for when yet another deceitful politician finally fulfils his promise and hears the voice of Donbas. If today we do not oppose this kind of brutal impunity, tomorrow we will be destroyed. (Iasinovatskii Vestnik, 2015a)

---

[4] 'Junta' refers to the government in Kyiv.

[5] Zakharchenko is referring to the fire in the Odesa Trade Unions building on May 2, 2014, in which 48 people died and around 250 were injured after the building caught fire from petrol bombs during clashes between groups of demonstrators. He likens this event to the Khatyn Massacre of 1940, in which forces of the Nazi Schultzmannschaft Battalion slaughtered, through the use of fire (and gunfire), nearly 150 adults and children in the Belarusian village of Khatyn.

Finally, articles about politics usually framed Ukraine as a weak state, subservient to the West (Europe, the United States, and/or NATO). Two main sub-themes dominated political discussions: US foreign policy and DNR/LNR elections. Discussions about US foreign policy mirrored discussions in parts of Russian and American media (Hutchings & Szostek, 2015; Mikhailova, 2017) that allude to a 'deep state', which, unbeholden to election results or the 'consent of the governed', is running the country behind the scenes (Lofgren, 2014). The United States was thus portrayed as a puppet master (Vetrova, 2017) that Ukraine was unable and unwilling to resist:

> The 'deep state' of the United States can no longer hold the world in the soft paws of the 'liberal world order'.[6] It needs enemies to show off its predator claws and strong beak for the edification of the disgruntled. And to achieve this goal, it does not hesitate to use even the 'last refuge of scoundrels' (*poslednee pribezhishche negodiaiev*),[7] which the Banderite Ukraine has now become.
>
> (Kazachii Vestnik, 2017b)

CONCLUSION

Three main narratives were identified in a large sample of DNR and LNR newspaper articles: business as usual, war and memory, and loss and guilt. Newspapers in the DNR and LNR to a large extent continued to perform 'typical' activities as a source of information for local communities, reporting on sports, entertainment, local affairs, and cultural events (Hindman, 1996; Nielsen, 2015). This was done without regularly infusing reports with explicit references to ingroup or outgroup identity.

Sports is a good example. Local sports can play a role in spurring community development, particularly during times of conflict (Porter, 2017; Waquet & Vincent, 2011). In the DNR and LNR, the authorities deemed it important to get sports back on the agenda as soon as possible after the outbreak of the conflict. And indeed, 'national' football teams and sports leagues were quickly established. However, while the motivation behind doing so may have been (in part) motivated by a need to establish a local collective identity, there is more evidence that this was done as a means to keep the local population entertained; one sign of this is that Ukrainian sports channels were quickly put back on air after local residents protested their being banned by the authorities along with all other Ukrainian television channels. Most sports reports were also descriptive, containing basic information about the match or tournament, accounting for who won or lost, and in the case of a

---

[6] Note that the language used here follows the far-right political scientist Aleksandr Dugin (Dugin, 2014), whose work I discussed in Chapter 2.

[7] 'Patriotism is the last refuge of a scoundrel' is a quote by Samuel Johnson, a seventeenth-century English writer and poet.

sports achievement by a local resident, elaborating on this person's success. But there is little indication that sports, writ large, was deployed as a tool for ideology building in the DNR and the LNR.

The same can be said for the other typical topics of discussion that make up the majority of DNR and LNR newspaper coverage: education, the weather, and the local economy. A significant proportion of newspaper space was dedicated to mundane topics like potholes, upcoming concerts, a coal mine's productivity, and so on. This practice indicates a partial mobilisation of local news as a means for identity building: while some identity discourse was present on the pages of DNR and LNR newspapers, it is decisively not the case that it permeated every topic of discussion.

Nonetheless, a significant part of by local newspapers did address and contribute to the shaping and development of collective identity. The Donbas War was, expectedly, a major topic of discussion, but it was explored primarily in two ways: (1) through reports of the damage wrought by the war, emphasising particularly Ukraine's ceasefire violations and acts of aggression and (2) by drawing connections between the current conflict and World War II. The frame of being under attack by a 'fascist' or 'neo-Nazi' invader was highly prevalent in this discussion. The actions of the outgroup, the invader – not the actions of the ingroup, the DNR and LNR troops – were the point of focus. Here, DNR and LNR media mimic Russian state media, which have relied heavily on collective memories of World War II to shape perceptions of the Euromaidan movement and the post-Euromaidan Ukrainian government (Cottiero et al., 2015; Gaufmann, 2015).

Public holidays were a common way of fostering, implicitly and explicitly, a collective commemoration, embrace, and celebration of identity (Billig, 1995). Here, too, there was a focus on past suffering, particularly in connection with World War II. The term 'Donbas' was in some cases used to draw a contrast between the DNR and LNR and Ukraine. At the same time, there was a relative absence of tropes connecting the DNR and LNR with Russian identity. 'Novorossiia' and the 'Russian World' played a small role in newspaper coverage. Only one publication (*Novorossiia*) paid significant attention to the former; other newspapers barely mentioned the term. This clear underemphasis in newspaper discourse problematises conventional wisdom about the importance of 'Novorossiia' in local identity (Laruelle, 2016; O'Loughlin et al., 2017). The concept of the 'Russian World', despite its common usage by important figures like Vladimir Putin, was also not as evident as some have assumed (O'Loughlin et al., 2016). Much the same can be said for the other references to historical identity that have been floated by the DNR and LNR leadership (see Chapter 2): indeed, 'Malorossiia', the Donetsk-Kryvyi Rih Soviet Republic, and the idea of Donbas as an independent region of industrial workers played almost no part in DNR and LNR newspapers. The Soviet Union, meanwhile, was also almost entirely absent: there is not much indication that these newspapers hearkened back to the Soviet era as an important precursor to the emergence of the DNR and LNR.

The Russian language, described as the 'language of the land' in the DNR and LNR, was held in high regard. At the same time, Ukrainian was portrayed as a language that people in the DNR and LNR had little use for, despite being officially recognised as a 'state' language in both territories until early 2020. This latter point was emphasised as a way to draw a contrast with Ukraine, which was portrayed as acting in discriminatory fashion towards Russian-speaking people in terms of its language policy.

The above discussion leads to the conclusion that ingroup identity remained impoverished. The DNR and LNR were instead defined only by their counterparts: more attention was paid to what they were not than to what they were or wanted to be. This conclusion is in line with that of Kateryna Boyko, who argues that the newspaper *Novorossiia* projected an incoherent ideology to its readers, devoid of a consistent set of ideals (Boyko, 2016). This incoherence is perhaps best exemplified by a speech by Aleksandr Zakharchenko from 2025, which is worth quoting in full:

At the start of the war, when I was communicating with my comrades, my friends, I asked them a question: what are we fighting for? I wanted to hear the opinion of various residents of our state. The answers were very diverse, but for the most part they overlapped: we are fighting for our home, for our family, for our land, for our Motherland, for Russia, for freedom.... The most important thing we're fighting for is the freedom (*svoboda*) of Donbas. And then a second word appeared: 'justice' (*spravedlivost*). We have risen up for the justice that we regard as the cornerstone of our soul, our statehood. In addition to that, in a fair society, it is very important to achieve universal equality (*ravenstvo*) at all levels. Later, when talking to students, we brought up another important concept of our ideology – 'conscience' (*sovest*). Any Russian wants to live according to his conscience, and live in a state based on the principles of conscience. These words formed the basis of the ideology that I submitted to society for discussion. If you take the first letters of these words – 'freedom' (*svoboda*), 'justice' (*spravedlivost*), 'conscience' (*sovest*), 'equality' (*ravenstvo*) – and put them together, you get 'SSSR' [the Russian acronym for the USSR]. We will not argue over whether this project was successful or not, but it was an attempt to build a fair state on the basis of equality. Today we have the opportunity to do this. Not to repeat it, but to build it from scratch. Therefore, these words formed the basis of the ideology that I have been carrying in my heart all this time. Without ideology, a state cannot exist. We can be successful in a war, we can build an economy, but when there is no essence, no inner fulfilment, any such process is doomed to fail. People need to understand what we do, for what purpose, and, most importantly, how we will do it. Can you name at least one state that in such a short time was able to accomplish the things that we have done? You cannot. All inhabitants of the Republic performed a miracle that no one has achieved before us. And our task is not only to create the right ideology, but also to bring it to every inhabitant. To make it so that these principles are already assimilated by children at school. Therefore, ideology implies both the lessons of statehood and the correct teaching of true history. A history in which the heroes – that is [Donbas-born infantry soldier and Hero of the Soviet Union Aleksandr Matveevich] Matrosov, the defenders of Stalingrad – and the winners are the soldiers who stormed the Reichstag. And the villains are the *Banderovtsy*[8] and the fascists. And the story must be true. We must remember that we had warriors who nailed a shield to the gates of Constantinople. We should not forget that our ancestors defeated the Swedes near Poltava.. . . Thousands of battles in which the heroism of our ancestors was glorified. We must remember the story that was: BAM,[9] DneproGES,[10] the Five-Year Plans, constructing a state. These are things that should not be forgotten. It is necessary to remember both the victories and the mistakes that were made.

(Makeevskii Rabochii, 2015c)

When asked about the DNR's ideology, Zakharchenko employed a wide variety of ideological phrases without settling on any one in particular. He flirted with the idea of the DNR being imbued with a post-Soviet legacy, while also reiterating the importance of World War II, the history's region of coal mining, and even the emergence of the Russian Empire in the early eighteenth century. The task at hand was to 'create the right ideology', indicating a lack of coherence in how to proceed with the construction of identity, despite acknowledging its importance.

This impoverished ingroup stands in contrast with the narrative of loss and guilt vis-à-vis the outgroup: Ukraine and specifically the 'Kyiv Regime'. Ukraine was perhaps the most significant object of discussion in DNR and LNR newspapers, a point of pivot between evolving definitions of ingroup and outgroup. It was variably portrayed as having been overtaken by a 'neo-Nazi' or 'fascist' invader, a 'junta', a 'right-wing radical government', and the result of an illegitimate 'coup d'état'. It is not the case, however, that Ukrainians or the idea of Ukraine were attacked per se. Rather, Ukrainians were represented as guilty of allowing their most radical elements to take over and doing nothing to stop the onslaught of repression against Donbas. Ukraine, its language, or its people were therefore not the object of discursive outgroup construction; instead, the focus lay on a narrative of usurpation in which a small group of people took hold of power and embarked on a process of destroying the country. Ultimately, this narrative is centred on behaviour rather than essence: Ukrainians had been led astray by nefarious forces, but reconciliation remained a possibility, provided certain actions are taken. What these actions are was left in the middle.

In the end, this narrative of loss and guilt seeks to provoke an emotional response: outrage at Ukraine's destruction of Donbas and fear of invading radical forces. This weaponisation of strong emotions such as fear and anger

---

[8] 'Banderovtsy' (after the Ukrainian nationalist and partisan Stepan Bandera, see Chapter 1) is a term commonly used in a derogative manner to describe Ukrainian nationalists.

[9] BAM most likely refers to the Baikalo-Amurskaia Magistral, or the Baikal-Amur Mainline, a broad-gauge railway that runs parallel to the famous Trans-Siberian Railway.

[10] DneproGES (ДнепроГЭС), or the Dnipro Hydroelectric Station, is the name of the largest hydroelectric dam on the Dnipro river.

is a common tactic in media coverage, as argued by David Altheide (1997) and evidenced recently in the context of Twitter news during the 2016 and 2020 US elections (Eady et al., 2023; Taninecz Miller, 2019). Within social identity theory, emotionally affective messages about outgroups that are directed towards ingroup members have been shown to significantly affect ingroup identification and predict higher levels of prejudice (D. A. Miller et al., 2004). Thus, the weaponisation of negative emotion directed at outgroups in media discourse can transform how group members view themselves as well as others. DNR and LNR newspaper coverage clearly followed this pattern, demonising the Ukrainian 'other' in the process.

In sum, newspaper readers in the DNR and LNR were largely exposed to a typical menu of coverage of local events and to an identity discourse without a sui generis, unifying coherence. Ideology comes into play not so much when talking about the DNR and LNR as 'national' entities, but rather when talking about those outside it, primarily Ukraine and to a smaller extent the Russian Federation. The matter of 'why we exist' was not answered in a consistent manner by neither journalists nor the DNR and LNR leadership.

5

Identity and Ideology in Online Media

INTRODUCTION

The internet makes possible the anonymous, rapid, and continuous dissemination of news content. The online sphere not only allows for political news to be consumed globally rather than locally; it also brings opportunities for enhanced dissemination (Crilley, 2001). Content can be shared, liked, reposted, and commented on. Articles, video clips, and social media posts can go viral, including through artificial amplification, for example, by using bots (Broniatowski et al., 2018) or so-called troll armies (Shao et al., 2017) – all of which makes the internet a useful vehicle for authorities and governments to disseminate and amplify political messages. Crucially, these messages can be directed at audiences from all parts of the world, whereas newspapers and television are primarily addressed to and consumed by locals.

Developing an online media presence is of particular importance during a military conflict. Two motivations inform the need for doing so: legitimising the grievances underlying one's participation in the conflict (Deacon & Golding, 1994; Edney, 2012; Salhani, 2006) and delegitimising the opponent by demoralising it or by demonising it in the eyes of third-party observers (Ingram, 2016; Szostek, 2017).

Between 2014 and 2018, forty news sites were set up by the DNR and LNR authorities, publishing primarily in Russian but also in English, French, and Swedish.[1] Most of these sites were updated daily, and ran accounts on social media pages such as Vkontakte, Odnoklassniki, Facebook, and Twitter. In addition, a number of other websites that existed prior to 2014 began publishing from a pro-DNR/LNR perspective around the start of the conflict.

The articles published on these news sites were then further disseminated and discussed on forums, in comment sections, and on social media pages. All

---

[1] For more detailed information, see the 'DNR and LNR Media Landscape Overview' in the online appendix. Link: https://osf.io/3846a/, in the 'Background Information' folder.

of them operated under a publishing licence and were officially approved or were run directly by the DNR or LNR authorities. Analysing the content of these news sites can therefore provide insight into the discursive strategies and themes employed by these authorities to inform external (as opposed to internal) audiences. In this chapter, as in the previous one, I will again focus on the role of group identity and ideology in this media coverage.

METHOD OF ANALYSIS

A total of 43,267 news articles, published between 2015 and late 2017, were collected from four different DNR and LNR news sites. To ensure a balance between sites operating from the DNR and LNR, one news website from each unrecognised republic was included (*DNR24* and *Lugansk1 Info*). The largest English-language news site operating from the DNR/LNR (*DONi News*) was included as well, in order to incorporate coverage intended for the international community. Finally, one official state-run news agency (*Luganskii Informatsionnyi Tsentr*) was included for three reasons: (1) news agencies provide other news organisations, including news sites, with source material and press releases, which they can choose to cover or not; (2) as the news agency is run directly by the (in this case) LNR authorities, its publications offer a direct window into the ways authorities attempt to formulate their own discourse online; and (3) the content published online by state-run news agencies is intended for online as well as offline use. Looking at the contrasts between a news agency and other news websites can thus highlight the differences in approach between online and offline media outlets towards identity construction in the DNR and LNR. See Appendix B for more details about each outlet.

The method of analysis is roughly the same as in Chapter 3: a quantitative topic modelling analysis was conducted using non-negative matrix factorisation (Kuang et al., 2015); see Appendix A. The categories identified by the topic modelling analysis were then grouped together into themes and narratives. These narratives were then analysed in-depth through qualitative close reading. See Figure 5.1.

The topic modelling analysis revealed three distinct narratives present in content published on DNR and LNR news sites: 'business as usual', 'the cost of the war', and 'shaming the enemy'. These narratives are in turn made up of six themes: (1) the local economy and (2) weather, culture, sports, and entertainment (of which both themes fall under the 'business as usual' narrative); (3) the Donbas War and (4) humanitarian aid (both part of 'the cost of the war' narrative); and (5) Ukrainian politics and (6) domestic and international politics (both part of 'shaming the enemy' narrative). While these narratives may seem similar to those identified in the previous chapter, there are important differences, which I will discuss below. See Table 5.1 for an overview.

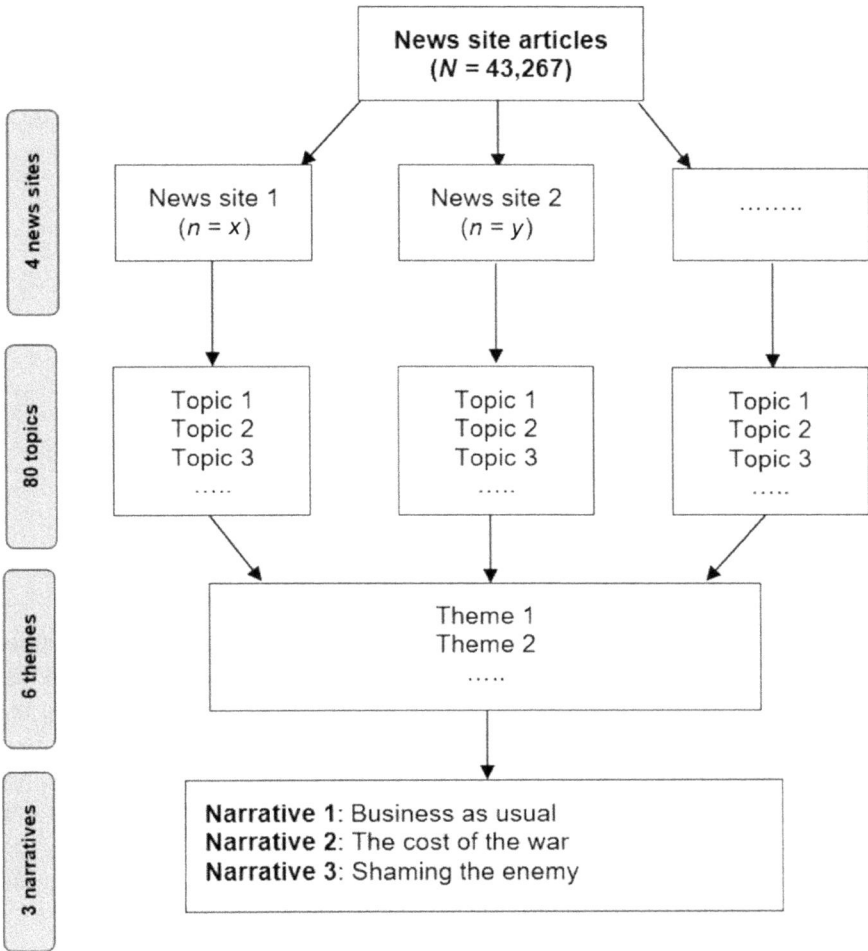

FIGURE 5.1 Schematic overview of the narrative analysis of DNR and LNR news sites.

BUSINESS AS USUAL?

I will first discuss themes that are not (or barely) imbued with ideological discourse. In its role as a press agency, *Luganskii Informatsionnyi Tsentr* did not publish daily reports about local affairs, unlike DNR and LNR newspapers. Instead, when it published material about locally relevant topics, the articles had some level of relevance beyond the DNR/LNR borders. For example, the press agency did not report on the results of competition football matches, but it did comment on 'international' matchups, when, for example, the LNR football team played against Abkhazia for the first time in 2015 (Luganskii Informatsionnyi Tsentr, 2015a). Weather reports were published mostly when weather conditions were somewhat exceptional, for example,

TABLE 5.1 Overview of narratives and themes in DNR and LNR news sites

Narrative	Theme	No. of topics	No. of news sites
Business as usual		**20 (25%)**	
	Local economy	10	4
	Weather, culture, sports, and entertainment	10	2
The cost of the war		**36 (45%)**	
	War	33	4
	Humanitarian aid	3	1
Shaming the enemy		**18 (22.5%)**	
	Ukrainian politics	5	4
	Domestic and international politics	13	4
Unclassified		**6 (7.5%)**	

when a new year's celebration was cancelled due to harsh winter weather (2014d). Articles about children or education often related directly to the authorities, for instance, when the LNR authorities proposed modelling the school curriculum after the Russian Federation's (2014a) or when Igor Plotnitskii went on a trip to Moscow with a few high-performing high school students (2016i). With regard to cultural activities, dispatches such as one about the opening of a new cinema were par for the course (2015b). In addition, the press agency published near-daily articles explaining what types of activities (film screenings, theatre performances, festivals, and concerts) were being organised throughout the region (2017b).

Similarly, as established in Chapter 4, the economy of the DNR and LNR was a salient point of discussion in DNR and LNR newspapers. The same is true for news websites, with articles covering topics such as deciding how to improve facilities for people with disabilities (2014b) or parliamentary discussions about tax reform (2016b). Unlike in local newspapers, however, discussions about the local economy were related primarily to the war and to the economic stabilisation of the two regions. Reports about how the DNR and LNR authorities planned to revive the region were common, particularly in *DONi News*:[2]

---

[2] In this chapter, I cite verbatim numerous articles published in English by *DONi News*, leaving intact some grammatical errors in the original publication as well as the original transliteration. Where necessary, I will offer additional contextual information.

Due to the stabilisation of the situation in the Republic, almost all the enterprises were able to profit in the current year. The heavy industry is also being developed. For example, Yasinovatskiy [*sic*] machine-building plant is returning to the Russian market. Now the plant has received an order from one of the enterprises from Ural to produce coal combines KSP-35.

(DONi News, 2015d)

In *DNR24*, *DONi News*, and *Lugansk1 Info*, the economy was discussed primarily within the context of the war to emphasise self-sufficiency; the DNR and LNR were cast as the victims of an economic blockade and a lack of official recognition (DNR24, 2016e), which made exporting products more difficult. Ukraine is represented in this material as a power that is squeezing DNR and LNR residents by not allowing trade to flourish, and by forcing the DNR and LNR to export almost exclusively to Russia (Lugansk1 Info, 2015). This narrative stands in contrast with the narratives identified in newspaper content (see Chapter 4): DNR and LNR newspapers discussed the economy not only in the context of the war, but also (to an extent) in the context of memory and identity. Coal mining and metallurgy, for example, were sometimes portrayed as sources of regional pride as well as sources of income (Kuromiya, 1998, 2008). Online, however, coal mining was primarily brought up within a technical context, with articles recounting the productivity of a mine or the effects of the war on production outputs (DNR24, 2016d). Articles about heavy industry and mining were much less present online than in newspapers, although not entirely absent: occasionally, articles did refer to the identity-building function of the mining industry, particularly around the Day of the Miner holiday on August 27 (Luganskii Informatsionnyi Tsentr, 2017e).

Another important topic of discussion was politics, both international and domestic. *Mir Luganshchine* ('Peace for Luhansk Region') was Igor Plotnitskii's social movement/political party. Between 2014 and 2017, it held a majority in the LNR 'People's Council'. *Luganskii Informatsionnyi Tsentr*, being the main press vehicle for the LNR authorities, paid a great deal of attention to *Mir Luganshchine*'s activities, covering its efforts to conduct 'youth diplomacy' (Luganskii Informatsionnyi Tsentr, 2015e), educational trips abroad for high school students (2015f), humanitarian and projects such as 'We will not forget, we will not forgive!' (*ne zabudem, ne prostim!*) (2016e) and 'Volunteer' (*voluntior*) (2016a), setting up a 'hotline' to report cases of corruption (2015h), and organising 'patriotic' public events such as 'Brianka sings with the heart!' (*Brianka poet serdtsem!*) (2016h), 'One thousand days of defiance' (*1,000 dnei vopreki*) (2017a), and 'Victory is ours!' (*pobeda za nami!*) (2015g). Such articles sometimes discussed the LNR's ideological underpinnings, for example, in a report about a competition for high school students entitled 'Unknown and known Donbas', organised by *Mir Luganshchine* in the town of Krasnyi Luch

(2016c). Another example was the announcement of a *subbotnik* (a day during which people sign up to do voluntary work, usually on some kind of public project), organised by the movement:

[*Mir Luganshchine*] invites all residents of the [LNR] to take part in a Republic-wide clean-up on April 28, 2017, under the motto 'Order in the Republic is peace at home'.... 'We [*Mir Luganshchine*], as the largest social movement in the Republic, with more than 87 thousand people in our ranks ... invite all concerned residents (*neravnodushnykh zhitelei*) to take active part in [this *subbotnik*]. Together, with combined effort, let's make the territory of our collective home – our Republic – beautiful,' said Nikolai Zaporozhtsev, acting Head of the Republican Executive Committee of *Mir Luganshchine*. 'As part of the *subbotnik*, trees will be planted in cities and districts of the LNR as a symbol of peace and new life, in which there is no place for war,' he added.

(Luganskii Informatsionnyi Tsentr, 2017c)

Mir Luganshchine representatives thus sometimes referred to patriotism and the idea of a homeland for LNR citizens. But while the events themselves may have been patriotic in nature, the rhetoric used to describe them was devoid of specificity; patriotism and love for the homeland were asserted but rarely explained in detail. Unlike DNR and LNR newspapers (see Chapter 4), *Luganskii Informatsionnyi Tsentr*'s online material rarely explored ideology and identity beyond the realm of banal descriptions.

This practice holds for the other news sites to an even greater extent, with internal politics receiving even less attention. Articles about domestic politics originated from press centres and were then copied or adapted by other news sites. *Lugansk1 Info*, for example, relied on *Luganskii Informatsionnyi Tsentr* as a source for articles about locally relevant political issues like fixing Luhansk's water supply (Lugansk1 Info, 2017e), speeches and public appearances by state officials (2017c), political and parliamentary reforms (2016f), and local cultural events and entertainment (2016e). But while *Luganskii Informatsionnyi Tsentr* was replete with articles about local affairs, the majority of its reports that were copied or used as a source by *Lugansk1 Info*, and even in some cases *DNR24* (2017h) and *DONi News* (2015g), were to do with the conflict; examples include the discovery of alleged Ukrainian spies (Lugansk1 Info, 2017a), ongoing discussions within the framework of the Minsk agreements (2016d), and an interview with a local activist group leader about Kyiv's 'terror attacks' against the LNR (2017f).

This point is indicative of a wider pattern present in DNR and LNR internet media: the discourse used to describe the ideology of these statelets was an anti-discourse, defined by what it was not, rather than by what it was or wanted to be. Terms that have a clear ideological connotation such as 'Novorossiia' show up from time to time, but the role these terms played in the ideology of the DNR and LNR was almost never explored. A good example is an interview with Nataliia Nikonorova, then-minister of foreign affairs of the DNR, published in 2016. Nikonorova was asked about the future of Novorossiia as a political project and the possibilities of forming a federation with the LNR (Lugansk1 Info, 2016h):

NIKONOROVA: For now we are bringing our legal frameworks in line with each other. But we're hoping for more, that is, if it is to be a federation, then with a much larger list of subjects. The idea of Novorossiia is good, but . . .

INTERVIEWER: But you still need a piece of the Rostov region?

N: No, we won't be going in that direction.

I: So do you expect that Kharkiv or other eastern regions of Ukraine will join you?

N: That would be nice.

I: And with whom is it better to unite, with Kharkiv or Rostov?

N: Everything will depend on the outcome of the Minsk process. If Kyiv fulfils its obligations, which I strongly doubt, it will be a completely different Ukraine.

Nikonorova weighed the pros and cons of 'Novorossiia' as a political negotiation, as opposed to an ideological mission. The term thus serves as a reference to an ideology without content. Articles delving into the relevance of 'Novorossiia' for the culture, history, or identity of Donbas or the DNR/LNR were almost non-existent.[3] The idea of Russian-ness and the 'Russian World' also received scant attention. Articles pondering the linkages between the DNR and LNR and the larger Russian space were rare, and instead some writers expressed their frustration with the lack of a coherent ideological framework to draw from. One article, for example, featured an opinion writer arguing that Donbas residents, suffering from a lack of culture and meaning, are looking for a 'happy Russian life' (Lugansk1 Info, 2016a). One exception is Elena Zaslavskaia, a well-known poet from Luhansk, who reflected on the effects of the war on her sense of identity in an interview:

Although my house was not completely destroyed, it did suffer during the shelling of the city. But I gained much more than I lost. I witnessed how my people resisted injustice and rose up to fight, for their language, for their traditions, for their heroes. The words 'Motherland' (*rodina*), 'Donbas character' (*donbasskii kharakter*), 'Russian world' (*russkii mir*), which used to be empty agitprop slogans, suddenly became full of meaning.

(Darenskii, 2016)

While Zaslavskaia did not elaborate further than this, her interview is a rare example of a clear invocation of collective identity. Thus, while on the

---

[3] See *Lugansk1 Info* (2016g) for an example.

surface internal politics were a common topic on DNR and LNR news sites, political discussions were almost entirely devoid of ingroup-focused discourse. Where this discourse did exist (mostly in articles published by *Luganskii Informatsionnyi Tsentr*), the statelets' ideological justifications were asserted as existing a priori, rather than explored in detail. Instead, news site discourse focused primarily on the conflict, and more specifically Ukraine's role in it.

Unlike newspapers, then, news sites in the DNR and LNR framed relevant issues not from a local but from a more international perspective. Topics like sports, the economy, culture, arts, education, and local history were less relevant online than in print and relatively devoid of references to community and local identity. In Chapter 4, I demonstrated that the inward-focused ideological discourse relating to these day-to-day topics was present but impoverished. Online, such discourse was absent altogether. In the next section, I explore what replaced it.

THE COST OF THE WAR

The Donbas War played an important role in DNR/LNR online news discourse. Thirty-six out of eighty topics in the topic model pertain to this theme, which includes articles about the material cost of the war (such as the destruction of infrastructure and houses), civilian casualties, military engagements including combat operations, and peace negotiations and conflict resolution. Unlike in DNR and LNR newspapers, World War II played a bit role.

A lot of articles focused on the actions of the enemy (i.e., the 'Kyiv regime'), for example, blaming them for ceasefire violations and other military infractions. *DNR24* and *DONi News* would often cite Eduard Basurin, deputy chief of the Operational Command of the DNR. Typical reports, which were published multiple times per week, would list the military activities undertaken by the Ukrainian Anti-Terrorist Operation:

> Over the past month, Ukrainian armed forces personnel carried out fourteen attacks in the direction of the positions of the Donetsk People's Republic. This was announced today at a briefing by the deputy commander of the operational command of the DNR, Eduard Basurin: 'In November 2016, the enemy carried out a total of 14 offensive strikes in the direction of our positions with the support of heavy artillery and armoured vehicles.'
>
> (DNR24, 2016b)

Basurin's press releases in *DONi News* typically mentioned both military engagements and Ukraine's alleged ceasefire violations:[4]

---

[4] See also *DONi News* (2015c, 2016c).

'The situation in the Donetsk People's Republic has remained tense over the past day. There were two ceasefire violations by the Ukrainian war criminals,' vice-commander of [DNR] army Eduard Basurin in Thursday [*sic*]. 'Donetsk airport was shelled from the positions of the 93 separate motorized rifle brigade under the command of Colonel Vladislav Klochkov with mortars of 82 mm calibre. The mines No. 6, 7 in Gorlovka were attacked from the town of Mayorsk with grenade machine guns.' The [DNR]'s intelligence constantly confirms the Minsk agreements violations by the Ukrainian side concerning the withdrawal of heavy weapons over 100 mm from the contact line.

(DONi News, 2015b)

In the LNR, the role of press officer was held by Andrei Marochko, variously referred to as a lieutenant-colonel, colonel, and major. While Marochko regularly addressed the press to talk about a variety of topics related to the ongoing conflict, his main role, like Basurin's, was to provide details on military engagements, casualties, and damage done to infrastructure and real estate. Typically, Marochko would also address the illegality of Ukraine's actions with reference to the Minsk agreements (Luganskii Informatsionnyi Tsentr, 2017d). More broadly, in all four outlets, the Minsk agreements were mentioned primarily within the context of Ukraine's alleged violations of it (Lugansk1 Info, 2017l).

Prisoner exchanges between Ukraine and the DNR/LNR were overseen by the OCSE Special Monitoring Mission (SMM) in the area (OSCE, 2015a). Fighters returning from Ukrainian captivity were occasionally interviewed by journalists for *Luganskii Informatsionnyi Tsentr*, after which these articles would be copied by other news sites. In such interviews, the fighters would often emphasise the bad treatment given to them by Ukrainian troops:

Supporters of the Donbas Republics, released yesterday . . . from Ukrainian captivity, told a journalist for *Luganskii Informatsionnyi Tsentr* about instances of torture in the Ukrainian security service and inhumane conditions in prisons. 'There was torture. They beat some kind of testimony out of us and then pinned entirely different charges on us. They tried to pin some homicide on me retroactively, but at that time I was already back in the DNR, and there was evidence for this,' said a Donetsk resident who had returned home.

(Lugansk1 Info, 2017k)

Another common object of discussion was the morale of Ukrainian troops, which was framed as being low due to bad working conditions and a lack of military accomplishments (DNR24, 2017g). In many cases, low morale was reported to result in criminal behaviour (DNR24, 2017b). Efforts were made to claim rampant alcoholism and other forms of irregular behaviour on the part of the Ukrainian troops (Luganskii Informatsionnyi Tsentr, 2016d, 2016g). The military accomplishments by DNR and LNR troops, by contrast, were covered less prominently than the disagreeable actions of the Ukrainian army; indeed, there were surprisingly few articles about DNR/LNR soldiers' feats of bravery or military victories (with some exceptions; see, for example, Luganskii Informatsionnyi Tsentr, 2015d). The focus of war-related coverage on DNR and LNR news sites was thus firmly on Ukraine. News articles often advanced claims about the illegality of Ukraine's actions under the Minsk agreements, its immoral behaviour towards non-combatants and prisoners of war, and the failure to maintain morale. In Chapter 4, I argued that in DNR and LNR newspapers, the commemor-ation of World War II was often employed to establish a discursive connec-tion between the Soviet Union's battle against Nazi Germany and the modern-day conflict, with the latter framed as a continuation of the fight against fascism. This connection was much less prominent online. For example, *DONi News* quoted Aleksandr Zakharchenko talking about how the city of Kyiv changed after 2014:

According to [Zakharchenko], now Kyiv faces hard times: 'Certainly in Kyiv there was the armed coup, and this city was given to the armed gangs of national radicals to be plundered. And if the usurpers have sent the armed punishers and bandits to our home, then Kyiv has undergone the improbable political terror, comparable unless with times of Nazi occupation during the Great Patriotic War.' The Head of the [DNR] has emphasized that Kyiv needs to be liberated as it was during the Great Patriotic War.

(DONi News, 2016d)

In both *DNR24* and *Lugansk1 Info*, however, World War II also did not play a meaningful role in the same way that it did in DNR and LNR newspapers; indeed, few direct comparisons were made between World War II and the present-day Donbas War. The conflict would be mentioned, for example, in the context of the destruction of a World War II monument in Dnipro (Lugansk1 Info, 2017b), a concert that was organised for World War II and Afghanistan war veterans (Lugansk1 Info, 2016b), a brief report about Victory Day celebrations on May 9 (DNR24, 2017d), and an article reminding audiences of the war crimes committed against Polish citizens by Ukrainian members of the SS in 1944 (DNR24, 2017k). Overall, however, reports mentioning the war were sparse, and even fewer drew a direct connection between the war years and the present-day conflict. This stands in stark contrast with DNR and LNR newspapers, where the war, while underspeci-fied, was part of an ideological discourse aimed at the local population.

SHAMING THE ENEMY

The third narrative relates to how the enemy (i.e., Ukraine) was portrayed, primarily through the trope of shame. I will do so by examining two salient themes in more detail: (1) international politics and (2) Ukrainian politics.

International Politics

A substantial number of articles covered US–Russia relations and the annex-ation of Crimea. As might be expected, articles about the United States,

Russia, and Crimea covered topics like military cooperation between the United States and Ukraine (DONi News, 2017c), European efforts to support Ukrainian reunification (DONi News, 2016a), US president Donald Trump's wariness of getting the United States involved in further foreign entanglements (DNR24, 2016c), and the supposed failure on the part of the international MH17 investigation team to involve Russia in the investigation (DNR24, 2017j). Broadly speaking, however, international politics was a significant topic of discussion only in *DONi News*, which covered, among other things, UN resolutions about Donbas. Its coverage recalls familiar tropes explored in Chapter 4, such as those conflating present-day Ukraine (and its Western allies) with Nazi Germany:

A UN General Assembly committee has passed a resolution 'combating glorification of Nazism', with 126 countries voicing their support. Meanwhile, the US, Ukraine and Canada voted against. Moscow has called the decision 'regrettable' and 'bewildering'. The resolution, which was initially proposed by Russia and co-authored by 52 states, including Brazil, China, India, and Kazakhstan, deals with measures to fight the glorification of Nazism, neo-Nazism, and other practices that facilitate the escalation of modern forms of racism, racial discrimination, xenophobia, and intolerance. Another 53 countries, including the European Union nations and NATO members abstained from the vote. Last year, 115 countries voted in support of a similar resolution, with three countries voting against – the US, Canada, and Ukraine.

(DONi News, 2015e)

On all news sites in the corpus, the West (meaning Europe and the United States) was portrayed as hypocritical in dealing with the Donbas and Crimea crises. Western journalists who disagreed with 'Western propaganda' about Ukraine, Crimea, and Donbas were praised for their convictions:

Those voices in European media that until recently were alone in singing that something was wrong with the best of all worlds (*luchshii iz mirov*), are now beginning to sound like a choir. A sobering choir (*khor otrezvleniia*), although not yet one of sobriety (*trezvost*). European non-propaganda (*nepropaganda*) has so thoroughly distorted the reality that public consciousness will have to take drastic measures against a hangover. Czech journalist Pavel Černocký, not sympathetic to Russia, has already come around to this fact. In his state of ideological hangover, he still thinks that Russia has captured Crimea and Donbas, but does already believe that peoples have the right to peaceful self-determination. Not much of a discovery (*ne bog vest kakoe otkrytie*), but still: 'The problem of territories breaking away [from the state] can be solved peacefully, for example, with the help of a referendum or agreement. To name an example: Slovakia. Of course, in Crimea and Donbas, most of the inhabitants are Russian, and they have the right to self-determination.'

(Lugansk1 Info, 2016j)

Another topic of discussion is the Syrian war, where the United States was portrayed as a warmonger that, inadvertently or not, supported radical forces in the region (DONi News, 2015a). This same frame was also identified in two studies about the framing of the Syrian War in Russian media (Abd El Rahman Kamal, 2017; Godefroidt, 2014). The discourse about the West on

DNR and LNR news sites thus appears to be in line with the historical 'anti-imperialist' sentiment that, as Hiroaki Kuromiya (2019) argues, has long been a key element of Donbas identity, although the target of this anti-imperialism has shifted towards being focused on the West, and the United States in particular. This discourse also closely mimicked Russian media's strategic narratives about the West as identified by Stephen Hutchings and Joanna Szostek (2015, p. 185), who write that 'characteristics attributed to western governments by the Russian media include hypocrisy, risibility, arrogant foolishness, and a lack of moral integrity to the point of criminality'. Anti-Westernism, according to Hutchings and Szostek, has been 'at the heart of efforts to establish the basis for national belonging' in Russia after the fall of the Soviet Union (2015, p. 189). On DNR and LNR news sites, anti-Westernism was a prominent trope, and discursively comparable to what has been observed in Russian media.

A second interpretation of this ostensible anti-Western discourse is that DNR and LNR internet media critique what Richard Sakwa calls Ukraine's shift towards 'European monism' as a source of identity (Sakwa, 2015b, 2015a, p. 86), in which the 'European Union is representative of what it means to be European', a view espoused by many within Ukraine, particularly since 2014.[5] From this point of view, the contested and as yet undecided question of what it means to be Ukrainian not only is debated and discussed within Ukraine itself but is influenced by outside forces such as the European Union and the NATO alliance. Following Sakwa, DNR and LNR online media discourse rejects European monist identity and instead 'seeks to retain historic links with Russia' as a means to contest what it sees as dominant Ukrainian nationalist narratives about Ukrainian identity. This conflation of Ukraine and the West, however, was not the most predominant frame, even within the theme of politics; here, Ukrainian politics took a much more central position.

Ukrainian Politics

Ukrainian politics took centre stage on DNR/LNR news sites relative to the attention that was paid to local (DNR/LNR) and international politics. Language and language policy were key elements in this discussion. In September 2017, the Ukrainian Verkhovna Rada passed the Law on Education (*zakon pro osvitu*). Article 7 of this law, pertaining to the regulation of the language of instruction in education (Council of Europe, 2017), evoked controversy both inside and outside Ukraine (Tulul, 2017). Politicians in Hungary and Romania expressed concern that the law would prohibit

---

[5] As witnessed, for example, by banners on Euromaidan saying 'Ukraine is Europe', alongside flags of the European Union.

Hungarian- and Romanian-language schools to teach subjects in these languages and would instead make teaching all subjects in Ukrainian mandatory.[6] The Venice Commission, an advisory body to the Council of Europe that consults countries in constitutional matters, in part agreed with this criticism, noting that the law lacked clarity and left too much room for interpretation, thus potentially putting minority rights at risk (Venice Commission, 2017). The discussion surrounding the law was also featured on the pages of DNR and LNR news sites. Specifically, discussions in Ukrainian media were re-reported, particularly when prominent Ukrainians expressed criticism of the law:

> The Law on Education, adopted by the Verkhovna Rada and signed by the President of Ukraine, constitutes a 'language raid', when at the expense of a different cultural space a monotony is introduced that will be deadly for Ukraine. This is according to the Kyiv-based, Russian-speaking poet Aleksandr Kabanov, writing in the commentary section of the publication *Gordon*. 'That this law rocks the societal boat during a time of war and economic collapse is without a doubt. Symon Petliura[7] was right: 'one shouldn't be so afraid of lice from Moscow so much as of nits from Ukraine'.
>
> (Lugansk1 Info, 2017g)

Another example is an article stating that 'the ministry of information of Ukraine submitted to the [Ukrainian Security Service] a list of sites to be banned for posing a threat to national security' (Lugansk1 Info, 2017d), which mocked the Ukrainian government's decision to ban what it calls 'popular websites in Ukraine' for 'spurious reasons'. Such articles would highlight the divisions within Ukrainian society and give voice to internal criticism of the Ukrainian government and armed forces. Other societal concerns within Ukraine were addressed as well. For example, crimes occurring throughout Ukraine were reported by DNR and LNR news sites with some regularity, emphasising especially the Ukrainian government's failure to prevent them:

> In Lviv oblast, several school teachers' partners were detained for arranging the trafficking of psychotropic substances and drugs from EU countries, according to the oblast police's communications department. 'Operatives of the Department of Counteracting Drug Crime of the National Police of Ukraine, together with investigators at the General Investigative Department for Procedural Guidelines of the Prosecutor General's Office, exposed the illegal activities of these drug trafficking spouses. The criminals, residents of Lviv oblast, established a channel to supply drugs and psychotropic substances from EU countries market them in Ukraine,' [the police said].
>
> (Lugansk1 Info, 2017h)

Other examples of articles about Ukraine's domestic problems include growing rates of tuberculosis (DNR24, 2017i), a lack of available vaccinations

---

[6] The law does allow for instruction in minority languages in pre-school and primary education (Law on Education, 2017).

[7] Symon Vasylovych Petliura was commander of the Ukrainian armed forces and Chairman of the Ukrainian Directorate between 1919 and 1926.

(Luganskı Info, 2017i), and an energy crisis due to coal shortages (DONi News, 2015f). Ukrainian media were also lambasted for their dishonest coverage of the situation in the DNR and LNR, as well as in Crimea, where life was said to be much better than portrayed (DNR24, 2017c). Such stories, which covered a wide range of problems and issues across the entire territory of Ukraine, contribute to a discourse framing Ukraine as being embroiled in a series of perpetual crises that it is unable to deal with, and a population that is being lied to about the 'real' situation in Donbas, Crimea, or Russia by a dishonest national media.

Not only the Ukrainian but also the international press was monitored for articles shaming Ukraine, in particular, Western media (Luganskı Info, 2016c, 2017j). One story on a French website was cited to highlight the Ukrainian government's attempts to rewrite history and deny its Russian imperial heritage:

> *Agora Vox*, a popular French online publication, has published a large article about the attempts of the Kyiv regime to rewrite the history of Ukraine, in which the authors remind Ukrainians that about 80% of their present lands were actually donated by the Russian tsars and Soviet secretaries general. The French publication also notes that with de-communisation, Ukraine is not only shooting itself in the foot, but is already putting a pistol to its temple.
>
> (DNR24, 2017e)

Another example is coverage of a non-binding referendum held in the Netherlands in April 2016 about Ukraine's association agreement with the European Union. Voters were asked to decide whether they supported the signing of a partnership deal between Ukraine and the EU, and rejected the proposal by around 61 to 39 per cent, with a turnout of about 30 per cent (BBC News, 2016a). The referendum result was cited by DNR and LNR websites to claim that the idea of Ukraine's integration into Europe was a 'fata morgana' (DNR24, 2017a) and that Europe 'does not need' Ukraine (Luganskii Informatsionnyi Tsentr, 2016f).

This shaming of Ukraine in media both inside and outside the country formed a cornerstone of these news sites' discourse. But while Ukraine's ceasefire violations and alleged war crimes were described in detail on both the Russian- and English-language news sites in the corpus, *DONi News* in particular would stress the role of the West in escalating the conflict:

> The cruel shelling of the civilian districts of the Lugansk People's Republic represents acts of pure state terrorism, conducted by the Western-backed Kyiv regime. The trend has been worrying in the past weeks and escalation of the situation in both Donbas republics, growth in all kind of provocations, in political and military spheres, have been witnessed,' believes [Janus] Putkonen.[8] The Finnish journalist emphasized that

---

[8] Putkonen was editor-in-chief of *DONi News* at the time of this article's publication.

apparently the West, led by US war hawks, has again chosen military solutions in its destructive agenda to fuel geopolitical standoff between the West and Russia.

(DONi News, 2017d)

The framing of coverage about demonstrations in Ukraine against the Poroshenko government makes use of similar tropes to the ones observed in the previous chapter, including an emphasis on Ukraine's 'neo-Nazi' affiliations and overabundance of radical political groups (Luganski Info, 2016i). Importantly, words such as 'fascist' were also used by high officials, such as former head of the LNR Igor Plotnitskii, to refer to the Ukrainian government (Luganskii Informatsionnyi Tsentr, 2014c). Similarly, *DNR24* employed terms such as 'junta', 'neo-Banderite', and 'neo-Nazi' to describe Ukrainian political figures and the Poroshenko government, as in the following opinion piece:

I think I'm not mistaken when I say that most experts and ordinary citizens of the former Soviet Union didn't expect to see what we all saw on May 9 in the Ukrainian territory that was seized by the neo-Banderite junta. People have finally begun to throw off the shackles of fear and psychological numbness that this neo-Banderite junta, led by Poroshenko, has put on them, psychologically speaking, between 2014 and 2015. The junta demonstrated its permissiveness, impunity, rudeness, violence, and the animalistic grin of neo-Nazi gangs who seized power and achieved what they did not manage to finish in 1941–1945: the destruction of the people.

(DNR24, 2017f)

DONi News would highlight the actions by Ukrainian volunteer battalions like Azov (2016b), which, while not officially being part of the Ukrainian army, nonetheless conducted military operations in Donbas under the command of the government. The outlet described it as an ultranationalist 'lunatic fringe group':[9]

How is Nazism reproduced in Ukraine? Ukrainians raise a new generation of pseudo-patriots. Despite the economic downfall, which started in 2014, Ukrainian radicals, who came to power, have no intention of solving those problems. However, they actively undertake massive youth recruitment. Thus, 'Azov' regiment's gunmen published a video of the new children's camp shift opening: boys and girls are inculcated Nazi ideology and hatred towards Russia from a very young age.

(DONi News, 2017b)

Here, again, Nazism, anti-Russian sentiments, and radical nationalism are framed as being central to Ukrainian politics and, importantly, society, despite them being marginal in sociological polls and electoral results.[10] The activities of such radical groups were framed as being against the will of ordinary people in Ukraine, who were shown to be questioning these groups' sincerity and capacity to bring the conflict to a close (DONi News, 2017a).

---

[9] This sentiment is shared by some Western scholars as well; see for example Umland (2019).
[10] See for example Shevel (2015) and Nemtsova (2018).

Alexandr Osipian argues that the 'fascist' and 'Banderite' tropes have roots in Ukrainian politics before the outbreak of the conflict, stating that the Party of Regions, the party of former president Viktor Yanukovych, began promoting these tropes as part of its campaign to build political support in Donbas (Osipian, 2015, p. 131). The attention that DNR and LNR media, particularly online, devoted to these tropes indicates a continuation of a process that was started before the conflict (rather than starting 'from scratch', as it were), the intensity of which was increased as the conflict broke out. On DNR and LNR news sites, there are thus three discursive elements when it comes to constructing Ukraine as the enemy: that of a government that is suppressing minorities, unable to deal with domestic problems, and being shunned by its foreign allies; of a society that is permanently riddled with economic and cultural problems; and of a political landscape that is dominated by and beholden to its most radical elements.

CONCLUSION

This chapter has examined the role of ideology in the content produced by four DNR and LNR news sites. At first glance, the findings appear similar to those from the previous chapter: internet content focused heavily on the conflict and Ukrainian internal affairs, while leaving collective identity underdefined and semantically impoverished. In addition, both newspapers and news sites weaponised emotional discourse, with a focus on evoking fear and anger among their readers. These conclusions, by themselves, show that the patterns observed in Chapter 4 can be extrapolated to written media content more broadly and that the discursive strategies online and offline display a significant degree of overlap.

With this in mind, there are a few differences worth exploring further. First, whereas in DNR/LNR newspapers more than half of all topics related to a narrative of 'business as usual' (e.g., sports, culture, infrastructure, etc.), they were much less evident online. *Luganskii Informatsionnyi Tsentr* was the only one out of four websites in this chapter's corpus that paid a significant amount of attention to local politics. On the other three news sites, almost no attention was given to such relatively banal affairs. Instead, such discourses were replaced with articles about the war, about which there were three dominant topics of discussion: Ukraine's alleged violations of the Minsk agreements, the Ukrainian army's putative immoral behaviour, and the failure of the Ukrainian leadership to maintain morale. Whereas in DNR and LNR newspapers, World War II was also a highly prevalent theme in which the connections between the Nazi occupation of the Soviet Union and the modern Donbas conflict were made explicit, this was not the case online.

Another major theme is the shaming of the enemy (Ukraine or, more specifically, the 'Kyiv regime') by paying attention to domestic issues, international affairs, and Ukrainian politics and society. The key difference with newspaper coverage is that there was no mention of a shared history or peaceful previous coexistence that Ukraine violated; instead, the focus was almost entirely on portraying Ukraine as a failed state, guilty of war crimes, which has no business continuing the war and which deliberately stymies all attempts at resolving the conflict peacefully. This theme shows a large degree of overlap with narratives about the post-Maidan Ukrainian government present in Russian state media (Cottiero et al., 2015; Gaufmann, 2015).

Intermixed with this political coverage were articles on patriotic and cultural events organised by the LNR's ruling political movement, *Mir Luganshchine*. Here, however, ingroup identity was asserted or assumed rather than explored in detail; articles that evoked patriotism or addressed cultural events or local politics rarely explored *why* readers should identify with the LNR. None of this is to say that ideology was never mentioned at all, only that a person reading any of these websites on a regular basis would likely not find ideological discourse to comprise a substantial part of what they were reading. This goes for all of the discursive 'usual suspects', including 'Novorossiia', the 'Russian World', and the history of Donbas as an independent-minded industrial region.

One important narrative element mostly absent online but very present in newspapers is the concept of guilt. In Chapter 4, I examined the prominent frame of Ukraine's guilt in betraying Donbas, the idea that Ukraine's actions were so egregious that they left the DNR and LNR no choice but to declare independence. Online, this sense of guilt and the lost potential for peaceful coexistence was replaced by outrage at Ukraine's alleged crimes, the difference being that there was no sense of a shared history of (relatively) peaceful coexistence whose loss was lamented. Exemplary of this point is the following quote, from an article in *Luganskı Info* about an interview with Ievgenii Kuznetsov, an elderly Luhansk resident who attended political rallies on a regular basis:

The presidency of Yanukovych is looked back on in a bad way. So the beginning of the demonstrations in Kyiv in 2013 did not raise too many objections. Yanukovych put the entire economy of the country under his 'family's' control, says Ievgenii, and was therefore forced to spin around like a political weathervane. This couldn't go on for very long. It was impossible to restrain [people's] dissatisfaction with the elites'[11] stupid greed. But Donbas, already educated by the bitter experience of the miner protests, understood: forcibly removing a snout from the trough will attract other snouts, but will also tear the country apart. The people of Donbas 'remained silent' and through sheer willpower continued to keep the economy going while getting ready to have their say in the elections. Donbas was also restrained from protesting by the fact that Ukrainian neo-Nazis became the shock troops for the saucepan-donning protesters on Maidan. This did not bother the 'Europeans'[12] at all, but for the east and

---

[11] Here written as 'ылиты' instead of 'элиты'.
[12] Here written as 'Эвропейцив', a Ukrainianised version of the Russian 'Европейцев', referring to pro-European protesters in Kyiv. The correct Ukrainian spelling is 'Європейців'.

south of the country such a union seemed diabolical, and rightfully so. For a citizen of Donbas, to lie with Ukrainian nationalism, and even more so with Nazism, was tantamount to abandoning one's self, one's history, culture, and faith. Already in February 2014, Ievgenii Kuznetsov was an active participant in rallies in Luhansk, where Russian banners were being flown. This prompted Kyiv's agitprop [to tell] Ukrainians that there were no Luhansk residents at these rallies, only 'people imported from adjacent regions of Russia'. But as Kuznetsov, as well as thousands of his fellow citizens knew: these people were his own.

(Chernov, 2016)

The passage above advances a common trope in DNR and LNR media coverage: that of ideology as an empty vessel whose contours are shaped by the enemy. Being a proponent or constituent of the DNR and LNR means, as Kuznetsov states, to *not* accept Ukrainian nationalism or, worse, Nazism into your home. The bounds of ideology are thus set by the bounds of a narrative in which Ukraine is met with shame and alienation. Whereas in newspaper coverage the possibility of reconciliation was left open, the key point of *shaming* (rather than blaming) the enemy is to discredit its essence rather than its behaviour (in contrast with the conclusions from Chapter 4).

The international reach of internet-based media was employed by DNR and LNR news sites to gain especially 'moral leverage' (Friman, 2015, p. 202)[13] over Ukraine in the eyes of international observers and audiences. As I hope to have shown, the point was not to leave open a space for reconciliation, but rather to demonise Ukraine before the eyes of the world. In Chapter 6, I will explore the consequences that this lack of ideological discourse and inconsistent efforts to build a collective identity provoked.

---

[13] Friman here cites Keck and Sikkink (1998, pp. 16–23).

6

The Consequences of Propaganda

INTRODUCTION

In this final chapter, I explore the consequences of the extensive propaganda campaign discussed in the previous chapters. I focus especially on changes in group identity and self-identification: To what extent did the discourse that emanated from the DNR/LNR and Russia about the Euromaidan revolution, the Donbas War, the 'Kyiv regime', and the 2022 invasion result in shifts in terms of how people in Ukraine felt about themselves? Did they come to feel less or more attached to Ukraine as a nation? Did they become more or less uncertain about their 'Ukrainian-ness' (especially Russian speakers who were seen as a key target group of Russian and DNR/LNR propaganda)? And what about people inside the DNR and LNR and in Russia?

    I begin this discussion with a case study of two local news outlets from Kramatorsk, a city in the northern part of Donetsk oblast with a population of approximately 160,000 (Roozenbeek, 2020a). Kramatorsk fell under DNR occupation in 2014, before returning to Ukrainian control several months later. I look at how these two outlets framed discussions around Ukrainian identity before, during, and after this period of occupation, and whether there was a shift towards a stronger sense of self-identification. I then examine discussions on Ukrainian social media before, during and after the 2022 invasion, and particularly social media engagement: Did posts derogating Russia and Russians get more 'likes' and shares, or was it pro-Ukrainian sentiments that best managed to go viral? After this, I discuss opinion polls conducted in Donbas and Russia: How many people in Donbas preferred to be part of Russia, inside and outside the occupied territories? And how can these poll results explain the 'failure of Russian propaganda' (Roozenbeek, 2022)?

A CASE STUDY OF TWO MEDIA OUTLETS IN KRAMATORSK

Founded as a small settlement by a minor railway station in the 1860s, Kramatorsk gradually grew into a large urban centre with heavy industry as its main source of economic activity. Over the years, Kramatorsk became one of the most economically vibrant cities in Donbas. The Kramatorsk machine building plant (NKMZ) designs and builds equipment for mining, metallurgy, steel rolling, and military-grade heavy weaponry. The city's metallurgical plant provided employment to thousands of residents until its closure in 2012.

On April 12, 2014, armed militiamen captured Kramatorsk's police station, airfield, and city council building. For the next few months, the city was occupied by the DNR, with parts of it changing hands periodically, until it was retaken by the Ukrainian army on July 5 (Butenko & Paton Walsh, 2014). After returning to Ukrainian control, it became the de facto administrative centre of Donetsk oblast. Apart from Mariupol, Kramatorsk is the largest urban centre in eastern Ukraine that was occupied by DNR or LNR militants before being recaptured (Mariupol fell under Russian occupation again in May 2022, whereas Kramatorsk did not; it remains under Ukrainian control as of this writing).

After the outbreak of the war in 2014, local media in Kramatorsk were placed under severe restrictions. DNR officials visited local newspaper offices, radio stations, and television channels, and used intimidation and sometimes violence to induce compliance (Horodetskii, 2014; Prigodich, 2015). Local media in Kramatorsk can therefore be a useful data source for investigating how the Donbas conflict has influenced Ukrainian and, more specifically, Donbas identity (Giuliano, 2018; Henrikson, 2016; Wilson, 2016).

For this case study, I analyse the content of two Kramatorsk-based media outlets published between late 2013 and 2016, *Tekhnopolis* and *Novosti Kramatorska*. *Tekhnopolis* is a small publication founded in 2001 (circulation ca. 20,000) with three permanent employees and a number of freelancers (Institut Masovoï Informatsiï, 2016b). During the occupation by Russian-backed militants, *Tekhnopolis'* office was hit with a mortar shell and partially destroyed. The paper did manage to keep publishing during the occupation, albeit less frequently than before. After Kramatorsk returned to Ukrainian control, it resumed its regular publication schedule.

Novosti Kramatorska is a newspaper (published under the name *Gazeta Privet*; circulation approximately 5,800) as well as a news site (Institut Masovoï Informatsiï, 2016b). Its printed version was suspended around mid-2016, but its website[1] continues to be updated daily with news and opinion articles. The paper was founded by the entrepreneur and later civil servant Aleksandr Tolstoguzov in 2005 (Novosti Kramatorska, 2017). In late May 2014, Tolstoguzov was forced to leave Donetsk oblast together with his family due to pressure from DNR representatives. The newspaper was then taken over by DNR activists, and part of the staff agreed to work

---

[1] www.hi.dn.ua.

for them until the end of the occupation in July (Institut Masovoï Informatsiï, 2014ck).

Both outlets are popular and well-read: *Tekhnopolis* is widely available in the kiosks that are dotted around town and is read by a large audience in the city, while *Novosti Kramatorska* is one of the city's most popular news sites. They are also distinctly local, catering almost exclusively to audiences in Kramatorsk, and are run by local residents and not owned by large media conglomerates, thus ensuring some degree of independence from local power structures. Also, while both *Tekhnopolis* and *Novosti Kramatorska* have a small number of permanent employees, they work with a large number of freelance journalists, and therefore offer a wide range of different perspectives.

In total, I obtained 9,973 articles from *Tekhnopolis* and 12,246 articles from *Novosti Kramatorska*, which I use as my data set for this case study. The below analysis is mostly qualitative, looking at representative news articles about a variety of themes in the periods before, during, and after the occupation of Kramatorsk. Specifically, I discuss arts and culture, local and national identity, and the framing of the war. These themes were identified using a methodology similar to the one used in Chapters 4 and 5.[2] For a more detailed explanation of this methodology, I refer to Roozenbeek (2020a).

Arts and Culture

In both outlets, coverage related to arts and culture came to be much more explicit in expressing pro-Ukrainian sentiments after the occupation was over. In 2013, a typical report in *Tekhnopolis* would cover (with some enthusiasm) upcoming holidays or cultural festivals: 'The favourite holidays of all citizens of Kramatorsk are approaching: the Day of the City (*den goroda*) and the Day of the Machine Engineers (*den mashinostroitelei*)!'[3] (Tehnopolis, 2013a). Local (as opposed to national Ukrainian) holidays were the main point of focus. This changed with the start of the occupation. On April 21, 2014, when the DNR had not yet taken full control over the city's media, a *Tekhnopolis* writer voiced his discontent with the DNR's lack of respect for cultural traditions: 'In Kramatorsk, the militants (*opolchentsy*) do not care about holidays' (Len'kov, 2014).

A few weeks later, the DNR was in more firm control of the city. According to one eyewitness account, the city was 'frozen', with people spending most of their time inside (Mikhailiuk, 2014). Holidays, festivals, and other cultural events became scarce, with one exception. Alina Mikhailiuk describes the festivities on Victory Day, celebrated annually on May 9 to

---

[2] Specifically, the themes discussed below were identified using dynamic topic modelling (Blei & Lafferty, 2006; Greene, 2016); see Appendix A.
[3] This was similar in *Novosti Kramatorska* (Monaenko, 2013).

commemorate the Soviet Union's victory over Nazi Germany (Mikhailiuk, 2014). However, her article makes no mention of the DNR or any of its representatives in the city, and unlike the period prior to the occupation, the article provides few further details, despite the historical relevance of the holiday in the region. Speaking more generally, articles that mention local cultural festivities organised by the DNR are rare.

When the occupation was over, however, its reports about cultural celebrations once again took on a more optimistic tone: 'On the city's central square ... there are currently mass celebrations going on. The "City of Craftsmen" is working again: the citizens of Kramatorsk are displaying their wide spectrum of talents' (Stadnichenko, 2014c). Importantly, unlike before and during the occupation, such reports now voiced explicit support for the Ukrainian army and government:

> On October 14, on the holiday of the Protection of Our Most Holy Lady Theotokos and Eternal Virgin Mary and the Cossacks, guests arrived at the Kramatorsk Ukrainian gymnasium: members of the military, led by the Chief Inspector of the Main Inspectorate of the Ministry of Defense, Colonel Valentin Fedichev.
>
> (Sidel'nikova, 2014)

The author of the above article describes the Intercession of the Theotokos and the Day of the Cossacks. The former is an Orthodox holiday stemming from the time of Kyivan Rus' (see Chapter 1). It was considered to be a holiday mainly for young girls and women, as most of the work that had to be done on the land would end around October, and it came time for them to look for a husband (Karp'iak, 2015). During the times of the Zaporizhian Sich (roughly the sixteenth to eighteenth centuries[4]), October 14 became an important holiday for Ukrainian Cossacks, who would elect a Hetman (commander) on this day. In later times, the holiday also began to symbolise and celebrate the history of the Ukrainian Insurgent Army (UPA), which waged guerrilla campaigns against Nazi, Soviet, and Polish occupiers of Western Ukraine during and around World War II (Magosci, 2010, pp. 695–697). The holiday was not mentioned at all by *Tekhnopolis* in 2013, and a 2011 article about the holiday was, if anything, critical of Ukraine's treatment of the Cossacks:

> It is worth mentioning that today's Cossacks are not going through the best of times. 'Previously, the Cossacks received more attention from the authorities, and our movement developed much more actively,' says the Hetman of the Kramatorsk Cossack regiment named after Skoropadskyi, Sergei Zadorozhnyi. 'At the moment, no law with regard to the Ukrainian Cossacks has been adopted for the creation of organisational, legal, financial, informational and other mechanisms for the Cossack movement.'
>
> (Sidorenko, 2011)

---

[4] For more information, see Magosci (2010, p. 193).

Starting in 2015, October 14 came to be celebrated as the 'Day of the Defender of Ukraine' (*den zakhisnika Ukraïny*), as ordered by President Poroshenko (Poroshenko, 2014). However, already in 2014, *Tekhnopolis* tied the celebration of this holiday to celebrations of Ukrainian independence and national identity, a clear indication of a shift towards a more explicitly pro-Ukrainian perspective.

Local and National Identity

The Euromaidan demonstrations were a contested subject within the city, but also served as a catalyst for discussing issues around local identity. *Tekhnopolis* published multiple stories and editorials about this topic from a variety of angles. Some articles expressed support for the Maidan demonstrations (Bondarev, 2013; Tehnopolis, 2013b). At the same time, demonstrations were organised in Kramatorsk decrying the supposed chaos in Kyiv. Local politicians and businesspeople voiced their concerns in front of gatherings of citizens, and placed local issues, not only in Kramatorsk but in Donbas more generally, at the centre of the discussion. Usually, they would come out in favour of the Yanukovych government:

While in the western regions [of Ukraine] people place candles in memory of those killed in Kyiv and seize regional administration buildings, the situation in the east is completely different. Obviously, the values and priorities in different regions of the country do not currently coincide. On January 25, a rally was held in the central square of Kramatorsk, organised by the local Party of Regions. There was one issue on the agenda: the current situation in Ukraine. About six thousand people attended the rally, mainly workers of industrial enterprises and budgetary organisations.... The general opinion expressed at the rally was that the east of Ukraine is looking at the events taking place both in Kyiv and in the western regions of the country with deep indignation, and asks President Viktor Yanukovych to take all necessary measures to restore order.

(Mironenko, 2014)

Just before the occupation, there was thus an ongoing discussion about eastern versus western Ukrainian identities, and a certain amount of concern that the demonstrations were primarily a western enterprise, while the east was left by the wayside. During the occupation, this focus on local issues shifted away from this 'east versus west' frame. Instead, *Tekhnopolis* published editorials about local people's experiences during the conflict, although both overt criticism and expressions of support for the DNR authorities were absent:

'As soon as they announced the Anti-Terrorist Operation, I left the city for a resort to survive this ordeal and heal,' says Kramatorsk resident Larisa Ivanovna. 'But the situation has become more complicated, and it is unknown how long it will last. Money is running out. My pensions aren't being paid. All the news I receive from Kramatorsk is discouraging. I talked with friends on the phone who are in [Kramatorsk] right now. All of them said that if it's at all possible, it's better not to return. Where do I go now? Opportunities are gone! I don't know whom to ask for help.'

(Chitak, 2014)

Ukrainian symbols began to take up a more central place in *Tekhnopolis'* coverage than they had before the start of the occupation:

For the second week in a row a People's *Veche*[5] was held near the statue of [Ukrainian national writer and poet] Taras Shevchenko. This time there were no representatives of the executive power, nor were there heads of local enterprises, who were invited to the last meeting. There were representatives of different political factions present, and the public was widely represented.

(Stadnichenko, 2014b)

Aside from this increased focus on national rather than regional identity, there was also a retrospective aspect to *Tekhnopolis'* coverage, looking back at the period of DNR control over the city. During the occupation, DNR officials took several measures intended to foster support for the new authorities; for example, the price of a bus ticket was lowered from 3.5 to 3 hryvnia. After the Ukrainian army regained control of the city, *Tekhnopolis* published an article arguing that this price decrease was, in effect, nothing but a public relations move:

As for the revision of transportation fares agreed upon during a session of the City Council, in the direction of reducing it, the conversation from the representatives of the DNR was short, and the decision was peremptory: people with machine guns in camouflage uniforms simply demanded that the transportation company's management reduce fares to three hryvnia. This turned out to be a spectacular PR move for the ordinary man in the street: 'Look! It was bad, and now it's good!' Looking back on the months when representatives of the DNR were leading the city, Sergei Dubovoi tells [*Tekhnopolis*] how it was necessary to organise eight buses to Kharkiv every day, and six to Berdiansk, just to get people out of the combat zone. DNR activists simply gave the drivers gasoline for the trip, without paying for their work and without taking into account depreciation costs. There were absurd situations when they demanded a bus to Rostov, and in the morning it turned out that they were to go to Voronezh.... People had to be taken out to Rostov under artillery fire. In this particular instance, one driver was wounded in the back.

(Stadnichenko, 2014a)

This article constitutes an attempt to explain retroactively some of the reasons why some Kramatorsk residents may have displayed little discontent (or perhaps even some enthusiasm) vis-à-vis the DNR authorities. Two things are worth noting here. First, as we saw in Chapters 4 and 5, there was a marked absence of ideological discourse during the period of occupation, such as about the 'Novorossiia' project, the 'Russian World', or Donbas identity. Second, even in hindsight there was no discussion about the identity aspect of

---

[5] *Veche* was a word for a popular assembly in medieval Slavic-speaking societies. It was later also used to mean 'parliament'.

the DNR project that Kramatorsk was briefly part of, neither in a positive nor in a negative light.

A similar pattern can be seen in *Novosti Kramatorska*. In December 2013, a *Novosti Kramatorska* writer expressed her reservations about the Euromaidan demonstrations and their increasingly political character, decrying the arrival of political activists from western Ukraine (Iurasova, 2013). Starting in late February, however, the same author began to express support for the Euromaidan protesters and discomfort with the 'Antimaidan' (or Anti-Euromaidan) demonstrations happening in the city (Iurasova, 2014a). In March, this discomfort that journalists expressed about the polarising effect that the demonstrations were having on the population became more explicit (Iurasova, 2014b). However, after the annexation of Crimea in mid-March, articles in *Novosti Kramatorska* became explicitly positive about Ukrainian nationalist sentiments. One article reported on a march held in favour of Ukrainian unity, and expressed approval of the diversity and supposed character of the demonstrators:

Today, near the fountain on Trade Unions Square, a march began for peace and unity and 'for a United Ukraine'. The march passed through the centre of Kramatorsk and ended on Parkovaia Street. Members of the organisation for disabled people 'Forum', the women's club 'Pani' and activists of the local Euromaidan all took part. It is symbolic that people with disabilities decided to show their citizenship in this way – even people in wheelchairs took part in the march. What's more, they were perhaps the most active participants of all.

(Iurasova, 2014c)

Novosti Kramatorska's coverage of the Ukrainian army and government became both more prominent and more positive. In October 2014, *Novosti Kramatorska* celebrated the Ukrainian parliamentary elections and expressed gratitude to the Ukrainian army for defending the city (Novosti Kramatorska, 2014c). Another article was published about Ukrainian Independence Day (celebrated annually on August 24), going into detail about the history of independent Ukraine (Monaenko, 2014). Outright patriotic coverage also became more common, for instance, about a 'patriotic action' called 'My homeland, my fatherland – our Ukraine!' that took place in the city between August 18 and 22 (Iurasova, 2014d).

The Framing of the War

Conflicts over the war and its relation to Ukrainian identity also played out on the pages of media outlets in Kramatorsk. *Novosti Kramatorska* journalists reported that there initially was a high degree of scepticism among Kramatorsk residents about the arrival of the Ukrainian army just after the start of the occupation (Novosti Kramatorska, 2014a). Protesters in the administration buildings were portrayed as local residents who had good reason to fear the Ukrainian army. A regiment of Ukrainian paratroopers from Dnipro (then called Dnipropetrovsk) was stopped by a group of locals and not allowed to proceed. It is not clear who these locals were or whom they supported, but *Novosti Kramatorska* pointed out the soldiers' low morale and poor preparation:[6]

Townspeople continue to detain security forces from Dnipropetrovsk at a railway crossing in the village of Pchelkino. According to sources, at 5 pm, twelve armoured personnel carriers with Ukrainian paratroopers were still standing still in the village. Despite the soldiers' requests to let them go to Dnipropetrovsk, the citizens reacted sceptically and did not let them leave. Residents of the village fed the soldiers, who, as it turned out, had not eaten for two days.

(Gurkovskaia, 2014a)

When the Kramatorsk airfield was recaptured by Ukrainian forces on April 17, this initial scepticism was abandoned. A *Novosti Kramatorska* report about this event called the action a 'liberation' (*osvobozhdenie*), and pointed out that no one was hurt or killed (Stepanova, 2014a). *Tekhnopolis* also made a clear distinction between citizens of Kramatorsk opposed to the occupation and DNR officials (Tehnopolis, 2014). Articles discussing the conflict and its aftermath thus did not focus on reconciliation, but rather the opposite. Those who participated in the occupation on the side of the DNR were described as 'criminal', and a sense of betrayal becomes visible in articles describing citizens of Kramatorsk who joined the DNR (openly or in secret).

The occupation proved to be a catalyst for local pride and self-identification. An op-ed in *Novosti Kramatorska* looked back on the battle for the airfield as a moment that put Kramatorsk on the map. The author referenced a 'meme' (*demotivator*) made by an anonymous local resident reflecting a sense of pride in Kramatorsk's position at the centre of attention; see Figure 6.1.

The occupation of the city was not over yet, however, as several administration buildings in Kramatorsk were still being occupied by assailants. On April 22, a *Novosti Kramatorska* journalist managed to talk to a few soldiers who were stationed at the airfield, which was then under Ukrainian control. She describes the chaotic situation in the city:

Having arrived at the roadblock close to the airfield, a journalist saw a couple dozen Kramatorsk residents, who were brought there after a demonstration on the square.... Some of them (about fifty people) went to the airfield, and another group, which had separated itself, went to the local city department and began shouting, 'The police is with the people!' After a few hours, the city department was again occupied by unknown individuals.

(Stepanova, 2014b)

---

[6] Even mentioning that Ukrainian soldiers were deserting to the DNR voluntarily (Novosti Kramatorska, 2014b).

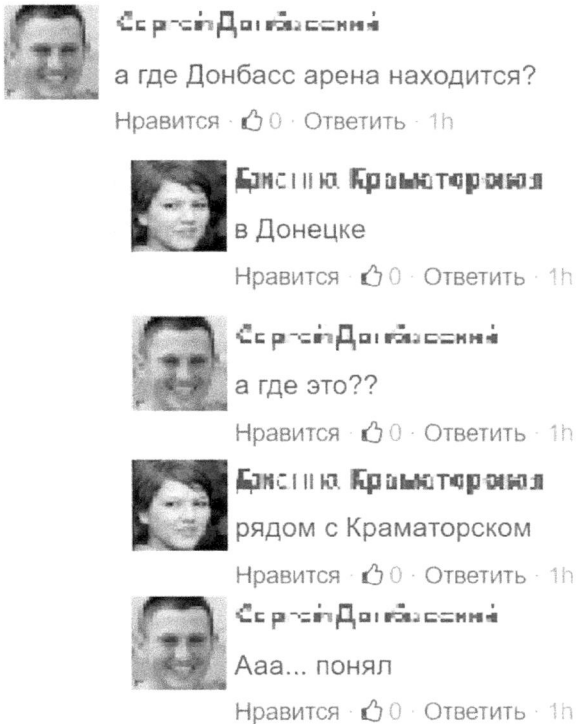

Сергій Донбасский

а где Донбасс арена находится?

Нравится · 👍 0 · Ответить · 1h

Виолия Краматорска

в Донецке

Нравится · 👍 0 · Ответить · 1h

Сергій Донбасский

а где это??

Нравится · 👍 0 · Ответить · 1h

Виолия Краматорска

рядом с Краматорском

Нравится · 👍 0 · Ответить · 1h

Сергій Донбасский

Ааа... понял

Нравится · 👍 0 · Ответить · 1h

FIGURE 6.1 Author's recreation of a meme reflecting the newfound fame of Kramatorsk. The text says: 'So where is the Donbas Arena located?' 'In Donetsk.' 'And where's that??' 'Next to Kramatorsk.' 'Ah right, got it' (adapted from Gurkovskaia, 2014b).

One Serhii Platyna posted a comment underneath this article that highlights the struggle to reconcile with the fact that the Ukrainian army was now fighting local residents:

May the arrival of holy Easter dispel the darkness over the city, and people will understand that these paratroopers from [Dnipro] – they are ours. They are our army. They are order and protection. And these vanquished goblins … they are also ours. Our shame.

The narrative in both newspapers before and during the occupation was thus ambiguous: reflecting local tensions and scepticism about the Euromaidan demonstrations, neither news outlet explicitly identified with either Euromaidan or the counterdemonstrations that were going on in Kramatorsk. Articles published during the period of occupation paid little or no attention to cultural or other celebrations organised by the DNR authorities, apart from the May 9 Victory Day celebration. There was also a sense of embarrassment that some locals had enthusiastically joined the side of the DNR. However, after this period of initial ambiguity, there was a sudden switch of support in favour of Ukraine once the occupation was over. This support proved sustainable, and patriotic coverage about the conflict and the army became commonplace.

These findings are in line with a growing volume of research into how the war has influenced Ukrainian identity (Bureiko & Moga, 2019; Kononov & Khobta, 2015; Malyutina, 2018; Pakhomenko, 2015). For example, Volodymyr Kulyk (2016) argues that Euromaidan and the Donbas War changed what it means to be Ukrainian, and resulted in 'increased alienation from Russia and the greater embrace of Ukrainian nationalism'. In another study, Kulyk (2018) identifies 'considerable changes in ethnolinguistic identifications, practices of language use, and preferences regarding language policies of the state, which can be seen as a kind of bottom-up de-Russification, a popular drift away from Russianness'. Elise Giuliano (2018) provides evidence that most ethnic Russians in Donbas didn't support the DNR and LNR separatists. And Lowell Barrington (2021, 2022b, 2022a) emphasises the strength of even Russian-speaking Ukrainians' attachment to Ukraine, and how weak their attachment was to Russia, even well before the 2022 invasion.[7]

THE 2022 INVASION

The above-mentioned work focuses on the consequences of the Euromaidan revolution and its aftermath, but there is indication that the 2022 full-scale invasion had an even more substantial impact on Ukrainian identity (Mazepus et al., 2023). This is illustrated by a recent study led by Yara Kyrychenko, a PhD student at the University of Cambridge whose work I've had the privilege of supervising (Kyrychenko et al., 2024). For one of her studies, Kyrychenko was interested in how the 2022 invasion influenced discussions on Ukrainian social media, particularly around group identity. To investigate this, she first obtained a total of about 1.75 million Facebook and Twitter posts, mostly from accounts run by Ukrainian news sources. She then looked at what types of identity language received the most engagement from Facebook users in the form of likes, shares, or reactions; Kyrychenko was particularly interested in people's engagement with expressions of support for Ukraine and Ukrainian identity (what she calls 'ingroup solidarity') versus expressions of antagonism towards Russia and Russians ('outgroup hostility'). The results are shown in Figure 6.2. Kyrychenko found that ingroup solidarity became by far the most important predictor of social media engagement after the invasion, with phrases such as *Slava Ukraïni!* (Glory

---

[7] It should be noted that although the Euromaidan revolution and the Donbas War may have served as a catalyst for the emergence of a more pro-Ukrainian (civic or national) identity, a shift away from Russian/Soviet identity and towards Ukrainian identity was also observed well before these events (e.g., see Taras et al., 2004).

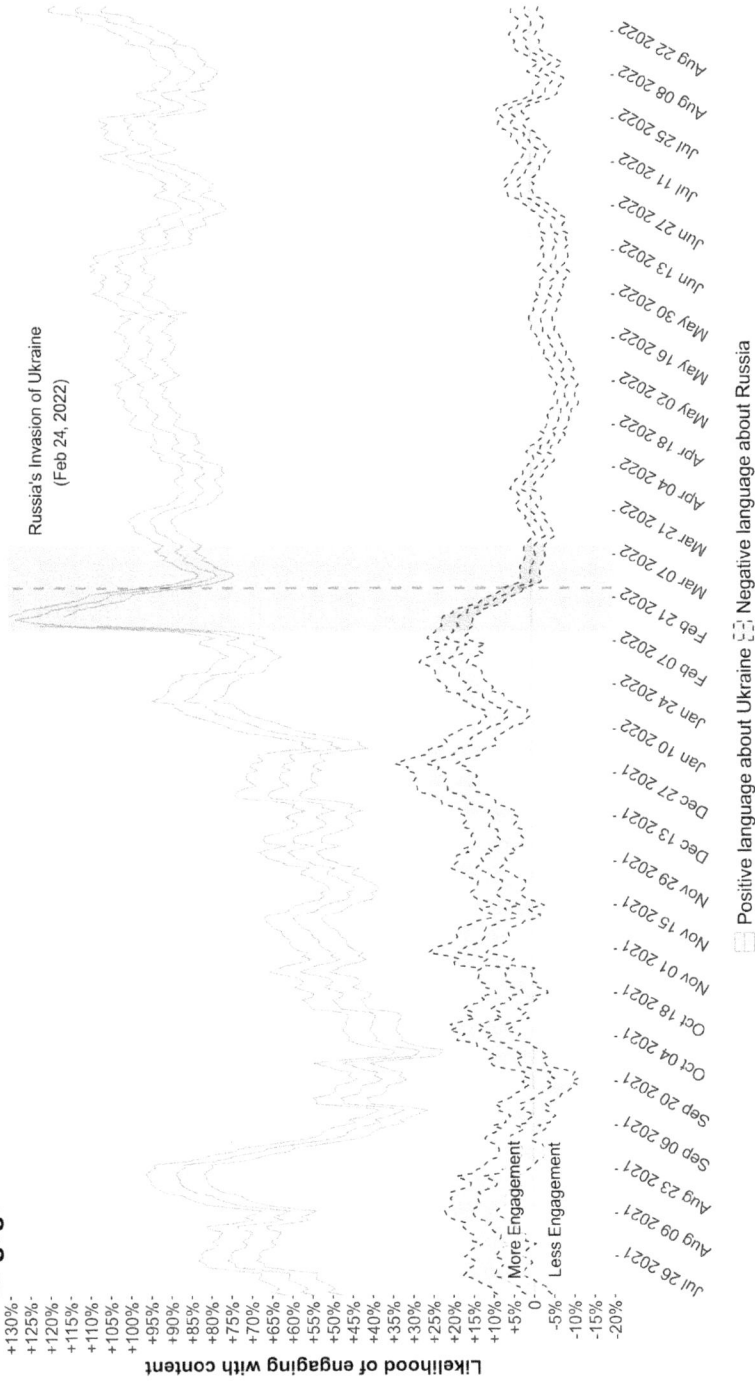

FIGURE 6.2 Engagement with various types of language on Ukrainian Facebook between July 2021 and August 2022. The *y*-axis shows how much more (above 0%) or less (below 0%) likely Facebook users are to engage with (e.g., "like" or share) a post containing positive language about Ukraine/Ukrainians (ingroup solidarity) or negative language about Russia/Russians (outgroup hostility). The figure shows that positive language about Ukraine (light grey, solid line) became by far the most important predictor of engagement after the 2022 full-scale invasion. Adapted from Kyrychenko et al. (2024).

to Ukraine!), feats of heroism by the Ukrainian military, and other positive expressions of pro-Ukrainian sentiments gaining huge amounts of likes and shares. Outgroup hostility, on the other hand, barely mattered; Ukrainian social media users were not much more prone to like or share posts derogating Russia or Russians than any other type of content. Here, too, we observe a clear pattern where Ukrainian identity becomes more popular after an important development (in this case the full-scale invasion), indicating that such events can serve as strong catalysts for the consolidation of group identity.

THE FAILURE OF PROPAGANDA?

Between 2016 and 2019, Gwendolyn Sasse and Alice Lackner (2018, 2019) conducted a series of large-scale surveys in Donbas, both the occupied and non-occupied territories, to investigate the degree of support for various possible outcomes of the conflict (for example, the DNR/LNR joining the Russian Federation, gaining increased authority within Ukraine, or keeping things as they were).[8] In one study (2018), they found that a fifth of their respondents from Kyiv-controlled Donbas reported feeling 'more Ukrainian' after the events that took place in the country between 2013 and 2016 (the Euromaidan revolution, the Crimea annexation, and the Donbas War). Using two waves of data collected in 2016 and 2019, Sasse and Lackner (2019) looked at public opinion in Donbas around questions such as the status of the DNR and LNR and identification with Russia and/or Ukraine (in terms of both civic and national identity). Because they collected data from both the DNR/LNR and government-controlled territory, they were able to make a comparison between DNR/LNR-occupied Donbas and the rest of the region. The results are shown in Figure 6.3.

Figure 6.3 reveals striking differences between the DNR/LNR and the parts of Donbas that remained under Ukrainian government control (at least prior to the 2022 invasion). For instance, 28.7 per cent of residents in government-controlled territories identified as ethnic Ukrainians (a substantial increase compared with 2016, which Sasse and Lackner note came at the expense of people identifying as Ukrainian citizens, indicative of a shift away from civic and

---

[8] One uncertain factor here is the degree to which opinion polls (in general, but particularly those conducted during active military conflict or in non-free societies) can be relied on for insights into people's actual opinions. For instance, it is possible that poll respondents give answers that are in line with what they believe the authorities, or perhaps their peers, would want to hear (or at least would not object to). It is therefore unwise to take opinion poll results for granted or accept them uncritically. At the same time, however, polls conducted correctly can be insightful even with these limitations in mind. In addition, the polls cited here were conducted with great attention to detail and with the above considerations in mind; I will therefore treat them as reflecting (to a degree) the actual opinions of Donbas residents at the time.

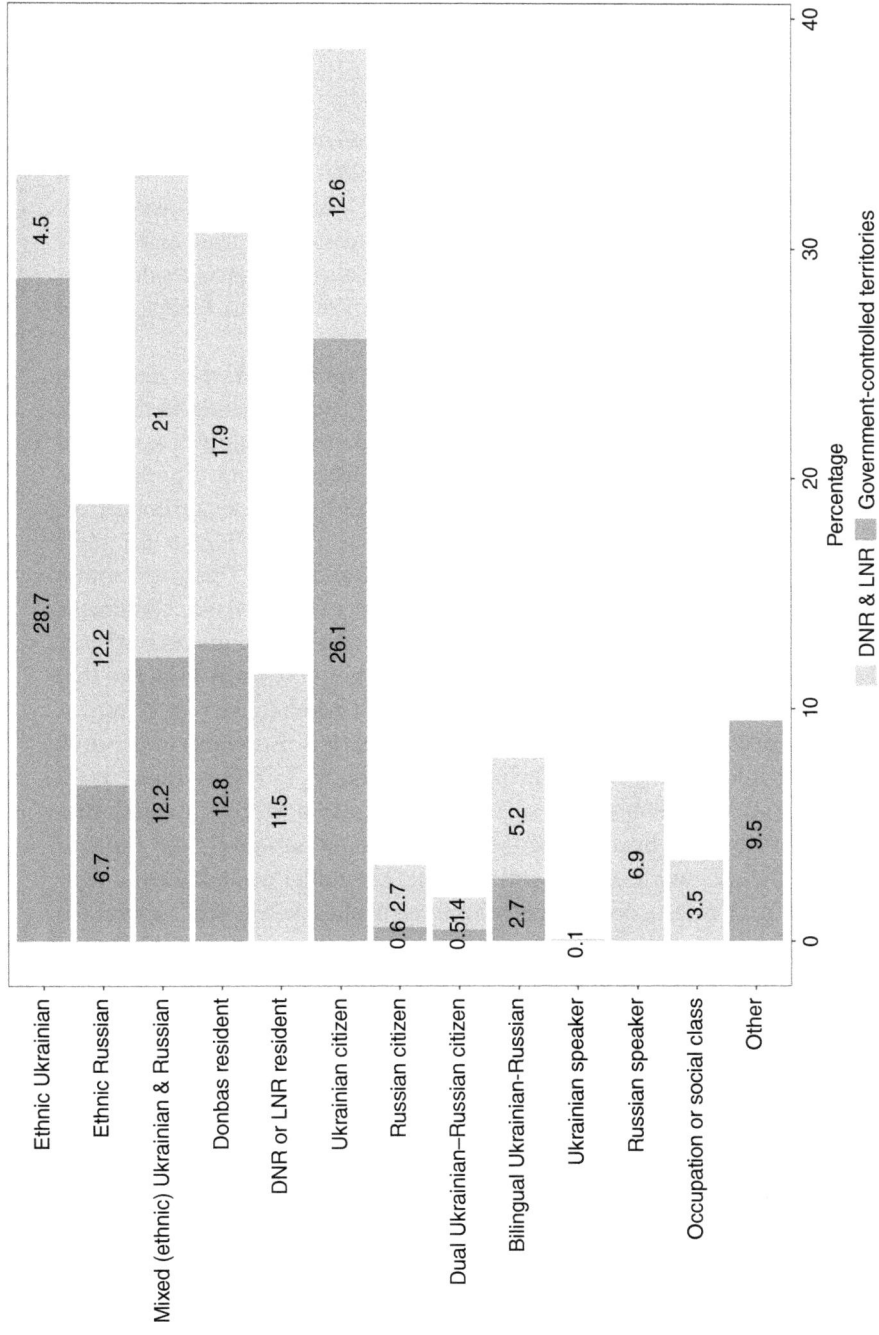

FIGURE 6.3 Comparison of respondents' first choice of identity between residents from the DNR/LNR (1,120 respondents) and government-controlled territories in Donbas (1,131 respondents), in 2019. Adapted from Sasse and Lackner (2019).

towards national identity), but this was only 4.5 per cent in the DNR/LNR. Similarly, many more people in the DNR/LNR identified as ethnic Russian or a Russian citizen, or as mixed Ukrainian and Russian, than outside the Republics. Overall, the pattern is very clear: after five years of occupation, people who lived in the DNR and LNR became substantially more pro-Russian compared with people in the unoccupied areas. It's therefore arguable that years of occupation (combined with years of propaganda) shifted DNR/LNR residents' opinions towards a somewhat more pro-Russian sense of self-identification. However, this is not the case in the rest of Donbas: support for Russia was stable and low, as witnessed (for example) by the fact that only 4.6 per cent of Donbas residents not living in the DNR/LNR supported any form of unification with Russia in 2019 (Sasse & Lackner, 2019, figure 6).

These findings, as well as those discussed above, are relevant when discussing the 'success' or 'failure' of Russia's (and the DNR/LNR's) propaganda. In the DNR and LNR, it can be said that propaganda was at least partly successful at fostering a more pro-Russian identity, assuming the polls are reliable (which is a problematic assumption due to the lack of freedom of expression in these territories; see Chapter 3). Within Russia itself, we see a similar pattern. Figure 6.4 plots Russians' attitudes towards Ukrainians between 1998 and 2021. This graph shows that Russians acquired dramatically more negative attitudes about Ukrainians after Euromaidan, an effect that was sustained for multiple years and exacerbated by the (run-up to) the 2022 invasion. While this is not necessarily evidence that Russia's efforts to demonise Ukraine and its post-revolutionary government through the media *caused* positive attitudes to plunge, it is reasonable to presume that it played at least some role (Hutchings & Szostek, 2015; Tolz & Teper, 2018; Yablokov, 2015).[9] In her book *Russia's War* (2023), Jade McGlynn argues that many Russians became heavily invested in propaganda narratives, and came to believe that the war was not foolhardy or futile but rather a fundamental fight against 'evil.' And indeed, opinion polls continue to show substantial support for the invasion (around 46 per cent 'full support' in mid- to late 2022; see Volkov & Kolesnikov, 2022), with opinion poll respondents parroting common media narratives: 'It's not like we are taking anything [that isn't ours]'; 'We're liberating [Ukraine] from Nazis and fascists'; and 'what other choice was there? . . . Negotiate with [the Ukrainians]? It was too late!' (Roozenbeek & van der Linden, 2024).

However, the outbreak of the conflict and the wave of propaganda that came with it, if anything, *backfired* in Donbas and other parts of Ukraine that have long

---

[9] Causation in media effects studies is notoriously difficult to establish due to the near-impossibility of conducting randomised experiments in naturalistic settings. However, there is good reason to assume that media coverage can affect attitudes, for instance, when it comes to coverage of a publication by Andrew Wakefield about childhood vaccinations being linked to autism (Motta & Stecula, 2021), the likely cause of a substantial drop in vaccination rates across various countries (Larson, 2020). For an extensive discussion, see my other book, *The Psychology of Misinformation*, which I wrote together with Sander van der Linden (Roozenbeek & van der Linden, 2024).

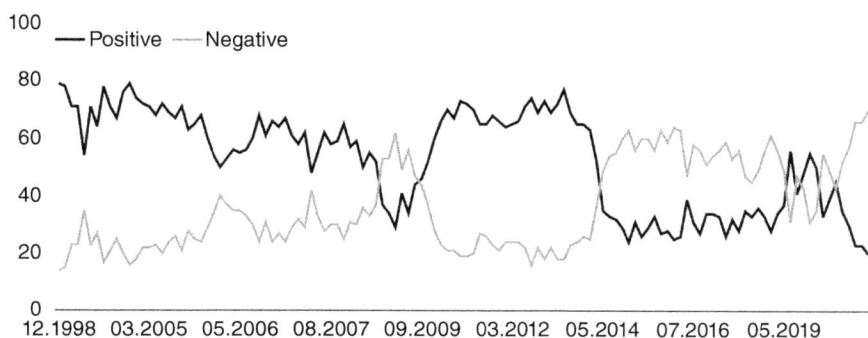

FIGURE 6.4 Russian citizens' attitudes towards Ukraine over time. The *y*-axis shows the percentage of respondents indicating a positive or negative attitude towards Ukraine. Source: Levada-Center (2022).

had 'no truck' with Ukrainian nationalism (Wilson, 1995, p. 280). Here, Ukrainian nationalism, which had previously been viewed with scepticism and sometimes even ridicule, became not only acceptable but even arguably dominant after Euromaidan and the Donbas War, and even more so after the 2022 invasion.

It is precisely this sustained consolidation of Ukrainian identity that Russian decision makers, including Putin, underestimated when planning their full-scale war. Around the start of the invasion, numerous commentators (Barrington, 2022c; Batta, 2022; Kilner, 2022) pointed out that there was little reason to expect Russian-speaking Ukrainians to be happy to see the Russian army arrive, much less join them in battle. Barrington (2022c) mentions the example of Oleksandr Vilkul, a politician from Kryvyi Rih who was known for his public support for the rights of Russian speakers in Ukraine. Vilkul had been approached by the Russians with an offer to join their side. In a full-throated defence of Ukrainian sovereignty, he told them to 'get lost'. Another telling example is that of an elderly woman from then-occupied Kherson, who angrily told a Russian soldier standing guard on a square: 'We will deal with our authorities (i.e., the government in Kyiv) on our own. We did not call you here!' (RTÉ News, 2022). The latter example is illustrative of a widespread sentiment among Russian-speaking Ukrainians: while they may want little to do with the kind of Ukrainian nationalism that is common in places such as Lviv and Zakarpattia, or even the country's pro-Western course, this makes them no less Ukrainian.[10] Few, it

[10] While not directly relevant to the present discussion, there is considerable evidence that Russia's efforts to influence attitudes and behaviours in other countries has been ineffective as well. For instance, Gregory Eady and colleagues (2023) found no evidence that exposure to content produced by the Russian Internet Research Agency (the 'troll factory') influenced US voters' attitudes and voting behaviour around the 2016 US elections. However, there is a lack of available research when it comes to the influence of Russian propaganda in other relevant countries such as India, South Africa, or Brazil, which have a high degree of geopolitical importance but are almost exclusively the domain of Russian, not Western, efforts of mass persuasion.

turns out, agree with Putin's assessment that Ukraine is only united as a nation by accident of history (Putin, 2022).

CONCLUSION

This chapter has explored the consequences of the propaganda campaign mounted by both Russia and the DNR and LNR between 2014 and 2023, focusing particularly on how they influenced Ukrainians' and Russians' sense of identity. This campaign was a half-failure: years of sustained effort by state media to portray Ukraine as a pro-fascist country with a US-installed puppet government were at least somewhat successful at fostering stronger anti-Ukrainian sentiments within Russia, and to an extent among Ukrainians in the DNR and LNR. This success has expressed itself as continued and sustained support among Russians for the invasion of Ukraine, many of whom have bought into propaganda narratives to the extent that they believe that military action against a previously friendly 'brother' nation is not only justified but even necessary. However, within Ukraine and especially among Russian-speaking Ukrainians, the propaganda backfired, and instead led to a strengthening of Ukrainian identity even among people who had been sceptical of Ukrainian nationalism prior to 2014.

Concluding Remarks

The goal of this book has been to understand the role of propaganda in the Russian-Ukrainian War. It's clear that since the outbreak of the war in 2014, Russia and its proxies in the DNR and LNR have invested a great deal of time and resources into media content production, and believe strongly in their ability to sow doubt, discord, and discontent. Almost immediately after seizing power, the DNR and LNR leadership and their Russian handlers began to set up a sprawling, organised, and well-funded propaganda machine. The purpose of this machine was not only to drown out pro-Ukrainian perspectives and paint a bleak picture of Ukraine and its 'Kyiv regime' but also to build support for the geopolitical shifts that the war brought about.

The leadership of the new Donbas 'Republics' was made up of a mix of ideologues, opportunists, and figures from the local underworld. Few had had media strategy training, and of those who hopped on board the DNR/LNR projects, almost none did so for ideological reasons. This lack of interest in ideology was reflected in the media content produced in the occupied territories: aside from a few haphazard efforts to find a historical justification for the DNR's and LNR's separation from the rest of Ukraine, such as Aleksandr Zakharchenko's ill-fated resuscitation attempt of 'Malorossiia' in 2017, ideology played a bit part in day-to-day media coverage. Especially after the MH17 disaster of July 2014, any serious efforts to foster DNR/LNR collective identity became irrelevant. Perhaps the most consistent narrative was a reinterpreting of Donbas' Soviet past, particularly the years between 1941 and 1945, but even this was contrasted against the DNR's and LNR's struggle against Ukrainian 'fascists', rather than serving as a referent for who 'we' are (Abibok, 2018).

This finding has implications for the legitimacy of the DNR and LNR: despite the Minsk agreements acknowledging their desire for autonomy (if not outright independence) from Ukraine, their disinterest in their own political and historical identity implies that the projects were artificial from the start. It's well-known that Russia supplied the DNR and LNR with arms, personnel, funding, and strategic input (Bellingcat, 2015). Nonetheless, the two statelets exhibited a degree of autonomy (see Chapters 2 and 3), and until just before the full-scale invasion there was a considerable amount of ambiguity over whether the DNR and LNR should be considered 'Russian'. For instance, leaked internal media strategy documents explicitly forbade DNR and LNR media from calling for unification with Russia (see Chapter 3). This book shows that this desire for autonomy, as expressed in, for example, the Minsk agreements, was not genuine, but rather reflected an uncertainty on the part of Kremlin officials as well as DNR and LNR decision makers about the future of Donbas. When this uncertainty was finally resolved, the 'solution' came in the form of annexation, not autonomy: at the end of the day, the Kremlin believed it had Russified Donbas and other parts of eastern and southern Ukraine enough to make annexation a palatable if not an attractive option, both in the occupied territories and in Russia proper.

This assumption was a mistake: between 2014 and 2022, only those who already supported the Kremlin, and especially heavy consumers of Russian and DNR/LNR state media, were convinced by the persistent efforts to derogate Ukraine and the 'Kyiv regime'. At the risk of evoking Godwin's law,[1] there is a historical parallel to this attitude change. In a study into anti-Semitic attitudes in Germany after World War II, Nico Voigtländer and Hans-Joachim Voth (2015) found that Germans who had come of age during the Nazi regime (1933–1945), and were thus exposed to Nazi propaganda during their formative years, continued to hold more anti-Semitic attitudes decades later compared with people who had grown up before or after the Nazis were in power. This effect was also stronger in regions of Germany where people had held more anti-Semitic beliefs before the war, demonstrating the power of propaganda to not necessarily change minds, but rather to tap into and exacerbate existing biases and attitudes. Russia's extensive propaganda campaign against Ukraine, for which the DNR and LNR served as a conduit, resulted in a similar outcome: overall, Russians (and some non-Russians) thus came to hold substantially negative (mis)beliefs about Ukraine and Ukrainians in part thanks to propaganda, to a point where all-out war was seen as an acceptable next step.

However, Russian propaganda was a tremendous failure in one key aspect: it never managed to convince those whom the Kremlin sees as a key potential ally, namely, Russian-speaking and Kyiv-sceptic Ukrainians. It could not make a dent into Ukrainians' development of a civic national identity, which had started in the 1990s and had been continuing into the 2000s and 2010s. Seeing the 2014 Euromaidan revolution as an opportunity to sow division in Ukraine and pull Russian-speaking Ukrainians further into its orbit, the Kremlin for years failed to understand that the revolution and its

---

[1] Godwin's Law of Nazi Analogies states that as a discussion, particularly on the internet, grows longer, the probability of Hitler or the Nazis being mentioned approaches 1.

aftermath only further spurred Ukrainian identity in the opposite direction, *towards* national unity. The attempts to create and popularise narratives with the goal of demonising and delegitimising Ukraine and the 'Kyiv regime' that I have documented in this book thus failed to achieve this key objective or to provide a meaningful alternative to Ukrainian nationhood even among those who felt little love for Ukraine's new powers that be. The Kremlin's colossal miscalculation was therefore to underestimate not only the unpopularity of its own actions in Donbas and Crimea, but also the impotence of its propaganda among the very people it professed to come save.

Appendices

Appendix A: A Note about Methodology

In Chapters 4–6, I analyse the content of around 100,000 newspaper and website articles, too many to read and digest individually. Content analysis is a staple method in sociology, psychology, media studies, and history, used to extract meaning from a corpus of text, images, sound, or video. A commonly used approach to tackling this problem is to infer categories with increasing levels of abstraction. Words and phrases are condensed into meaningful units. These units are categorised into codes, or labels, that describe what the condensed unit of meaning is about. Codes are then grouped together into categories by their content or their context. Categories are linked together into themes, comprised of two or more categories with a latent underlying meaning. And finally, themes comprise narratives, or the stories that are told through these themes (Dill & Neal, 2012; Erlingsson & Brysiewicz, 2017; Kohlbacher, 2006; Meyer, 2017).

Prior to the advent of the internet age, this process was necessarily done manually. Researchers would sift through and categorise large volumes of data by hand. Since the early 2000s, computer scientists have sought ways to automate (written) content analysis for purposes of convenience, replicability, and scale. This field of study, broadly defined, carries the name 'natural language processing'. By seeking to eliminate the unconscious (and sometimes conscious) biases of researchers, and in allowing for much larger volumes of data to be analysed, automated content analysis methodologies have brought about important contributions to the social sciences (Blei et al., 2003; Curiskis et al., 2019; Greene & Cross, 2016).

One of the most successful of these contributions is topic modelling. A topic modelling algorithm turns a corpus of texts (such as news articles) into a series of vectors (or a set of coordinates), in which each word is assigned a unique space in a multi-dimensional vector matrix. By iteratively calculating the proximity of each vector (or word) to every other vector in the corpus, a topic model can determine the semantic closeness between two words within a topic. Depending on the number of topics that the researcher asks the algorithm to extract, the model then puts out a series of topics in the form of lists of words ranked by their probability of occurring in that topic (Blei et al., 2003). To do so, the model requires as input a corpus of text, for example, in the form of news articles, social media posts, or film reviews. The output is a set of topics, each made up of a list of semantically related words. For example, the algorithm might decide that the words 'goal', 'corner', 'ball', and 'pass' are semantically related. The researcher then (manually) assigns a name to the topic (in this case 'football'). Topic models have been used in a wide range of social science research, for example, to look at conspiracy theories on Reddit (Klein et al., 2018), themes and motifs in Spanish poetry (Navarro-Colorado, 2018), and news articles about third-hand smoke pollutants in China (Liu et al., 2019).

A strong advantage of topic modelling is its agnosticism, which is of particular importance to the study of such a highly politicised and contested media landscape as Ukraine's. The researcher does not give the topic model any input in advance about what topics it will generate. The model can thus be seen as a fair representation of the topics of discussion present in the text corpus. If 80 per cent of all topics in a topic model relate to sports, then sports is a highly prevalent topic of discussion across the corpus. Because it's unknown what kinds of topic will emerge prior to starting the analysis, the topic model gives insight not only into what specific topics are discussed, but also in what proportion. This lowers the risk of selection bias.

There are various ways to construct a topic model. The most well-known and well-established methods are latent dirichlet allocation (LDA), latent semantic analysis with singular value decomposition (LSA), and non-negative matrix factorisation (NMF). Their differences can be found in the way that they determine the semantic closeness of words in documents; this can be done statistically (as is the case with LDA) or algebraically (as with LSA and NMF). The utility and preferability of each method depends on the type of corpus. Factors such as the average length of each document (whether the corpus consists of Twitter posts or Wikipedia entries, for example) and the corpus language (different languages have different syntactic structures) can make a significant difference to the accuracy and interpretability of the model (Zhao et al., 2011).

In Chapters 4 and 5, NMF was used as the main topic modelling method (Kuang et al., 2015; Singh, 2019). This was done because a test showed that the NMF method yielded the most coherent results compared with LDA and LSA (Roozenbeek, 2020b). In Chapter 6, I draw on a slightly different method called dynamic topic modelling, which is capable of measuring the change of specific topics over time (Blei & Lafferty, 2006). For a detailed explanation of how these methods work at the mathematical level, see Roozenbeek (2020b, section 0.1.5.2).

A topic in a topic model is analogous to a category (see above), as it is the result of a statistical or algebraic grouping process of words with underlying semantic similarities. After this point, however, the process of structuring topics (or categories) into themes is not (or not yet) within the grasp of natural language processing methods. This part of content analysis remains largely qualitative. The process of distilling the categories (i.e., topics) into themes and narratives (see Tables 4.1 and 5.1) was therefore done qualitatively (Kohlbacher, 2006), following the steps set out by Erlingsson and Brysiewycz (2017).

Appendix B: Chapters 4 and 5: Newspapers and News Sites

This appendix contains a list of newspapers and news sites whose contents were scraped and analysed for the purpose of topic modelling and narrative analyses (see Chapters 3 and 4). Relevant information about each outlet's management, circulation, et cetera, is provided where possible. This appendix does not cover *all* DNR and LNR media outlets (some news papers and websites, but also radio stations and television channels are not listed here); for this, I refer to the online appendix (https://osf.io/3846a/). Table A.1 shows an overview of how many articles from each outlet were included in the data analysis for Chapters 4 and 5, as well as the total word count.

NEWSPAPERS

- *Boevoe Znamia Donbassa*
  A weekly newspaper (circulation of around 2,550) published by the DNR Ministry of Defence. It was the main publication for members of the military, purporting to 'provide correct information to the international community, adequately cover ongoing events for the population of the Republic, and [produce] the timely dissemination of operations-related information among service members' (Boevoe Znamia Donbassa, 2014).
- *Debaltsevskie Vesti*
  This paper was founded in mid-2016 as a replacement for the old *Tribuna* newspaper in Debaltsevo. It was run by editor-in-chief Nelly Saidini and had a circulation of around 1,000 (Online Debal'tsevo, 2016).
- *Donetsk Vechernii*
  A long-running newspaper based in Donetsk. On June 2, 2014, its then-editor-in-chief Leonid Lapa was arrested by DNR officials, interrogated, and held captive for several hours. The newspaper's office was heavily

TABLE A.1 Overview of news outlets (newspapers and news sites) used for data analysis

Type	No. of articles	Word count
Newspapers (Chapter 4)		
Boevoe Znamia Donbassa	67	44,439
Debaltsevskie Vesti	67	22,109
Donetsk Vechernii	252	194,936
Enakievskii Rabochii	446	170,089
Golos Respubliki	822	415,805
Iasinovatskii Vestnik DNR	18	9,359
Informatsionnyi Biulleten Dokuchaevsk	29	4,401
Kazachii Vestnik	1,302	515,540
Kochegarka DNR	544	148,228
Makeevskii Rabochii	7,246	960,065
Narodnaia Tribuna	6	1,772
Nashe Vremia	29	4,401
Novaia Niva	1,644	452,274
Novaia Zhizn	741	307,346
Novorossia	169	170,274
Novye Gorizonty	272	70,048
Novyi Luch	553	178,265
Rodina	1,008	459,671
Rodnoe Priazovie	926	287,178
Snezhnianskie Novosti	1,277	480,181
Torezskii Gorniak	190	47,259
Vash Ilovaisk	273	102,055
Vestnik DNR	318	180,045
XpressKlub	19,543	1,099,793
XXI Vek	3,758	1,006,154
Znamia Pobedy	923	362,481
Total	42,423	7,694,168
Median	382	174,269.5
Average	1,631.65	295,929.54
Websites (Chapter 5)	**No. of articles**	**Word count**
DNR24	2,606	570,119
DONi News agency	1,276	413,355
Lugansk1 Info	8,668	1,828,824
Luganskii Informatsionnyi Tsentr	30,717	7,553,627
Total	43,267	10,365,925
Median	5,637	1,199,471.5
Average	10,816.75	2,591,481.25

damaged. Lapa was forced to retire. In October 2015, the paper resumed publication under Mikhail Kononenko and received accreditation to operate as an 'official' DNR newspaper (Administratsiia Goroda Donetska, 2016).

- *Enakievskii Rabochii*
  A weekly newspaper from Enakievo that began publication in March 2015. It was run by editor-in-chief A. A. Pologovoi as an 'official' DNR newspaper (Gorlovka.ua, 2016).
- *Golos Respubliki*
  An 'official' Donetsk-based weekly newspaper run by editor-in-chief Rostislav Shinkarenko. It was linked to a news website, *Golos Naroda* (Rasporiazhenie Glavy Donetskoi Narodnoi Respubliki 'O Pooshchrenii', 2016).
- *Iasinovatskii Vestnik DNR*
  An 'official' newspaper from Iasinovataia, run by editor-in-chief Vitalii Korablev. It had been unable to operate between the start of the conflict and September 2015, after which it resumed publication (Rasporiazhenie Glavy Donetskoi Narodnoi Respubliki 'O Pooshchrenii', 2016).
- *Informatsionnyi Biulleten Dokuchaevsk*
  This paper is the official bulletin for the Dokuchaevsk city administration. Up until December 2015, it had a circulation of around 500, until it suspended its regular publication for unknown reasons (Dokuchaevskii gorodskoi otdel Iustitsii, 2016).
- *Kazachii Vestnik*
  A Luhansk-based newspaper that fell under the 'Kazach'a Media Gruppa', which includes outlets like *Kazach'e Radio*, *Kazachiy Vestnik*, and the TV channel *Novyi Kanal Novorossii*. Its founder, Pavel Dremov, also a commander in the LNR army, was killed in a car explosion on December 12, 2015. The paper had a circulation of around 5,500 (Kirillov & Dergachev, 2015).
- *Kochegarka DNR*
  A newspaper in Gorlovka originally called *Kochegarka*. In May 2014 its employees resigned in protest of the DNR's takeover. On May 3, 2015, the paper resumed publication under the old name and banner, slightly renaming it to *Kochegarka DNR* (Leoshko, 2015).
- *Makeevskii Rabochii*
  One of the largest newspapers published inside DNR/LNR territory, with a circulation of around 11,000 prior to the start of the conflict. After the DNR takeover in June 2014, publication was suspended and then-editor-in-chief Mariia Semenova was fired. It resumed publication in October 2014, rebranding itself as *Makeevskii Rabochii DNR* and becoming an 'official' DNR newspaper (Vremia Chitat', 2019).
- *Narodnaia Tribuna*
  The first pro-DNR print publication in Debaltsevo, run by the Ukrainian language teacher Tatiana Ochapovskaia. After a few editions, it was taken out of print and replaced by *Debal'tsevskie Vesti* (Gorlovka. ua, 2016).

- *Nashe Vremia*
  A weekly newspaper from Dokuchaevsk, with a circulation of around 1,050. It began publication on September 1, 2016, as an 'official' DNR newspaper (Gosudarstvennoe Predpriatie 'Pochta Donbassa', 2017).
- *Novaia Niva*
  A newspaper based in Telmanovo run by editor-in-chief Natalia Zubach. It was founded in early 2015 with the help of the DNR Ministry of Information, and has since become an 'official' outlet. It had a circulation between 1,500 and 2,180 in 2016 (Zubach, 2016).
- *Novaia Zhizn*
  A weekly newspaper published in and around Starobeshevo, run by editor-in-chief Alina Kosse. It was originally founded in 1932 as *Sotsialiticheskaia Pobeda*, but took on the name *Novaia Zhizn* in 1963. Under DNR rule, it became an 'official' newspaper (Spravochnik DNR, 2019a).
- *Novorossia*
  A Donetsk-based newspaper that began publication in June 2014 under the auspices of former 'People's Governor' of the DNR Pavel Gubarev. It was then taken over by editor-in-chief Dmitri Dezortsev. There was also an actively publishing news site (Novorossia, 2019).
- *Novye Gorizonty*
  A relatively small newspaper in Kirovskoe with a circulation between 2,050 and 3,500, run by editor-in-chief Liliia Starushenko. Its first issue was published in January 2016, after which it became an 'official' DNR outlet (Spravochnik DNR, 2019b).
- *Novyi Luch*
  A weekly newspaper distributed in Novyi Luch and Amvrosivka with a circulation between 1,000 and 2,350, run by editor-in-chief Regina Gadyeva. It began publishing in early 2015 and became an 'official' DNR outlet (Spravochnik DNR, 2019c).
- *Rodina*
  An 'official' newspaper in Khartsyzk with a circulation of around 5,000, run by Sergei Pavlienko. Its first issue was published in 1936 (Spravochnik DNR, 2019d).
- *Rodnoe Priazovie*
  An 'official' newspaper in Novoazovsk with a circulation of 3,650. Editor-in-chief Sergei Shvedko had harboured pro-Russian sympathies since before the events of 2014. In 2014, he directed his newspaper to publish reports calling for a Donbas independence referendum. After Novoazovsk was recaptured by Ukrainian forces, he fled to Kuban in Russia. When the city was subsequently recaptured by DNR separatists, he was able to return (Vlasenko, 2016).

- *Snezhnianskie Novosti*
  The 'official' DNR newspaper in the city of Snezhnoe, run by Olga Vasilieva and Oleg Koronev. It began publishing in December 2014, with a circulation of 3,250 (Spravochnik DNR, 2019e).
- *Torezskii Gorniak*
  A long-running 'official' newspaper from Torez. On May 6, 2014, DNR officials entered the *Gorniak* offices and damaged it, warning the journalists present to change their editorial line, which they refused. On June 6, a local holiday called the 'Day of the Journalist', separatists came into the office and burned it down. The post of editor-in-chief was then taken over by Anna Mititela (Horodetskii, 2014; Novosti Donbassa, 2014e; Pro Gorod, 2014).
- *Vash Ilovaisk*
  An 'official' DNR newspaper founded in April 2016 covering events in the DNR and the town of Ilovaisk. It had three employees in 2016: editor-in-chief Olga Babych, a journalist, and an accountant (Informatsionnoe Soprotivlenie, 2016).
- *Vestnik DNR*
  A free Donetsk-based newspaper run by editor-in-chief Valerii Gerlandets. Gerlandets also moonlighted as a poet, publishing among other things a volume of poems titled 'Donbas in My Heart' (Mel'nikova, 2016).
- *XpressKlub*
  A commercial-heavy newspaper from Luhansk, also distributed in surrounding cities. It is part of a larger conglomerate of newspapers including *Ekspress Novosti*, *Mir Novostei*, and *RIO-Plius*. It had a circulation of around 3,000 throughout Luhansk Oblast, and had been publishing continuously since the early 1990s. It was run by Liudmila Kulinchenko (Xpress-Klub, 2019).
- *XXI Vek*
  A large daily newspaper in and around Luhansk with a circulation of around 25,000. It was run by Iurii Iurov, the former press secretary of Aleksandr Efremov, the former governor of Luhansk Oblast. It was the first newspaper to obtain an official accreditation from the new authorities in the LNR, in July 2015 (Luganskii Informatsionnyi Tsentr, 2015c).
- *Znamia Pobedy*
  A newspaper based in the town of Shakhtersk, run by editor-in-chief Liudmila Polianskaia, with a circulation of around 3,750. The first edition of the paper came out on May 9, 1946, in commemoration of the USSR's victory over Nazi Germany (Spravochnik DNR, 2019f).

NEWS SITES

- *DNR24*
  A news site founded in late 2016 providing daily news updates. In its own words, all information on the site is provided for 'informative or educational purposes only' (DNR24, 2016a).
- *Donetsk International News Agency (DONi News)*
  The main English-language publication from the DNR, founded by Russian businessman Andrei Stepanenko and launched on July 15, 2015 (Shandra, 2016). It was run by the Finnish former journalist Janus Putkonen. It employed a variety of people from different European countries such as France and the United Kingdom. The website went offline in 2018 (DONi News, 2018).
- *Lugansk1 Info*
  An information portal that started in 2015, focused on 'the economy, politics, social life, and the war in Donbas' (Lugansk1 Info, 2019).
- *Luganskii Informatsionnyi Tsentr*
  The official state press agency of the LNR, providing press releases, interviews, and news and opinion articles. It publishes primarily in Russian, but there was also an English-language version available (Luganskii Informatsionnyi Tsentr, 2019).

Appendix C: Timeline of Media-Related Events in (Eastern) Ukraine, 2014–2022

This appendix provides a timeline, ordered more or less chronologically, detailing relevant media-related incidents such as the deaths of journalists, physical assaults, attacks on editorial offices, kidnappings, the introduction of accreditation procedures, instances of journalists fleeing their hometown due to pressure, et cetera. The focus is primarily on Donetsk and Luhansk oblasts between 2014 and 2022, but other regions of the country are mentioned where relevant. The efforts by the Ukrainian *Institut Masovoï Informatsiï* to meticulously document ongoing events were a highly useful source for putting together this timeline.

DECEMBER 2013

- **27/12/2013** Oleksyi Matsuka, editor-in-chief of *Novosti Donbassa*, reports on his Facebook page that local media in Donetsk are preparing to purge journalists who are supportive of EuroMaidan. In his words, 'Kompromat' is collected on journalists who share Euromaidan's values, if they communicate with editors of independent media as a side job, if they participate in Euromaidan-related public events, or if they attend meetings of pro-Euromaidan committees or public organisations (Matsuka, 2013).

FEBRUARY 2014

- **28/02/2014** In Artemivsk, Donetsk oblast, female journalists working for the publication *06274.com.ua* are attacked by a group of youngsters at the Avangard Stadium who are preparing an anti-Maidan protest scheduled for March 1. As a result, one of the journalists received an injury to the arm. The youngsters also took away the camera's memory card (06274, 2014; Institut Masovoï Informatsiï, 2014f).

- **03/02/2014** Jan Hunin, a journalist working for the Dutch newspaper *De Volkskrant*, is denied access to a press conference held by the head of the Donetsk regional state administration, Andriy Shyshatskyi, because he did not pass the accreditation procedure (Hunin, 2014; Institut Masovoï Informatsiï, 2014a).
- **21/02/2014** Sergei Vaganov, a correspondent for the news site *o62.ua*, is attacked in the centre of Donetsk. He was taking pictures of workers who were welding steel sheets to the entrances and windows in a building operated by the Donetsk Regional Council and the Regional State Administration (62.ua, 2014a; Institut Masovoï Informatsiï, 2014e; Vaganov, 2014).
- **08/02/2014** In Pokrovsk (formerly Krasnoarmeisk), Donetsk oblast, unknown assailants break the windows of the building in which the regional television channel *Kapri* has its studio. The assailants reportedly threw three bottles containing a flammable mixture through the windows (Institut Masovoï Informatsiï, 2014c; Telebachennia KAPRI, 2014).
- **10/02/2014** The editorial board of the online edition of *Novosti Donbassa*, located in Donetsk, is evicted from its office. According to Oleksiy Matsuka, editor-in-chief, no reasons were mentioned for the eviction. Instead, the contract was simply terminated (Detektor Media, 2014; Institut Masovoï Informatsiï, 2014b).

MARCH 2014

Threats

- **02/03/2014** Journalists working for *Radio Liberty*, *Pervyi Delovoi*, and *URA-Inform.Donbass* are attacked by protesters during protests in Kharkiv and Donetsk. Police officers do not intervene (Mijatović, 2014b).
- **03/03/2014** Iuliia Bozhko, who works in Donetsk for the television channel *Channel 5*, claims that working as a journalist for *Channel 5* is becoming increasingly dangerous. She relates the story of a co-worker who is trying to leave the city in fear for her life. Bozhko asks media experts to put out advice on how journalists can protect themselves when covering mass demonstrations in Ukraine (Institut Masovoï Informatsiï, 2014j).
- **04/03/2014** At a rally in Donetsk, Pavel Gubarev, the self-declared governor of the Donetsk region, publicly threatens to capture the television and radio companies *Iunion* and *Donbass* (Institut Masovoï Informatsiï, 2014n; N'iuman, 2014).

Violence

- **02/03/2014** At a rally in Donetsk against the newly installed Ukrainian government, protesters assault journalists Pavlo Stepanenko and Serhii Volskyi, who worked for the television channel *Pershyi Dilovyi*, as well as Oleksandr Peremot, a journalist working for the website *URA-Inform.Donbass* (Institut Masovoï Informatsiï, 2014i; Interfaks-Ukraina, 2014a; Telegraf.by, 2014).

- **02/03/2014** *Radio Svoboda* reports that its journalist Valeriia Dubova was approached by an unknown assailant during a rally near the Taras Shevchenko monument in Donetsk, who took her camera from her hands and pushed her (Insider, 2014a; Institut Masovoï Informatsiï, 2014g; Radio Svoboda, 2014a).
- **10/03/2014** In Luhansk, near the Regional State Administration building, participants at a pro-Russian rally break journalists' equipment. The video cameras of two teams of journalists working for *TRK Ukraina* and *NTN* are damaged (24 Kanal, 2014a; Institut Masovoï Informatsiï, 2014p; Radio Svoboda, 2014c).
- **15/03/2014** Denis Khvostikov, a journalist working for the news site *Guru. ua*, reports that pro-Russian protesters attacked him and took two of his flash drives in Mariupol: 'I was taking pictures, looking at the crowd, but then the crowd began to act inappropriately towards me. I was surrounded, they grabbed for my tripod and held me there. I could not escape. They took the flash drives from the camera and camcorder, but the equipment was returned' (Institut Masovoï Informatsiï, 2014u).
- **15/03/2014** Mykola Lesohor, a journalist working for the Association of Journalists, Publishers and Broadcasters, as well as *Novomedia*, reports that he was attacked by unknown assailants during a pro-Russian rally in Mariupol (Institut Masovoï Informatsiï, 2014u).

Blocking Access

- **03/03/2014** A correspondent working for *UkrInform* reports that a crowd of pro-Russian demonstrators led by the self-declared governor Pavel Gubarev has locked about seventy media representatives inside the hall of the regional council in Donetsk (Institut Masovoï Informatsiï, 2014h; Matsuka, 2014b; Novosti Donbassa, 2014a).
- **03/03/2014** Several Donetsk-based news sites report that their websites are experiencing access problems, including *Ostrov*, *Novyny Donbasu*, and *URA-Inform.Donbass*. The journalists also note that the problems appeared to become apparent just as an extraordinary session began in the Donetsk Regional Council (ITAR-TASS, 2014a; Upolnomochennyi po pravam cheloveka v Rossiiskoi Federatsii, 2014).
- **06/03/2014** At the Donetsk airport, journalists and camera crews working for Russian television channels, including *NTV*, *TV Tsentr*, and *Vesti*, are denied entry into Ukraine (Mijatović, 2014b).
- **09/03/2014** Sergei Fadeichev, a photojournalist with the Russian news agency *Itar-Tass*, is denied entry at the Donetsk airport, supposedly for the reason of having insufficient funds.(ITAR-TASS, 2014a; Upolnomochennyi po pravam cheloveka v Rossiiskoi Federatsii, 2014).

- **11/03/2014** The National Television and Radio Broadcasting Council of Ukraine orders all cable operators to stop broadcasting the Russian television channels *Rossiia 24*, *ORT*, *RTR Planeta*, and *NTV-Mir*. On May 14, the Kyiv Magistrate Court of Appeals upholds the ruling (Mijatović, 2014b).
- **15/03/2014** Crowds of people gathered at a pro-Russian rally near the Ukrainian Secret Service building in Donetsk refuse to let Ukrainian journalists into the building, where self-proclaimed governor Pavel Gubarev is working (Institut Masovoï Informatsiï, 2014r).

Attacks on Offices

- **01/03/2014** Armed police are sent to protect the entrance to the studio and office of the television company *Simon*, after reports of a possible attack (Alekseev, 2014; Institut Masovoï Informatsiï, 2014k).
- **05/03/2014** In Donetsk, the television and radio company *Donbas* briefly interrupts its broadcast due to unknown pro-Russian demonstrators entering the studio and allegedly demanding more coverage of their activities (Institut Masovoï Informatsiï, 2014m; TSN Ukraina, 2014a).
- **10/03/2014** Unknown people refuse entry to four journalists into the premises in Kharkiv where a press conference by the leader of the UDAR party, Vitalii Klychko, was to take place (Institut Masovoï Informatsiï, 2014o; Radio Svoboda, 2014b).
- **11/03/2014** In Luhansk, pro-Russian assailants capture the building of the *IRTA TV* television company, according to *IRTA-Fax*. A crowd of people allegedly knocked down the front door, rummaged through the offices, took away the fire extinguishers, and threatened to burn down the building (Institut Masovoï Informatsiï, 2014q).
- **16/03/2014** Mykhailo Chernov, a correspondent for *NTV*, is injured in Kharkiv during a pro-Russian rally on the Freedom Square (Fedorkova, 2014; Institut Masovoï Informatsiï, 2014s; Ukraïns'ka Pravda, 2014a).
- **23/03/2014** Viacheslav Mavrich, a journalist working for *ICTV*, is beaten up during a clash between pro-European and pro-Russian protesters in Kharkiv (Institut Masovoï Informatsiï, 2014t; Mavrichev, 2014; Pyrlik, 2014).
- **23/03/2014** *Radio Svoboda* journalist Volodymyr Noskov is forcefully removed from a rally by pro-Russian demonstrators, who allegedly thought he was an American spy (Dontsiak, 2014).

APRIL 2014

Refugees

- **30/04/2014** Tetiana Zavorna, a journalist working for the newspaper *Gazeta Po-Ukraiins'ki*, flees Donetsk out of fear of reprisals: 'I left a few weeks ago, somewhere on April 10. When they captured our regional state administration, we started living with a Euromaidan activist, and then moved a week later to Kyiv, because we realized that this person was also in danger. Today, too, I call up many people, saying that they should not stay at home today because I have information that there might be purges of activists, of patriots. After all, the entire police base is at the disposal of the bandits' (Institut Masovoï Informatsiï, 2014bb).

Blocking Access

- **07/04/2014** Andrei Ivanov, with the Russian agency *RT Ruptly*, is denied entry into Donetsk (Mijatović, 2014a).
- **08/04/2014** Andrei Malyshkin, with the Russian *RIA Novosti*, is denied entry into Luhansk. His colleague Aleksei Kudenko is denied entry into Donetsk, along with Stanislav Bernvald and Konstantin Krylov from the Russian *Channel 5* and Maksim Dodonov with *TV Zvezda* (Mijatović, 2014a).

Abductions and Disappearances

- **12/04/2014** In Sloviansk, separatists arrest Serhii Hrishin, a *Hromads'ke TV* journalist, and ban him from working inside the city, covering events under the administration of the Interior Ministry and other activities. *Lenta.ru* journalist Il'ia Azar is also arrested (Institut Masovoï Informatsiï, 2014aa; Ukraïns'ka Pravda, 2014b).
- **13/04/2014** In Sloviansk, Artem Deinehu, a citizen-journalist broadcasting the storming of the Ukrainian Security Service building by pro-Russian demonstrators, goes missing from his apartment (Iarovaia, 2014; Institut Masovoï Informatsiï, 2014ak; Sidorenko, 2014).
- **14/04/2014** In Gorlovka, pro-Russian activists kidnap the editor of the city site *Gorlovka.ua* Oleksandr Bilinskyi, according to the site's Vkontakte page (Institut Masovoï Informatsiï, 2014ac).
- **14/04/2014** In Donetsk, pro-Russian activists detain Aleksei Iaroslavtsev, a journalist working for *Poriad z Vami*, allegedly for taking pictures of events taking place near the Donetsk Regional State Administration Building (Institut Masovoï Informatsiï, 2014ad).
- **16/04/2014** Pro-Russian demonstrators in Sloviansk take independent journalist Serhii Lefter captive. He is accused of espionage and involvement with the Right Sector (Pravyi Sektor), a Ukrainian nationalist group. Lefter is released a few weeks later, on May 8 (Institut Masovoï Informatsiï, 2014ah; Karpins'ka, 2014; Maystrenko, 2014).
- **19/04/2014** Journalists in Sloviansk are forced to suspend their journalistic activities, according to Oleh Zontov, the editor-in-chief of *Slov'iansk'ki Vidomosti* and head of the local branch of the Independent Union of Journalists of Ukraine (Novosti Donbassa, 2014c).
- **21/04/2014** French journalist Paul Gogo, Italian journalist Kossimo Attanasio, and Belorusian journalist Dmitryi Galko are detained in

Sloviansk. They are held briefly and released after their documents were checked (Institut Masovoï Informatsiï, 2014am; Kazanskii, 2014; Kyiv Post, 2014).

- **22/04/2014** American journalist Simon Ostrovsky, working for *Vice News*, is detained in Donetsk by pro-Russian separatists along with British cameraman Frederick Paxton, *Time* correspondent Simon Shuster, and a Ukrainian cameraman, but released two days later (Dettmer, 2014; McAllester, 2014; McVeigh, 2014).
- **22/04/2014** Ievhen Hapych, a journalist working for the Ivano-Frankivsk-based newspaper *Reporter*, is taken captive in Sloviansk and released after two days (Institut Masovoï Informatsiï, 2014ap; IPress.ua, 2014; Mijatović, 2014a).
- **24/04/2014** Ievheniia Supricheva, a correspondent for the newspaper *Komsomol'skaia Pravda v Ukraine*, is detained for two days by pro-Russian demonstrators in Sloviansk (Institut Masovoï Informatsiï, 2014ar; Suprycheva, 2014).
- **25/04/2014** Iuryi Leliavs'kyi, freelance correspondent for the television channel *ZIK*, is detained in Sloviansk by unknown individuals (Galkin, 2014; Institut Masovoï Informatsiï, 2014at).
- **25/04/2014** Iulia Shustraia and Mikhail Pudovkin, a journalist and a camera operator working for the Russian channel *LifeNews*, are reported missing in Donetsk. It is later revealed that they were captured by armed men and deported from Ukraine (Mijatović, 2014a).
- **26/04/2014** Serhii Shapovalov, a journalist for *VolynPost*, is taken captive in Sloviansk. He is released on May 19 (Institut Masovoï Informatsiï, 2014av; Podrobnosti, 2014a, 2014c).
- **28/04/2014** Journalist Ruslan Kukharchuk, with the *Novomedia Association*, spends thirteen hours in captivity in Sloviansk, where he was interrogated, allegedly with a bag over his head (Institut Masovoï Informatsiï, 2014ax).

Threats and Intimidation

- **11/04/2014** An unknown person sets fire to the car of Oleksyi Matsuka, editor-in-chief of the internet news site *Novosti Donbassa*. At around 12:30 am, an unknown man approached Matsuka's car, which was parked near his house in Donetsk, poured a combustible substance over it, and set it on fire (Detektor Media, 2014; Institut Masovoï Informatsiï, 2014z).
- **13/04/2014** Employees of the television channel *Donbas* are reported to have left Donetsk due to threats of the channel being captured by pro-Russian activists (Institut Masovoï Informatsiï, 2014ab; Ostrov, 2014a).
- **15/04/2014** Oleh Poplavskyi, the editor-in-chief of Gorlovka-based internet television channel *Smena*, reports that pro-Russian activists are preparing to seize regional media outlets. He advised his employees to go into

hiding if they did not want to cooperate (Gordon, 2014a; Institut Masovoï Informatsiï, 2014ae).

- **19/04/2014** Journalists in Sloviansk are forced to suspend their activities due to consistent threats, according to Oleh Zontov, the editor-in-chief of the newspaper *Slavianskie Vedomosti* (Institut Masovoï Informatsiï, 2014aj; Korrespondent, 2014).
- **29/04/2014** The pro-separatist armed group *Armiia Iugo-Vostoka* (Southeastern Army) threatens to seize the local government television company and radio-television centre in Luhansk (Espreso.tv, 2014; Institut Masovoï Informatsiï, 2014ay).
- **29/04/2014** During a mass demonstration near the building of the Regional State Administration in Luhansk, unknown individuals threaten Ievgenii Spirin, a journalist working for the site *0642*. Spirin claims he was taking pictures when a couple of youngsters approached him, who began to move him out of the area and forbade him from taking more pictures (Institut Masovoï Informatsiï, 2014bg).

Physical Attacks

- **06/04/2014** During a rally near the building of the SBU in Luhansk, a pro-Russian activist strikes the head of Aleksei Movsenian, a cameraman working for the local state television channel *LOT* (Institut Masovoï Informatsiï, 2014aq).
- **06/04/2014** Hrihoryi Pyrlyk, a journalist working for the television channel *Ukraina*, is attacked by protesters while livestreaming a demonstration on Kharkiv's Freedom Square (Institut Masovoï Informatsiï, 2014w).
- **9/04/2014** Oles' Borozenka, a correspondent for the Belarusian television channel *Belsat*, is beaten by unknown assailants in Donetsk (Institut Masovoï Informatsiï, 2014y; MoiBY, 2014).
- **13/04/2014** Pro-Russian activists in Kramatorsk attack the local blogger and activist Stanislav Chernohor, taking his equipment and breaking one of his ribs (Institut Masovoï Informatsiï, 2014af; Novosti Donbassa, 2014b).
- **16/04/2014** In Sloviansk, armed men confiscate the documentation and equipment of journalist Roman Huba during a nightly search (Hromadske, 2014; Institut Masovoï Informatsiï, 2014ai).
- **17/04/2014** A TV crew working for the Polish public television channel *TVP* is almost assaulted by participants to a protest near the regional administration building in Donetsk (Institut Masovoï Informatsiï, 2014ag).
- **21/04/2014** Unknown assailants assault and injure Maksim Danil'chenko, a journalist working for *Tochka Opora*, who was taking pictures of a pro-Russian demonstration taking place near the occupied SBU building in Luhansk (Institut Masovoï Informatsiï, 2014al).
- **24/04/2014** Mykola Riabchenko, a well-known journalist, is injured during the storming of the local city council building in Mariupol. His

equipment is destroyed (Institut Masovoï Informatsiï, 2014aq; TSN Ukraina, 2014b).

- **28/04/2014** Pro-Russian activists in Donetsk hit *Dzerkalo Tyzhnia* journalist Ievhen Shibalov over the head during a demonstration for Ukrainian unity (Institut Masovoï Informatsiï, 2014aw).
- **28/04/2014** Richard Gaisford and Simon Llewellyn, both working for the British television channel *ITV*, and Ievhen Shibalov with *Zerkalo Nedeli*, are attacked at knifepoint by pro-Russian activists during a demonstration in Donetsk (Gaisford, 2014; Institut Masovoï Informatsiï, 2014az).
- **29/04/2014** Serhii Davidov, editor-in-chief of the newspaper *Hrivna Plius* and a member of the Luhansk city council, is assaulted by unknown assailants during a demonstration by the regional state administration building in Luhansk (CityNews, 2014; Institut Masovoï Informatsiï, 2014ba).
- **29/04/2014** Iurii Leliavs'kyi, a freelance correspondent for *ZIK*, and Serhii Shapovalov, a journalist with the Luts'k-based news portal *VolynPost*, are detained for two weeks in Sloviansk. Ruslan Kukharchuk, with the *Novomedia* journalists' association, is also detained in the city but released after thirteen hours (Mijatović, 2014b).

Attacks on Editorial Offices

- **07/04/2014** Unknown individuals unsuccessfully attempt to take over the Regional State Television and Radio Company in Donetsk, according to its director Oleh Dzholos (Institut Masovoï Informatsiï, 2014v).
- **07/04/2014** Three security guards at the local television channel *IRTA* are injured in Luhansk, after around a dozen unknown men attempted to enter the building (Institut Masovoï Informatsiï, 2014x).
- **17/04/2014** A television tower in Sloviansk owned by *Kontsern RRT* that provides broadcasting signal to neighbouring towns, including Kramatorsk, Gorlovka, and Makeevka, is captured by armed individuals.
- **18/04/2014** In Torez, unknown individuals attack and set fire to the office of the local newspaper *Pro Horod*, according to its editor-in-chief Ihor Abizov (Institut Masovoï Informatsiï, 2014an; Novosti Donbassa, 2014d).
- **22/04/2014** Unknown assailants attack the office of the local newspaper *Provintsiia* in Konstantynivka with Molotov cocktails, resulting in a fire and damage to the office and equipment (Dozhd TV, 2014a; Institut Masovoï Informatsiï, 2014ao).
- **25/04/2014** In Donetsk, eight men in balaclavas carrying batons enter the building where the editorial office of the website *62.ua* is located (Institut Masovoï Informatsiï, 2014as).
- **27/04/2014** The DNR flag is raised over the building of the Donetsk Regional Television and Radio Company. Protesters are reported to chant

'Shame to the mass media' (Institut Masovoï Informatsiï, 2014au; Mijatović, 2014b; Ostrov, 2014b).

- **29/04/2014** Armed, uniformed men seize the building of the Donetsk Regional Television and Radio Company and replace some of the ongoing broadcasts with the Russian television channel *Rossiia-24* (Mijatović, 2014b).

Accreditation

- **27/04/2014** Unofficial local leaders in Sloviansk introduce new accreditation procedures for journalists seeking to work in the city. Journalists without accreditation are denied entry into administration buildings, cannot attend press briefings, and may be refused entry into the city (Mijatović, 2014b).

MAY 2014

Deaths

- **24/05/2014** Italian photo-correspondent Andrea Rocchelli and his translator die during a mortar shelling in the village of Andriivka, near Sloviansk (Committee to Protect Journalists, 2014; Institut Masovoï Informatsiï, 2014ch; Seneghini, 2014). Vitalii Markiv, a Ukrainian-Italian member of Ukraine's National Guard, was initially convicted (in Italy) of ordering the fatal strike, but was later acquitted by the Italian supreme court (Ukrainska Pravda, 2021).

Abductions and Disappearances

- **02/05/2014** Mike Giglio, a reporter working for *Buzzfeed*, and his translator Olena Hlazunova briefly go missing in Sloviansk, claiming to have been taken captive by separatists (Giglio, 2014; Institut Masovoï Informatsiï, 2014bd; Mijatović, 2014b).
- **02/05/2014** Camera crews for *Sky News* and *CBS* disappear briefly in various parts of Donetsk oblast (Institut Masovoï Informatsiï, 2014be).
- **06/05/2014** Journalist Mykola Riabchenko goes missing near Manhush, Donetsk oblast (Institut Masovoï Informatsiï, 2014bk; OSCE Representative on Freedom of the Media, 2014a).
- **08/05/2014** A camera crew for *ICTV* is stopped by pro-Russian separatists at a roadblock in Sloviansk. They are questioned for several hours before being released (Institut Masovoï Informatsiï, 2014bq).
- **11/05/2014** Pavel Kanygin, a correspondent working for the Russian newspaper *Novaia Gazeta*, is kidnapped in Artemivs'k together with the German journalist Stefan Scholl (Bartlby, 2014; Institut Masovoï Informatsiï, 2014bw).
- **18/05/2014** Marat Saichenko and Oleg Sidiakin, journalists working for the Russian channel *LifeNews*, are arrested by Ukrainian military forces (Mijatović, 2014b).

- **20/05/2014** Graham Phillips, a British freelance journalist working for *RT*, is arrested by Ukrainian law enforcement and released after around thirty-six hours (Mijatović, 2014b).
- **21/05/2014** Milana Omelchuk, a photo correspondent, returns to Kyiv after two weeks of imprisonment in Donetsk (24 Kanal, 2014b; Institut Masovoï Informatsiï, 2014cd; Mijatović, 2014b).
- **25/05/2014** Viacheslav Bondarenko, a journalist working for the Luhansk-based internet news site *Obzor.lg.ua*, and Maksim Osobskyi with *Spilno.tv* are detained by pro-Russian separatists at a roadblock in the city of Shchastie, close to Luhansk, and taken to the occupied SBU building in Luhansk (Informator Media, 2014; Institut Masovoï Informatsiï, 2014cj).
- **29/05/2014** *STB* Journalist Dmitro Litvinenka and camera operator Oleksandr Razkevych are detained for approximately twelve hours in Donetsk by pro-Russian separatists (Institut Masovoï Informatsiï, 2014cs).

Refugees

- **08/05/2014** *Ostrov* journalist Iaroslav Kohushev and his wife Olena, vice-president of *UNIAN* in Donetsk, relocate to Lviv oblast in western Ukraine due to the unstable situation for journalists in Donetsk (Institut Masovoï Informatsiï, 2014bl; Panchyshyn, 2014).
- **13/05/2014** *Moi Gorod*, a news site in Severodonets'k, temporarily suspends its activities due to the risk of kidnapping. Several journalists working for the outlet leave the city (Alkerchin, 2014; Institut Masovoï Informatsiï, 2014bz).
- **26/05/2014** Oleksandr Tolstohuzov, the publisher and editor-in-chief of the Kramatorsk-based news outlet *Novosti Kramatorska*, is forced to leave Donetsk oblast together with his family, due to pressure from representatives of the DNR. The newspaper was captured by DNR activists, and part of the staff agreed to work with them due to the threats issued, according to Tolstohuzov (Ekho Moskvy, 2014; Institut Masovoï Informatsiï, 2014ck).
- **27/05/2014** The editorial staff of the news site *Segodnia v Severodonetske* is forced to leave Severodonetsk for Kyiv after pressure from the so-called South-eastern Army (*Armiia Iugo-Vostoka*) (Institut Masovoï Informatsiï, 2014co).

Threats

- **02/05/2014** Hermine Kotanjyan, the Sloviansk correspondent for the Russian channel *LifeNews*, receives death threats via social media (Mijatović, 2014b).
- **14/05/2014** Journalists working in Donbas who do not wish to follow the directives of the DNR are threatened with execution, according to Olena Maliutina, the press secretary of the Donetsk Regional Administration (Institut Masovoï Informatsiï, 2014ca).

- **22/05/2014** Representatives of the DNR threaten employees of the Donetsk-based newspaper *Segodnia* and its website *Segodnya.ua*, forcing them to withdraw the newspaper from local kiosks (Institut Masovoï Informatsiï, 2014ce).

Physical Attacks

- **05/05/2014** In Donetsk, unknown assailants fire at the summer house of Serhii Harmash, the editor-in-chief of *Ostrov* and the coordinator of the Committee of Patriot Forces of Donbas (KPSD), using automatic rifles (Institut Masovoï Informatsiï, 2014bh).
- **06/05/2014** In Luhansk, unknown assailants open fire near the house of Roman Landyk, the co-owner of the local television and radio company *IRTA* and Party of Regions MP in the Luhansk city council (Institut Masovoï Informatsiï, 2014bj).
- **06/05/2014** Svetlana Evseeva, a correspondent for the local advertising and information weekly *Telegazeta*, receives injuries to her hand in Stakhanov (Institut Masovoï Informatsiï, 2014bi).
- **09/05/2014** A freelance correspondent working for the Russian television channel *RT* is injured during a shooting in Mariupol (Institut Masovoï Informatsiï, 2014bs; Simon'ian, 2014).
- **24/05/2014** William Roguelon, a French freelance journalist who was travelling with Andrea Rocchelli and Andrei Mironov when they were killed, is injured in a shootout close to the village of Andriivka (Institut Masovoï Informatsiï, 2014cg; Reuters, 2014).

Attacks on Editorial Offices

- **06/05/2014** Around fifty unknown individuals wearing masks and armed with sticks and bats destroy the office of the regional newspaper *Torezskii Gorniak* (Horodetskii, 2014; Mijatović, 2014b).
- **06/05/2014** The website of the Kramatorsk-based newspaper *Kramatorskaia Pravda* suspends publication. The paper reports that journalists working for the paper were stuck on the fourth floor of the occupied local administration buildings, and did not have unhindered access to their files and equipment. The paper's editor-in-chief and accountant were outside the city limits at the start of the Ukrainian Army's operation to take control over the city, and unable to get back into town (Podrobnosti, 2014b; Shtal', 2014).
- **08/05/2014** Armed men block access to the office of the Konstantynivka-based newspaper *Provintsiia*. Editor-in-chief Mikhailo Razutko and the paper's founder Halina Razutko are told by DNR officers that they no longer work for the paper (Institut Masovoï Informatsiï, 2014bm; Mijatović, 2014b).
- **08/05/2014** Representatives of the DNR occupy the building of the *Iunion* television channel. Members of the self-declared Committee for Television

and Radio Broadcasts of the DNR enter the channel's premises and take control of the equipment (Institut Masovoï Informatsiï, 2014bn).

- **08/05/2014** The editorial board of *Novosti Kramatorska* and *Gazeta Privet* suspends its activities, vacates its office, and leaves Kramatorsk, after receiving threats about burning down the building (Institut Masovoï Informatsiï, 2014br; Mijatović, 2014b).
- **19/05/2014 and 20/05/2014** The television tower in Sloviansk is shelled twice in two days (Institut Masovoï Informatsiï, 2014cc; Tymchuk, 2014) .
- **22/05/2014** Five DNR soldiers enter the office of the *Novyi Svit* printing office in Donetsk, demanding that they cease the dissemination of newspapers that criticise separatist activities, such as *Segodnia, Donetskie Novosti*, and *Priazovskyi Rabochyi* (Institut Masovoï Informatsiï, 2014ce; Segodnya.ua, 2014a).
- **25/05/2014** In Donetsk, around fifteen armed men enter the office of television channel *Iunion*, demanding a meeting with the management (Institut Masovoï Informatsiï, 2014n; Segodnya.ua, 2014b).
- **30/05/2014** Luhansk-based television channel *IRTA* is taken off-air; it is announced during a press conference by the head of the LNR, Valerii Bolotov (Institut Masovoï Informatsiï, 2014cm).

Closing of Local Channels

- **01/05/2014** Ukraine's *Channel 1* is replaced with the Russian *Rossia-24* in Luhansk (Institut Masovoï Informatsiï, 2014bc; Mijatović, 2014b; Sxid. info, 2014).
- **03/05/2014** *Channel 1+1* and *Channel 5* are closed down in Luhansk (Institut Masovoï Informatsiï, 2014bf).
- **08/05/2014** Television channel *1+1* closes down in Lysychansk (Institut Masovoï Informatsiï, 2014bo).
- **08/05/2014** In Severodonetsk, *Vokar Holding*, a company providing cable television services and is part of the *Lanet* network, suspends the broadcasting of Ukrainian TV channels *Inter, Ukraina, 1+1, ICTV, STB, Novyi Kanal*, and *112 Ukraina* (Institut Masovoï Informatsiï, 2014bp; Lanet, 2014).
- **10/05/2014** In Krasnyi Luch, local cable operator *TRK Luch* suspends the broadcasting of a number of Ukrainian television channels, including *ICTV, TRK Ukraina, STB*, and *112 Ukraina*. One week prior, *TRK Luch* had also suspended *Channel 1, 1+1, Channel 5*, and *Channel 24* (Delo.ua, 2014; Institut Masovoï Informatsiï, 2014bu).
- **10/05/2014** Due to threats of closure, the Konstantynivka-based newspaper *Provintsiia* appoints a new deputy editor-in-chief, Volodymyr Averin, an active supporter of the DNR (Institut Masovoï Informatsiï, 2014bt; Wikipedia, 2019).
- **12/05/2014** *Channel 1+1* is closed down in the cities of Artemivs'k and Konstantynivka. In Konstantynivka, local channel *TET* is also

suspended. Both are replaced with *Rossiia-24* (Institut Masovoï Informatsiï, 2014bv).

- **12/05/2014** *Radio Era FM*, a radio station in Donetsk, is closed down after armed men enter the office (Institut Masovoï Informatsiï, 2014by; Ukraïns'ki Novyny, 2014).
- **13/05/2014** Valerii Bolotov, the self-appointed governor of the Luhansk region and head of the LNR, orders the closure of what he calls television channels with a 'pro-fascist' orientation (Biznes Online, 2014; Institut Masovoï Informatsiï, 2014bx).
- **15/05/2014** The Severodonetsk-based local cable television operator *vokar Holding* also shuts down *Channel 5* and *TVi* (Institut Masovoï Informatsiï, 2014cb; Ukraine News One Russian, 2014).
- **22/05/2014** In Donetsk, armed men seize a car containing part of the day's edition of the information bulletin for miners *Po-Horniatski* (Institut Masovoï Informatsiï, 2014cf).
- **22/05/2014** In Donetsk, separatists seize *Novyi Mir*, a printing office where *Segodnia* and *Po-Horniatski* are printed. Two employees are taken captive (Podrobnosti, 2014d).
- **23/05/2014** In Alchevs'k, Luhansk oblast, five Ukrainian television channels are taken off air: *1+1*, *Channel 1*, *Channel 5*, *Channel 24*, and *112 Ukraina* (Institut Masovoï Informatsiï, 2014ci).
- **27/05/2014** In Severodonetsk, local representatives of the LNR carry out a 'cleaning operation' of the local information sector of the internet (Institut Masovoï Informatsiï, 2014ct).
- **28/05/2014** The Luhansk cable television company again takes channel *1 +1* off air, after transmission had been restored briefly two days prior (Institut Masovoï Informatsiï, 2014cl).
- **30/05/2014** Television channels *ICTV*, *STB*, *Inter*, and *IRTA* are taken off the air in Luhansk (Institut Masovoï Informatsiï, 2014cn).

JUNE 2014

Deaths

- **17/06/2014** Igor Korneliuk, a correspondent working for the Russian channel *VGTRK*, suffers lethal injuries during the shelling of the town of Myrnyi, near Luhansk. Anton Voloshin, a video engineer also working for *VGTRK*, also perishes in the same attack (BBC Russian, 2014; Institut Masovoï Informatsiï, 2014cx).
- **30/06/2014** Anatolyi Klian, a camera operator working for the Russian *Channel 1* (*Pervyi Kanal*), dies after coming under fire in the vicinity of a Ukrainian military unit in Donetsk oblast, where his crew was filming a reportage (NTV, 2014; OSCE Representative on Freedom of the Media, 2014b).

Refugees

- **17/06/2014** Danilo Aheev, editor of the Luhansk-based internet news site *CityNews*, is forced to relocate to Lutsk. The Institute of Mass Media reports that another fifteen journalists are in similarly difficult positions due to the escalating situation in eastern Ukraine (Institut Masovoï Informatsiï, 2014cw).

Kidnappings

- **02/06/2014** In Donetsk, armed men enter the building of the publishing house Donechchina and take away Oleksandr Brizh, the editor-in-chief of the newspaper *Donbass*, and Leonid Lapa, editor-in-chief of *Vechernyi Donetsk* (Institut Masovoï Informatsiï, 2014cq).
- **05/06/2014** The Konstantynivka-based blogger Artur Golubev is captured by representatives of the DNR. He is freed from captivity on June 21 (Dozhd TV, 2014b).
- **17/06/2014** In Makiivka, armed representatives of the DNR take captive Larisa Butova, the director of the local publishing house Presa Makiivki, and Maria Semenova, the editor of the local paper *Vecherniaia Makeevka*, for approximately ten hours (Institut Masovoï Informatsiï, 2014cy).
- **17/06/2014** In Donetsk, Aleksandr Peremot, a journalist working for *URA-Inform.Donbass*, a news site, is kidnapped by representatives of the DNR while filming near the prosecutor's office (URA-Inform.Donbass, 2014a).
- **26/06/2014** Oleksandr Chernov, a doctor and freelance correspondent working for *Ostrov*, is detained in Enakievo (Gordon, 2014b).
- **27/06/2014** Boris Iuzhik, editor-in-chief of the Druzhkovka-based newspaper *Druzhkovskyi Rabochyi*, is detained by DNR representatives and taken to an unknown location (Insider, 2014b).
- **30/06/2014** In Luhansk, Nastia Stanko, a journalist working for *Hromad'ske TV*, and cameraman Ilia Bezkorovainyi are taken captive by representatives of the LNR (Institut Masovoï Informatsiï, 2014da).

Threats

- **13/06/2014** The DNR leadership ask local internet service providers to provide their customers' registration data (62.ua, 2014b).
- **24/06/2014** Oleksyi Svetikov, the editor of *Segodnia v Severodonetske*, a local news site in Severodonetsk, asks the Ukrainian police to intervene after receiving repeated threats at his home address (Institut Masovoï Informatsiï, 2014cz).

Attacks on Editorial Offices

- **02/06/2014** Armed individuals enter the building of the publishing house Donechchina in Donetsk, stating that they are placing the building under surveillance (Institut Masovoï Informatsiï, 2014cp).

- **06/06/2014** The office of the newspaper *Torezskii Gorniak* in Torez is burned down during the night (Horodetskii, 2014).
- **18/06/2014** Around six to eight unknown armed men enter the premises of television company *TRK Donbas* in Donetsk and try to shut down ongoing activities (Donetskie Novosti, 2014).
- **26/06/2014** Armed men enter the office of the newspaper *Pro Gorod* in Torez, confiscate equipment, and warn those present to suspend publication (Novosti Donbassa, 2014d).
- **30/06/2014** A television tower on Karachun mountain, near Sloviansk, collapses as a result of artillery shelling (Institut Masovoï Informatsiï, 2014db).

Closing of Local Channels

- **02/06/2014** Representatives of the DNR close down five television channels in Makiivka, including *Channel 1*, *Rada*, and *Donbas* (@21brklyn, 2014; Institut Masovoï Informatsiï, 2014cr).
- **02/06/2014** Four television channels are closed down in Donetsk by cable operator *TRK Mis'ke Budivnytstvo*, including *Channel 5*, *UT-1*, *Rada*, and *Donbas* (Ostrov, 2014c).
- **03/06/2014** DNR representatives demand a change in editorial policy from Oleksandr Brizh, editor-in-chief of the newspaper *Donbass*, during their negotiations after Brizh was released from captivity (Institut Masovoï Informatsiï, 2014cu).
- **05/06/2014** In Donetsk, the telecommunications company MATRIX is forced by DNR representatives to suspend broadcasting *Channel 5*, *1+1*, *Donbas*, *UBR*, and *News24* (Matrix Home, 2014).
- **10/06/2014** In Luhansk, cable operator Luhanske Kabelne Telebachennia resumes broadcasting *Channel 1+1*, but remains off the air during news broadcasts (Institut Masovoï Informatsiï, 2014cv).
- **26/06/2014** In Donetsk, the Ukrainian television channels *ICTV* and *Channel 12* are replaced with Russian ones after pressure from unknown armed men (Interfaks-Ukraina, 2014b).
- **30/06/2014** The telecommunications company Luhanske Kabelne Telebachennia from Luhansk take the television channels *Inter*, *ICTV*, and *STB* off the air, and replace them with Russian channels (Institut Masovoï Informatsiï, 2014dd).

Accreditation

- **27/06/2014** The press service of the DNR announces that all mass media outlets broadcasting within the territory under DNR control must obtain a registration from the ministry of information and communication of the DNR (Zhurdom, 2014).

JULY 2014

Physical Attacks

- **06/07/2014** In Luhansk, unknown men armed with automatic rifles and dressed in camouflage outfits assault and arrest Serhii Sakadinskyi, the editor of the website *Polityka 2.o.* The paper's office is raided (Institut Masovoï Informatsiï, 2014dh; Pogukai, 2014).
- **19/07/2014** After the downing of Malaysian Airlines flight 17 on July 14, ten foreign journalists are taken captive by representatives of the DNR. They are released by July 20 (Greenslade, 2014).
- **20/07/2014** Piotr Andryszczak, a Polish journalist working for *Nowa Europa Vschodnia*, is briefly detained and then released in Donetsk (Institut Masovoï Informatsiï, 2014dj).
- **22/07/2014** Freelance journalist Anton Skib, working as a fixer for *CNN*, is taken captive in Donetsk (Podrobnosti, 2014e).
- **23/07/2014** Iurii Leliavs'kyi, a Lviv-based journalist and freelance correspondent for *ZIK*, is taken captive in Luhansk oblast (ZIK, 2014).
- **31/07/2014** LNR soldiers take captive journalists Ievhen Shliakhtin and Ievhen Timofeev (Institut Masovoï Informatsiï, 2014dm).

Gun-Related Incidents

- **01/07/2014** Special correspondent Denis Kulag and camera operator Vadim Iunin, both working for the Russian television channel *REN TV*, are injured during an exchange of fire near the village of Izarino, close to Luhansk (Institut Masovoï Informatsiï, 2014dc).
- **10/07/2014** Oleksandr Zahorodnyi, working for television channel *1+1*, and his colleagues are injured during a shooting close to the village of Siverska, Donetsk oblast (TSN Ukraina, 2014d).
- **08/07/2014** Roban Bochkal, war correspondent for the television channel *Inter*, and camera operator Vasil Menovshchikov are involved in an exchange of fire near Luhansk. Bochkal suffered injuries, Menovshchikov remained unharmed (Institut Masovoï Informatsiï, 2014de).
- **11/07/2014** Valerii Moroz, a camera operator working for the Russian channel *LifeNews*, is injured during an exchange of fire in Luhansk (Institut Masovoï Informatsiï, 2014df).
- **15/07/2014** Natalia Filatova, a journalist working for Novosti Donbassa, is attacked at the train station in Donetsk (Institut Masovoï Informatsiï, 2014di).
- **27/07/2014** Bianka Zalewska, a Polish citizen and correspondent working for *Espreso TV*, is injured when militia members allied with the DNR and LNR open fire near Starobelsk, Luhansk oblast (Interfaks-Ukraina, 2014c).

Attacks on Editorial Offices

- **04/07/2014** Armed insurgents capture the building of the Luhansk regional television and radio company, and announce that it would henceforth be operating in a new format (Radio Svoboda, 2014d).

Closing Down of Local Channels

- **15/07/2014** All Ukrainian television channels are taken off the air in Donetsk (Institut Masovoï Informatsiï, 2014dg; Segodnia.ua, 2014).
- **24/07/2014** The leadership of the DNR issues a decree prohibiting journalists from working in the conflict zone (BBC Ukrainian, 2014).
- **29/07/2014** Practically all cable providers in Donetsk have ceased broadcasting Ukrainian television channels in the Donetsk region, including entertainment channels (Institut Masovoï Informatsiï, 2014dk).
- **30/07/2014** In Luhansk, the broadcasting of Ukrainian television channels is suspended, and radio channels play pro-DNR/LNR songs (Institut Masovoï Informatsiï, 2014dl).

AUGUST 2014

Deaths

- **22/08/2014** Representatives of the DNR announce that they discovered the remains of Andrei Stenin, a Russian photojournalist who had gone missing (Institut Masovoï Informatsiï, 2014dt).

Kidnappings

- **02/08/2014** Camera operator Oleksandr Osadchyi, working for the television channel *NTN*, is detained in Donetsk (Fakty, 2014).
- **17/08/2014** Roman Cheremskyi, a Kharkiv-based journalist working for *Ukraïnskyi Prostir*, is taken captive by representatives of the LNR (Interfaks-Ukraina, 2014d).
- **21/08/2014** Journalist Hanna Ivanenko and camera operator Nazar Zotsenko, both working for the television channel *112 Ukraina*, are detained for two and a half weeks by representatives of the LNR, and released after an intervention by *LifeNews* (112 Ukraina, 2014).
- **25/08/2014** Journalist Iehor Vorobiov and camera operator Taras Chkan, both working for *Espreso TV*, and Rostislav Shaposhnikov, a journalist working for *Dorozhnyi Kontrol'*, are detained near the town of Ilovaisk, Donetsk oblast, allegedly by Russian troops (Institut Masovoï Informatsiï, 2014dv; Shaposhnikov, 2014).

Arrests

- **01/08/2014** Roman Hnatiuk, a reporter for *112 Ukraina* who had previously livestreamed the events surrounding the downing of Malaysia Airlines flight 17 on July 14, goes missing near Donetsk, despite having accreditation to work inside the DNR, along with Sergei Belous (working for the Serbian weekly *Pecat*) and freelance journalist Serhii Boiko (Pervyi Kanal, 2014).
- **10/08/2014** Beata Bubinets, a Russian documentary film maker, is arrested by the Ukrainian authorities near the city of Shchastie in Luhansk oblast (Institut Masovoï Informatsiï, 2014do).
- **25/08/2014** In Shchastie, the Aidar Batallion detains the Luhansk-based journalist Oksana Lashchonova, editor-in-chief of *Luhans'ka Pravda*, accusing her of 'supporting terrorism' (LB.ua, 2014b).
- **25/08/2014** Journalists Evheniia Koroliova and Maksim Vasilenko, working for the weekly *Krymskii Telegraf*, are detained by members of the Right Sector movement (Institut Masovoï Informatsiï, 2014du; RIA Novosti, 2014).

Physical Attacks

- **21/08/2014** During an exchange of fire in the city of Ilovaisk, freelance photographer Oleksandr Gliadelov and blogger Dmitro Riznychenko are injured (LB.ua, 2014a).

Attacks on Editorial Offices

- **02/08/2014** *TRK Iunion*, a television channel in Donetsk, is captured by armed DNR members (Institut Masovoï Informatsiï, 2014dn).

Threats

- **09/08/2014** The parents of Viktoriia Ishchenko, a journalist in Donetsk, are arrested by DNR representatives, after which she was forced to leave the city (Institut Masovoï Informatsiï, 2014dp).
- **15/08/2014** Members of the *Armiia Iugo-Vostoka* (South-eastern Army) in Krasnodon prohibit capturing photo and video footage in public places (Institut Masovoï Informatsiï, 2014dq).

Attacks on Infrastructure

- **19/08/2014** Three television towers in Luhansk and Donetsk oblast are under DNR/LNR control (Institut Masovoï Informatsiï, 2014dr).

SEPTEMBER 2014

Physical Attacks

- **07/09/2014** Dmitro Potekhin, a local journalist, is taken captive by DNR representatives in Donetsk (NV Ukraina, 2014).

- **15/09/2014** Valeriia Olifiruk, a girl from Donetsk, is arrested by DNR representatives after she published pictures of damaged buildings and infrastructure in Khartsyzk on social media (Novosti Donbassa, 2014f).
- **17/09/2014** Local journalist Oleksandr Bilokobylskyi goes missing in Luhansk. He is released from jail shortly after (Osadcha, 2014; RIA Novosti Ukraina, 2014).
- **22/09/2014** Serhii Sakadinskyi remains in LNR captivity in Luhansk (Hromads'ke Radio, 2016).
- **22/09/2014** Members of the special forces of the DNR arrest Serhii Boiko, a freelancer preparing publications for *Vesti* and *Reporter*, as well as the photojournalist Oleksandr Harmatenko, in Antratsit (Institut Masovoï Informatsiï, 2014dx).

Arrests

- **01/09/2014** Members of the Azov Batallion arrest Timur Olevskyi, a a Russian journalist working for the television channel *Dozhd*, and Orkhan Dzhemal, who was working for the Russian edition of *Forbes*. Both are released after a few hours (Dozhd TV, 2014c).

Censorship

- **16/09/2014** The Ministry of Information and Communications of the DNR orders local internet provider to block twenty-seven Donetsk-based news sites, including *Novosti Donbassa* and *Donetskaia Pravda* (Institut Masovoï Informatsiï, 2014dy; Matsuka, 2014a).

Accreditation

- **12/09/2014** Local media outlets in Donetsk are told to register with the DNR ministry of information (Institut Masovoï Informatsiï, 2014dw).

OCTOBER 2014

Physical Attacks

- **22/10/2014** Oleksyi Ishchenko, a journalist working for the television programme *Absatz*, is injured in his chest covering the battle for the Donetsk airport (Abzats, 2014).

Attacks on Editorial Offices

- **11/10/2014** In Lysychansk, a group of armed men tries to capture the local television and radio company *Aktsent* (Institut Masovoï Informatsiï, 2014ea).

Blocking of Local Channels

- **15/10/2014** DNR representatives circulate a list of Ukrainian news sites that they consider blocking (Institut Masovoï Informatsiï, 2014dz).

Other

- **01/10/2014** On the former frequency of channel *1+1*, DNR representatives begin broadcasting their own (amateur) television channel in Donetsk (Tsenzor.net, 2014).
- **30/10/2014** OSCE Representative on Freedom of the Media Dunja Mijatović condemns an incident of Russian actor Mikhail Porechenkov being filmed in Donetsk firing a large-calibre machine gun while wearing a helmet marked with press insignia, stating that this put journalists at great risk (OSCE, 2014d).

NOVEMBER 2014

Deaths

- **29/11/2014** Crime reporter Aleksandr Kuchinskii, editor-in-chief of *Kriminal Ekspress*, and his wife are found dead near Sloviansk. They were reportedly stabbed to death (Obozrevatel', 2014).

Intimidation

- **18/11/2014** Serhii Ivanov, a well-known blogger from Luhansk, reports that unknown individuals are shadowing him on his daily commute in Kyiv (Institut Masovoï Informatsiï, 2014eb).

DECEMBER 2014

- **01/12/2014** The Donetsk-based news site *URA-Inform.Donbass* suspends its activities. Up until this day, the outlet had continued to operate in Donetsk and other cities in the DNR/LNR (URA-Inform.Donbass, 2014b).
- **10/12/2014** All media content producers inside the DNR, including bloggers, are henceforth obliged to obtain a registration before being allowed to operate (Radio Maksimum, 2014).
- **26/12/2014** The deputy head of the People's Front of Novorossiia, Konstantin Dolgov, accuses Bianka Zalewska, a Polish journalist working for *Espreso TV* who was injured during the previous summer, of being a sniper working for the Aidar Battalion (Institut Masovoï Informatsiï, 2014ec).

JANUARY 2015

- **13/01/2015** Independent unions for journalists in Ukraine (the NMPU and the NSZhU) state that the mandatory accreditation procedure for journalists working in the conflict zone is in violation of journalists' rights, and call on the SBU and Ministry of Defence to end the policy (Natsional'na spilka zhurnalistiv Ukraïny, 2015).

FEBRUARY 2015

Deaths

- **25/02/2015** Serhii Nikolaev, a photo correspondent for *Segodnia*, dies in the hospital after being injured in a shelling near the village of Pisky in Donetsk oblast (Hromadske, 2015).

Physical Attacks

- **07/02/2015** In Avdiivka, Donetsk oblast, locals attack a camera crew working for *112 Ukraina* and break one of their cameras (Institut Masovoï Informatsiï, 2015a).
- **15/02/2015** Soldiers working for Arsen Pavlov (also known as Motorola) briefly detain Danilo Elia and Cosimo Attanasio, two Italian journalists in Donetsk (Elia, 2015; Institut Masovoï Informatsiï, 2014d).
- **25/01/2015** DNR soldiers briefly detain Paweł Pieniążek, a Polish journalist working for *Krytyka Polityczna* (Institut Masovoï Informatsiï, 2015b).

Accreditation

- **12/02/2015** The Verkhovna Rada revokes by decree the accreditation of journalists working for certain Russian media outlets for the duration of the Anti-Terrorist Operation. The action is condemned by OSCE Representative on Freedom of the Media Dunja Mijatović (OSCE, 2015c; Verkhovna Rada Ukraïny, 2015).

MARCH 2015

- **06/03/2015** In Krasnyi Luch, two Ukrainian television channels and the Russian channel *Dozhd* are shut down by LNR soldiers, in order to 'protect national interests of the LNR' (Institut Masovoï Informatsiï, 2014l; RIA Novosti, 2015a).
- **21/03/2015** Journalist Olga Kalynovska and camera operator Serhii Klymenko, both working for *Channel 5*, are fired at by snipers while filming near the frontline village of Stanitsiia Luhanska in Luhansk oblast (5 Kanal, 2015).
- **16/03/2015** Vice-speaker of the People's Council of the DNR, Denis Pushilin, announces that no Ukrainian media that took part in igniting the conflict in Donbas will be allowed inside DNR territory (Institut Masovoï Informatsiï, 2015d).

- **17/03/2015** Viktoriia Ivleva, a photographer and author working for *Novaia Gazeta*, is briefly detained at a checkpoint near Stantsiia Luhanska, and released after her documentation, money, and equipment were confiscated (Novaia Gazeta, 2015a).

APRIL 2015

Deaths

- **15/04/2015** Olga Moroz, editor-in-chief of *Neteshinskii Vestnik*, is found dead in Kyiv (DP.ru, 2015).
- **16/04/2015** Serhii Sukhobok, founder of the newspaper *Viddzerkalennya* and several other (online) publications, is shot to death in a dacha outside Kyiv (Telekrytyka, 2015).
- **17/04/2015** Oles Buzina, a pro-Russian activist and blogger, is shot to death by masked men in Kyiv (Sydney Morning Herald, 2015).

Attacks on Editorial Offices

- **27/04/2015** In Konstantynivka, unknown individuals break the windows of the office of local newspaper *Provintsiia* (Institut Masovoï Informatsiï, 2015e).

MAY 2015

- **14/05/2015** In Donetsk, DNR soldiers destroy the apartment of Bohdan Dolgopolskyi, a freelancer working for *Hromadske TV Donbasu*, injuring him in the process (Institut Masovoï Informatsiï, 2015f).
- **25/05/2015** The Luhansk regional television and radio company *LOT* resumes broadcasting (Hromads'ke Radio, 2015).

JUNE 2015

- **09/06/2015** On order of DNR officials, the Donetsk Cable Television Company blocks access to thirty-nine internet news sources, including *Radio Svoboda*, *Tsenzor.net*, *Hromads'ke*, and other Ukrainian media outlets (Institut Masovoï Informatsiï, 2015g).
- **16/06/2015** DNR officials arrest Pavel Kanigin, special correspondent for *Novaia Gazeta*, in Donetsk (Novaia Gazeta, 2015b).

AUGUST 2015

- **10/08/2015** The People's Council of the DNR prohibits Ukrainian media outlets from receiving official information about the local elections in the DNR (Institut Masovoï Informatsiï, 2015h).

SEPTEMBER 2015

- **07/09/2015** Monika Andruszewska, a Polish journalist working for *Tygodnik Powszechny* as a conflict zone correspondent, reports receiving regular threats from unknown individuals (Andruszewska, 2015; Institut Masovoï Informatsiï, 2015i).
- **18/09/2015** DNR and LNR officials prohibit foreign journalists from showing footage of Russian troops operating inside DNR/LNR territory (Institut Masovoï Informatsiï, 2015j).

OCTOBER 2015

- **01/10/2015** The law 'On Amendments to Several Laws of Ukraine on Ensuring the Transparency of Media Ownership and Implementing the Principles of State Policy in the Sphere of Television and Radio Broadcasting' comes into effect in Ukraine (OSCE, 2015d).
- **20/10/2015** Unknown individuals destroy the office of *06239.com.ua*, a local news site for the cities of Pokrovsk (formerly Krasnoarmiisk) and Dimitrov, both in Luhansk oblast (Institut Masovoï Informatsiï, 2015k).

NOVEMBER 2015

- **13/11/2015** Viacheslav Stoliarenko, the LNR minister of information, issues a decree banning the broadcasting of Ukrainian television channels that discredit the LNR (Institut Masovoï Informatsiï, 2015l).
- **24/11/2015** The Verkhovna Rada adopts the law 'On Reforming State and Communal Print Mass Media', which aims to limit state and communal ownership of print media outlets in Ukraine (OSCE, 2015e).

DECEMBER 2015

- **16/12/2015** The signal of the Ukrainian radio station *Hromadske Radio* is blocked in Luhansk and replaced with *Kazache Radio*, which broadcasts pro-LNR content (Institut Masovoï Informatsiï, 2015m).
- **29/12/2015** The signal of the Ukrainian radio station *Radio 24* is blocked in Luhansk (Institut Masovoï Informatsiï, 2015n).

JANUARY 2016

- **13/01/2016** In the LNR, 113 Ukrainian news sites are blocked by decree from the ministry of information of the LNR (BBC Ukrainian, 2016).

FEBRUARY 2016

- **10/02/2016** The DNR authorities order the blocking of almost all Ukrainian television channels for having an extremist character (Institut Masovoï Informatsiï, 2016a).

MAY 2016

- **11/03/2016** The Ukrainian freelance journalist Roman Stepanovych reports receiving threats from unknown individuals, after his name was published on the doxxing site *Mirotvorets* as being accredited to work in the DNR (Institut Masovoï Informatsiï, 2016c).
- **11/03/2016** Journalists working for Ukrainian and international media, as well as Reporters without Borders, the OSCE, and the Committee for the Protection of Journalists, condemn the publication by *Mirotvorets* of personal information of journalists with a DNR or LNR accreditation, and demand the removal of this information from its website (Committee to Protect Journalists, 2016; Deutsche Welle, 2016a; Institut Masovoï Informatsiï, 2016d; Radio Svoboda, 2016).
- **20/03/2016** Doxxing site *Mirotvorets* publishes a new list of journalists with an accreditation to work in the DNR, apologising for its earlier version not being entirely up to date (Mirotvorets, 2016).
- **24/03/2016** In response to *Mirotvorets*, the pro-LNR website *Okkupatsiia. net* publishes a list, dated October 10, 2014, of Ukrainian and international journalists with an accreditation for covering events in the conflict zone (Institut Masovoï Informatsiï, 2016e).

JULY 2016

- **20/07/2016** In Kyiv, the well-known journalist Pavlo Sheremet dies after the car he was sitting in exploded. The car belonged not to Sheremet, but to the Olena Prytula, the owner of *Ukrainska Pravda* (Institut Masovoï Informatsiï, 2016f).

AUGUST 2016

- **02/08/2016** The broadcasting of Ukrainian television channels in the DNR and LNR suffers from continued interruptions (Interfaks-Ukraina, 2016).

SEPTEMBER 2016

- **02/09/2016** The analogue signal of Ukrainian television channels *1+1* and *Novyi Kanal* are blocked by the DNR throughout Donbas, with the help of specialised equipment (Institut Masovoï Informatsiï, 2016g).

- **12/09/2016** Representatives of the DNR, referring to internal intelligence data, claim that the Ukrainian security service is sending saboteurs into DNR territory under the guise of being journalists. A DNR official states that the DNR would do its utmost best to detect and destroy these saboteurs (RIA Novosti, 2016).

OCTOBER 2016

- **18/10/2016** The personal information of three members of the board of the Donetsk regional department of the National Television and Radio Company of Ukraine (NKTU) is published on the pro-separatist website *Tribunal* (Institut Masovoï Informatsiï, 2016h).

NOVEMBER 2016

- **21/11/2016** In Luhansk, representatives of the ministry of state security of the LNR arrest the local pro-Ukrainian blogger Eduard Nedeliaev, who under the pseudonym Edward Ned wrote about life in Luhansk on social media. He is subsequently sentenced to fourteen years in prison for 'espionage' (Anna News, 2016; Institut Masovoï Informatsiï, 2017d).
- **25/11/2016** *Dozhd* correspondents Sergei Ierzhenkov and Vasilii Polonskyi go missing in Donetsk, and are later expelled from the area (Dozhd TV, 2016).

DECEMBER 2016

- **12/12/2016** Christian Trippe, the Kyiv correspondent for *Deutsche Welle*, together with his camera crew are refused entry into the DNR (Deutsche Welle, 2016b).
- **21/12/2016** Vladislav Ovcharenko, a blogger from Luhansk, has been held captive inside LNR territory since October 2016. Ovcharenko went missing after going out to meet a girl. Shortly after his disappearance, representatives of the ministry of state security of the LNR conducted a search of his house and confiscated his computer, claiming that Ovcharenko was a supporter of the Azov Batallion (Institut Masovoï Informatsiï, 2016j).
- **27/12/2016** LNR representatives arrest the Luhansk-based blogger Gennadii Benitskyi for spreading extremist materials online (Novosti Donbassa, 2016).
- **27/12/2016** The personal information of Roman Koshmal, a Kramatorsk-based journalist, is published on *Tribunal*, a pro-separatist doxxing site (Institut Masovoï Informatsiï, 2016i).

FEBRUARY 2017

- **02/02/2017** Christopher Nunn, a British photographer, is injured as a result of a shelling in Avdiivka (Romanyshyn, 2017).

MARCH 2017

- **23/03/2017** The Anti-Terrorist Center of the Security Service of Ukraine bans all citizens from capturing video, film, and photo footage of armed forces personnel, law enforcement officers, military equipment, and defence facilities, in connection with the aggravation of the situation in the area of the anti-terrorist operation, the increased risk of sabotage, and penetration of the operation by reconnaissance groups (Institut Masovoï Informatsiï, 2017a).

APRIL 2017

- **27/04/2017** The LNR ministry of internal affairs issues a search warrant for *Inter* correspondents Hennadii Vivchenko and Ruslan Smeshchuk, camera operator Serhii Dubinin, and former editor Roman Bochkal (Institut Masovoï Informatsiï, 2017b).

MAY 2017

- **15/05/2017** Ukrainian president Petro Poroshenko signs a decree blocking access to Russian social networks Vkontakte and Odnoklassniki and the Russian search engine Yandex in all of Ukraine (Institut Masovoï Informatsiï, 2017c).

JUNE 2017

- **02/06/2017** Stanyslav Vasin (Aseev), a journalist and author, goes missing in Donetsk. Amnesty International, the OSCE, and other international organisations issue statements demanding his release (OSCE, 2017a; Radio Svoboda, 2017a; UNIAN, 2017a).
- **19/06/2017** All pro-DNR and most Russian television channels in Donetsk briefly go off the air, including *Oplot TV* and *Novorossiia TV*. Radio channels also play white noise (Segodnia.ua, 2017).

AUGUST 2017

- **29/08/2017** Spanish journalists Antonio Pampliega and Manuel Ángel Sastre are refused entry into Ukraine for anti-Ukrainian activities (El Mundo, 2017).

SEPTEMBER 2017

- **18/09/2017** DNR officials introduce a classification system for journalists working inside DNR and LNR territory: yellow for neutral journalists, orange for journalists who should be placed under surveillance by the security service, and red for journalists who should be deported or detained (Obshchestvennoe TV Donbassa, 2017a).

DECEMBER 2017

- **04/12/2017** *Radio Svoboda*, a Ukrainian radio station, accuses Dejan Berić, a Serbian mercenary who fought on behalf of the DNR, of issuing threats against journalists working for *Donbas.Realii*, a *Radio Svoboda* journalism project, after they published an article entitled 'Serbian Mercenaries in Donbas: How Russia Recruits Serbs into the Ranks of Militants', which mentioned Berić (Radio Svoboda, 2017b).

FEBRUARY 2018

- **22/02/2018** In Rivne (Rivne oblast), an unknown assailant throws bottles containing a flammable substance into the editorial office of *Chetverta Vlada*. No one was hurt (Institut Masovoï Informatsiï, 2018a).

AUGUST 2018

- **31/08/2018** The 'Ministry of State Security' of the LNR, along with the websites *Istok* and *Russkaia Vesna*, publish the personal information (including phone numbers) of Ukrainian journalists working for eleven different news outlets (Institut Masovoï Informatsiï, 2018b).

NOVEMBER 2018

- **05/11/2018** Kateryna Handziuk, a Ukrainian journalist from Kherson, dies after she was attacked with sulphuric acid. Her journalistic work had focused on exposing corruption in the Kherson region; protesters in Kyiv demanded a full investigation into her death (New York Times, 2018).

FEBRUARY 2019

- **28/02/2019** Oleksyi Bratushchak, a journalist from the newspaper *Detali*, writes on his blog on *Ukrainska Pravda* that he is being fired due to 'censorship' imposed by President Poroshenko (Institut Masovoï Informatsiï, 2019a).

MAY 2019

- **04/05/2019** Vadym Komarov, an investigative journalist living and working in Cherkasy known for investigating local corruption, is attacked by unknown assailants and severely beaten. He dies as a result of his injuries on June 20, 2019 (Human Rights Watch, 2019).

JUNE 2019

- **14/06/2019** Several journalists and managers resign from the TV channel *ZIK* after the announcement that Taras Kozak, a politician for the Opposition Bloc, would become its new owner. Kozak was a known associate of businessman Viktor Medvedchuk (Institut Masovoï Informatsiï, 2019b).

APRIL 2020

- **07/04/2020** In Donetsk oblast, unknown assailants open fire on a car carrying several journalists working for the TV channel *Ukraina*. According to Oleksandr Makhov, one of the journalists involved, a drone deliberately dropped a projectile onto the car from above. No one is injured (Institut Masovoï Informatsiï, 2020).

DECEMBER 2020

- **04/12/2020** The Ukrainian TV channel *Nash* airs a talk show with Rodion Miroshnik, a member of the LNR leadership, as a guest. An investigation is opened by Ukraine's National Council (Natsrada) (Institut Masovoï Informatsiï, 2021).

MARCH 2022

- **01/03/2022** Yevhenii Sakun, a camera operator working for the TV channel *LIVE* in Kyiv, dies in a Russian attack on the Kyiv TV tower (International Press Institute, 2022).
- **01/03/2022** Ukrainian photojournalists and documentary photographers Maks Levin and Oleksyi Chernyshov go missing near the village of Huta Mezhyhirska, Kyiv oblast. Levin's body is found on April 1 (Ukrinform, 2022).
- **13/03/2022** Brent Renaud, an award-winning documentary filmmaker and journalist who had previously worked for the *New York Times*, dies after being shot by Russian soldiers at a checkpoint in Irpin, Bucha Raion, north of Kyiv (Sampson, 2022).

- **14/03/2022** Pierre Zakrzewski, an Irish photojournalist and cameraman working for *Fox News*, along with Oleksandra Kuvshynova (a Ukrainian freelancer also working with *Fox*), are killed when the vehicle they are travelling in comes under fire in Horenka, Kyiv oblast. British journalist Benjamin Hall (also working for *Fox*) is injured (Flood, 2022).
- **23/03/2022** Oksana Baulina, an independent Russian journalist working for *The Insider* (and having previously worked with Aleksei Navalny), dies in a Russian shelling of the Podilskyi District in Kyiv (BBC News, 2022a).

APRIL 2022

- **02/04/2022** Mantas Kvedaravičius, a Lithuanian documentary filmmaker and professor of anthropology, dies while trying to leave the besieged city of Mariupol (The Economist, 2022).

MAY 2022

- **26/05/2022** Roman Zhuk, a photographer and videographer, dies in combat after volunteering for the Ukrainian Armed Forces (Institut Masovoï Informatsiï, 2022).
- **30/05/2022** Frédéric Leclerc-Imhoff, a French journalist working for *BFM TV*, dies after receiving a shrapnel wound while following a humanitarian operation in Luhansk oblast (Fisher, 2022).

REFERENCES

5 Kanal. (2015, March 22). Zhurnalisty '5 kanalu' potrapyly pid vohon' snaipera poblyzu zruhnovanoho mostu cherez Sivers'kyi Donets'. *5.ua.* www.5.ua/atona-shodi/zhurnalisty-5-kanalu-potrapyly-pid-vohon-snaipera-poblyzu-zruinova noho-mostu-cherez-siverskyi-donets-74125.html

@21brklyn. (2014, June 1). Post. *Twitter.com.* https://twitter.com/21brklyn/status/473110238175170560/photo/1

24 Kanal. (2014a, March 10). Sutychky u Luhans'ku: Pobyly zhurnalistiv ta zakhopyly telekanal. *24tv.ua.* https://24tv.ua/sutichki_u_lugansku_pobili_zhurnalistiv_ta_zahopili_telekanal_n419368

24 Kanal. (2014b, May 20). Ukrainskuiu fotokorrespondentku osvobodili iz plena v Donetske. *24tv.ua.* https://24tv.ua/ru/ukrainskuyu_fotokorrespondentku_osvobo dili_iz_plena_v_donetske_n444832

62.ua. (2014a, February 21). V Donetske napali na zhurnalista, kotoryi fotografiroval oblgosadministratsiiu (FOTO, VIDEO). *62.ua.* www.62.ua/news/480212/v-doneckenapali-na-zurnalista-kotoryj-fotografiroval-oblgosadministraciu-foto-video

62.ua. (2014b, June 13). Donetskie separatisty namereny 'vychisliat' neugodnykh v Internete. *62.ua.* www.62.ua/news/554643

112 Ukraina. (2014, September 3). S'emochnaia gruppa '112 Ukraina' popala v plen boevikov, snimaia reportazh po pros'be Minoborony. Video. *YouTube.com.* https://youtu.be/dXNz3lhDh1A

06274. (2014, February 28). Napadenie 'Titushek' na zhurnalistov saita 06274, ili kogo nuzhno boiat'sia v Artemovske? *06274.com.ua.* www.06274.com.ua/news/485763/napadenie-titusek-na-zurnalistov-sajta-06274-ili-kogo-nuzno-boatsa-v-artemovske

Abd El Rahman Kamal, M.-A. H. (2017). *The Syrian Public Opinion versus Frames in News Media.* American University in Cairo.

Abibok, Y. (2018, June 5). Identity policy in the self-proclaimed republics in east Ukraine. *OSW Commentary.* www.osw.waw.pl/en/publikacje/osw-commentary/2018-06-06/identity-policy-self-proclaimed-republics-east-ukraine-0

Abibok, Y. (2019, February 19). The republic lives on and is managed by rumours. *Open Democracy.* www.opendemocracy.net/en/odr/the-republics-east-ukraine-donetsk-luhansk/

Abzats. (2014, October 21). Vypusk seredy 'Abzats!' prysviatyt' 'Kibohram'. *Abzats. novy.tv.* https://abzats.novy.tv/ua/news/2014/10/21/vipusk-seredi-abzats-prisvyatit-kiborgam/

Administratsiia Goroda Donetska. (2016, May 6). V Kalininskom raione pozdravili redaktsiu gazety 'Donetsk Vechernii'. *Gorod-Donetsk.com.* http://gorod-donetsk.com/novosti/5635-v-kalininskom-rajone-pozdravili-redaktsiyu-gazety-donetsk-vechernij

Alekseev, G. (2014, March 3). Posle shturma Doma sovetov neizvestnye pytalis' prorvat'sia v ofis telekompanii Simon. *Archive.Objectiv.tv.* http://archive.objectiv.tv/030314/93943.html

Alkerchin, A. (2014, May 12). Obrashchenie k grahdanskim zhurnalistam saita 'Moi gorod'. *Severodonetsk.Info.* http://sever.lg.ua/2014-05-13-obrashchenie-k-grazhdanskim-zhurnalistam-saita-moi-gorod

Altheide, D. L. (1997). The news media, the problem frame, and the production of fear. *The Sociological Quarterly, 38*(4), 647–668.

Anderson, G. (2023). *Natopolitanism: The Atlantic Alliance since the Cold War.* Verso Books.

Andruszewska, M. (2015, September 7). Post. *Facebook.com.* www.facebook.com/monikandruszewska/posts/952688021444507?fref=nf

Anna News. (2016, November 29). MGB LNR zaderzhan luganskii bloger, izvestnyi pod nikneimom 'Edward Ned'. Video. *YouTube.com.* www.youtube.com/watch?v=HtjcLEKQkqs

Antoniuk, D. (2020, February 7). Ex-Russian official becomes 'prime minister' of Donetsk militants. *Kyiv Post.* www.kyivpost.com/post/7966

Applebaum, A. (2017). *Red Famine: Stalin's War on Ukraine.* Penguin Books.

Arel, D. (2018). How Ukraine has become more Ukrainian. *Post-Soviet Affairs, 34*(2–3), 186–189. https://doi.org/10.1080/1060586X.2018.1445460

Artem'ev, A., Ul'ianova, Z., Makutina, M., & Khimshiashvili, P. (2014, October 30). Ogranichennyi vybor: Golosovanie v Donbasse proidet pochti bez konkurentsii. *RBC.ru.* www.rbc.ru/politics/30/10/2014/54511705cbb20f139df5ae6e

Asmus, R. (2009). *A Little War That Shook the World: Georgia, Russia, and the Future of the West.* Palgrave Macmillan.

Atanasov, V. (2017, July 17). Reporting from Ukraine's separatist areas is becoming more difficult. *Indexoncensorship.org.* www.indexoncensorship.org/2017/07/reporting-ukraines-separatist-areas-becoming-difficult/

Babiak, M. (2014, May). *Welcome to New Russia.* Ukrainian Policy. http://ukrainianpolicy.com/welcome-to-new-russia/

Barrington, L. (2021). Citizenship as a cornerstone of civic national identity in Ukraine. *Post-Soviet Affairs, 37*(2), 155–173. https://doi.org/10.1080/1060586X.2020.1851541

Barrington, L. (2022a). A new look at region, language, ethnicity and civic national identity in Ukraine. *Europe–Asia Studies, 74*(3), 360–381. https://doi.org/10.1080/09668136.2022.2032606

Barrington, L. (2022b). Is the regional divide in Ukraine an identity divide? *Eurasian Geography and Economics, 63*(4), 465–490. https://doi.org/10.1080/15387216.2021.1899835

Barrington, L. (2022c, May 23). Putin's key mistake? Not understanding Ukraine's blossoming national identity – Even in the Russian-friendly southeast. *The Conversation*. https://theconversation.com/putins-key-mistake-not-understand ing-ukraines-blossoming-national-identity-even-in-the-russian-friendly-south east-183576

Bartlby. (2014, May 12). Post. *Twitter.com*. https://twitter.com/A3AP/status/ 465713037199294464

Batta, A. (2022, February 28). Are the Russian speakers in Ukraine on Putin's side? *Wild Blue Yonder*. www.airuniversity.af.edu/Wild-Blue-Yonder/Article-Display/ Article/2949512/are-the-russian-speakers-in-ukraine-on-putins-side/

BBC News. (2014a, April 7). Ukraine Crisis: Protesters declare 'Donetsk People's Republic'. *BBC.com*. www.bbc.com/news/world-europe-26919928

BBC News. (2014b, July 24). Ukraine rebel leader Borodai admits to Russia links. *BBC. com.uk*. www.bbc.co.uk/news/world-europe-28450303

BBC News. (2014c, August 26). Captured Russian troops 'in Ukraine by accident'. *BBC.com.uk*. www.bbc.co.uk/news/world-europe-28934213

BBC News. (2014d, October 13). East Ukraine rebel leader Gubarev unconscious after ambush. *BBC.com.uk*. www.bbc.co.uk/news/world-europe-29593949

BBC News. (2016a, April 7). Netherlands rejects EU-Ukraine partnership deal. *BBC. com.uk*. www.bbc.co.uk/news/world-europe-35976086

BBC News. (2016b, August 7). Ukraine crisis: Blast injures Luhansk rebel leader Plotnitsky. *BBC.com.uk*. www.bbc.co.uk/news/world-europe-37000601

BBC News. (2016c, October 17). 'Motorola': Ukraine rebels accuse Kiev over commander's death. *BBC.com.uk*. www.bbc.co.uk/news/world-europe-37676607

BBC News. (2017a, February 4). Ukraine conflict; Rebel commander killed in bomb blast. *BBC.com*. www.bbc.com/news/world-europe-38868600

BBC News. (2017b, February 8). Ukraine conflict: Rebel leader Givi dies in rocket attack. *BBC.com.uk*. www.bbc.co.uk/news/world-europe-38905110

BBC News. (2017c, July 19). Ukraine conflict: Russia rejects new Donetsk rebel 'state'. *BBC.com.uk*. www.bbc.co.uk/news/world-europe-40653913

BBC News. (2018, August 31). Ukraine conflict: Blast kills top Donetsk rebel Zakharchenko. *BBC.com.uk*. www.bbc.co.uk/news/world-europe-45371270

BBC News. (2022a, March 23). Ukraine war: Russian journalist Oksana Baulina killed in Kyiv shelling. *BBC.com.uk*. www.bbc.co.uk/news/world-europe-60855732

BBC News. (2022b, March 26). Russia targets east Ukraine, says first phase over. *BBC. com*. www.bbc.com/news/world-europe-60872358

BBC News. (2022c, October 13). Ukraine war: UN General Assembly condemns Russia annexation. *BBC.com*. www.bbc.com/news/world-63237669

BBC Russian. (2014, June 17). Dvoe sotrudnikov Rossiiskoi VGTRK pogibli pod Luganskom. *BBC.com*. www.bbc.com/russian/international/2014/06/140617_ journalist_vgtrk_ukraine_korneliuk

BBC Russian. (2018a, August 31). Lidera DNR Aleksandra Zakharchenko vzorvali v Donetske. *BBC.com*. www.bbc.com/russian/news-45374142

BBC Russian. (2018b, August 31). Vzryv v 'Separe'. Versii gibeli Aleksandra Zakharchenko. *BBC.com*. www.bbc.com/russian/news-45375642

BBC Ukrainian. (2014, July 23). U 'DNR' zhurnalistam zaboronyly pratsiuvaty v zoni boiovykh dii. *BBC.com/Ukrainian*. www.bbc.com/ukrainian/news_in_brief/2014/07/140723_sa_dnr_journalists.shtml

BBC Ukrainian. (2016, January 13). U 'LNR' ne pratsiuiut' ukraïns'ki novynni saity. *BBC.com/Ukrainian*. www.bbc.com/ukrainian/news_in_brief/2016/01/160113_hk_lnr_internet

Bellingcat. (2015). *Russia's Path(s) to War: A Bellingcat Investigation*. www.bellingcat.com/app/uploads/2015/09/russia_s_path_s__to_war.pdf

Bellingcat. (2018). *Russian Officers and Militants Identified as Perpetrators of the January 2015 Mariupol Artillery Strike*.

Bessonova, I. (2015, October 31). Futbol v 'DNR-LNR': Patriotichno, nezavisimo, pechal'no. *112.ua*. https://112.ua/statji/futbol-v-dnr-lnr-patriotichno-nezavisimo-pechalno-267785.html

Billig, M. (1995). *Banal Nationalism*. SAGE Publications.

Bittner, J., Ginzel, A., & Hock, A. (2016, September 29). Glückspropaganda und Hass auf Befehl. *Die Zeit*. www.zeit.de/2016/41/russland-propaganda-ostukraine-separatisten-e-mails

Biznes Online. (2014, May 13). 'Narodnyi gubernator' Luganskoi oblasti vvel chrezvychainoe polozhenie v regione. *M.Business-Gazeta.ru*. https://m.business-gazeta.ru/news/444046

Blei, D. M., & Lafferty, J. D. (2006). Dynamic topic models. In *Proceedings of the 23rd International Conference on Machine Learning*, 113–120. https://doi.org/10.1145/1143844.1143859

Blei, D. M., Ng, A. Y., & Jordan, M. I. (2003). Latent Dirichlet allocation. *Journal of Machine Learning Research*, 3, 993–1022.

Boevoe Znamia Donbassa. (2014, November 13). Vas privetstvuet 'Boevoe Znamia Donbassa'! *Boevoe Znamia Donbassa*.

Boevoe Znamia Donbassa. (2015, August 6). Gorlovka otmechaet den' VDV. *Boevoe Znamia Donbassa*. http://gazeta-dnr.ru//?p=678

Boevoe Znamia Donbassa. (2016, February 12). MChS DNR napominaet o merakh bezopasnosti na vodnykh ob"ektakh v zimnii period! *Boevoe Znamia Donbassa*. http://gazeta-dnr.ru//?p=21582

Bondarev, I. (2013, December 4). Napriazhenie. *Tehnopolis.com.ua*. https://tehnopolis.com.ua/index.php?option=com_content&view=article&id=5056:2013-12-15-220831&catid=59:2011-01-11-21-18-52&Itemid=15

Boyko, K. (2016). Mediating alternative statehood: A case study of Dabiq and Novorossiya publications. Master's thesis, Södertörn University.

Broniatowski, D. A., Jamison, A. M., Qi, S., AlKulaib, L., Chen, T., Benton, A., Quinn, S. C., & Dredze, M. (2018). Weaponized health communication: Twitter bots and Russian trolls amplify the vaccine debate. *American Journal of Public Health*, 108 (10), 1378–1384. https://doi.org/10.2105/AJPH.2018.304567

Bulanov, K. (2016, September 24). V LNR zaiavili o samoubiistve eks-prem'era respubliki Tsypkalova. *RBC.ru*. www.rbc.ru/politics/24/09/2016/57e67bb69a7947715563f478

Bureiko, N., & Moga, T. L. (2019). The Ukrainian–Russian linguistic dyad and its impact on national identity in Ukraine. *Europe–Asia Studies*, *71*(1). https://doi.org/10.1080/09668136.2018.1549653

Butenko, V., & Paton Walsh, N. (2014). Ukrainian authorities: Separatists cleared from 2 eastern cities. *CNN*. https://edition.cnn.com/2014/07/05/world/meast/ukraine-crisis/index.html

Butko, A. (2017, May 28). File: Flag Interdvizheniia Donbassa.svg. *Commons. Wikimedia.org*. https://commons.wikimedia.org/wiki/File:Флаг_Интердвижения_Донбасса.svg

Chernov, A. (2016, March 11). Okopnaia pravda Evgeniia Kuznetsova. *Lugansk1.Info*. https://web.archive.org/web/20160322091203/http://lugansk1.info/11392-okopnaya-pravda-evgeniya-kuznetsova/

Chitak, M. (2014, June 26). Dolgo li, korotko li Kamatorchanam razblokirovat' pensiiu? *Tehnopolis.com.ua*. https://tehnopolis.com.ua/index.php?option=com_content&view=article&id=7064:2014-06-26-07-42-58&catid=59:2011-01-11-21-18-52&Itemid=15

CityNews. (2014, April 30). Kak sdavali Lugansk, ili Nastoiashchii boi eshche vperedi. *Citynews.net.ua*. www.citynews.net.ua/polit/33458-kak-sdavali-lugansk-ili-nastoyaschiy-boy-esche-vperedi.html

Committee to Protect Journalists. (2014, May 25). Andrea Rocchelli. *CPJ.org*. https://cpj.org/data/people/andrea-rocchelli/

Committee to Protect Journalists. (2016, May 11). Hackers, lawmaker put reporters at risk in Ukraine. *CPJ.org*. https://cpj.org/2016/05/hackers-lawmaker-put-reporters-at-risk-in-ukraine.php

Cottiero, C., Kucharski, K., Olimpieva, E., & Orttung, R. W. (2015). War of words: The impact of Russian state television on the Russian Internet. *Journal of Nationalism and Ethnicity*, *43*(4), 533–555. https://doi.org/10.1080/00905992.2015.1013527

Council of Europe. (2017). The Law on Education (*) (Adopted by the Verkhovna Rada on September 5, 2017). 902/2017.

Coynash, H. (2019, February 22). Why are Ukrainian pensioners from Donbas forced to fight or die for their pensions? *Kharkiv Human Rights Protection Group*. http://khpg.org/en/index.php?id=1550413831

Coynash, H. (2020a, March 11). Ukrainian stripped of official language status in Russian proxy Donbas 'republic'. *Human Rights in Ukraine*. https://khpg.org/en/1583536107

Coynash, H. (2020b, June 9). Ukrainian language removed from schools in Russian proxy Luhansk 'republic'. *Human Rights in Ukraine*. https://khpg.org/en/1591317237

Crilley, K. (2001). Information warfare. New battle fields: Terrorists, propaganda and the Internet. *Aslib Proceedings*, *53*(7), 250–264. https://doi.org/10.1108/EUM0000000007059

Curiskis, S. A., Drake, B., Osborn, T. R., & Kennedy, P. J. (2019). An evaluation of document clustering and topic modelling in two online social networks: Twitter and Reddit. *Information Processing & Management*. https://doi.org/10.1016/j.ipm.2019.04.002

Danilin, O. (2002). On the way to decline: The development of the Donbass coal-mining industry from the 1950s to the 1980s. *Mining Technology*, *111*(3), 167–171. https://doi.org/10.1179/mnt.2002.111.3.167

Darch, C. (2020). *Nestor Makhno and Rural Anarchism in Ukraine, 1917–1921*. Pluto Press.

Darenskii, V. (2016, February 5). Elena Zaslavskaia: Poeziia novogo mira. *Lugansk1. Info.* https://web.archive.org/web/20160208162332/http://lugansk1.info/7394-elena-zaslavskaya-poeziya-novogo-mira/

Deacon, D., & Golding, P. (1994). *Taxation and Representation*. John Libby.

Delo.ua. (2014, May 13). V Luganskoi oblasti provaideram prikazali otkliuchit' nekotorye ukrainskie kanaly. *Delo.ua.* https://delo.ua/business/v-luganskoj-oblasti-provajderam-skazali-otkljuchit-nekotorye-ukr-235953/

Demirjian, K. (2014, July 20). Watch: Ukraine's pro-Russian rebels discuss MH17's black box in secret recording. *Washington Post.* www.washingtonpost.com/news/worldviews/wp/2014/07/20/watch-ukraines-pro-russian-rebels-discuss-mh17s-black-box-in-secret-recording/?noredirect=on

Dergachev, V. (2017, July 18). Ideia Zakharchenko o Malorossii byla vydvinuta bez soglasovaniia s Kremlem. *RBC.ru.* www.rbc.ru/politics/18/07/2017/596de6549a794753426d8657?utm_source=pushc

Dergachev, V., & Kartsev, D. (2015, February 6). DNR nashla sebe istoriiu. *Gazeta.ru.* www.gazeta.ru/politics/2015/02/06_a_6402557.shtml?updated

Detektor Media. (2014, February 10). Redaktsiiu vydannia 'Novosti Donbassa' vyseliaiut' z ofisu. Kolektyv tse pov'iazuie z vysvitlenniam Ievromaidanu. *Detektor. media.* https://detector.media/community/article/90282/2014-02-10-redaktsiyu-vidannya-novosti-donbassa-viselyayut-z-ofisu-kolektiv-tse-povyazue-z-visvitle nnyam-evromaidanu/

Dettmer, J. (2014, April 23). Putin's men in Ukraine seize U.S. Journalist. *Thedailybeast.com.* www.thedailybeast.com/putins-men-in-ukraine-seize-us-journalist

Deutsche Welle. (2016a, April 20). 'Reportery bez kordoniv': Ti, khto opryliudnyv dani zhurnalistiv, maiut' postaty pered sudom. *DW.com.* www.dw.com/uk/репортери-без-кордонів-ті-хто-оприлюднив-дані-журналістів-мають-постати-перед-судом/a-19248953

Deutsche Welle. (2016b, December 12). Boiovyky 'DNR' ne propustyly znimal'nu hrupu DW cherez Mar'inku. *DW.com.* www.dw.com/uk/бойовики-днр-не-пропустили-знімальну-групу-dw-через-марїнку/a-36743276?maca=ukr-rss-ukr-all-1496-rdf

Dialog UA. (2016, July 15). Byvshii glavar' 'LNR' Valerii Bolotov 'obradoval' reanimatsiei proekta 'Novorossiia' i svoim vozvrashcheniem v politiku. *Dialog.ua.* www.dialog.ua/news/91693_1468598386

Digital Security Lab Ukraine. (2018). Rezul'taty vymiriuvan' internet-blokuvan'. Lugans'k, Donets'k, serpen' 2018. Google Drive document. https://docs.google.com/spreadsheets/d/1qZ5cKfiTv_67TE2ottAqYwPjo5VlQmwoYhoVqQgpXEk/edit#gid=1489080196

Digital Security Lab Ukraine. (2019, June 24). Findings of analysis of Internet blocking in Ukraine (March 2019). *Medium.com.* https://medium.com/@cyber labukraine/findings-of-analysis-of-internet-blocking-in-ukraine-march-2019-b20e23c17aee

Dikoe Pole. (2019). Prazdniki LNR. *Dikoe-Pole.Info.* www.dikoe-pole.info/gosudarst vennye-i-professionalnye-prazdniki-lnr/

Dill, K. E., & Neal, M. R. (2012). *Media Content Analysis: Qualitative Methods.* www .oxfordhandbooks.com/10.1093/oxfordhb/9780195398809.001.0001/oxfordhb-9780195398809-e-29

Dmytruk, A. (2017, June 11). V SBU pidtverdyly znyknennia publitsysta Aseeva u Donets'ku i povidomyly pro ioho poshuku. *Hromadske.ua.* https://hromadske .ua/posts/v-sbu-pidtverdyly-znyknennia-publitsysta-asieieva-u-donetsku-i-povi domyly-pro-ioho-poshuky

DNR Today. (2014, November 3). TsIK DNR oglasil itogovye tsifry rezul'tatov vyborov 2 noiabria. *DNR.Today.* https://web.archive.org/web/20141104053933/http://dnr .today/news/cik-dnr-oglasil-itogovye-cifry-rezultatov-vyborov-2-noyabrya/

DNR24. (2016a). Otkaz ot otvetstvennosti. *DNR24.com.* https://dnr24.com/disclaimer .html

DNR24. (2016b, December 2). VSU za noiabr' sovershili 14 boevykh vylazok na territoriiu DNR, poteri dostigli 25 silovikov. *DNR24.com.* https://dnr24.com/ main/25801-vsu-za-noyabr-sovershili-14-boevyh-vylazok-na-territoriyu-dnr-poteri-dostigli-25-silovikov.html

DNR24. (2016c, 7 December 7). Tramp otkazalsia vmeshivat'sia v konflikt na vostoke Ukrainy. *DNR24.com.* https://dnr24.com/main/25860-tramp-otkazalsya-vmeshi vatsya-v-konflikt-na-vostoke-ukrainy.html

DNR24. (2016d, December 10). Uchenye DNR pridumali, kak prodlit' srok sluzhby makeevskoi shakhte 'Kholodnaia balka' na 30 let. *DNR24.com.* https://dnr24 .com/main/25890-uchenye-dnr-pridumali-kak-prodlit-srok-sluzhby-makeevs koy-shahte-holodnaya-balka-na-30-let.html

DNR24. (2016e, December 16). 'Aidar' i 'Donbass' prigrozili nachat' blokadu DNR i LNR. *DNR24.com.* https://dnr24.com/main/25975-aydar-i-donbass-prigrozili-nachat-blokadu-dnr-i-lnr.html

DNR24. (2017a, January 12). Ukraina–SShA: Khitrye plany dvukh P. *DNR24.com.* https://dnr24.com/main/26217-ukraina-ssha-hitrye-plany-dvuh-p.html

DNR24. (2017b, January 17). P'ianyi boets VSU rasstrelial sosluzhivtsev v 'zone ATO', semero pogibli —Narodnaia militsiia LNR. *DNR24.com.* http://lugansk1.info/ 26512-pyanyj-boets-vsu-rasstrelyal-sosluzhivtsev-v-zone-ato-semero-pogibli-nar odnaya-militsiya-lnr/

DNR24. (2017c, April 2). 'Ukrainskii proryv': Kto i zachem edet v Krym. *DNR24.com.* https://dnr24.com/main/26985-ukrainskiy-proryv-kto-i-zachem-edet-v-krym.html

DNR24. (2017d, April 19). Den' Pobedy v stolitse DNR otmetiat paradom voennoi tekhniki vremen VOV – komandovanie. *DNR24.com.* https://dnr24.com/main/ 27157-den-pobedy-v-stolice-dnr-otmetyat-paradom-voennoy-tehniki-vremen-vov-komandovanie.html

DNR24. (2017e, April 23). Frantsuzskie SMI: 80% territorii Ukrainy podareny Moskvoi. *DNR24.com.* https://dnr24.com/main/27188-francuzskie-smi-80-terri torii-ukrainy-podareny-moskvoy.html

DNR24. (2017f, May 11). 'Besspmertnyi polk': 9 maia na Ukraine proizoshel perelom. *DNR24.com.* https://dnr24.com/main/27322-bessmertnyy-polk-9-maya-na-ukraine-proizoshel-perelom.html

DNR24. (2017g, June 13). Nizkii moral'nyi dukh boitsov VSU privel k ocherednym neboevym poteriam. *DNR24.com.* https://dnr24.com/main/27554-nizkiy-moral nyy-duh-boycov-vsu-privel-k-ocherednym-neboevym-poteryam.html

DNR24. (2017h, July 4). V Donetske predotvrashchen terakt, organizovannyi ukrains-kimi spetssluzhbami —Komandovanie DNR. *DNR24.com*. https://dnr24.com/main/27681-v-donecke-predotvraschen-terakt-organizovannyy-ukrainskimi-specsluzhbami-komandovanie-dnr.html

DNR24. (2017i, August 30). Rospotrebnadzor predupredil o rasprostranenii tuberku-leza na Ukraine. *DNR24.com*. https://dnr24.com/main/27994-rospotrebnadzor-predupredil-o-rasprostranenii-tuberkuleza-na-ukraine.html

DNR24. (2017j, August 30). Unichtozhenie reisa MH17. Neozhidannyi povorot. *DNR24.com*. https://dnr24.com/main/27998-unichtozhenie-reysa-mn17-neozhi dannyy-povorot.html

DNR24. (2017k, November 4). Kiev otvetil na reshenie Varshavy ne puskat' ukraint-sev v 'mundirakh SS'. *DNR24.com*. https://dnr24.com/main/28383-kiev-otvetil-na-reshenie-varshavy-ne-puskat-ukraincev-v-mundirah-ss.html

DNR-Online. (2019). Prazdnichnye dni i professional'nye prazdniki Donetskoi Narodnoi Respubliki. *DNR-Online.ru*. https://dnr-online.ru/prazdnichnye-dni-i-professionalnye-prazdniki-donetskoj-narodnoj-respubliki/

Dokuchaevskii gorodskoi otdel Iustitsii. (2016, February 2). Sozdan Dokuchaevskii otdel tekhnicheskoi inventarizatsii. *Dokuchaevskga.ucoz.org*. http://dokuchaevskga.ucoz.org/news/sozdan_dokuchaevskij_otdel_tekhnicheskoj_inventarizacii/2016-02-02-302

Domańska, M., Wiśniewska, I., & Żochowski, P. (2023, October 25). Caught in the jaws of the 'russkiy mir': Ukraine's occupied regions a year after their annexation. *Raam Op Rusland*. www.raamoprusland.nl/dossiers/oekraine/2486-caught-in-the-jaws-of-the-russkiy-mir-ukraines-occupied-regions-a-year-after-their-annexation

Donetskaia Narodnaia Respublika – Glava Respubliki. (2016). *Rasporiazhenie glavy Donetskoi Narodnoi Respubliki 'O pooshchrenii'*. https://web.archive.org/web/20180304193932/https://av-zakharchenko.su/documents/rasporiazh/2016/rasporiazhGlavaN58_05052016.pdf

Donetskaia Narodnaia Respublika. (2016, August 7). Perechen likvidirovannykh ili zapreshchennykh obshchestvennykh i religioznykh ob'edinenii, inykh organizat-sii. www.Dnr-Online.Ru https://web.archive.org/web/20190401045239/http://dnr-online.ru/perechen-zapreshhennyx-obshhestvennyx-i-religioznyx-obedine nij-inyx-organizacij/

Donetskie Novosti. (2014, June 20). Telekanal 'Donbass': Pod pritselom. *Dnews.dn.ua*. www.dnews.dn.ua/news/550039

Donetskie Novosti. (2017a, July 17). Boks v 'DNR': My eshche ni razu ne ekipirovali nashikh rebiat, net deneg. *Dnews.dn.ua*. www.dnews.dn.ua/news/631259

Donetskie Novosti. (2017b, October 2). 'Prezident federatsii khokkeia DNR' prome-nial 'respubliku' na Rossiiu. *Dnews.dn.ua*. https://dnews.dn.ua/news/649547

Donetskoe Agenstvo Novostei. (2018, July 12). Elena Nikitina, vozglavliavshaia v 2014–2017 godakh Mininform DNR, predstavila v Donetske knigu menuarov. *Dan-News.Info*. https://dan-news.info/politics/elena-nikitina-vozglavlyavshaya-v-2014-2017-godax-mininform-dnr-predstavila-v-donecke-knigu-memuarov.html

DONi News. (2015a, October 13). Washington airdrops tons of weapons to rebels in Syria. *Dnipress.com*. https://dnipress.com/en/posts/washington-airdrops-tons-of-weapons-to-rebels-in-syria/

DONi News. (2015b, October 15). Situation in Donetsk remains tense —DPR SitRep. *Dnipress.com.* https://dnipress.com/en/posts/situation-in-donetsk-remains-tense-dpr-sitrep-15.10.2015/%0A

DONi News. (2015c, October 18). Harsh conditions in Ukrainian occupied territory in front of elections —DPR SitRep 18.10. *Dnipress.com.* https://dnipress.com/en/posts/harsh-conditions-in-ukrainian-occupied-territory-in-front-of-elections-dpr-sitrep-18.10/%0A

DONi News. (2015d, October 30). In the midst of conflict: Donetsk Defence Ministry drew attention to peaceful life in free Donbass —DPR SitRep 30.10. *Dnipress. com.* https://dnipress.com/en/posts/in-the-midst-of-conflict-donetsk-defence-ministry-drew-attention-to-peaceful-life-in-free-donbass/%0A

DONi News. (2015e, November 21). US, Canada, Ukraine reject again UN resolution condemning glorification of Nazism. *Dnipress.com.* https://dnipress.com/en/posts/us-canada-ukraine-reject-again-un-resolution-condemning-glorification-of-nazism/

DONi News. (2015f, December 8). Ukraine's coal reserves will last 3 weeks at most. *Dnipress.com.* https://dnipress.com/en/posts/ukraines-coal-reserves-will-last-3-weeks-at-most/

DONi News. (2015g, December 18). Supported by NATO Kiev may escalate the conflict in Donbass. *Dnipress.com.* https://dnipress.com/en/posts/supported-by-nato-kiev-may-escalate-the-conflict-in-donbass/

DONi News. (2016a, January 22). Poroshenko says no to federalization: The trident will return to Donbass and to the Crimea. *Dnipress.com.* https://dnipress.com/en/posts/poroshenko-says-no-to-federalization-the-trident-will-return-to-donbass-and-to-the-crimea/

DONi News. (2016b, February 26). Mass brawl with Ukrainian military in Donbass. *Dnipress.com.* https://dnipress.com/en/posts/mass-brawl-with-ukrainian-military-in-donbass/

DONi News. (2016c, March 12). Donetsk SitRep: JCCC and OSCE's cynicism and indifference amid suffering and deaths in Donbass – 12.03. *Dnipress.com.* https://dnipress.com/en/posts/donetsk-sitrep-jccc-and-osces-cynicism-and-indifference-amid-suffering-and-deaths-in-donbass-12.03/

DONi News. (2016d, June 17). Zakharchenko to hold direct line with Kiev on June 22. *Dnipress.com.* https://dnipress.com/en/posts/zakharchenko-to-hold-direct-line-with-kiev-on-june-22/

DONi News. (2017a, June 22). Participants of the so-called 'ATO' protest in Kiev [video]. *Dnipress.com.* https://dnipress.com/en/posts/participants-of-the-so-called-ato-protest-in-kiev-video/

DONi News. (2017b, July 13). Ukrainian Nazis recruit children [video]. *Dnipress.com.* https://dnipress.com/en/posts/https-dninews.com-content-ukrainian-nazis-recruit-children-video/

DONi News. (2017c, August 13). US begins deliveries of anti-tank weapons to Ukraine —Document leak. *Dnipress.com.* https://dnipress.com/en/posts/us-begins-deliveries-of-anti-tank-weapons-to-ukraine-document-leak/

DONi News. (2017d, December 19). Shelling of LPR represents acts of Ukrainian state terrorism —Finnish journalist. *Dnipress.com.* https://dnipress.com/en/posts/shelling-of-lpr-represents-acts-of-ukrainian-state-terrorism-finnish-journalist/

DONi News. (2018). *Donetsk International Press Center.* www.dnipress.com/

Dontsiak, T. (2014, March 24). Osobaia voina: Pochemu zhurnalisty – Glavnyi ob'ekt dlia napadeniia. *Atn.ua.* https://atn.ua/obshchestvo/osoba ya-voyna-pochemu-zhurnalisty-glavnyy-obekt-dlya-napadeniya

Dozhd TV. (2014a, April 23). Redaktsiiu gazety v Donetskoi oblasti zabrosali 'kokteiliami Molotova'. *Tvrain.ru.* https://tvrain.ru/news/redaktsiju_gazety_v_donets koj_oblasti_zabrosali_koktejljami_molotova-367407/

Dozhd TV. (2014b, June 22). Zhurnalist Maistrenko ob osvobozhdenii zalozhnikov: 'Boeviki postoianno meniaiut svoi resheniia, im nuzhny plennye i rabotniki'. *Tvrain.ru.* https://tvrain.ru/teleshow/here_and_now/boeviki_postojanno_menja jut_svoi_reshenija_im_nuzhny_plennye_nuzhny_rabotniki_redaktor_gazety_ kovrovskaja_iskra_viktor_majstrenko_o_tom_kak_osvobozhdajut_zalozhnikov-370372/

Dozhd TV. (2014c, September 1). Timur Olevskii i Orkhan Dzhemal' vyshli na sviaz'. *Tvrain.ru.* https://tvrain.ru/news/timur_olevskij_i_orhan_dzhemal_vyshli_na_ svjaz-374855/

Dozhd TV. (2016, November 25). V Donetske propala s'emochnaia gruppa telekanala Dozhd'. *Tvrain.ru.* https://tvrain.ru/news/zaderzhali_zhurnalistov_dozhdja-421907/?utm_source=facebook&utm_medium=social&utm_campaign=news& utm_term=421907

DP.ru. (2015, April 17). Na Ukraine ubita zhurnalist Ol'ga Moroz. *DP.ru.* www.dp.ru/ a/2015/04/17/Na_Ukraine_ubita_zhurnalis

Dugin, A. (2014, May 22). Rozhdenie Novorossii. *Novorossia.su.* https://web.archive .org/web/20171109134821/https://novorossia.su/news/rozhdenie-novoroccii

Dyczok, M. (2016). *Ukraine's Euromaidan: Broadcasting through Information Wars with Hromadske Radio.* E-International Relations Publishing.

Eady, G., Pashkalis, T., Zilinsky, J., Bonneau, R., Nagler, J., & Tucker, J. A. (2023). Exposure to the Russian Internet Research Agency foreign influence campaign on Twitter in the 2016 US election and its relationship to attitudes and voting behavior. *Nature Communications, 14*(62). https://doi.org/10.1038/s41467-022-35576-9

Eckel, M. (2021, May 19). Did the West promise Moscow that NATO would not expand? Well, it's complicated. *Radio Free Europe/Radio Liberty.* www.rferl.org/ a/nato-expansion-russia-mislead/31263602.html

The Economist. (2014, May 11). Ukraine's bogus referendums: Alternate realities. *Economist.com.* www.economist.com/eastern-approaches/2014/05/11/alternate-realities

The Economist. (2022, May 19). Mantas Kvedaravicius was killed while filming the war in Ukraine. www.economist.com/culture/2022/05/19/mantas-kvedaravicius-was-killed-while-filming-the-war-in-ukraine

Edney, K. (2012). Soft power and the Chinese propaganda system. *Journal of Contemporary China, 21*(78), 899–914. https://doi.org/10.1080/10670564.2012 .701031

Edwards, M. (2014, June 9). Symbolism of the Donetsk People's Republic. *Open Democracy.* www.opendemocracy.net/en/odr/symbolism-of-donetsk-peoples-republic-flag-novorossiya/

Edwards, M. (2017, July 19). Little Russia, big dreams. *Open Democracy*. www
.opendemocracy.net/en/odr/little-russia-big-dreams-0/

Ekho Moskvy. (2014, May 30). Zapiski iz podpol'ia: Kak rabotaiut ukrainskie SMI na
Donbasse. *Echo.Msk.ru*. https://echo.msk.ru/blog/echomsk/1330988-echo/

El Mundo. (2017, August 25). Ucraina deporta a los periodistas españoles Antonio
Pampliega y Manuel Ángel Sastre tras ser retenidos durante 20 horas. *Elmundo.
es*. www.elmundo.es/television/2017/08/25/59a01663468aebe3258b462a.html

Elia, D. (2015, February 15). Post. *Twitter.com*. https://twitter.com/daniloeliatweet/
status/566916567762755584

Enakievskii Rabochii. (2015a, August 8). Evgeniia Samokhina provela priem v
Enakievo. *Enakievskii Rabochii*. http://gazeta-dnr.ru//?p=1032

Enakievskii Rabochii. (2015b, August 8). S miru po nitke. *Enakievskii Rabochii*. http://
gazeta-dnr.ru//?p=1051

Enakievskii Rabochii. (2016, February 11). Nalogovaia inspektsiia v g. Enakievo MDS
DNR informiruet. *Enakievskii Rabochii*. http://gazeta-dnr.ru//?p=20839

Erlingsson, C., & Brysiewicz, P. (2017). A hands-on guide to doing content analysis.
African Journal of Emergency Medicine, 7(3), 93–99. https://doi.org/10.1016/j
.afjem.2017.08.001

Espreso.tv. (2014, April 29). Luhans'ki separatysty pohrozhuiut' zakhopyty oblasne
telebachennia. *Espreso.tv*. https://espreso.tv/news/2014/04/29/luhanski_separa
tysty_pohrozhyuyut_zakhopyty_oblasne_telebachennya

Euromaidan Press. (2016, September 13). Soviet tactics: 'DNR' and 'LNR' 'embassies'
pop up in the EU. *Euromaidanpress.com*. http://euromaidanpress.com/2016/09/
13/soviet-tactics-another-dnr-lnr-embassy-pops-up-in-europe/

Euronews. (2022, September 28). Ukraine 'referendums': Full results for annexation
polls as Kremlin-backed authorities claim victory. www.euronews.com/2022/09/
27/occupied-areas-of-ukraine-vote-to-join-russia-in-referendums-branded-a-
sham-by-the-west

Fakty. (2014, August 6). Na Donbasse boeviki pokhitili predstavitelei Krasnogo
Krestea (video, foto). *Fakty.ua*. http://fakty.ua/185961-na-donbasse-boeviki-pohi
tili-predstavitelej-krasnogo-kresta-video-foto

Fedirko, T. (2020). Self-censorships in Ukraine: Distinguishing between the silences of
television journalism. *European Journal of Communication*, 35(1), 12–28. https://
doi.org/10.1177/0267323119897424

Fedirko, T. (2021). Liberalism in fragments: Oligarchy and the liberal subject in
Ukrainian news journalism. *Social Anthropology/Anthropologie Sociale*, 29(2),
471–489.

Fedorkova, T. (2014, March 16). Post. *Facebook.com*. www.facebook.com/photo.php?
fbid=616095688444185&set=a.200694316650993.55459.100001312796893&
type=1&stream_ref=10

Financial Times. (2015, February 12). Full text of the Minsk agreement. *FT.com*. www
.ft.com/content/21b8f98e-b2a5-11e4-b234-00144feab7de

Finnin, R. (2011). Nationalism and the lyric, or How Taras Shevchenko speaks to
compatriots dead, living, and unborn. *The Slavonic and East European Review*, 89
(1), 29–55. https://doi.org/10.5699/slaveasteurorev2.89.1.0029

Fisher, M. (2022, May 30). Frédéric Leclerc-Imhoff: French BFMTV journalist killed in Ukraine. *BBC News*. www.bbc.co.uk/news/world-europe-61638049

Flood, B. (2022, March 15). Fox News cameraman Pierre Zakrzewski killed in Ukraine: 'Absolutely heartbroken at the loss of a legend'. *Fox News*. www.foxnews.com/media/pierre-zakrzewski-fox-news-ukraine

Forbes. (2014, July 4). Glava LNR otpravil pravitel'stvo v otstavku. *Forbes.ru*. www.forbes.ru/news/261801-glava-lnr-otpravil-pravitelstvo-v-otstavku

Foxall, A. (2015). *The Ceasefire Illusion: An Assessment of the Minsk II Agreement between Ukraine and Russia* (Henry Jackson Society Policy Paper). Russia Studies Centre.

Freeden, M. (2001). Ideology: Political aspects. In N. J. Smelser & B. Baltes, eds., *International Encyclopedia of the Social & Behavioral Sciences* (pp. 7174–7177). Elsevier.

Friman, H. R. (2015). *The Politics of Leverage in International Relations: Name, Shame, and Sanction*. Palgrave Macmillan.

Futbol'nyi Soiuz Donetskoi Narodnoi Respubliki. (2019). Chempionat DNR Sezon 2016. *Fsdnr.com*. http://fsdnr.com/chempionat-dnr/chempionat-dnr-2016

Gaisford, R. (2014, April 28). Post. *Twitter.com*. https://twitter.com/richardgaisford/status/460815254361223168/photo/1

Galkin, V. (2014, April 25). Post. *Facebook.com*. www.facebook.com/vikgalkin/posts/745433815488050?stream_ref=10

Gatehouse, G. (2014, February 20). Ukraine crisis: Sniper fires from Ukraine media hotel. *BBC News*. www.bbc.co.uk/news/av/world-europe-26284100

Gati, C. (1999). Review: NATO Enlargement: Who, why, and how? *SAIS Review (1989–2003)*, *19*(2), 211–217.

Gaufmann, E. (2015). World War II 2.0: Digital memory of fascism in Russia in the aftermath of Euromaidan in Ukraine. *Journal of Regional Security*, *10*(1), 17–36.

Gazeta.ru. (2017, March 22). SMI: v Gretsii otkrylos' predstavitel'stvo DNR. *Gazeta.ru*. www.gazeta.ru/politics/news/2017/03/22/n_9826481.shtml

Gibbons-Neff, T. (2015, October 27). The unusual difficulty of tracking Russia's dead in Ukraine and Syria. *Washington Post*. www.washingtonpost.com/news/checkpoint/wp/2015/10/27/the-unusual-difficulty-of-tracking-russias-dead-in-ukraine-and-syria/?noredirect=on

Giglio, M. (2014, May 2). I should kill you right here. *Buzzfeed*. www.buzzfeednews.com/article/mikegiglio/i-should-kill-you-right-here

Giuliano, E. (2018). Who supported separatism in Donbas? Ethnicity and popular opinion at the start of the Ukraine crisis. *Post-Soviet Affairs*, *34*(2–3), 158–178. https://doi.org/10.1080/1060586X.2018.1447769

Glava Luganskoi Narodnoi Respubliki. (2014). *Ukaz o formirovanii Soveta Ministrov Luganskoi Narodnoi Respubliki*.

Godefroidt, A. (2014). *What's in a Frame? Framing of the Syrian War: A Comparative Analysis of European, American and Russian Newspapers* [KU Leuven]. www.academia.edu/9515903/What_s_in_a_Frame_Framing_of_the_Syrian_war

Goldgeier, J., & Itzkowitz Shifrinson, J. R. (2023). *Evaluating NATO Enlargement: From Cold War Victory to the Russia–Ukraine War*. Palgrave Macmillan.

Golos Respubliki. (2015a, November 12). Bor'ba za kubki zavershilas'. *Golos Respubliki*. http://gazeta-dnr.ru//?p=9433

Golos Respubliki. (2015b, November 20). 111 semei poluchat novye doma. *Golos Respubliki*. http://gazeta-dnr.ru//?p=10960

Gordeev, I. (2017, April 19). Rabota fonda Edinyi Donbass. *Gorlovka News*. http://gorlovka-news.su/novosti/novosti-gorlovki/1838-rabota-fonda-edinyj-donbass

Gordo, O., & Gal'skaia, O. (2017, July 18). Chto dlia donchan budet znachit' Malorossiia? *Komsomol'skaia Pravda*. www.kompravda.eu/daily/26706/3731023/

Gordon. (2014a, April 14). Donetskii zhurnalist: V Gorlovke gotoviatsia 'razrulit'' situatsiiu s neugodnymi SMI. *Gordonua.com*. http://gordonua.com/news/politics/doneckiy-zhurnalist-v-gorlovke-seychas-okazyvaetsya-davlenie-na-smi-18300.html

Gordon. (2014b, July 1). SMI: Pokhishchennogo zhurnalista donetskogo izdaniia 'OstroV' Chernova boeviki 'DNR' zastavili ryt' okopy. *Gordonua.com*. http://gordonua.com/news/war/smi-pohishchennogo-zhurnalista-doneckogo-izdaniya-ostrov-chernova-terroristy-iz-dnrzastavili-ryt-okopy-29779.html

Gorlovka.ua. (2016, September 20). Telekanaly, gazety i saity v okkupirovannykh gorodakh Donbassa: Kto govorit i pokazyvaet v Enakievo, Debal'tsevo, Toreze? (Chast' 1). *Gorlovka.ua*. http://gorlovka.ua/news/article/10457/

Gosudarstvennoe Predpriatie 'Pochta Donbassa'. (2017). Nashe vremia – Ezhenedel'naia gazeta goroda Dokuchaevska. *Postdonbass.com*. https://postdonbass.com/periodicheskie_izdaniya/nashe-vremya

Government of the Netherlands. (2018, May 25). MH17: The Netherlands and Australia hold Russia responsible. *Government.nl*. www.government.nl/latest/news/2018/05/25/mh17-the-netherlands-and-australia-hold-russia-responsible

Grant, T. D. (2015). Annexation of Crimea. *The American Journal of International Law, 109*(1), 68–95.

Greene, D. (2016). Dynamic-nmf: Dynamic topic modelling. *Github.com*. https://github.com/derekgreene/dynamic-nmf

Greene, D., & Cross, J. P. (2016). Exploring the political agenda of the European Parliament using a dynamic topic modeling approach. *CoRR, abs/1607.0*. http://arxiv.org/abs/1607.03055

Greenslade, R. (2014, July 21). Swedish reporters detained while reporting on MH17 tragedy. *Guardian*. www.theguardian.com/media/greenslade/2014/jul/21/press-freedom-malaysia-airlines-flight-mh17

Guardian. (1999, March 25). Yeltsin: Russia will not use force against NATO. *Guardian*. www.theguardian.com/world/1999/mar/25/russia

Gurkovskaia, N. (2014a, April 16). Dnepropetrovskie voennye, zablokirovannye na Pchelkino, prosiatsia domoi. *Novosti Kramatorska*. https://hi.dn.ua/index.php?option=com_content&view=article&id=45916&catid=55:kramatorsk&Itemid=147

Gurkovskaia, N. (2014b, April 18). Chem Kramatorsk zapomnitsia vsemu miru? (VIDEO). *Novosti Kramatorska*. https://hi.dn.ua/index.php?option=com_content&view=article&id=45969&catid=55:kramatorsk&Itemid=147

Haaretz. (2015, February 3). Ukraine led by 'miserable Jews,' says rebel leader. *Haaretz*. www.haaretz.com/jewish/2015-02-03/ty-article/ukraine-led-by-miserable-jews/0000017f-e6cb-d62c-a1ff-fefbc8430000

Hauter, J. (2021). *Civil War? Interstate War? Hybrid War? Dimensions and Interpretations of the Donbas Conflict in 2014–2020.* ibidem.

Hauter, J. (2023). *Russia's Overlooked Invasion: The Causes of the 2014 Outbreak of War in Ukraine's Donbas.* ibidem.

Henrikson, M. (2016). Nation-building in times of conflict: The discursive construction of Russian national identity through the Russo–Georgian war. PhD dissertation, University of Manchester.

Hindman, D. B. (1996). Community newspapers, community structural pluralism, and local conflict with nonlocal groups. *Journalism & Mass Communication Quarterly*, 73(3), 708–721. https://doi.org/10.1177/107769909607300315

Horodetskii, M. (2014, May 8). Torezskuiu gazetu 'Gorniak' razgromili separatisty. *Day.Kyiv.ua.* http://day.kyiv.ua/ru/article/media/torezskuyu-gazetu-gornyak-razgromili-separatisty

Hromadske. (2014, April 15). Roman Huba pro sytuatsiiiu v Slov'ians'ku. Video. *YouTube.com.* www.youtube.com/watch?v=ZRYyCtoNKWQ

Hromadske. (2015, February 28). Na Donechchyni zahynuv fotokor Serhii Nikolaev. *Hromadske.ua.* https://hromadske.ua/posts/na-donechchyni-zahynuv-fotokor-serhii-nikolaiev

Hromads'ke Radio. (2015, May 25). Luganskaia OGTRK vozobnovliaet veshchanie v Severodonetske – Gendirektor Shapovalov. *Hromadske.Radio.* https://hromadske.radio/en/podcasts/lyudy-donbasu/luganskaya-ogtrk-vozobnovlyaet-veshchanye-v-severodonecke-gendyrektor-shapovalov

Hromads'ke Radio. (2016). 104 dnia v plenu i kniga-ispoved' Sergeia Sakadynskogo. *Hromadske.Radio.*

Hryn, H. (2005). The executed Renaissance Paradigm revisited. *Harvard Ukrainian Studies*, 27(1/4). www.jstor.org/stable/41036862

Human Rights Watch. (2019, June 25). Ukraine: Investigate journalist's killing. *HRW.org.* www.hrw.org/news/2019/06/25/ukraine-investigate-journalists-killing

Hunin, J. (2014, February 6). Journalisten lusten ze hier rauw. *De Volkskrant.* www.volkskrant.nl/nieuws-achtergrond/journalisten-lusten-ze-hier-rauw~ba868007/

Hutchings, S., & Szostek, J. (2015). Dominant narratives in Russian political and media discourse during the Ukraine crisis. In A. Pikulicka-Wilcewska & R. Sakwa (eds.), *Ukraine and Russia.* E-International Relations Publishing.

Iarovaia, M. (2014, March 28). V plen popal programmist, kotoryi vel transliatsii iz Slavianska. *Ain.ua.* https://ain.ua/2014/04/28/v-slavyanske-vzyali-v-plen-programmista-kotoryj-strimil-zaxvat-sbu/

Iasinovatskii Vestnik. (2015a, December 6). Nachalo Donetskoi Narodnoi Respubliki (Aleksandr Zakharchenko). *Iasinovatskii Vestnik.* http://gazeta-dnr.ru//?p=13500

Iasinovatskii Vestnik. (2015b, December 9). Oda ob orekhe. *Iasinovatskii Vestnik.* http://gazeta-dnr.ru//?p=13904

Il'f, I., & Petrov, I. (2016). *Zolotoi Telenok.* Tekst.

Informator Media. (2014, May 25). 'Opolchentsami' s blokposta v Schast'e pokhishcheny luganskii zhurnalist, strimer i ikh voditel'. *Informator.Media.* http://informator.media/archives/258

Informatsionnoe Soprotivlenie. (2016, April 23). V Ilovaiske zapustili propagandistskuiu gazetu dlia zapudrivaniia mozgov mestnym zhiteliam, – IS. *Sprotyv.Info*. https://sprotyv.info/news/v-ilovajske-zapustili-propagandistskuju-gazetu-dlja-zapudrivanija-mozgov-mestnym-zhiteljam-is

Informatsionnyi Biulleten' Dokuchaevsk. (2015a, September 30). Spartakiadad 'Zdorovaia Molodezh' – Dostoianie Respubliki'. *Informatsionnyi Biulleten' Dokuchaevsk*. http://gazeta-dnr.ru//?p=5232

Informatsionnyi Biulleten' Dokuchaevsk. (2015b, November 19). I v Dokuchaevske est' svoi 'Zolotoi golos'. *Informatsionnyi Biulleten' Dokuchaevsk*. http://gazeta-dnr.ru//?p=10833

Ingram, H. J. (2016). *A Brief History of Propaganda during Conflict* (ICCT Research Paper). International Centre for Counter-Terrorism.

Insider. (2014a, March 2). U Donets'ku na prorosiis'komu mitingu napaly na zhurnalistiv tr'okh vydan'. *Theinsider.ua*. www.theinsider.ua/politics/5313846421723/

Insider. (2014b, June 28). V Donetskoi oblasti pokhitili dvukh ukrainskikh zhurnalistov, – OBSE. *Theinsider.ua*. www.theinsider.ua/rus/politics/53aeb2a69febc/

Institut Masovoï Informatsiï. (2014a, February 3). U Donets'ku inozemnoho zhurnalista ne pustili na pres-konferentsiiu gubernatora. *Imi.org.ua*. https://imi.org.ua/news/u-donetsku-inozemnogo-jurnalista-ne-pustili-na-pres-konferentsiyu-gubernatora/

Institut Masovoï Informatsiï. (2014b, February 10). Redaktsiiu 'Novostei Donbassa' vygnaly z prymishchennia, iake arenduvalos' pid ofis. *Imi.org.ua*. https://imi.org.ua/news/redaktsiyu-novostey-donbassa-vignali-z-primischennya-yake-arenduvalos-pid-ofis/

Institut Masovoï Informatsiï. (2014c, February 11). Na Donechchyny nevidomi zakydaly ofis telekanalu 'Kapri' zaimystymy pliashkami. *Imi.org.ua*. https://imi.org.ua/news/na-donechchini-nevidomi-zakidali-ofis-telekanalu-kapri-zaymistimi-plyashkami/

Institut Masovoï Informatsiï. (2014d, February 17). Boiovyky 'Motoroly' zatrymaly u Donets'ku Italiis'kykh zhurnalistiv. Zhodom vidpustyly. *Imi.org.ua*. http://imi.org.ua/news/boyoviki-motoroli-zatrimali-u-donetsku-italiyskih-jurnalistiv-zgodom-vidpustili/

Institut Masovoï Informatsiï. (2014e, February 21). U Donets'ku napaly na zhurnalista iakyi fotohrafuvav oblderzhadministratsiiu. *Imi.org.ua*. https://imi.org.ua/news/u-donetsku-napali-na-jurnalista-yakiy-fotografuvav-oblderjadministratsiyu/

Institut Masovoï Informatsiï. (2014f, February 28). V Artemivs'ku molodyky napaly na zhurnalistok. *Imi.org.ua*. https://imi.org.ua/news/v-artemivsku-molodiki-napali-na-jurnalistok/

Institut Masovoï Informatsiï. (2014g, March 3). U Donets'ku nevidomyi nakynuvsia na zhurnalistku Radio Svoboda, vyrvavshy fotokameru. *Imi.org.ua*. http://imi.org.ua/news/u-donetsku-nevidomiy-nakinuvsya-na-jurnalistku-radio-svoboda-virvavshi-fotokameru/

Institut Masovoï Informatsiï. (2014h, March 3). U Donets'ku pislia vyboriv holovy oblrady pochavsia shturm. Zablokovani bliz'ko 70 predstavnykiv ZMI (onovleno). *Imi.org.ua*. http://imi.org.ua/news/43288-u-donetsku-pislya-viboriv-

golovi-oblradi-pochavsya-shturm-zablokovani-blizko-70-predstavnikiv-zmi
.html
Institut Masovoï Informatsiï. (2014i, March 3). U Donets'ku protestuval'nyky pobyly
zhurnalistiv 'Pershoho dilovoho' i 'URA-Inform.Donbas'. *Imi.org.ua.* http://imi
.org.ua/news/u-donetsku-protestuvalniki-pobili-jurnalistiv-pershogo-dilovogo-i-
ura-informdonbas/
Institut Masovoï Informatsiï. (2014j, March 3). Zhurnalist 5 kanalu zaiavliaie, shcho u
Donets'ku na znimal'nu grupu vidkryto spravzhnie poliuvannia. *Imi.org.ua.*
http://imi.org.ua/news/jurnalist-5-kanalu-zayavlyae-scho-u-donetsku-na-zni
malnu-grupu-vidkrito-spravjne-polyuvannya/
Institut Masovoï Informatsiï. (2014k, March 4). U Kharkovi posylyly okhoronu
telekanalu SIMON cherez pohrozy nevidomykh. *Imi.org.ua.* https://imi.org.ua/
news/u-harkovi-posilili-ohoronu-telekanalu-simo-cherez-pogrozi-nevidomih-
i7613
Institut Masovoï Informatsiï. (2014l, March 6). Boiovyky zzalyshyly Krasnyi Luch bez
dvokh Ukraïns'kykh telekanaliv. *Imi.org.ua.* http://imi.org.ua/news/boyoviki-
zalishili-krasniy-luch-bez-dvoh-ukrajinskih-telekanaliv/
Institut Masovoï Informatsiï. (2014m, March 6). Telekanal 'Donbas' pereryvav efir
cherez zakhoplennia prorosiis'kymy aktyvistamy. *Imi.org.ua.* https://imi.org.ua/
news/telekanal-donbas-pererivav-efir-cherez-zahoplennya-prorosiyskimi-
aktivistami/
Institut Masovoï Informatsiï. (2014n, March 6). U Donets'ku prorosiis'ki syly
pohrozhuiut' zakhopyty kanaly 'Iunion' i 'Donbas'. *Imi.org.ua.* http://imi.org
.ua/news/u-donetsku-prorosiys-sili-pogrojuyut-zahopiti-kanali-yunion-i-
donbas/
Institut Masovoï Informatsiï. (2014o, March 11). U Kharkovi nevidomi ne puskali zhurnalistiv na pres-konferentsiiu Klichka. *Imi.org.ua.* https://imi.org
.ua/news/u-harkovi-nevidomi-ne-puskali-jurnalistiv-na-pres-konferentsiyu-
klichka-i7698
Institut Masovoï Informatsiï. (2014p, March 11). U Luhans'ku prorosiis'ki aktyvisty
poshkodyly zhurnalistam 'Ukraïny' ta NTN videokamery i vyhnaly z mitingu.
Imi.org.ua. http://imi.org.ua/news/u-lugansku-prorosiyski-aktivisti-poshkodili-
jurnalistam-ukrajini-ta-ntn-videokameri-i-vignali-z-mitingu/
Institut Masovoï Informatsiï. (2014q, March 11). U Luhans'ku prorosiis'ki aktyvisty
zakhopyly telekompaniiu 'IRTA'. *Imi.org.ua.* http://imi.org.ua/news/u-lugansku-
prorosiyski-aktivisti-zahopili-telekompaniyu-irta/
Institut Masovoï Informatsiï. (2014r, March 15). Prorosiis'ki mitinguval'nyky v
Donets'ku ne propuskaiut' ukraïns'kykh zhurnalistiv v SBU, de utrymuiut'
samoprogoloshenoho hubernatora. *Imi.org.ua.* http://imi.org.ua/news/proro
siyski-mitinguvalniki-v-donetsku-ne-propuskayut-ukrajinskih-jurnalistiv-v-sbu-
de-utrimuyut-samoprogoloshenogo-gubernatora/
Institut Masovoï Informatsiï. (2014s, March 17). U Kharkovi pid chas prorosiis'koho
mitinhu postrazhdav zhurnalist NTV. *Imi.org.ua.* https://imi.org.ua/news/u-har
kovi-pid-chas-prorosiyskogo-mitingu-postrajdav-jurnalist-ntv-i7783
Institut Masovoï Informatsiï. (2014t, March 25). U Kharkovi prorosiis'ki protestuval'nyky pobyly zhurnalista 'nazvychainykh novyn'. *Imi.org.ua.* https://imi.org

.ua/news/u-harkovi-prorosiyski-protestuvalniki-pobili-jurnalista-nadvzichaynih-novin-i7856

Institut Masovoï Informatsiï. (2014u, March 27). U Mariupoli prorosiis'ki mitinhuval'nyky napaly na dvokh zhurnalistiv. *Imi.org.ua.* https://imi.org.ua/news/u-mariupoli-prorosiyski-mitinguvalniki-napali-na-dvoh-jurnalistiv/

Institut Masovoï Informatsiï. (2014v, April 7). U Donets'ku namahalysia zakhopyty ODTRK. *Imi.org.ua.* https://imi.org.ua/news/u-donetsku-namagalisya-zahopiti-odtrk-i7939

Institut Masovoï Informatsiï. (2014w, April 7). U Kharkovi prorosiis'ki mitynhuval'-nyky napaly na zhurnalista 'Ukraïny'. *Imi.org.ua.* http://imi.org.ua/news/u-har kovi-prorosiyski-mitinguvalniki-napali-na-jurnalista-ukrajini/

Institut Masovoï Informatsiï. (2014x, April 7). U Luhans'ku na 'IRTI' nevidomi poranyly tr'okh okhorontsiv. Vlasnyku kanalu pohrozhuiut' spalyty dim. *Imi.org.ua.* http://imi.org.ua/news/u-lugansku-na-irti-nevidomi-poranili-troh-ohor ontsiv-vlasniku-kanalu-pogrojuyut-spaliti-dim/

Institut Masovoï Informatsiï. (2014y, April 10). U Donets'ku nevidomi pobyly bilorus'koho zhurnalista. *Imi.org.ua.* http://imi.org.ua/news/u-donetsku-nevidomi-pobili-biloruskogo-jurnalista/

Institut Masovoï Informatsiï. (2014z, April 12). U Donets'ku nevidomyi pidpalyv avto holovreda 'Novostei Donbassa'. *Imi.org.ua.* http://imi.org.ua/news/u-donetsku-nevidomiy-pidpaliv-avto-golovreda-novostey-donbassa/

Institut Masovoï Informatsiï. (2014aa, April 12). U Slov'ians'ku ozbroeni separatysty zakhopyly zhurnalistiv i zaboronyly pratsiuvaty. *Imi.org.ua.* https://imi.org.ua/news/u-slovyansku-ozbroeni-separatisti-zahopili-jurnalistiv-i-zaboronili-pratsyu vati-i7993

Institut Masovoï Informatsiï. (2014ab, April 13). Cherez zahrozu zakhoplennia u Donets'ku evakiuvaly spivrobitnykiv telekanalu 'Donbas'. *Imi.org.ua.* https://imi .org.ua/news/cherez-zagrozu-zahoplennya-u-donetsku-evakuyuvali-spivrobitni kiv-telekanalu-donbas-i7994

Institut Masovoï Informatsiï. (2014ac, April 14). U Horlivtsi vykraly redaktora saitu Gorlovka.ua (onovleno). *Imi.org.ua.* https://imi.org.ua/news/u-gorlivtsi-vikrali-redaktora-saytu-gorlovkaua-i8004

Institut Masovoï Informatsiï. (2014ad, April 15). U Donets'ku za ziomku pid ODA prorosiis'ki aktyvisty zatrymaly dvokh zhurnalistiv. *Imi.org.ua.* https://imi.org.ua/news/u-donetsku-za-zyomku-pid-oda-prorosiyski-aktivisti-zatrimali-dvoh-jurnalis tiv-i8012

Institut Masovoï Informatsiï. (2014ae, April 15). U horlivtsi holovred internet-TV poradyv svoïm zhurnalistam skhovatysia cherez vidmovu spivpratsiuvaty z separatystamy. *Imi.org.ua.* http://imi.org.ua/news/u-gorlivtsi-golovred-inter net-tb-poradiv-svojim-jurnalistam-shovatisya-cherez-vidmovu-spivpratsyu vati-z-separatistami/

Institut Masovoï Informatsiï. (2014af, April 15). U Kramators'ku hopniky pohrabu-valy mistsevoho blohera ta zlamaly iomu rebro. *Imi.org.ua.* https://imi.org.ua/news/na-vihidnih-u-kramatorsku-mistsevi-gopniki-pograbuvali-mistsevogo-blo gera-ta-zlamali-yomu-rebro-i8014

Institut Masovoï Informatsiï. (2014ag, April 17). Prorosiis'ki aktyvisty ledve ne pobyly u Donets'ku pol'skykh zhurnalistiv. *Imi.org.ua.* https://imi.org.ua/news/proro siyski-aktivisti-ledve-ne-pobili-u-donetsku-polskih-jurnalistiv-i8034

Institut Masovoï Informatsiï. (2014ah, April 17). U Slov'ians'ku separatysty vzialy v polon zhurnalista Serhiia Leftera. *Imi.org.ua.* https://imi.org.ua/news/u-slo vyansku-separatisti-vzyali-v-polon-jurnalista-sergiya-leftera-i8040

Institut Masovoï Informatsiï. (2014ai, April 18). U Slov'ians'ku separatysty pid chas nichnoho obshuku pohrabuvaly zhurnalista. *Imi.org.ua.* http://imi.org.ua/news/ u-slovyansku-separatisti-pid-chas-nichnogo-obshuku-pograbuvali-jurnalista/

Institut Masovoï Informatsiï. (2014aj, April 19). Zhurnalisty v Slov'ians'ku pryzupnyly robotu cherez peresliduvannia i pohrozy. *Imi.org.ua.* http://imi.org.ua/news/slo vyansk-opinivsya-v-informatsiyniy-blokadi-nsju/

Institut Masovoï Informatsiï. (2014ak, April 22). Ponad tyzhden' separatysty trymaiut' u Slov'ians'ku strimera, iakii transliuvav shturm SBU. *Imi.org.ua.* http://imi.org .ua/news/ponad-tijden-separatisti-trimayut-u-slovyansku-strimera-yakiy-trans lyuvav-shturm-sbu/

Institut Masovoï Informatsiï. (2014al, April 22). U Luhans'ku pobyly zhurnalista, iakyi znimav mitynh separatystiv. *Imi.org.ua.* http://imi.org.ua/news/u-lugansku-pobili-jurnalista-yakiy-znimav-miting-separatistiv/

Institut Masovoï Informatsiï. (2014am, April 22). U Slov'ians'ku vykraly tr'okh inozem-nykh zhurnalistiv, ale zhodom vidpustyly. *Imi.org.ua.* https://imi.org.ua/news/u-slovyansku-vikrali-troh-inozemnih-jurnalistiv-ale-zgodom-vidpustili-i8053

Institut Masovoï Informatsiï. (2014an, April 22). U Torezi rozhromyly ta pidpalyly redaktsiiu hazety 'Pro Horod'. *Imi.org.ua.* http://imi.org.ua/news/u-torezi-rozgro mili-ta-pidpalili-redaktsiyu-gazeti-pro-gorod/

Institut Masovoï Informatsiï. (2014ao, April 23). Na Donechchyni hazetu 'Provintsiia' zakydaly 'kokteiliamy Molotova'. *Imi.org.ua.* http://imi.org.ua/news/na-donech chini-gazetu-provintsiya-zakidali-kokteylyami-molotova/

Institut Masovoï Informatsiï. (2014ap, April 23). U Horlivtsi znyk fotozhurnalist Ievhen Hapych. *Imi.org.ua.* https://imi.org.ua/news/u-gorlivtsi-znik-fotojurnal ist-evgen-gapich-i8072

Institut Masovoï Informatsiï. (2014aq, April 24). Pid chas sthturmu u Mariupoli nevidomi napaly na zhurnalista ta rozbyly tekhniku. *Imi.org.ua.* https://imi.org.ua/news/pid-chas-shturmu-u-mariupoli-nevidomi-napali-na-jurnalista-ta-rozbili-tehniku/

Institut Masovoï Informatsiï. (2014ar, April 24). U Slov'ians'ku zhurnalistku 'Komsomolky' dva dni protrymaly u kameri. *Imi.org.ua.* https://imi.org.ua/news/u-slovyansku-jurnalistku-komsomolki-dva-dni-protrimali-u-kameri-i8081

Institut Masovoï Informatsiï. (2014as, April 25). Separatysty uvirvalysia do ofisu Donets'koho saitu. *Imi.org.ua.* http://imi.org.ua/news/separatisti-uvirvalisya-do-ofisu-donetskogo-saytu/

Institut Masovoï Informatsiï. (2014at, April 25). U Slov'ians'ku zakhopyly zhurnalista ZIK. *Imi.org.ua.* https://imi.org.ua/news/u-slovyansku-zahopili-jurnalista-zik-i8108

Institut Masovoï Informatsiï. (2014au, April 27). Separatysty zakhopyly Donets'ku ODTRK i televezhu. *Imi.org.ua.* http://imi.org.ua/news/separatisti-zahopili-donetsku-odtrk-i-televeju/

Institut Masovoï Informatsiï. (2014av, April 27). U Slov'ians'ku znyk zhurnalist Volyn'Post Serhii Shapoval. *Imi.org.ua.* http://imi.org.ua/news/u-slovyansku-znik-jurnalist-volinpost-sergiy-shapoval/

Institut Masovoï Informatsiï. (2014aw, April 28). U Donets'ku prorosiis'ki aktyvisty rozbyly holovu zhurnalistu 'Dzerkala Tyzhnia'. *Imi.org.ua.* http://imi.org.ua/news/u-donetsku-na-mitingu-prorosiyski-aktivisti-rozbili-golovu-jurnalistu-dzer kala-tijnya/

Institut Masovoï Informatsiï. (2014ax, April 28). U slov'ians'ku zhurnalista Ruslana Kukharchuka dopytuvaly z paketom na holovi ta pohrozhuvaly vbyby. *Imi.org. ua.* https://imi.org.ua/news/u-slovyansku-jurnalist-ruslan-kuharchuk-potrapiv-v-polon-dopituvali-z-paketom-na-golovi-ta-i8120

Institut Masovoï Informatsiï. (2014ay, April 29). Luhans'ki separatysty pohrozhuiut'-zakhoipyty oblasne telebachennia. *Imi.org.ua.* http://imi.org.ua/news/luganski-separatisti-pogrojuyut-zahopiti-oblasne-telebachennya/

Institut Masovoï Informatsiï. (2014az, April 29). U Donets'ku z nozhem napaly na zhurnalistiv Brytans'koho kanalu ITV. *Imi.org.ua.* http://imi.org.ua/news/u-donetsku-z-nojem-napali-na-jurnalistiv-britanskogo-kanalu-itv/

Institut Masovoï Informatsiï. (2014ba, April 30). U Luhans'ku pid chas aktsiï pobyly holovreda hazety 'Hryvna Plius'. *Imi.org.ua.* http://imi.org.ua/news/u-lugansku-pid-chas-aktsiji-pobili-golovreda-gazeti-grivna-plyus/

Institut Masovoï Informatsiï. (2014bb, April 30). Zhurnalistka 'Hazety po-Ukraïns'ky' vyïkhala z Donets'ka cherez zahrozu zhyttiu (onovleno). *Imi.org.ua.* http://imi .org.ua/news/jurnalistka-gazeti-po-ukrajinski-vijihala-z-donetsku-cherez-zagrozu-jittyu/

Institut Masovoï Informatsiï. (2014bc, May 1). U Luhans'ku ozbroeni liudy zamist' pershoho natsional'noho vvimknuly 'Rossiiu 24'. *Imi.org.ua.* http://imi.org.ua/news/u-lugansku-ozbroeni-lyudi-zamist-pershogo-natsionalnogo-vvimknuli-ros siyu-24/

Institut Masovoï Informatsiï. (2014bd, May 2). Separatysty vykraly amerikans'koho zhurnalista v Slov'ians'ku. *Imi.org.ua.* http://imi.org.ua/news/separatisti-vikrali-amerikanskogo-jurnalista-v-slovyansku/

Institut Masovoï Informatsiï. (2014be, May 2). V Donets'kii oblasti znykly znimal'ni hrupy SkyNews (Brytaniia) i CBS (SShA). *Imi.org.ua.* http://imi.org.ua/news/na-donechchini-propali-znimalni-grupi-skynews-britaniya-i-cbs-ssha/

Institut Masovoï Informatsiï. (2014bf, May 3). V Luhans'ku vidkliuchyly '1+1', 5 kanal ta pershyi natsional'nyi. *Imi.org.ua.* http://imi.org.ua/news/v-lugansku-vidklyu chili-11-5-kanal-ta-pershiy-natsionalniy/

Institut Masovoï Informatsiï. (2014bg, May 4). U Luhans'ku napaly na zhurnalista. *Imi.org.ua.* http://imi.org.ua/news/u-lugansku-napali-na-jurnalista/

Institut Masovoï Informatsiï. (2014bh, May 6). U Donets'ku obstrilialy dachu holov-noho redaktora 'Ostrova'. *Imi.org.ua.* http://imi.org.ua/news/u-donetsku-obstri lyali-dachu-golovnogo-redaktoru-ostrovva/

Institut Masovoï Informatsiï. (2014bi, May 6). U Stakhanovi likari vpravlialy ruku zhurnalistsi, na iaku nakynulasia ahresyvna zhinka. *Imi.org.ua.* http://imi.org.ua/news/u-stahanovi-likari-vpravlyali-ruku-jurnalisttsi-na-yaku-nakinulasya-agre sivna-jinka/

Institut Masovoï Informatsiï. (2014bj, May 7). U Luhans'ku nevidomi obstrilialy budynok spivvlasnyka telekompaniï IRTA. *Imi.org.ua.* http://imi.org.ua/news/u-lugansku-nevidomi-obstrilyali-budinok-spivvlasnika-telekompanji-irta/

Institut Masovoï Informatsiï. (2014bk, May 7). Znyk Mariupol's'kyi zhurnalist Mykola Riabchenko. *Imi.org.ua.* http://imi.org.ua/news/znik-donetskiy-jurnalist-mikola-ryabchenko/

Institut Masovoï Informatsiï. (2014bl, May 8). Cherez peresliduvannia dvoe Donets'kikh zhurnalistiv pereïkhaly na L'vivshchynu. *Imi.org.ua.* http://imi.org.ua/news/cherez-peresliduvannya-dvoe-donetskih-jurnalistiv-perejihali-na-lvivschinu/

Institut Masovoï Informatsiï. (2014bm, May 8). Ozbroeni separatysty, pohgozhuiuchy zhhurnalistam, zakryly hazetu 'Provintsiia'. *Imi.org.ua.* http://imi.org.ua/news/ozbroeni-separatisti-pogrojuyuchi-jurnalistam-zakrili-gazetu-provintsiya/

Institut Masovoï Informatsiï. (2014bn, May 9). U Donets'ku separatysty zakhopyly telekanal 'Iunion'. *Imi.org.ua.* http://imi.org.ua/news/u-donetsku-separatisti-zahopili-telekanal-yunion/

Institut Masovoï Informatsiï. (2014bo, May 9). U Lysychans'ku vidkliuchyly '1+1'. *Imi.org.ua.* http://imi.org.ua/news/u-lisichansku-vidklyuchili-11/

Institut Masovoï Informatsiï. (2014bp, May 9). U Severodonets'ku separatysty pid zahrozoiu rozpravy zmusyly vidkliuchyty Ukraïns'ki telekanaly. *Imi.org.ua.* http://imi.org.ua/news/u-severodonetsku-separatisti-pid-zagrozoyu-rozpravi-zmusili-vidklyuchiti-ukrajinski-telekanali/

Institut Masovoï Informatsiï. (2014bq, May 9). U Slov'ians'ku boiovyky dekil'ka hodyn trymaly u poloni zhurnalistiv ICTV. *Imi.org.ua.* http://imi.org.ua/news/u-slovyansku-boyoviki-dekilka-godin-trimali-u-poloni-jurnalistiv-ictv/ https://ictv.ua/ru/index/read-news/id/1514513/

Institut Masovoï Informatsiï. (2014br, May 10). U Kramators'ku chereez pohrozy pidpalu zakrylas' hazeta 'Privet/Novosty Kramatorska'. *Imi.org.ua.* http://imi.org.ua/news/u-kramatorsku-cherez-pogrozi-pidpalu-zakrilas-gazeta-privet-novosti-kramatorska/

Institut Masovoï Informatsiï. (2014bs, May 10). U Mariupoli poraneno zhurnalista kanalu RT. *Imi.org.ua.* http://imi.org.ua/news/u-mariupoli-poraneno-jurnalista-kanalu-rt/

Institut Masovoï Informatsiï. (2014bt, May 12). Pid tyskom separatystiv kerivnytstvo 'Provintsiï' pryznachylo zastupnykom holovreda liudynu DNR. *Imi.org.ua.* http://imi.org.ua/news/pid-tiskom-separatistiv-kerivnitstvo-provintsiji-priznachilo-zastupnikom-golovreda-lyudinu-dnr/

Institut Masovoï Informatsiï. (2014bu, May 12). U Krasnomu Luchi naperedodni psevdoreferendumu provaider vymknuv Ukraïns'ki telekanaly. *Imi.org.ua.* http://imi.org.ua/news/u-krasnomu-luchi-naperedodni-psevdoreferendumu-provayder-vimknuv-ukrajinski-telekanali/

Institut Masovoï Informatsiï. (2014bv, May 12). V Artemivs'ku ta Konstiantynivtsi vikliuchyly kanaly '1+1 Media'. *Imi.org.ua.* http://imi.org.ua/news/v-artemivsku-ta-kostyantinivtsi-vidklyuchili-kanali-11-media/

Institut Masovoï Informatsiï. (2014bw, May 12). V Artemivs'ku vykraly rosiis'koho zhurnalista Pavla Kanyhina. *Imi.org.ua.* http://imi.org.ua/news/v-artemivsku-vikrali-rosiyskogo-jurnalista/

Institut Masovoï Informatsiï. (2014bx, May 13). Samoprohloshenyi 'Hubernator' Luhanshchiny nakazav vidkliuchyty ukraïns'ki 'profashists'ki telekanaly'. *Imi. org.ua.* http://imi.org.ua/news/samoprogolosheniy-gubernator-luganschini-naka zav-vidklyuchiti-ukrajinski-profashistski-telekanali/

Institut Masovoï Informatsiï. (2014by, May 13). U Donets'ku ozbroeni boiovyky zmusyly vymknuty 'Radio Era FM'. *Imi.org.ua.* http://imi.org.ua/news/u-donetsku-ozbroeni-boyoviki-zmusili-vimnkuti-radio-era-fm/

Institut Masovoï Informatsiï. (2014bz, May 13). Zhurnalisty Severedonets'koho saitu 'Moi Horod' vyïkhaly z mista cherez mozhlyvist' vykradennia. *Imi.org.ua.* http:// imi.org.ua/news/jurnalisti-severodonetskogo-saytu-moy-gorod-vijihali-z-mista-cherez-mojlivist-vikradennya/

Institut Masovoï Informatsiï. (2014ca, May 14). Zhurnalistam, iaki ne pidkoriaiut'sia Donets'kii psevdorespublitsi, pohrozhuiut' rozpravoiu. *Imi.org.ua.* http://imi.org .ua/news/jurnalistam-yaki-ne-pidkoryayutsya-donetskiy-psevdorespublitsi-pogrojuyut-rozpravoyu/

Institut Masovoï Informatsiï. (2014cb, May 16). U Severodonets'ku operator znovu vymknuv 5 kanal ta TVI. *Imi.org.ua.* http://imi.org.ua/news/u-severodonetsku-operator-pid-zagrozoyu-rozpravi-vimknuv-5-kanal-ta-tvi/

Institut Masovoï Informatsiï. (2014cc, May 19). Terorysty u cherhovyi raz obstrilialy televezhu poblyzu Slov'ians'ka. *Imi.org.ua.* http://imi.org.ua/news/teroristi-u-chergoviy-raz-obstrilyali-televeju-poblizu-slovyanska/

Institut Masovoï Informatsiï. (2014cd, May 21). Terorysty dva tyzhni trymaly u poloni u Donets'ku Ukraïns'ku zhurnalistku. *Imi.org.ua.* http://imi.org.ua/news/teror isti-dva-tijni-trimali-u-poloni-u-donetsku-ukrajinsku-jurnalistku/

Institut Masovoï Informatsiï. (2014ce, May 22). DNR pohrozhue redaktsiï 'Segodnia' u Donets'ku i zmushue pospryiaty zniaty hazetu z prodazhu. *Imi.org.ua.* http:// imi.org.ua/news/predstavniki-dnr-pogrojuyut-redaktsiji-segodnya-u-donetsku-ta-zmushuyut-pospriyati-znyati-gazetu-z-prodaju/

Institut Masovoï Informatsiï. (2014cf, May 23). DNR vykrala chastynu tyrazhu donets'koho profspilkovoho biuletenia. *Imi.org.ua.* http://imi.org.ua/news/dnr-vikrala-chastinu-tiraju-donetskogo-profspilkovogo-byuletenya/

Institut Masovoï Informatsiï. (2014cg, May 25). Frantsuz'kii fotohraf poranenyi pid Slov'ians'kom. *Imi.org.ua.* http://imi.org.ua/news/frantsuzkiy-fotograf-porane niy-pid-slovyanskom/

Institut Masovoï Informatsiï. (2014ch, May 25). Pid Slov'ians'kom vbyto italiis'koho fotoreportera. *Imi.org.ua.* https://imi.org.ua/news/pid-slovyanskom-vbito-italiys kogo-fotoreportera/

Institut Masovoï Informatsiï. (2014ci, May 25). V Alchevs'ku na vymohu terorystiv vidkliuchyly 5 ukraïns'kykh telekaniv. *Imi.org.ua.* http://imi.org.ua/news/v-alchevsku-na-vimogu-teroristiv-vidklyuchili-5-ukrajinskih-telekaniv/

Institut Masovoï Informatsiï. (2014cj, May 26). Cherez Ukraïns'kii prapor terorysty vzialy u zaruchnyky dvokh zhurnalistiv. *Imi.org.ua.* http://imi.org.ua/news/cherez-ukrajinskiy-prapor-separatisti-vzyali-u-zaruchniki-pid-luganskom-dvoh-jurnalistiv/

Institut Masovoï Informatsiï. (2014ck, May 26). Holovred 'Novosti Kramatorska' vyïkhav z Donechchyny. Redaktsiia pratsioe pid tyskom DNR. *Imi.org.ua.*

http://imi.org.ua/news/golovred-novosti-kramatorska-vijihav-z-donechchini-redaktsiya-pratsyue-pid-tiskom-dnr/

Institut Masovoï Informatsiï. (2014cl, May 27). U Luhans'ku kabel'nyi operator pvernuv '1+1' u svoiu merezhu. *Imi.org.ua.* http://imi.org.ua/news/u-lugansku-kabelniy-operator-povernuv-11-u-svoyu-mereju/

Institut Masovoï Informatsiï. (2014cm, May 31). LNR prypynyla diial'nist' telekanalu IRTA. *Imi.org.ua.* https://imi.org.ua/news/lnr-pripinila-diyalnist-telekanalu-irta-i8434

Institut Masovoï Informatsiï. (2014cn, May 31). U Luhans'ku znykly chotyty Ukraïns'ki telekanaly. *Imi.org.ua.* http://imi.org.ua/news/u-lugansku-znikli-cho tiri-ukrajinski-telekanali/

Institut Masovoï Informatsiï. (2014co, June 2). Cherez tysk terorystiv zhurnalisty 'Segodnia v Severodonetske' vyïkhaly z Luhanshchyny. *Imi.org.ua.* http://imi .org.ua/news/cherez-tisk-teroristiv-jurnalisti-segodnya-v-severodonetske-viji hali-z-luganschini/

Institut Masovoï Informatsiï. (2014cp, June 2). Ozbroeny boiovyky u Donets'ku uvyshli do vydavnytstva i zaiavyly, shcho berut' ioho 'pid okhoronu'. *Imi.org.ua.* http://imi .org.ua/news/ozbroeni-boyoviki-u-donetsku-uvishli-do-vidavnitstva-i-zayavili-scho-berut-yogo-pid-ohoronu/

Institut Masovoï Informatsiï. (2014cq, June 2). Terorysty vyvezly golovreda 'Vechernoho Donetska' u nevidomomu napriamku. *Imi.org.ua.* http://imi.org .ua/news/ozbroeni-boyoviki-zablokuvali-redaktsiyu-vechernego-donetska-i-vima gayut-zustrichi-z-golovredom/

Institut Masovoï Informatsiï. (2014cr, June 2). U Makiïvtsy terorysty DNR vidkliuchyly dekil'ka Ukraïns'kykh telekanaliv. *Imi.org.ua.* http://imi .org.ua/news/u-makijivtsi-teroristi-dnr-vidklyuchili-dekilka-ukrajinskih-telekanaliv/

Institut Masovoï Informatsiï. (2014cs, June 2). U poloni terorystiv u Donets'ku pivdoby proviv zhurnalist STB. *Imi.org.ua.* http://imi.org.ua/news/u-poloni-teror istiv-u-donetsku-pivdobi-proviv-jurnalist-stb/

Institut Masovoï Informatsiï. (2014ct, June 2). U Severodonets'ku 'zachystyly' mistsevyi internet. *Imi.org.ua.* http://imi.org.ua/news/u-severodonetsku-zachistili-mistseviy-internet/

Institut Masovoï Informatsiï. (2014cu, June 3). Gazety 'Donbass' i 'Vechernyi Donetsk' zakrylys' cherez vymohu boiovykiv zminyty redaktsiinu polityku. *Imi.org.ua.* http://imi.org.ua/news/gazeti-donbass-i-vecherniy-donetsk-zakri lis-cherez-vimogu-boyovikiv-zminiti-redaktsiynu-politiku/

Institut Masovoï Informatsiï. (2014cv, June 10). U Luhans'ku kabel'nyi operator vymykae '1+1' na vypuskakh novyn. *Imi.org.ua.* http://imi.org.ua/news/u-lugansku-kabelniy-operator-vimikae-11-na-vipuskah-novin/

Institut Masovoï Informatsiï. (2014cw, June 17). Luhans'kyi zhurnalist zmushenyi buv zalyshyty dim ta pereïkhav do Luts'ka. *Imi.org.ua.* http://imi.org.ua/news/lugans kiy-jurnalist-zmusheniy-buv-zalishiti-dim-i-perejihav-do-lutska/

Institut Masovoï Informatsiï. (2014cx, June 17). Pomer poranennyi zhurnalist VGTRK ta zahynuv zvukorezhyser telekanalu. *Imi.org.ua.* http://imi.org.ua/news/pomer-poraneniy-jurnalist-vgtrk/

Institut Masovoï Informatsiï. (2014cy, June 17). U Makiïvtsi boiovyky DNR vidvezly redaktora hazety i dyrektora vydavnytstva u nevidomomu napriamku. *Imi.org. ua.* http://imi.org.ua/news/u-makijivtsi-boyoviki-dnr-vidvezli-redaktora-gazeti-u-nevidomomu-napryamku/

Institut Masovoï Informatsiï. (2014cz, June 25). Redaktor vydannia 'S'ohodni v Severodonets'ku' zaiavliaie pro pohrozy i prosyt' militsiiu ioho zakhystyty. *Imi. org.ua.* http://imi.org.ua/news/redaktor-vidannya-sogodni-v-severodonetsku-zayavlyae-pro-pogrozi-i-prosit-militsiyu-yogo-zahistiti/

Institut Masovoï Informatsiï. (2014da, July 1). Boiovyky LNR vzialy v polon zhurnalistku ta operatora Hromads'koho TV (onovleno). *Imi.org.ua.* http://imi.org.ua/news/boyoviki-lnr-vzyali-v-polon-jurnalistku-ta-operatora-gromadskogo-tb/

Institut Masovoï Informatsiï. (2014db, July 1). Pid Slov'ians'kom u rezul'tati obstrilu obvalylasia televezha. *Imi.org.ua.* http://imi.org.ua/news/pid-slovyanskom-u-rezultati-obstrilu-obvalilasya-televeja/

Institut Masovoï Informatsiï. (2014dc, July 1). Rosiis'kyi REN TV zaiavliae, shcho na Luhanshchyni kontuzheni ïkh korespondente i operator. *Imi.org.ua.* http://imi.org.ua/news/rosiyskiy-ren-tv-zayavlyae-scho-na-luganschini-kontujeni-jih-korespondent-i-operator/

Institut Masovoï Informatsiï. (2014dd, July 1). U Luhans'ku znykla nyzka Ukraïns'kykh telekanaliv. *Imi.org.ua.* http://imi.org.ua/news/u-lugansku-znikla-nizka-ukrajinskih-telekanaliv/

Institut Masovoï Informatsiï. (2014de, July 9). Znimal'na hrupa 'Intera' potrapyla pid minometnyi obstril. *Imi.org.ua.* http://imi.org.ua/news/znimalna-grupa-intera-potrapila-pid-minometniy-obstril/

Institut Masovoï Informatsiï. (2014df, July 14). Rosiis'ki zhurnalisty potrapyly pid obstril u Luhans'ku. *Imi.org.ua.* http://imi.org.ua/news/rosiyski-jurnalisti-potrapili-pid-obstril-u-lugansku/

Institut Masovoï Informatsiï. (2014dg, July 16). U Donets'ku vidkliuchyly usi Ukraïns'ki kanaly. *Imi.org.ua.* http://imi.org.ua/news/u-slovyansku-ponovili-movlennya-pershogo-natsionalnogo-i-5-kanalu/

Institut Masovoï Informatsiï. (2014dh, July 17). U Luhans'ku terorysty pobyly redaktora i pohrabuvaly redaktsiiu saitu 'Polityka-2.0'. *Imi.org.ua.* http://imi.org.ua/news/u-lugansku-teroristi-pobili-redaktora-i-pograbuvali-redaktsiyu-saytu-politika-20/

Institut Masovoï Informatsiï. (2014di, July 22). U Donets'ku terorysty napaly na zhurnalistku 'Novosti Donbassa'. *Imi.org.ua.* http://imi.org.ua/news/u-donetsku-teroristi-napali-na-jurnalistku-novosti-donbassa/

Institut Masovoï Informatsiï. (2014dj, July 23). U Donets'ku terorysty zatrymaly pol's'koho zhurnalista. Zhodom vidpustyly. *Imi.org.ua.* http://imi.org.ua/news/u-donetsku-teroristi-zatrimali-polskogo-jurnalista-yakiy-fotografuvav-budivlyu-zaliznitsi/

Institut Masovoï Informatsiï. (2014dk, July 30). Terorysty u Donets'ku vymahaiut' vid provaideriv vidkliuchyty vsi Ukraïns'ki kanali, v tomu chysli i rozvazhal'ni. *Imi. org.ua.* http://imi.org.ua/news/teroristi-u-donetsku-vimagayut-vid-provayderiv-vidklyuchiti-vsi-ukrajinski-kanali-v-tomu-chisli-i-rozvajalni/

Institut Masovoï Informatsiï. (2014dl, July 31). U Luhans'ku vidkliuchyly Ukraïns'ki telekanaly, a po radio klychut' u separatysty. *Imi.org.ua.* http://imi.org.ua/news/u-lugansku-vidklyuchili-ukrajinski-telekanali-a-po-radio-klichut-u-separatisti/

Institut Masovoï Informatsiï. (2014dm, August 1). U Stakhanovi vykraly dvokh zhurnalistiv. *Imi.org.ua*. http://imi.org.ua/news/u-stahanovi-vikrali-dvoh-jurnalistiv/

Institut Masovoï Informatsiï. (2014dn, August 3). U Donets'ku ozbroeni Dniprivtsi zakhopyly telekanal 'Iunion'. *Imi.org.ua*. http://imi.org.ua/news/u-donetsku-ozbroeni-dnrivtsi-zahopili-telekanal-yunion/

Institut Masovoï Informatsiï. (2014do, August 11). Na Luhanshchyni aresthtuvaly rosiis'ku dokumentalistku Beatu Bubinets'. V ATO zaznachyly, shcho ne aresthuvaly, a zupynyly. *Imi.org.ua*. http://imi.org.ua/news/na-luganschini-areshtu vali-rosiysku-dokumentalistku-beatu-bubinets-v-ato-zaznachili-scho-ne-areshtu vali-a-zupinili/

Institut Masovoï Informatsiï. (2014dp, August 12). Terorysty vykraly u Donets'ku bat'kiv mistsevoï zhurnalistky. *Imi.org.ua*. http://imi.org.ua/news/teroristi-vik rali-u-donetsku-batkiv-jurnalistki/

Institut Masovoï Informatsiï. (2014dq, August 15). U Krasnodoni tereorysty zabor-onyly fotohrafuvaty pid strakhom 'trybunalu'. *Imi.org.ua*. http://imi.org.ua/news/ u-krasnodoni-teroristi-zaboronili-fotografuvati-pid-strahom-tribunalu/

Institut Masovoï Informatsiï. (2014dr, August 19). Terorysty utrymuiut' z televezhi v zoni ATO. *Imi.org.ua*. http://imi.org.ua/news/teroristi-utrimuyut-3-televeji-v-zoni-ato/

Institut Masovoï Informatsiï. (2014ds, August 22). V 'DNR' rozpovily, shcho znaishly bilia Snizhnoho obhorile tilo rosiis'koho zhurnalista Stenina. *Imi.org.ua*. http:// imi.org.ua/news/v-dnr-rozpovili-scho-znayshli-bilya-snijnogo-obgorile-tilo-rosiyskogo-jurnalista-stenina/

Institut Masovoï Informatsiï. (2014dt, August 22). V 'DNR' rozpovily, shcho znaishly bilia snizhnoho obhorile tilo Rosiis'koho zhurnalista Stenina. *Imi.org.ua*. http:// imi.org.ua/news/v-dnr-rozpovili-scho-znayshli-bilya-snijnogo-obgorile-tilo-rosiyskogo-jurnalista-stenina/

Institut Masovoï Informatsiï. (2014du, August 26). Pid Donets'kom znykly dva zhurnalisty tyzhnevyka 'Krymskyi Telegraf'. *Imi.org.ua*. http://imi.org.ua/news/ pid-donetskom-znikli-dva-jurnalisti-tijnevika-kryimskiy-telegrafy/

Institut Masovoï Informatsiï. (2014dv, September 2). Ukraïns'kyi zhurnalist pidtverdyv, shcho buv u poloni rossis'kykh viis'kovykh. *Imi.org.ua*. http:// imi.org.ua/news/ukrajinskiy-jurnalist-pidtverdiv-scho-buv-u-poloni-rosiys kih-viyskovih/

Institut Masovoï Informatsiï. (2014dw, September 15). 'DNR' vymahae vid Donets'kykh ZMI reestruvatysia u 'ministersetvi informatsiï'. *Imi.org.ua*. http:// imi.org.ua/news/dnr-vimagae-vid-donetskih-zmi-reestruvatisya-u-ministerstvi-informatsiji

Institut Masovoï Informatsiï. (2014dx, September 30). Do polonu 'LNR' potrapyly zhurnalist 'vestei' Serhii Boiko i fotoreporter Oleksandr Harmatenko. *Imi.org.ua*. http://imi.org.ua/news/do-polonu-lnr-potrapili-jurnalist-vestey-sergiy-boyko-i-fotoreporter-oleksandr-garmatenko/

Institut Masovoï Informatsiï. (2014dy, September 30). Terorysty 'DNR' vymahaiut' vid provaideriv zablokuvaty 27 Donets'kykh saitiv. *Imi.org.ua*. http://imi.org.ua/ news/teroristi-dnr-vimagayut-vid-provayderiv-zablokuvati-27-donetskih-saytiv/

Institut Masovoï Informatsiï. (2014dz, October 8). Zhytlovyi kompleks ta robota zhurnalista. De mezha mizh pryvatnistu ta publichnistiu? *Imi.org.ua.* http://imi .org.ua/news/v-dnr-stvoryuyut-reestr-ukrajinskih-saytiv-yaki-mayut-namir-zablokuvati-timchuk/

Institut Masovoï Informatsiï. (2014ea, October 13). U Lysychans'ku namahalysia zakhopyty teleradiokompaniiu 'Aktsent'. *Imi.org.ua.* http://imi.org.ua/news/u-lisichansku-namagalisya-zahopiti-teleradiokompaniyu-aktsent/

Institut Masovoï Informatsiï. (2014eb, November 19). Luhans'kyi bloher zaiavyv, shcho za nym stezhat' nevidomi. *Imi.org.ua.* http://imi.org.ua/news/luganskiy-bloger-zayaviv-scho-za-nim-stejat-nevidomi/

Institut Masovoï Informatsiï. (2014ec, December 26). Separatysty vvazhaiut' zhurnalistku Espreso.tv zalevs'ku snaiperom i diznavachem, ta zbyraiut'sia ïï pokaraty. *Imi.org.ua.* http://imi.org.ua/news/separatisti-vvajayut-jurnalistku-espresotv-zalevsku-snayperom-i-diznavachem-ta-zbirayutsya-jiji-pokarati/

Institut Masovoï Informatsiï. (2015a, February 9). V Avdiïvtsi prybichnyky 'DNR'napaly na znimal'nu hrupu '112 Ukraïna'. *Imi.org.ua.* http://imi.org.ua/news/v-avdijivtsi-pribichniki-dnr-napali-na-znimalnu-grupu-112-ukrajina/

Institut Masovoï Informatsiï. (2015b, February 27). Terorysty 'DNR' zatrymuvaly dlia perevirky pol'skoho zhurnalista Pavla Pen'onzheka. *Imi.org.ua.* http://imi.org.ua/news/teroristi-dnr-zatrimuvali-dlya-perevirki-polskogo-jurnalista-pavla-penonjeka/

Institut Masovoï Informatsiï. (2015c, February 28). U piskakh unaslidok obstrilu zahynuv fotohraf 'Segodnia' Serhii Nikolaev. *Imi.org.ua.* https://imi.org.ua/news/u-piskah-zaginuv-fotograf-segodnya-sergiy-nikolaev/

Institut Masovoï Informatsiï. (2015d, March 16). Boiovyky 'DNR' pohrozhuiuit' ne puskaty na pidkontrol'ni ïm terytoriï Ukraïns'ki ZMI. *Imi.org.ua.* http://imi.org .ua/news/boyoviki-dnr-pogrojuyut-ne-puskati-na-pidkontrolni-jim-teritoriji-ukrajinski-zmi/

Institut Masovoï Informatsiï. (2015e, April 27). *U Konstiantynivtsi nevidomi pobyly vikna u redaktsiï hazety 'Provintsiia'.* http://imi.org.ua/news/u-kostyantinivtsi-nevidomi-pobili-vikna-u-redaktsiji-gazeti-provintsiya/

Institut Masovoï Informatsiï. (2015f, May 14). U Donets'ku boiovyky 'DNR' rozhromyly kvartyru zhurnalista 'Hromads'koho TV Donbasu'. *Imi.org.ua.* http://imi .org.ua/news/u-donetsku-boyoviki-dnr-rozgromili-kvartiru-jurnalista-gromads kogo-tb-donbasu/

Institut Masovoï Informatsiï. (2015g, June 9). Na vymohu 'DNR' Donets'kyi internet-provaider zablokuvav dostup do 39 ZMI. *Imi.org.ua.* http://imi.org.ua/news/na-vimogu-dnr-donetskiy-internet-provayder-zablokuvav-dostup-do-39-zmi/

Institut Masovoï Informatsiï. (2015h, August 10). 'DNR' zaboronyla Ukraïns'kym ZMI vysvitliuvaty khid 'Mistsevykh vyboriv'. *Imi.org.ua.* http://imi.org.ua/news/dnr-zaboronila-ukrajinskim-zmi-visvitlyuvati-hid-mistsevih-viboriv/

Institut Masovoï Informatsiï. (2015i, September 7). Pol's'ka zhurnalistka, iaka pyshe z ATO, zaiavliae pro pohrozy. *Imi.org.ua.* http://imi.org.ua/news/polska-jurna listka-yaka-pishe-z-ato-zayavlyae-pro-pogrozi/

Institut Masovoï Informatsiï. (2015j, September 18). Terorysty 'DNR' ta 'LNR' zaboroniaiut' inozemnym zhurnalistam pokazuvaty video z Rosiis'kym viis'kovymy—

Popova. *Imi.org.ua*. http://imi.org.ua/news/teroristi-dnr-ta-lnr-zaboronyayut-ino
zemnim-jurnalistam-pokazuvati-video-z-rosiyskim-viyskovimi-popova/
Institut Masovoï Informatsiï. (2015k, October 20). Na Donechchyni nevidomi rozbyly
vikna v ovisi saitu 06239. *Imi.org.ua*. http://imi.org.ua/news/na-donechchini-
nevidomi-rozbili-vikna-v-ofisi-saytu-06239/
Institut Masovoï Informatsiï. (2015l, November 13). V 'LNR' zaboronyly movlennia
Ukraïns'kykh telekanaliv. *Imi.org.ua*. http://imi.org.ua/news/v-lnr-zaboronili-
movlennya-nizki-ukrajinskih-telekanaliv/
Institut Masovoï Informatsiï. (2015m, December 16). 'Hromads'ke Radio' u
Luhans'ku boiovyky hlushat' 'Kazach'ym Radio'. *Imi.org.ua*. http://imi.org.ua/
news/gromadske-radio-u-lugansku-boyoviki-zaglushili-kazachim-radio/
Institut Masovoï Informatsiï. (2015n, December 29). U Luhans'ku separatysty hlushat'
'Radio 24'. *Imi.org.ua*. http://imi.org.ua/news/u-lugansku-separatisti-glushat-
radio-24/
Institut Masovoï Informatsiï. (2016a, February 10). V 'DNR' rozporiadylysia vikliu-
chyty maizhe vsi Ukraïn'ki telekanaly. *Imi.org.ua*. https://imi.org.ua/news/v-dnr-
rozporyadilasya-vidklyuchiti-mayje-vsi-ukrajinski-telekanali/
Institut Masovoï Informatsiï. (2016b, March 11). Analysis of media-situation in
southern and eastern oblasts of Ukraine: Donetsk oblast. *Imi.org.ua*. https://imi
.org.ua/en/articles/analysis-of-media-situation-in-southern-and-eastern-oblasts-
of-ukraine-donetsk-oblast/
Institut Masovoï Informatsiï. (2016c, May 11). Zhurnalist, iakyi e u spysku
'akredytovanykh' u 'DNR', zaiavyv pro pohrozy. *Imi.org.ua*. http://imi.org
.ua/news/jurnalist-yakiy-e-u-spisku-akreditovanih-u-dnr-zayaviv-pro-
pogrozi/
Institut Masovoï Informatsiï. (2016d, May 11). Zhurnalisty vymahaiut' vydalyty z
saitu 'Myrotvorets"informatsiiu pro svoïkh koleh. *Imi.org.ua*. http://imi.org.ua/
news/jurnalisti-vimagayut-vidaliti-z-saytu-mirotvorets-informatsiyu-pro-svojih-
koleg/
Institut Masovoï Informatsiï. (2016e, May 25). Separatysts'kyi sait vyklav spysky
zhurnalistiv, iaki otrymuvaly akreditatsiiu v zonu ATO. *Imi.org.ua*. http://imi
.org.ua/news/separatistskiy-sayt-viklav-spiski-jurnalistiv-yaki-otrimuvali-akredi
tatsiyu-v-zonu-ato/
Institut Masovoï Informatsiï. (2016f, July 20). U Kyevi vnaslidok vybukhu v mashyni
zahynuv zhurnalist Pavlo Sheremet (dop.). *Imi.org.ua*. http://imi.org.ua/news/u-
kievi-vid-vibuhu-v-mashini-zaginuv-jurnalist-pavlo-sheremet/
Institut Masovoï Informatsiï. (2016g, September 5). 'DNR' zablokuvala na Donbasi
movlennia '1+1' ta novoho kanalu. *Imi.org.ua*. http://imi.org.ua/news/dnr-zablo
kuvala-na-donbasi-movlennya-11-ta-novogo-kanalu/
Institut Masovoï Informatsiï. (2016h, October 18). Personal'ni dani zhurnalistiv
Donets'koï NTKU rozmistyly na saiti separatystiv. *Imi.org.ua*. http://imi.org.ua/
news/personalni-dani-jurnalistiv-donetskoji-ntku-rozmistili-na-sayti-
separatistiv/
Institut Masovoï Informatsiï. (2016i, December 27). Dani Kramators'koho zhurnalista
rozmistyly na saiti separatystiv. *Imi.org.ua*. http://imi.org.ua/news/dani-krama
torskogo-jurnalista-rozmistili-na-sayti-separatistiv/

Institut Masovoï Informatsiï. (2016j, December 27). U poloni 'LNR' znakhodyt'sia shche odyn luhans'kyi bloher. *Imi.org.ua.* http://imi.org.ua/news/u-poloni-lnr-znahoditsya-sche-odin-luganskiy-bloger/

Institut Masovoï Informatsiï. (2017a, March 23). Na terytoriï Donechchyny ta Luhanshchyny vvely obmezhennia dliia foto i videoziomky. *Imi.org.ua.* http://imi.org.ua/news/na-teritoriji-donechchini-ta-luganschini-vveli-obmejennya-dlya-foto-i-videozyomki/

Institut Masovoï Informatsiï. (2017b, April 27). 'LNR' oholosyla u rozshuk viis'kovykh korespondentiv 'Intera'. *Imi.org.ua.* http://imi.org.ua/news/lnr-ogolosila-u-rozshuk-viyskovih-korespondentiv-intera/

Institut Masovoï Informatsiï. (2017c, May 16). Poroshenko pidpysav ukaz pro blokuvannia v Ukraïni 'Vkontakte', 'Odnoklassnikov' ta Iandeksa. *Imi.org.ua.* http://imi.org.ua/news/poroshenko-pidpisav-ukaz-pro-blokuvannya-v-ukrajini-vkontakte-odnoklassnikov-ta-yandeksa/

Institut Masovoï Informatsiï. (2017d, December 27). Z polonu 'LNR' zvil'neno blohera Eduarda Nedeliaeva. *Imi.org.ua.* http://imi.org.ua/news/z-polonu-lnr-zvilneno-blohera-eduarda-njedjelyajeva/

Institut Masovoï Informatsiï. (2018a, March 7). Barometr Svobody Slova Za Liutyi 2018 Roku (Onovleno). *Imi.org.ua.* https://imi.org.ua/monitorings/barometr-svobody-slova-za-lyutyj-2018-roku-i28360

Institut Masovoï Informatsiï. (2018b, September 4). Barometr Svobody Slova za Serpen' 2018 Roku. *Imi.org.ua.* https://imi.org.ua/monitorings/barometr-svobody-slova-za-serpen-2018-roku-i28334

Institut Masovoï Informatsiï. (2019a, March 4). Barometr Svobody Slova za Liutyi 2019 Roku. *Imi.org.ua.* https://imi.org.ua/monitorings/barometr-svobody-slova-za-liutyy-2019-roku-i28314

Institut Masovoï Informatsiï. (2019b, July 4). Barometr Svobody Slova za Cherven' 2019 Roku. *Imi.org.ua.* https://imi.org.ua/monitorings/barometr-svobody-slova-za-cherven-2019-roku-i28279

Institut Masovoï Informatsiï. (2020, May 6). Barometr Svobody Slova za Kviten 2020 Roku. *Imi.org.ua.* https://imi.org.ua/monitorings/barometr-svobody-slova-za-kviten-2020-roku-i32940

Institut Masovoï Informatsiï. (2021, March 5). Barometr Svobody Slova za Liutyi 2021 Roku (Onovleno). *Imi.org.ua.* https://imi.org.ua/monitorings/barometr-svobody-slova-za-lyutyj-2021-roku-i37963

Institut Masovoï Informatsiï. (2022, May 30). Photographer and videographer Roman Zhuk killed in the war with Russia. *Imi.org.ua.* https://imi.org.ua/en/news/photographer-and-videographer-roman-zhuk-killed-in-the-war-with-russia-i45843

Interfaks-Ukraina. (2014a, March 2). V Donetske protestuiushchie izbili dvukh zhurnalistov. *Interfaks-Ukraina.* https://interfax.com.ua/news/general/193821.html

Interfaks-Ukraina. (2014b, June 27). Pod davleniem boevikov telekanaly ICTV i '12 kanal' v Donetske zamenili na rossiiskie —SNBO Ukrainy. *Interfax.com.ua.* https://interfax.com.ua/news/general/211240.html

Interfaks-Ukraina. (2014c, July 27). V zone ATO tiazhelo ranena korrespondent Espreso TV, grazhdanka Pol'shi —Press-tsentr ATO. *Interfax.com.ua.* https://interfax.com.ua/news/general/215631.html

Interfaks-Ukraina. (2014d, August 29). Roman Cherems'kyi potrapyv u polon do prybichnykiv samoproholoshenoï 'Luhans'koï narodnoï respubliky'. *Ua. Interfax.com.ua.* https://ua.interfax.com.ua/news/general/220667.html

Interfaks-Ukraina. (2016, August 1). U zoni ATO prodovzhuiut 'hlushyty' transliatsiiu ukraïns'kykh kanaliv. *Ua.Interfax.com.ua.* https://ua.interfax.com.ua/news/general/361342.html

Interfax-Ukraine. (2011, September 5). EU–Ukraine association deal might hit ratification problems if Tymoshenko situation remains unchanged. *Kyiv Post.* https://archive.kyivpost.com/article/content/ukraine-politics/eu-ukraine-association-deal-might-hit-ratification-112197.html

Interfax-Ukraine. (2014, April 7). Ukraine's Party of Regions expels presidential hopefuls Tigipko, Tsariov and Boiko. *En.Interfax.com.ua.* https://en.interfax.com.ua/news/general/199490.html

International Press Institute. (2022, March 1). Ukrainian camera operator Yevhenii Sakun killed in bombing of Kyiv TV tower. *Ipi.Media.* https://ipi.media/alerts/camera-operater-killed-in-bombing-of-a-kyiv-tv-tower/

IPress.ua. (2014, April 23). V Gorlovke ischez eshche odin zhurnalist —Foto. *Ipress. ua.* https://ipress.ua/ru/news/v_gorlovke_yschez_eshche_odyn_zhurnalyst__foto_61125.html

ITAR-TASS. (2014a, March 9). Fotokorrespondent ITAR-TASS zaderzhan v aeroportu Donetska i otpravlen obratno v Moskvu. *Tass.ru.* https://tass.ru/obschestvo/1032584

ITAR-TASS. (2014b, April 10). Demonstrators in Donetsk plan to create 'people's army'. *Tass.com.* https://tass.com/world/727352/amp

ITAR-TASS. (2014c, May 13). Na narodnogo gubernatora Luganskoi oblasti sversheno pokushenie. *Tass.ru.* https://tass.ru/mezhdunarodnaya-panorama/1183110

ITAR-TASS. (2014d, May 18). Glavoi provozglashennoi Luganskoi narodnoi respubliki izbran Valerii Bolotov. *Tass.ru.* https://tass.ru/mezhdunarodnaya-panorama/1195149

ITAR-TASS. (2014e, August 18). V DNR sozdano ministerstvo informatsii i sviazi. *Tass.ru.* https://tass.ru/mezhdunarodnaya-panorama/1386960

Iurasova, O. (2013, December 2). Na Kramatorskom evromaidane poiavilis' politicheskie flagi. *Novosti Kramatorska.* https://hi.dn.ua/index.php?option=com_content&view=article&id=40338&catid=55:kramatorsk&Itemid=147

Iurasova, O. (2014a, February 23). Maidanovtsev zabrosali iaitsami – Provokatsiia ne udalas'. *Novosti Kramatorska.* https://hi.dn.ua/index.php?option=com_content&view=article&id=43576&catid=55:kramatorsk&Itemid=147

Iurasova, O. (2014b, March 11). Gorozhane khotiat referenduma? *Novosti Kramatorska.* https://hi.dn.ua/index.php?option=com_content&view=article&id=44333&catid=55:kramatorsk&Itemid=147

Iurasova, O. (2014c, March 22). Organizatsiia invalidov i 'Pani' proshli marsh mira. *Novosti Kramatorska.* https://hi.dn.ua/index.php?option=com_content&view=article&id=44831&catid=55:kramatorsk&Itemid=147

Iurasova, O. (2014d, August 29). V patrioty s pelenok. *Novosti Kramatorska.* https://hi.dn.ua/index.php?option=com_content&view=article&id=49547&catid=55:kramatorsk&Itemid=147

Janowitz, M. (1967). *The Community Press in an Urban Setting: The Social Elements of Urbanism*. University of Chicago Press.

Joint Investigation Team. (2018, May 24). Update in criminal investigation MH17 disaster. *Politie.nl*. www.politie.nl/en/news/2018/mei/24/update-in-criminal-investigation-mh17disaster.html

Kalinina, E., & Menke, M. (2016). Negotiating the past in hyperconnected memory cultures: Post-Soviet nostalgia and national identity in Russian online communities. *International Journal of Media & Cultural Politics*, 12(1), 59–74.

Kanashevich, S., & Ul'ianova, Z. (2014, August 14). Glava LNR 'vremenno' ushel v otstavku iz-za raneniia. *RBC.ru*. www.rbc.ru/politics/14/08/2014/570420a89a794760d3d40b1a

Karp'iak, O. (2015, October 14). Pokrova: Prazdnik voinov, khristian i iazychnikov. *BBC Ukraina*. www.bbc.com/ukrainian/ukraine_in_russian/2015/10/151014_ru_s_pokrova_holiday

Karpins'ka, V. (2014, April 17). U Slov'ians'ku separatysty vzialy v polon zhurnalista. *Zaxid.net*. https://zaxid.net/u_slovyansku_separatisti_vzyali_v_polon_zhurnalista_n1306836

Kazachii Vestnik. (2016a, October 19). Opasnaia pereprava. *Kazachii Vestnik*. http://kazache.ru/#newspaper/kazachiy-vestnik-100/opasnaja-pereprava-9

Kazachii Vestnik. (2016b, November 2). Poekhali! *Kazachii Vestnik*. http://kazache.ru/#newspaper/kazachiy-vestnik-102/

Kazachii Vestnik. (2017a, February 15). Verny svoemu gorodu. *Kazachii Vestnik*. http://kazache.ru/#newspaper/kazachiy-vestnik-117/

Kazachii Vestnik. (2017b, August 9). Ni shagu nazad: V Narodnoi militsii LNR oprovergli informatsiiu o prodvizhenii VSU na Svetlodarskoi duge. *Kazachii Vestnik*. http://kazache.ru/#newspaper/kazachiy-vestnik-142/

Kazanskii, D. (2014, April 21). Post. *Facebook.com*. www.facebook.com/den.kazansky/posts/634478379965011?stream_ref=10

Kazanskii, D. (2020, February 5). Post. *Facebook.com*. www.facebook.com/photo.php?fbid=2811532862259541&set=a.180274162052104&type=3&theater

Keck, M. E., & Sikkink, K. (1998). *Activists beyond Borders: Advocacy Networks in International Politics*. Cornell University Press. www.jstor.org/stable/10.7591/j.ctt5hh13f

Kendall, B. (2014, March 19). Crimea crisis: Russian President Putin's speech annotated. *BBC News*. www.bbc.co.uk/news/world-europe-26652058

Kilner, J. (2022, March 6). Vladimir Putin overestimated the support he'd receive from Russian-speaking Ukrainians. *Telegraph*. www.telegraph.co.uk/world-news/2022/03/06/vladimir-putin-overestimated-support-receive-russian-speaking/

Kim, L. (2014, April 11). The Battle of Ilovaisk: Details of a massacre inside rebel-held eastern Ukraine. *Newsweek*. www.newsweek.com/2014/11/14/battle-ilovaisk-details-massacre-inside-rebel-held-eastern-ukraine-282003.html

Kirillov, D., & Dergachev, V. (2015, December 12). 'Batia' ne doekhal do svad'by. *Novaya Gazeta*. www.gazeta.ru/politics/2015/12/12_a_7962323.shtml

Klein, C., Clutton, P., & Polito, V. (2018). Topic modeling reveals distinct interests within an online conspiracy forum. *Frontiers in Psychology*, 9, 189. https://doi.org/10.3389/fpsyg.2018.00189

Klimova, M. (2015, September 19). Ukraina – Sakral'naia zhertva. *Makeevskii Rabochii.* http://gazeta-dnr.ru//?p=4227%0A

Kochegarka DNR. (2015, September 14). Nas ne dogoniat. *Kochegarka DNR.* http://gazeta-dnr.ru//?p=3997

Kohlbacher, F. (2006). The use of qualitative content analysis in case study research. *Forum Qualitative Sozialforschung/Forum: Qualitative Social Research, 7*(1). https://doi.org/10.17169/fqs-7.1.75

Kohut, Z. E. (1986). The development of a Little Russian identity and Ukrainian nationbuilding. *Harvard Ukrainian Studies, 10*(3–4), 559–576.

Kononov, I., & Khobta, S. (2015). Public opinion in the Donbas and Halychyna on the Ukraine's upheavals of winter 2013–summer 2014. In Viktor Stepanenk & Yaroslav Pylynskyi, eds., *Ukraine after the Euromaidan: Challenges and Hopes* (Vol. 13). Peter Lang. https://doi.org/10.3726/978-3-0351-0798-2

Korrespondent. (2012, July 13). Glavred gazety Rodnoe Priazov'e ne svyazyvaet isk Gazmanova s Korolevskoi. *Korrespondent.net.* https://korrespondent.net/ukraine/politics/1371729-glavred-gazety-rodnoe-priazove-ne-svyazyvaet-isk-gazmanova-s-korolevskoj

Korrespondent. (2014, April 19). Zhurnalisty zaiavliaiut o nevozmozhnosti rabotat' v Slavianske. *Korrespondent.net.* https://korrespondent.net/ukraine/politics/3351907-zhurnalysty-zaiavliauit-o-nevozmozhnosty-rabotat-v-slavianske

Korrespondent. (2015, July 18). *Zakharchenko zaiavil, chto zauvazhal Pravyi Sektor.* https://korrespondent.net/ukraine/politics/3541010-zakharchenko-zaiavyl-chto-zauvazhal-pravyi-sektor

Kostadinova, T. (2000). East European public support for NATO membership: Fears and aspirations. *Journal of Peace Research, 37*(2), 235–249.

Kotenko, A. L., Martyniuk, O. V., & Miller, A. I. (2011, August 16). 'Maloross': Evoliutsiia poniatiia do pervoi mirovoi voiny. *Novoe Literaturnoe Obozrenie.* http://aej.org.ua/analytics/1125.html

Kots, A. (2017, November 18). Zakhar Prilepin: Tsel' Malorossii – Ob'edinennoe gosudarstvo s Rossiei i Belorussiei. *Komsomol'skaia Pravda.* www.penza.kp.ru/daily/26705/3731002/

Kramer, A. E. (2014, November 2). Rebel-backed elections to cement status quo in Ukraine. *New York Times.* www.nytimes.com/2014/11/03/world/europe/rebel-backed-elections-in-eastern-ukraine.html?_r=0

Krutov, M. (2018, February 22). Byl v medaliakh, teper v 'Krestakh'. Soobshcheniia ob areste Igoria Plotnitskogo. *Radio Svoboda.* www.rbc.ru/rbcfreenews/6050e9789a79472c101f0fdc

Kuang, D., Choo, J., & Park, H. (2015). Nonnegative matrix factorization for interactive topic modeling and document clustering. In M. Celebi (ed.), *Partitional Clustering Algorithms* (pp. 215–243). Springer. https://doi.org/10.1007/978-3-319-09259-1_7

Kulyk, V. (2001). The politics of ethnicity in post-Soviet Ukraine: Beyond Brubaker. *Journal of Ukrainian Studies, 26*(1–2), 197–221.

Kulyk, V. (2006). Constructing common sense: Language and ethnicity in Ukrainian public discourse. *Ethnic and Racial Studies, 29*(2), 281–314. https://doi.org/10.1080/01419870500465512

Kulyk, V. (2011). Language identity, linguistic diversity and political cleavages: Evidence from Ukraine. *Nations and Nationalism*, *17*(3), 627–648. https://doi.org/10.1111/j.1469-8129.2011.00493.x

Kulyk, V. (2016). National identity in Ukraine: Impact of Euromaidan and the war. *Europe–Asia Studies*, *68*(4), 588–608. https://doi.org/10.1080/09668136.2016.1174980

Kulyk, V. (2018). Shedding Russianness, recasting Ukrainianness: The post-Euromaidan dynamics of ethnonational identifications in Ukraine. *Post-Soviet Affairs*, *34*(2–3), 119–138. https://doi.org/10.1080/1060586X.2018.1451232

Kuromiya, H. (1998). *Freedom and Terror in the Donbas: A Ukrainian-Russian Borderland, 1870s–1990s*. Cambridge University Press.

Kuromiya, H. (2008). The Donbas: The last frontier of Europe? In O. Schmidtke & S. Yekelchyk (eds.), *Europe's Last Frontier? Belarus, Moldova, and Ukraine between Russia and the European Union* (pp. 97–114). Palgrave Macmillan US. https://doi.org/10.1007/978-1-137-10170-9

Kuromiya, H. (2016, March 20). Pavel Gubarev as a 'Little Russian'. *Historians.ua*. www.historians.in.ua/index.php/en/avtorska-kolonka/1839-hiroaki-kuromiya-pavel-gubarev-as-a-little-russian

Kuromiya, H. (2019). The war in the Donbas in historical perspective. *The Soviet and Post-Soviet Review*, *46*(3), 245–262. https://doi.org/10.1163/18763324-04603003

Kuzio, T. (2017). Ukraine 'experts' in the West and Putin's military aggression: A new academic 'orientalism'? Cicero Foundation Great Debate Paper, 17/06.

Kyiv Post. (2014, May 5). Twenty-four people remain hostages in Donetsk Oblast. *Kyivpost.com*. www.kyivpost.com/article/content/war-against-ukraine/twenty-four-people-remain-hostages-in-donetsk-oblast-346360.html?cn-reloaded=1

Kyrychenko, Y., Brik, T., & Roozenbeek, J. (2024). In-group solidarity drives engagement on social media during intergroup conflict. Under review.

Landelijk Parket. (2018, May 24). Update in criminal investigation MH17 disaster. *Om.nl*. www.om.nl/onderwerpen/mh17-crash/@103196/update-criminal-o/

Lanet. (2014, May 8). Vynuzhdennoe otkliuchenie telekanalov. *Lanet.ua*. https://sdonetsk.lanet.ua/news/channels-off/

Larson, H. J. (2020). *Stuck: How Vaccine Rumors Start – And Why They Don't Go Away*. Oxford University Press.

Laruelle, M. (2015). *The 'Russian World': Russia's Soft Power and Geopolitical Imagination*. Center on Global Interests.

Laruelle, M. (2016). The three colors of Novorossiya, or The Russian nationalist mythmaking of the Ukrainian crisis. *Post-Soviet Affairs*, *32*(1), 55–74. https://doi.org/10.1080/1060586X.2015.1023004

LB.ua. (2014a, August 21). 'Dnipro-1' i armiia pryishly na dopomohu do sylovykiv v Ilovais'ku. *Lb.ua*. https://ukr.lb.ua/society/2014/08/21/276841_dnepr1_armiya_prishli_pomoshch.html

LB.ua. (2014b, August 26). Batal'on 'Aidar' zaderzhal glavreda 'Luganskoi pravdy' po podozreniiu v posobnichestve 'LNR'. *Lb.ua*. https://lb.ua/news/2014/08/26/277194_batalon_aydar_zaderzhal_glavreda.html

Len'kov, S. (2014, April 21). Kramatorskie opolchentsy sobralis' pered Gorotdelom. *Tehnopolis.com.ua.* https://tehnopolis.com.ua/index.php?option=com_content& view=article&id=5689:2014-04-21-14-19-00&catid=59:2011-01-11-21-18-52& Itemid=15

Lenta.ru. (2016, January 24). MVD Ukrainy soobshchilo o planakh Zakharchenko i Plotnitskogo ubit' drug druga. *Lenta.ru.* https://lenta.ru/news/2016/01/24/ skiryak/

Lenta.ru. (2017a, January 17). Zakharchenko ob'iasnil nevozmozhnost' ob'edineniia DNR i LNR. *Lenta.ru.* https://lenta.ru/news/2017/01/17/lnr_dnr/

Lenta.ru. (2017b, August 9). Zakharchenko priznal nezhelatel'nost' upotrebleniia slova 'Malorossiia'. *Lenta.ru.* https://lenta.ru/news/2017/08/09/dnr/

Leoshko, V. (2015, April 8). Redaktor gazety 'Vecherniaia Gorlovka': 'Ranshe pressu pressovali – Teper "otzhimaiut"'. *Glavnoe.in.Ua.* https://glavnoe.in.ua/news/ n221066

Lesiv, M. (2016, July 15). Eks-glavar' 'LNR' anonsiroval vozrozhdenie proekta 'Novorossiia'. *Pl.com.ua.* https://pl.com.ua/eks-glavar-lnr-anonsiroval-vozrozhde nie-proekta-novorossiya/

Levada Tsentr. (2018). Nostal'gia po SSSR. *Levada.ru.* www.levada.ru/2018/12/19/ nostalgiya-po-sssr-2/?fromtg=1

Levada-Center. (2022). The attitude of Russians to countries: November 2022. *Levada. ru.* www.levada.ru/en/2022/12/16/the-attitude-of-russians-to-countries-novem ber-2022/

Liber, G. (1982). Language, literacy, and book publishing in the Ukrainian SSR, 1923–1928. *Slavic Review, 41*(4), 673–685. https://doi.org/10.2307/2496868

Liu, Q., Chen, Q., Shen, J., Wu, H., Sun, Y., & Ming, W.-K. (2019). Data analysis and visualization of newspaper articles on thirdhand smoke: A topic modeling approach. *JMIR Medical Informatics, 7*(1), e12414–e12414. https://doi.org/10 .2196/12414

Lofgren, M. (2014). Anatomy of the deep state. *BillMoyers.com.* https://billmoyers .com/2014/02/21/anatomy-of-the-deep-state/

Lugansk 24. (2014, May 11). Lugansk 24. Referendum 11 Maia 2014 g. Oleg Tsarev. Video. *YouTube.com.* www.youtube.com/watch?v=-c103dZ-_j4

Lugansk1 Info. (2015, December 21). S nachala 2015 goda Lutuginskii zavod prokat-nykh valkov realizoval produktsii na 180 mln rublei. *Lugansk1.Info.* http:// lugansk1.info/2234-2234/

Lugansk1 Info. (2016a, January 17). Beglaia moshennitsa iz Sverdlovska rassazyvaet nebylitsy o Respublike (video). *Lugansk1.Info.* http://lugansk1.info/5279-russkoj-schastlivoj-zhizni-iskali-v-malokulturnyh-gorodah-donbassa-zhurnalist/

Lugansk1 Info. (2016b, February 15). Veteranov Velikoi Otechestvennoi 'afgantsev' pozdravili kontsertom v Luganskoi filarmonii. *Lugansk1.Info.* http://lugansk1 .info/8176-veteranov-velikoj-otechestvennoj-i-afgantsev-pozdravili-kontsertom-v-luganskoj-filarmonii/

Lugansk1 Info. (2016c, April 3). Donbassu grozit eskalatsiia konflikta pri otstutstvii politicheskogo protsessa —L'Opinion. *Lugansk1.Info.* http://lugansk1.info/ 16407-donbassu-grozit-eskalatsiya-konflikta-pri-otsutstvii-politicheskogo-prot sessa-lopinion/

Lugansk1 Info. (2016d, April 5). Uchastniki Kontaktnoi gruppy nachali zasedanie v Minske. *Lugansk1.Info.* http://lugansk1.info/17065-uchastniki-kontaktnoj-gruppy-nachali-zasedanie-v-minske/

Lugansk1 Info. (2016e, April 11). Bolee 500 knig peredali v detskii priiut i dom prestarelykh zhiteli Antratsita. *Lugansk1.Info.* http://lugansk1.info/18799-bolee-500-knig-peredali-v-detskij-priyut-i-dom-prestarelyh-zhiteli-antratsita/

Lugansk1 Info. (2016f, April 11). Plotnitskii anonsiroval sokrashchenie chisla ministerstv i perestanovki v rukovodstve regionov. *Lugansk1.Info.* http://lugansk1.info/18525-plotnitskij-anonsiroval-sokrashhenie-chisla-ministerstv-i-perestanovki-v-rukovodstve-regionov/

Lugansk1 Info. (2016g, April 13). Novorossiia ot Luganska do Odessy eshche ne proigrana. *Lugansk1.Info.* http://lugansk1.info/19486-novorossiya-ot-luganska-do-odessy-eshhyo-ne-proigrana/

Lugansk1 Info. (2016h, April 18). Ukraina ob"iasniaet tormozhenie 'Minska-2' otsutstviem bezopasnosti na Donbasse —Ministr MID DNDR. *Lugansk1.Info.* https://web.archive.org/web/20191130123809/http://lugansk1.info/21105-ukraina-obyasnyaet-tormozhenie-minska-2-otsutstviem-bezopasnosti-na-don basse-ministr-mid-dnr/

Lugansk1 Info. (2016i, November 21). Ukrainskie neonatsisty zaiavili o massovykh antipravitel'stvennykh aktsiiakh protesta v Kieve. *Lugansk1.Info.* http://lugansk1.info/23718-ukrainskie-neonatsisty-zayavili-o-massovyh-antipravitelstvennyh-aktsiyah-protesta-v-kieve/

Lugansk1 Info. (2016j, December 8). Varianty real'nosti v real'nosti bez variantov. *Lugansk1.Info.* https://web.archive.org/web/20191229234323/http://lugansk1.info/24753-varianty-realnosti-v-realnosti-bez-variantov/

Lugansk1 Info. (2017a, March 22). Politsiia obnaruzhila nedaleko ot tsentra Luganska tainik ukrainskikh diversantov —Igor' Kornet. *Lugansk1.Info.* http://lugansk1.info/29614-politsiya-obnaruzhila-nedaleko-ot-tsentra-luganska-tajnik-ukrains kih-diversantov-igor-kornet/

Lugansk1 Info. (2017b, April 21). Skul'pturu Neizvestnogo ofitsera raspilili dlia sdachi na metallolom v Dnepropetrovskoi oblasti. *Lugansk1.Info.* http://lugansk1.info/30571-skulpturu-neizvestnogo-ofitsera-raspilili-dlya-sdachi-na-metallolom-v-dnepropetrovskoj-oblasti/

Lugansk1 Info. (2017c, May 18). Ukraina stal iarkim primerom degradatsii instituta gosudarstvennosti —Plotnitskii. *Lugansk1.Info.* http://lugansk1.info/31989-ukraina-stala-yarkim-primerom-degradatsii-instituta-gosudarstvennosti-plotnitskij/

Lugansk1 Info. (2017d, June 19). Mininform Ukrainy peredal v SBU spisok saitov, ugrozhashchikh svidomizmu, dlia zapreta. *Lugansk1.Info.* http://lugansk1.info/33936-mininform-ukrainy-peredal-v-sbu-spisok-sajtov-ugrozhashhih-svido mizmu-dlya-zapreta/

Lugansk1 Info. (2017e, July 31). Vostochnye raiony Luganska budut poluchat' vodu v techenie vsego dnia —Sergei Ivanushkin. *Lugansk1.Info.* http://lugansk1.info/36632-vostochnye-rajony-luganska-budut-poluchat-vodu-v-techenie-vsego-dnya-sergej-ivanushkin/

Lugansk1 Info. (2017f, September 19). Ustraivaia terakty, Kiev pokazyvaet svoiu negotovnost' k mirnomu dialogu s Donbassom—Aktivist. *Lugansk1.Info.* http://

lugansk1.info/39440-ustraivaya-terakty-kiev-pokazyvaet-svoyu-negotovnost-k-mirnomu-dialogu-s-donbassom-aktivist/

Lugansk1 Info. (2017g, September 28). Ukrainskii zakon 'Ob obrazovanii' iavliaetsia 'movnym reiderstvom' —Kievskii poet. *Lugansk1.Info*. https://web.archive.org/web/20170929182907/http://lugansk1.info/40064-ukrainskij-zakon-ob-obrazova nii-yavlyaetsya-movnym-rejderstvom-kievskij-poet/

Lugansk1 Info. (2017h, December 19). Suprugi-uchitelia v L'vovskoi oblasti naladili postavki narkotikov iz Evrosoiuza. *Lugansk1.Info*. https://web.archive.org/web/20191130123755/http://lugansk1.info/44230-suprugi-uchitelya-v-lvovskoj-oblasti-naladili-postavki-narkotikov-iz-evrosoyuza/

Lugansk1 Info. (2017i, December 23). Na Ukraine slozhilas' katastroficheskaia situatsiia s vaktsinami protiv poliomielita. *Lugansk1.Info*. http://lugansk1.info/44480-na-ukraine-slozhilas-katastroficheskaya-situatsiya-s-vaktsinami-protiv-poliomielita/

Lugansk1 Info. (2017j, December 26). Der Spiegel: Skazki o zlykh russkikh – Patologicheskaia politika Zapada. *Lugansk1.Info*. http://lugansk1.info/44620-der-spiegel-skazki-o-zlyh-russkih-patologicheskaya-politika-zapada/

Lugansk1 Info. (2017k, December 28). Osvobozhdennye iz ukrainskogo plena stor-onniki respublik Donbassa rasskazali o pytkakh SBU. *Lugansk1.Info*. https://web .archive.org/web/20180318062018/http://lugansk1.info/44792-osvobozhdennye-iz-ukrainskogo-plena-storonniki-respublik-donbassa-rasskazali-o-pytkah-sbu/

Lugansk1 Info. (2017l, December 29). Za god kievskimi silovikami v LNR razrusheno okolo 70 domostroenii i ob"ektov infrastruktury. *Lugansk1.Info*. http://lugansk1 .info/44866-za-god-kievskimi-silovikami-v-lnr-razrusheno-okolo-70-domostroe nij-i-obektov-infrastruktury/

Lugansk1 Info. (2019). Lugansk1.Info – Main page. *Lugansk1.Info*. http://lugansk1 .info/

Luganskii Informatsionnyi Tsentr. (2014a, November 18). Ministerstvo obrazovaniia LNR gotovo k perekhodu na obuchenie shkol'nikov po rossiiskim programmam. *Lug-Info.com*. http://lug-info.com/news/one/pogoda-ne-isportit-luganchanam-novogodnie-prazdniki-771

Luganskii Informatsionnyi Tsentr. (2014b, November 26). V Ministerste sotsial'noi politik ikhotiat vvesti dolzhnost' spetsialista po delam invalidov. *Lug-Info.com*. http://lug-info.com/news/one/121

Luganskii Informatsionnyi Tsentr. (2014c, December 17). Fashistskie idei v Kieve budut iskoreneny, uveren glava LNR Igor' Plotnitskii. *Lug-Info.com*. http://lug-info.com/news/one/534

Luganskii Informatsionnyi Tsentr. (2014d, December 30). Pogoda ne isportit lugan-chanam novogodnie prazdniki. *Lug-Info.com*. http://lug-info.com/news/one/pogoda-ne-isportit-luganchanam-novogodnie-prazdniki-771

Luganskii Informatsionnyi Tsentr. (2015a, March 19). Futbolisty LNR sygrali pervyi mezhdunarodnyi match. *Lug-Info.com*. http://lug-info.com/news/one/futbolisty-lnr-sygrali-pervyi-mezhdunarodnyi-match-2122

Luganskii Informatsionnyi Tsentr. (2015b, June 11). Zhiteli Luganska v techenie leta smogut besplatno poseshchat' letnii kinoteatr v kvartale Iuzhnyi. *Lug-Info.com*. http://lug-info.com/news/one/zhiteli-luganska-v-techenie-leta-smogut-bes platno-poseschat-letnii-kinoteatr-na-kvartale-yuzhnyi-3866

Luganskii Informatsionnyi Tsentr. (2015c, July 8). Gazeta 'XXI vek' stala pervym izdaniem, zaregistrirovannym v LNR. *Lug-Info.com.* http://lug-info.com/news/one/gazeta-xxi-vek-stala-pervym-zaregistrirovannym-v-lnr-izdaniem-4647

Luganskii Informatsionnyi Tsentr. (2015d, August 31). 'Urok muzhestva' dlia molodezhi proshel v Luganskom aeroportu v godovshchinu ego osvobozhdeniia. *Lug-Info.com.* http://lug-info.com/news/one/urok-muzhestva-dlya-molodezhi-lnr-proveli-na-ruinakh-luganskogo-aeroporta-osvobozhdennogo-god-nazad-6234

Luganskii Informatsionnyi Tsentr. (2015e, September 3). Molodezhnaia diplomatiia v LNR uzhe rabotaet —Aktivist. *Lug-Info.com.* http://lug-info.com/news/one/molo dezhnaya-diplomatiya-v-lnr-uzhe-rabotaet-aktivist-6339

Luganskii Informatsionnyi Tsentr. (2015f, September 21). Talantlivye deti Respubliki vernulis' iz poezdki v Moskvu. *Lug-Info.com.* http://lug-info.com/news/one/talan tlivye-deti-respubliki-vernulis-iz-poezdki-v-moskvu-6868

Luganskii Informatsionnyi Tsentr. (2015g, October 9). Narodnyi forum 'Pobeda za nami!' sostoitsia v Luganske na stadione 'Avangard' 10 oktiabria. *Lug-Info.com.* http://lug-info.com/news/one/forum-pobeda-za-nami-sostoitsya-v-luganske-na-stadione-avangard-10-oktyabrya-7497

Luganskii Informatsionnyi Tsentr. (2015h, November 23). 'Mir Luganshchine' budet reagirovat' na vse fakty korruptsii, postupaiushchie ot zhitelei —Glava LNR. *Lug-Info.com.* http://lug-info.com/news/one/mir-luganschine-budet-reagirovat-na-vse-fakty-korruptsii-postupayuschie-ot-zhitelei-glava-lnr-8517

Luganskii Informatsionnyi Tsentr. (2015i, December 26). Mininform v 2015 godu zaregistriroval v Respublike 92 SMI. *Lug-Info.com.* http://lug-info.com/news/one/mininform-v-2015-godu-zaregistriroval-v-respublike-92-smi-ministr-9493

Luganskii Informatsionnyi Tsentr. (2016a, January 20). Shkola Sverdlovska poluchila shefskuiu pomoshch' ot blagotvoritel'nogo fonda iz Ekaterinburga. *Lug-Info.com.* http://lug-info.com/news/one/shkola-sverdlovska-poluchila-shefskuyu-pomosch-ot-blagotvoritelnogo-fonda-iz-ekaterinburga-9992

Luganskii Informatsionnyi Tsentr. (2016b, February 6). Narodnyi Sovet mozhet priniat' 'nalogovye' popravki uzhe na sleduiushchei needle —Drobot. *Lug-Info.com.* http://lug-info.com/news/one/narodnyi-sovet-mozhet-prinyat-nalogovye-popravki-uzhe-na-sleduyuschei-nedele-drobot-10502

Luganskii Informatsionnyi Tsentr. (2016c, February 19). Organizatory podveli itogi konkursa 'Neizvestnyi–Izvestnyi Donbass' v Krasnom Luche. *Lug-Info.com.* http://lug-info.com/news/one/organizatory-podveli-itogi-konkursa-neizvestnyi-izvestnyi-donbass-v-krasnom-luche-10936

Luganskii Informatsionnyi Tsentr. (2016d, March 26). Voennosluzhashchii VSU stal zhertvoi p'ianykh 'razborok' kievskikh silovikov —Narodnaia militsiia. *Lug-Info.com.* http://lug-info.com/news/one/voennosluzhaschii-vsu-stal-zhertvoi-pya nykh-razborok-kievskikh-silovikov-narodnaya-militsiya-11931

Luganskii Informatsionnyi Tsentr. (2016e, April 7). Radioperedachi proekta 'ne zabudem, ne prostim!' pomogaiut zhiteliam LNR otstaivat' ikh prava. *Lug-Info.com.* http://lug-info.com/news/one/radioperedachi-proekta-ne-zabudem-ne-pros tim-pomogayut-zhitelyam-lnr-otstaivat-ikh-prava-12346

Luganskii Informatsionnyi Tsentr. (2016f, April 10). Referendum v Niderlandakh pokazal, chto Zapad otvernulsia ot Ukrainy —Plotnitskii. *Lug-Info.com.* http://

lug-info.com/news/one/referendum-v-gollandii-pokazal-chto-zapad-otvernul sya-ot-ukrainy-plotnitskii-12445

Luganskii Informatsionnyi Tsentr. (2016g, May 4). Kievskie SMI podtverdili rost neboevykh poter' v VSU iz-za p'ianstva —Narodnaia militsiia. *Lug-Info.com.* http://lug-info.com/news/one/kievskie-smi-podtverdili-rost-neboevykh-poter-v-vsu-iz-za-pyanstva-narodnaya-militsiya-13218

Luganskii Informatsionnyi Tsentr. (2016h, May 6). Zhiteli Brianki 'speli serdtsem' pesniu 'Den' Pobedy'. *Lug-Info.com.* http://lug-info.com/news/one/zhiteli-bryanki-speli-serdtsem-pesnyu-den-pobedy-13312

Luganskii Informatsionnyi Tsentr. (2016i, August 2). Luchshie shkol'niki Respubliki pobyvali v stolnitse Rossii. *Lug-Info.com.* http://lug-info.com/news/one/luchshie-shkolniki-respubliki-pobyvali-v-stolitse-rossii-15806

Luganskii Informatsionnyi Tsentr. (2017a, January 9). Fleshmob v ramkakh respublikanskoi aktsii '1000 dnei vopreki' sostoialsia v Krasnoluchskoi Novopavlovke (FOTO). *Lug-Info.com.* http://lug-info.com/news/one/fleshmob-v-ramkakh-respublikanskoi-aktsii-1000-dnei-vopreki-sostoyalsya-v-krasnoluchskoi-novopav lovke-foto-20524

Luganskii Informatsionnyi Tsentr. (2017b, February 15). Luganskaia afisha. *Lug-Info. com.* http://lug-info.com/news/one/luganskaya-afisha-21533

Luganskii Informatsionnyi Tsentr. (2017c, April 24). 'Mir Luganshchine' priglashaet zhitelei LNR 28 aprelia priniat' uchastie v respublikanskom subbotnike. *Lug-Info. com.* http://lug-info.com/news/one/mir-luganschine-priglashaet-zhitelei-28-apre lya-prinyat-uchastie-v-respublikanskom-subbotnike-23755

Luganskii Informatsionnyi Tsentr. (2017d, August 4). VSU za nedeliu vypustili po territorii LNR bolee 700 boepripasov —Narodnaia militsiia. *Lug-Info.com.* http:// lug-info.com/news/one/vsu-za-nedelyu-vypustili-po-territorii-lnr-bolee-700-boe pripasov-narodnaya-militsiya-27017

Luganskii Informatsionnyi Tsentr. (2017e, August 23). 'Mir Luganshchine' k Dniu shakhtera provodit internet-fleshmob 'Im pokoriaietsia Zemlia'. *Lug-Info.com.* http://lug-info.com/news/one/mir-luganschine-k-dnyu-shakhtera-provodit-inter net-fleshmob-im-pokoryaetsya-zemlya-27587

Luganskii Informatsionnyi Tsentr. (2017f, November 24). Zaiavlenie Pasechnika L.I. *Lug-Info.com.* http://lug-info.com/news/one/zayavlenie-pasechnika-li-30162

Luganskii Informatsionnyi Tsentr. (2019). Luganskii Informatsionnyi Tsentr – Main page. *Lug-Info.com.* http://lug-info.com/

Luganskii Telegraf. (2016, September 20). Glava LNR soobshchil o raskrytom zagovore protiv Respubliki. *Lgt.su.* https://lgt.su/main/5791-glava-lnr-soobschil-o-raskrytom-zagovore-protiv-respubliki.html

Lugansk-Online. (2014, November 3). Na vyborakh v LNR bol'shinstvo golosov nabrali Igor' Plotnitskii i obshchestvennoe dvizhenie 'Mir Luganshchine'. *Lugansk-Online.Info.* https://archive.is/20141103192620/http://lugansk-online .info/news/na-vyborah-v-lnr-bolshinstvo-golosov-nabrali-igor-plotnitskii-i-obshchestvennoe-dvizhenie-mir-luganshchine

Luhn, A. (2014, July 20). Three pro-Russia rebel leaders at the centre of suspicions over downed MH17. *Guardian.* www.theguardian.com/world/2014/jul/20/three-pro-russia-rebel-leaders-suspects-over-downed-mh17

Luxmoore, M. (2017, July 22). Rival factions battle for control in Eastern Ukraine. *New York Times.* www.nytimes.com/2017/11/22/world/europe/luhansk-ukraine-feuding.html

Magosci, P. R. (2010). *A History of Ukraine: The Land and Its Peoples.* University of Toronto Press.

Makeevskii Rabochii. (2015a, September 1). Istsepit' rasteniem. *Makeevskii Rabochii.* http://gazeta-dnr.ru//?p=2608

Makeevskii Rabochii. (2015b, September 10). Snova derzhim udar. *Makeevskii Rabochii.* http://gazeta-dnr.ru//?p=3475

Makeevskii Rabochii. (2015c, December 30). Volnuiushchie voprosy –Obstoiatel'nye otvety. *Makeevskii Rabochii.* http://gazeta-dnr.ru//?p=16406

Malyutina, D. (2018). The impact of the armed conflict in the east of Ukraine on relationships among scholars of Ukraine across Europe. *Ideology and Politics Journal, 11*(3), 58–85.

Mareš, P., & Šmídová, I. (2000). Public opinion research data on the entry of the Czech Republic into NATO. *Czech Sociological Review, 8*(1), 103–116.

Marples, D. R. (2006). Stepan Bandera: The resurrection of a Ukrainian national hero. *Europe–Asia Studies, 58*(4), 555–566.

Matrix Home. (2014, June 5). 5 Kanal, 1+1, Telekanal 'Donbass', UBR, News24. *Matrixhome.net.* www.matrixhome.net/donetsk/news/?id=617

Matsuka, O. (2013). Post. *Facebook.com.* www.facebook.com/oleksiy.matsuka/posts/10202863577096545

Matsuka, O. (2014a, March 3). Post. *Facebook.com.* www.facebook.com/oleksiy.matsuka/posts/10203341291959118?stream_ref=10

Matsuka, O. (2014b, September 29). Post. *Facebook.com.* www.facebook.com/photo.php?fbid=10204985423981391&set=a.1834267382518.2107971.1415440582&type=1&theater

Mavrichev, S. (2014, March 23). Post. *Facebook.com.* www.facebook.com/photo.php?fbid=608499739241009&set=a.223824147708572.52620.100002429640300&type=1&stream_ref=10

Maystrenko, V. (2014, May 8). Plen. Sergei Lefter. Slaviansk. Vse pravdivo. Video. *YouTube.com.* www.youtube.com/watch?v=j9oez1Zzpac

Mazepus, H., Osmudsen, M., Bang-Petersen, M., Toshkov, D., & Dimitrova, A. (2023). Information battleground: Conflict perceptions motivate the belief in and sharing of misinformation about the adversary. *PLoS ONE, 18*(3), e0282308. https://doi.org/10.1371/journal.pone.0282308

McAllester, M. (2014, April 23). Time, Vice journalists detained by separatists in Eastern Ukraine. *Time Magazine.* https://time.com/73522/time-vice-journalists-detained-ukraine/

McFaul, M. (2001, October 24). U.S.–Russia relations after September 11, 2001. *Carnegie Endowment for International Peace.* https://carnegieendowment.org/2001/10/24/u.s.-russia-relations-after-september-11-2001-pub-840

McGlynn, J. (2003). *Russia's War.* Cambridge: Polity Press.

McVeigh, K. (2014, April 24). US journalist released by pro-Russian gunmen in Ukraine, Vice confirms. *Guardian.* www.theguardian.com/world/2014/apr/24/us-journalist-simon-ostrovsky-released-ukraine

Meduza. (2018, September 7). Parlament DNR smenil ispolniaiushchego obiazannosti glavy respubliki. https://meduza.io/news/2018/09/07/parlament-dnr-smenil-ispol nyayuschego-obyazannosti-glavy-respubliki

Mel'nikova, L. V. (2016). Literatura rodnogo kraia: V. I. Gerlanets. *Kabruss.Blogspot. com.* http://kabruss.blogspot.com/2016/12/blog-post_38.html

Meyer, E. T. (2017). What is content analysis? *Oxford Microsites.* http://microsites.oii .ox.ac.uk/tidsr/kb/54/what-content-analysis

MGBPLNR. (2017a, November 22). Eks-predsedatel' Soveta Ministrov LNR Genadii Tsypkalov umer ot pytok —Sledovatel' Genprokuratury. *MGBLNR.org.* http:// mgblnr.org/media/133f496d-42ee-4905-8cd8-8a10c9334ef3

MGBPLNR. (2017b, November 22). Novosti i svodki MGB DNR '22.22.2017'. *MGBDNR.ru.* https://mgbdnr.ru/news.php?id=20171122_00&img_num=0

Mijatović, D. (2014a). Media freedom under siege in Ukraine. *Organization for Security and Co-operation in Europe.* www.osce.org/fom/118990?download= true

Mijatović, D. (2014b). Report by the OSCE Representative on freedom of the media: 'Media freedom under siege in Ukraine'. *Organization for Security and Co-operation in Europe.* www.osce.org/fom/118990?download=true

Mikhailiuk, A. (2014, July 2). Ukhodiashchii Kramatorsk: Reportazh po pamiati zhitel'nitsy razrushennogo goroda. *Novaya Gazeta.* www.novayagazeta.ru/art icles/2014/07/02/60195-uhodyaschiy-kramatorsk

Mikhailova, Y. R. (2017). Sravnitel'nyi analiz Osveshcheniia Rosiiskimi i Amerikanskimi SMI krizisa v Donbase. *Alleia Nauki, 11.*

Miller, C. (2014, August 8). Russian resigns to make way for Ukrainian as new head of 'Donetsk People's Republic'. *Guardian.* www.theguardian.com/world/2014/aug/ 08/russian-resigns-ukrainian-head-donetsk-peoples-republic

Miller, C. (2017, November 22). What in the world is going on in the Russia-backed separatist Luhansk 'Republic'? *RFE/RL.* www.rferl.org/a/ukraine-luhansk-armed-masked-men-what-is-going-on-kornet-plotnitsky/28870308 .html

Miller, C., Ward, A., & Forgey, Q. (2022, May 26). Putin's 'Russification' of Ukraine. *Politico.* www.politico.com/newsletters/national-security-daily/2022/05/26/ putins-russification-of-ukraine-00035500

Miller, D. A., Smith, E. R., & Mackie, D. M. (2004). Effects of intergroup contact and political predispositions on prejudice: Role of intergroup emotions. *Group Processes & Intergroup Relations, 7*(3), 221–237. https://doi.org/10.1177/ 1368430204046109

Ministerstvo Informatsii Donetskoi Narodnoi Respubliki. (2018, September 6). Postanovlenie Soveta Ministrov Donetskoi Narodnoi Respubliki ot 10.08.2018 G. No 10-37 'Ob utverzhdenii polozheniia o ministerstve informatsii Donetskoi Narodnoi Respubliki'. Opublikovano 06.09.2018. *Mininfodnr.ru.* http:// mininfodnr.ru/postanovlenie-soveta-ministrov-donetskoj-narodnoj-respubliki-ot-10-01-2015g-1-18-ob-utverzhdenii-polozheniya-o-ministerstve-informatsii-donetskoj-narodnoj-respubliki/

Ministerstvo Osvity i Nauky Ukraïny. (2017, September 5). *Law on Education.* https:// mon.gov.ua/ua/npa/law-education

Minzagov, S. (2022, September 27). Za vkhozhdenie v Rossiiu progolosovali ot 87% do 99% uchastnikov chetyrekh referendumov. *Forbes*. www.forbes.ru/society/478269-za-vhozdenie-v-rossiu-progolosovali-ot-87-do-99-ucastnikov-cetyreh-referendumov

MIPMKLNR. (2015). *O zaprete rasprostraneniia informatsii s informatsionnykh saitov, rasprostroniaiushchikh informatsiiu s narusheniem zakonodatel'stva Luganskoi Narodnoi Respubliki.*

Mironenko, N. (2014, January 25). Miting vozmushcheniia. *Tehnopolis.com.ua*. https://tehnopolis.com.ua/index.php?option=com_content&view=article&id=5206:2014-01-25-180009&catid=59:2011-01-11-21-18-52&Itemid=15

Mirotvorets. (2016, May 10). Obnovlennyi spisok zhurnalistov, akkreditovannykh terroristicheskoi organizatsiei DNR. *Psb4ukr.org*. https://psb4ukr.org/587351-izvineniya-kollektiva-centra-mirotvorec-po-povodu-publikacii-10-05-2016-spiska-zhurnalistov-akkreditovannyx-terroristicheskoj-organizaciej-dnr/#more-587351

Mitchell, L. A. (2012). *The Color Revolutions*. University of Pennsylvania Press.

Mitin, E. (2016, November 16). Osobennosti shakhmatnoi biografii Donbassa. *Donetskoe Vremia*. http://dnr-news.com/pressa/37081-osobennosti-shahmatnoy-biografii-donbassa.html

Mitrokhin, N. (2015). Gang warfare and state building: The future of the Donbass [Bandenkrieg und Staatsbildung: Zur Zukunft des Donbass]. *Osteuropa*, *65*(1–2), 5–19.

Mitrokhin, N. (2017). Transfer of dictatorship: 'State building' in Russia's 'People's Republics' [Diktaturtransfer im Donbass: Gewalt und 'Staatsbildung' in Russlands 'Volksrepubliken']. *Osteuropa*, *67*(3–4), 41–55.

MIuDNR, (2017, August 28). Respublikanskii spisok ekstremistskikh materialov, www.Minjust-Dnr.Ru https://web.archive.org/web/20170828124144/www.minjust-dnr.ru/wp-content/uploads/2017/08/SPISOK-EKSTR.-MATERIALOV-na-01.08.2017.pdf.

MKSMLNR. (2019). Edinyi kalendarnyi plan respublikanskikh fizkul'turnykh i sportivnykh meropriiatii luganskoi narodnoi respubliki na 2019 god. *Mklnr.su*. https://mklnr.su/ekp-sport-2019.html

MoiBY. (2014, April 9). Karespondenta 'Belsatu' zbili u Danetsku. *Moyby.com*. www.moyby.com/video/15078/

Monaenko, V. (2013, October 8). Segodnia 8 oktiabria, vtornik. Pogoda, narodnye primety, den' v istorii. *Novosti Kramatorska*. https://hi.dn.ua/index.php?option=com_content&view=article&id=38371&catid=55:kramatorsk&Itemid=147

Monaenko, V. (2014, August 24). S Dnem nezavisimosti Ukrainy! *Novosti Kramatorska*. https://hi.dn.ua/index.php?option=com_content&view=article&id=49380&catid=55:kramatorsk&Itemid=147

Montiel, C. J., Salvador, A. M. O., See, D. C., & Leon, M. M. D. (2014). Nationalism in local media during international conflict: Text mining domestic news reports of the China–Philippines maritime dispute. *Journal of Language and Social Psychology*, *33*(5), 445–464. https://doi.org/10.1177/0261927X14542435

Morris, J. (2005). The empire strikes back: Projections of national identity in contemporary Russian advertising. *The Russian Review*, *64*(4), 642–660.

Motta, M., & Stecula, D. (2021). Quantifying the effect of Wakefield et al. (1998) on skepticism about MMR vaccine safety in the U.S. *PLOS ONE*, *16*(8), e0256395. https://doi.org/10.1371/journal.pone.0256395

MSMKLNR. (2015, July 28). Press-konferentsiia o sozdanii ministerstva sviazi LNR. *Mslnr.su.* https://mslnr.su/8-press-konferenciya-o-sozdanii-ministerstva-svyazi-lnr.html

MSMKLNR. (2016, March 22). O vnesenii izmenenii v prikaz ministerstva informatsii, pechati i massovykh kommunikatsii Luganskoi Narodnoi Respubliki ot 22 marta 2016 goda No 10-OD. *Sovminlnr.ru.* https://sovminlnr.ru/akty-ispolni telnyh-organov/ministerstvo-svyazi/4292-o-vnesenii-izmeneniy-v-prikaz-minis terstva-informacii-pechati-i-massovyh-kommunikaciy-luganskoy-narodnoy-respubliki-ot-22-marta-2016-goda-10-od.html

Narodnyi Sovet Donetskoi Narodnoi Respubliki. (2015, February 5). Memorandum donetskoi narodnoi respubliki ob osnovakh gosudarstvennogo stroitel'stva, politicheskoi i istoricheskoi preemstvennosti. *Dnrsovet.Su.* https://web.archive.org/web/20160316070936/https://dnrsovet.su/zakonodatelnaya-deyatelnost/memorandumy/

Narodnyi Sovet Donetskoi Narodnoi Respubliki. (2018). Konstitutsiia Donetskoi Narodnoi Respubliki. *GB-DNR.com.* http://gb-dnr.com/normativno-pravovye-akty/3977/

Narodnyi Sovet Luganskoi Narodnoi Respubliki. (2014a). Konstitutsiia Luganskoi Narodnoi Respubliki. *NSLNR.su.* https://nslnr.su/zakonoda telstvo/konstitutsiya/

Narodnyi Sovet Luganskoi Narodnoi Respubliki. (2014b, June 25). O sisteme ispolnitel'nykh organov gosudarstvennoi vlasti Luganskoi Narodnoi Respubliki. *NSLNR.su.* https://nslnr.su/zakonodatelstvo/normativno-pravo vaya-baza/600/

NATO. (1997, May 27). Founding act on mutual relations, cooperation and security between NATO and the Russian Federation signed in Paris, France. *NATO.int.* www.nato.int/cps/cn/natohq/official_texts_25468.htm

Natsional'na spilka zhurnalistiv Ukraïny. (2015, January 14). Polozhennia pro akreditatsiiui zhurnalistiv u zoni ATO porushue prava zhurnalistiv. *NSJU.org.* http://nsju.org/article/view/4629

Navarro-Colorado, B. (2018). On poetic topic modeling: Extracting themes and motifs from a corpus of Spanish poetry. *Frontiers in Digital Humanities, 5*, 15. https://doi.org/10.3389/fdigh.2018.00015

Necro Mancer. (2017, November 21). Post. *Twitter.com.* https://twitter.com/666_mancer/status/932994937662078977?ref_src=twsrc%255Etfw&ref_url=https%253A%252F%252Fmedium.com%252Fmedia%252F9d475c0841cab64d4981d9500443d6de%253FpostId%253Dc77705325e38

Nemtsova, A. (2018, May 2). The frightening far-right militia that's marching in Ukraine's streets, promising to bring 'order'. *Daily Beast.* www.thedailybeast.com/the-frightening-far-right-militia-thats-marching-in-ukraines-streets-prom ising-to-bring-order

New York Times. (2018, November 5). Kateryna Handziuk, Ukrainian activist, dies from acid attack. *New York Times.* www.nytimes.com/2018/11/05/world/europe/kateryna-handziuk-dies-ukraine.html

Nielsen, R. K. (2015). Local newspapers as keystone media: The increased importance of diminished newspapers for local political information environments. In R. K. Nielsen (ed.), *Local Journalism: The Decline of Newspapers and the Rise of Digital Media* (pp. 51–72). I. B. Tauris.

Nikolayenko, O. (2008). Contextual effects on historical memory: Soviet nostalgia among post-Soviet adolescents. *Communist and Post-Communist Studies, 41*, 243–259.

N'iuman, D. (2014, March 9). Donetsk: Kak arestovali 'narodnogo gubernatora' Gubareva. *BBC Russian*. www.bbc.com/russian/international/2014/03/140309_donetsk_gubarev_arrest

NOS. (2022, November 17). Drie keer levenslang in MH17-strafproces, eenmaal vrijspraak. *NOS.nl*. https://nos.nl/collectie/13835/artikel/2452782-drie-keer-levenslang-in-mh17-strafproces-eenmaal-vrijspraak

Novaia Gazeta. (2015a, March 17). Zaderzhannuiu pod luganskom fotografa Viktoriiu Ivlevu otpustili. *Novayagazeta.ru*. www.novayagazeta.ru/news/2015/03/17/110874-zaderzhannuyu-pod-luganskom-fotografa-viktoriyu-ivlevu-otpustili

Novaia Gazeta. (2015b, June 17). Spetskora 'Novoi Gazety' Pavla Kanygina zaderzhali 'organy gosbezopasnosti DNR'. Zaiavlenie redaktsii. *Novayagazeta.ru*. www.novayagazeta.ru/articles/2015/06/16/64550-spetskora-171-novoy-gazety-187-pavla-kanygina-zaderzhali-171-organy-gosbezopasnosti-dnr-187-zayavlenie-redaktsii

Novaia Niva. (2016a, April 28). Bessmertnyi Polk. *Novaia Niva*. http://gazeta-dnr.ru//?p=29186

Novaia Niva. (2016b, June 23). Slovo – Za nami! *Novaia Niva*. http://gazeta-dnr.ru//?p=33847

Novaia Niva. (2016c, September 26). Aleksandr Zakharchenko: 'My stali splochennee'. *Novaia Niva*. http://gazeta-dnr.ru//?p=41101

Novaia Zhizn'. (2015, August 6). Tirazh raionki rastet. *Novaia Zhizn'*. http://gazeta-dnr.ru//?p=560

Novorossia. (2014, May 23). PROGRAMMA Obshchestvenno-politicheskogo drizheniia 'Partiia NOVOROSSIIA'. *Novorossia.su*. https://web.archive.org/web/20171123082931/http://novorossia.su/news/programma-obshchestvenno-politicheskogo-dvizheniya-partiya-novorossiya

Novorossia. (2016a, August 27). Katastrofa v nebe. *Novorossia*. https://web.archive.org/web/20160404190812/http://novopressa.ru/articles/katastrofa-v-nebe.html

Novorossia. (2016b, August 27). Za chto srazhaetsia Novorossiia. *Novorossia*. https://web.archive.org/web/20160404191855/http://novopressa.ru/articles/za-chto-srazhaetsya-novorossiya.html

Novorossia. (2016c, December 11). Tridtsat' synovei leitenanta Shmidta. *Novorossia*. https://web.archive.org/web/20161022024928/http://novopressa.ru/articles-450.html

Novorossia. (2019). Kontaktnaia Informatsiia. *Novopressa.ru*. http://novopressa.ru/contacts.html

Novosti Donbassa. (2014a, March 3). Chast' Donetskoi OGA zaniata prorossiiskimi aktivistami – Vse video. *Novosti.dn.ua*. http://novosti.dn.ua/article/4796-chast-doneckoy-oga-zanyata-prorossyyskymy-aktyvystamy-vse-vydeo

Novosti Donbassa. (2014b, April 13). V Kramatorske bandity napali na obshchestvennogo aktivita. *Novosti.dn.ua*. http://novosti.dn.ua/news/205465-v-kramatorske-bandyty-napaly-na-obshhestvennogo-aktyvyta

Novosti Donbassa. (2014c, April 19). Slaviansk: Russkie boeviki ustanovili informatsionnuiu blokadu. *Novosti.dn.ua*. http://novosti.dn.ua/news/206087-slavyansk-russkye-boevyky-ustanovyly-ynformacyonnuyu-blokadu

Novosti Donbassa. (2014d, April 20). V Toreze neizvestnye razgromili redaktsiiu mestnoi gazety —Foto/video. *Novosti.dn.ua.* http://novosti.dn.ua/news/206135-v-toreze-neyzvestnye-razgromyly-redakcyyu-mestnoy-gazety-foto/vydeo

Novosti Donbassa. (2014e, June 6). Budni 'DNR': V Toreze sozhgli ofis gazety 'Gorniak'. *Novosti.dn.ua.* http://novosti.dn.ua/news/209637-budny-dnr-v-tor eze-sozhgly-ofys-gazety-gornyak

Novosti Donbassa. (2014f, September 12). Ochevidtsy: V Donbasse mogut rasstreliat' iz-za stranitsy v sotsseti. *Novosti.dn.ua.* http://novosti.dn.ua/article/5023-oche vydcy-v-donbasse-mogut-rasstrelyat-yz-za-stranycy-v-socsety

Novosti Donbassa. (2016, December 26). 'LNR' zaderzhala eshche odnogo luganskogo blogera. *Novosti.dn.ua.* http://novosti.dn.ua/news/264964-lnr-zaderzhala-eshhe-odnogo-luganskogo-blogera

Novosti Donbassa. (2017a, September 16). 'DNR' vvela praktiku raznotsvetnykh spiskov dlia zhurnalistov. *Novosti.dn.ua.* http://novosti.dn.ua/news/274327-dnr-vvela-praktyku-raznocvetnykh-spyskov-dlya-zhurnalystov

Novosti Donbassa. (2017b, November 30). Kornet rasskazal o podgotovke pokush-eniia na Zakharchenko. *Novosti.dn.ua.* http://novosti.dn.ua/news/277002-kornet-rasskazal-o-podgotovke-pokushenyya-na-zakharchenko

Novosti Donbassa. (2021, January 28). 'L-DNR' predstavili svoiu 'doktrinu': Bez vkhozdeniia v Rossiiu, no s zakhvatom vsego Donbassa. *Novosti.dn.ua.* https:// novosti.dn.ua/ru/news/308202-l-dnr-predstavyly-svoyu-doktrynu-bez-vkhozhde nyya-v-rossyyu-no-s-zakhvatom-vsego-donbassa

Novosti Donetskoi Respubliki. (2017a, July 18). Glava DNR o sozdanii Malorossii: Donbass ne poidet v Ukrainu, eto Ukraina prisoedinitsia k Donbassu. *DNR-News.com.* http://dnr-news.com/intervyu/41311-glava-dnr-o-sozdanii-maloros sii-donbass-ne-poydet-v-ukrainu-eto-ukraina-prisoedinitsya-k-donbassu.html

Novosti Donetskoi Respubliki. (2017b, July 18). Initsiativa sozdaniia Malorossii iavliaetsia nesvoevremennoi —Deinego. *DNR-News.com.* http://dnr-news.com/dnr/41314-ini ciativa-sozdaniya-malorossii-yavlyaetsya-nesvoevremennoy-deynego.html

Novosti Kramatorska. (2014a, April 16). Mer Kramatorska nedopustil provedenie voennoi operatsii protiv mirnykh zhitelei. *Novosti Kramatorska.* https://hi.dn .ua/index.php?option=com_content&view=article&id=45872&catid=55:krama torsk&Itemid=147

Novosti Kramatorska. (2014b, April 16). 'V Kramatorske na storonu DNR pereshli voennye s tekhnikoi' —Ochevidets. *Novosti Kramatorska.* https://hi.dn.ua/index .php?option=com_content&view=article&id=45880&catid=55:kramatorsk& Itemid=147

Novosti Kramatorska. (2014c, October 26). 'Novosti Kramatorska' predstsavliaiut: Vybory-online. *Novosti Kramatorska.* https://hi.dn.ua/index.php?option=com_ content&view=article&id=51083&catid=55:kramatorsk&Itemid=147

Novosti Kramatorska. (2017, February 13). Komu prinadlezhat kramatorskie SMI i kto opredeliaet ikh redaktsionnuiu politiku i soderzhanie. *Hi.dn.ua.* https://hi.dn .ua/index.php?option=com_content&view=article&id=72966:2017-02-12-14-48-49&catid=55.:kramatorsk&Itemid=147

Novye Gorizonty. (2015, August 6). Kanikuly s pol'zoi. *Novye Gorizonty.* http:// gazeta-dnr.ru//?p=723

Novyi Luch. (2015, August 5). Tol'ko vmeste my – Sila. *Novyi Luch.* http://gazeta-dnr .ru//?p=422

NTV. (2014, June 30). Zhurnalist Pervogo kanala pogib u vorot donetskoi voinskoi chasti s kameroi v rukakh. *NTV.ru.* www.ntv.ru/novosti/1086217/

NV Ukraina. (2014, September 28). Bloger Dmitrii Potekhin rasskazal o svoem prebyvanii v plenu. *NV.ua.* https://nv.ua/ukraine/bloger-dmitriy-potehin-rasska zal-o-svoem-prebyvanii-v-plenu-13819.html

Obozrevatel'. (2014, November 29). Na Donbasse ubili zhurnalista. Vmeste s zhenoi. *Obozrevatel.com.* www.obozrevatel.com/politics/40852-v-slavyanskom-rajone-ubityi-izvestnyij-zhurnalist-i-ego-zhena.htm

Obshchestvennoe TV Donbassa. (2017a, September 6). Aresty blogerov organizat-siiami 'L-DNR'. Video. *YouTube.com.* www.youtube.com/watch?v=yIJumwn9jys

Obshchestvennoe TV Donbassa. (2017b, September 16). Okruzhenie Zakharchenko. Kto eti liudi? Video. *YouTube.com.* www.youtube.com/watch?v=JufQFeItR6E

Okkupatsiia.net. (2016, June 15). Rozhdenie zhurnalistiki LNR: ne govorit' pravdu ne mogli (VIDEO). *Okkupatsiya.net.* http://okkupatsiya.net/7294-rozhdenie-zhurna listiki-lnr-ne-govorit-pravdu-ne-mogli-video/

O'Loughlin, J., Toal, G., & Kolosov, V. (2016). Who identifies with the 'Russian world'? Geopolitical attitudes in southeastern Ukraine, Crimea, Abkhazia, South Ossetia, and Transnistria. *Eurasian Geography and Economics*, *57*(6), 745–778. https://doi.org/10.1080/15387216.2017.1295275

O'Loughlin, J., Toal, G., & Kolosov, V. (2017). The rise and fall of 'Novorossiya': Examining support for a separatist geopolitical imaginary in southeast Ukraine. *Post-Soviet Affairs*, *33*(2), 124–144. https://doi.org/10.1080/1060586X.2016.1146452

Online Debal'tsevo. (2016, September 24). Obzor agitatsionnoi pressy v Debal'tsevo. *Debaltsevo.com.* https://debaltsevo.com/news/2016-09-24-1875

Onuch, O. (2014). *Mapping Mass Mobilizations: Understanding Revolutionary Moments in Argentina and Ukraine.* Palgrave Macmillan.

Onuch, O. (2017). The revolution on the granite. *New Eastern Europe*, *27*(3–4). https://neasterneurope.eu/product/issue-3-42017/

Onuch, O., & Hale, H. E. (2018). Capturing ethnicity: The case of Ukraine. *Post-Soviet Affairs*, *34*(2–3), 84–106. https://doi.org/10.1080/1060586X.2018.1452247

Onuch, O., Hale, H. E., & Sasse, G. (2018). Studying identity in Ukraine. *Post-Soviet Affairs*, *34*(2–3), 79–83. https://doi.org/10.1080/1060586X.2018.1451241

Orlova, D. (2016). Ukrainian media after the EuroMaidan: In search of independence and professional identity. *Publizistik*, *61*, 441–461. https://doi.org/10.1007/ s11616-016-0282-8

Osadcha, I. (2014, September 16). Post. *Facebook.com.* www.facebook.com/guculka/ posts/10152694992009726?fref=nf

OSCE. (2014a, August 22). Latest from OSCE Special Monitoring Mission (SMM) to Ukraine based on information received as of 18:00 (Kyiv time), 21 August 2014. *OSCE.org.* www.osce.org/ukraine-smm/122920

OSCE. (2014b, September 1). Protokol po itogam konsul'tatsii Trekhstoronnei kon-taktnoi gruppy otnositel'no sovmestnykh shagov, napravlennykh na implemen-tatsiiu Mirnogo plana Prezidenta Ukrainy P.Poroshenko i initsiativ Prezidenta Rossii V.Putina. *OSCE.org.* www.osce.org/ru/home/123258?download=true

OSCE. (2014c, September 19). Memorandum ob ispolnenii polozhenii Protokola po itogam konsul'tatsii Trekhstoronnei kontaktnoi gruppy otnositel'no shagov, napravlennykh na implmementatsiiu Mirnogo plana Prezidenta Ukrainy P.Poroshenko i initsiativ Prezidenta Rossii V.Putina. *OSCE.org.* www.osce.org/ ru/home/123807?download=true

OSCE. (2014d, October 31). Abuse of press insignia unacceptable, says Official Representative following incident in eastern Ukraine. *OSCE.org.* www.osce.org/ fom/126223

OSCE. (2014e, October 31). So-called elections not in line with Minsk Protocol, says OSCE Chair, calling for enhanced efforts and dialogue to implement all commitments. *OSCE.org.* www.osce.org/cio/126242

OSCE. (2015a). Latest from OSCE Special Monitoring Mission (SMM) to Ukraine based on information received as of 19:30 (Kyiv time), 10 July 2015. *OSCE.org.* www.osce.org/ukraine-smm/171856

OSCE. (2015b, February 12). OSCE Chairperson-in-Office gives full backing to Minsk package. *OSCE.org.* www.osce.org/cio/140196

OSCE. (2015c, February 26). Restrictive measures toward Russian journalists reporting from Ukraine excessive, OSCE Representative says. *OSCE.org.* www .osce.org/fom/142896

OSCE. (2015d, October 1). OSCE Representative welcomes law on transparency of media ownership in Ukraine as it comes into force. *OSCE.org.* www.osce.org/ fom/187956

OSCE. (2015e, November 24). OSCE media freedom representatives welcomes print media privatization law in Ukraine. *OSCE.org.* www.osce.org/fom/203431

OSCE. (2017a, July 28). OSCE media freedom representative for immediate release of detained Donetsk journalist Stanislav Aseev. *OSCE.org.* www.osce.org/fom/ 333066

OSCE. (2017b, November 22). Latest from the OSCE Special Monitoring Mission to Ukraine (SMM), based on information received as of 19:30, 21 November 2017. *OSCE.org.* www.osce.org/special-monitoring-mission-to-ukraine/358186

OSCE Representative on Freedom of the Media. (2014a, April 24). New attacks on media in eastern Ukraine, warns OSCE representative. *OSCE.org.* www.osce.org/ fom/117985

OSCE Representative on Freedom of the Media. (2014b, October 30). OSCE representative warns about appalling journalists' safety situation in eastern Ukraine after death of one more journalist, calls for thorough investigation. *OSCE.org.* www.osce.org/fom/120566

Osipian, A. L. (2015). Historical myths, enemy images, and regional identity in the Donbass insurgency. *Journal of Soviet and Post-Soviet Politics and Society*, 1(1), 109–140.

Ostrov. (2014a, March 5). V Donetske TRK 'Donbass' prervala efir iz-za vorvavshikh-sia v studiiu agressivnykh liudei. *Ostro.org.* www.ostro.org/general/politics/news/ 439333/

Ostrov. (2014b, April 27). Flag samoprovozglashennoi Donetskoi respubliki podniat nad zdaniem Donetskoi oblastnoi teleradiokompanii (Foto). *Ostro.org.* www .ostro.org/general/society/news/443481/

Ostrov. (2014c, June 2). V Donetske po prikazu DNR otkliuchaiut ukrainskie kanaly. *Ostro.org.* www.ostro.org/general/society/news/446136/

Ostrov. (2014d, June 14). Pomoshchnik Pushilina Richard Yali, ranennyi v rezul'tate vzryva vozle Donetskoi OGA, umer v bol'nitse. *Ostro.org.* www.ostro.org/regions/37/society/news/article-446954/

Pakhomenko, S. (2015). Identity factor in terms of the Ukrainian crisis (the example of the Donbas region). *Bezpieczeństwo. Teoria i Praktyka.*, *3*, 95–102.

Panchyshyn, O. (2014, May 7). Zhurnalisty z Donets'ka cherez peresliduvannia pereïkhaly na L'vivshchynu. *Zakhid.net.* https://zaxid.net/zhurnalisti_z_donetska_cherez_peresliduvannya_pereyihali_na_lvivshhinu_n1308152

Parliamentary Assembly of the Council of Europe. (2023, April 27). The forcible transfer and 'russification' of Ukrainian children shows evidence of genocide, says PACE. *PACE.COE.int.* https://pace.coe.int/en/news/9075/the-forcible-transfer-and-russification-of-ukrainian-children-shows-evidence-of-genocide-says-pace

Pauly, M. D. (2014). *Breaking the Tongue: Language, Education, and Power in Soviet Ukraine, 1923–1934.* University of Toronto Press.

Peremitin, G. (2014, May 15). V Luganskoi i Donetskoi oblastiakh podveli itogi referenduma. *RBC.ru.* https://web.archive.org/web/20140515002538/http://top.rbc.ru/politics/12/05/2014/923136.shtml

Perlez, J. (1997, November 17). Hungarians approve NATO membership. *New York Times.* www.nytimes.com/1997/11/17/world/hungarians-approve-nato-membership.html

Pervyi Kanal. (2014, August 6). Stalo izvestno, chto nashelsia korrespondent Kievskogo telekanala '112-Ukraina' Roman Gnatiuk. *1tv.ru.* www.1tv.ru/news/2014-08-06/38916-stalo_izvestno_chto_nashelsya_korrespondent_kievskogo_telekanala_112_ukraina_roman_gnatyuk

Pirie, P. S. (1996). National identity and politics in southern and eastern Ukraine. *Europe–Asia Studies*, *48*(7), 1079–1104.

Plokhy, S. (2014). *The Last Empire: The Final Days of the Soviet Union.* Basic Books.

Plokhy, S. (2015). *The Gates of Europe: A History of Ukraine.* Penguin Random House.

Plokhy, S. (2019). *Chernobyl: History of a Tragedy.* Penguin Books.

Plokhy, S. (2023). *The Russo–Ukrainian War.* Penguin Books.

Podrobnosti. (2014a, April 28). Propavshii v Slavianske zhurnalist Sergei Shapoval vyshel na sviaz'. *Podrobnosti.ua.* https://podrobnosti.ua/973533-propavshij-v-slavjanske-zhurnalist-sergej-shapoval-vyshel-na-svjaz.html

Podrobnosti. (2014b, May 6). V Kramatorske prekrashchaiut vypusk gazet. *Podrobnosti.ua.* http://podrobnosti.ua/974644-v-kramatorske-prekraschajut-vypusk-gazet.html

Podrobnosti. (2014c, May 19). Zhurnalist s Volyni Sergei Shapoval osvobozhden iz plena v Donetske. *Podrobnosti.ua.* https://podrobnosti.ua/976616-zhurnalist-s-volyni-sergej-shapoval-osvobozhden-iz-plena-v-donetske.html

Podrobnosti. (2014d, May 22). Pokhishchennykh rabotnikov donetskoi tipografii vyvezli v Lugansk. *Podrobnosti.ua.* http://podrobnosti.ua/977184-pohischennyh-rabotnikov-donetskoj-tipografii-vyvezli-v-lugansk.html

Podrobnosti. (2014e, July 27). Terorysty vidpustyly donets'koho zhurnalista Antona Skybu (video). *Podrobnosti.ua*. http://podrobnosti.ua/986462-teroristi-vdpustili-donetskogo-zhurnalsta-antona-skibu-vdeo.html

Pogukai, T. (2014, July 16). Post. *Facebook.com*. www.facebook.com/csomvd/posts/568981056543545

Politrada. (2019). Purgin, Andrei Ievgen'evich. *Politrada.com*. http://politrada.com/dossier/Andrey-Evgenevich-Purgin/

Pop-Eleches, G., & Robertson, G. B. (2018). Identity and political preferences in Ukraine – Before and after the Euromaidan. *Post-Soviet Affairs, 34*(1–2), 107–118. https://doi.org/10.1080/1060586X.2018.1452181

Poroshenko, P. (2014). UKAZ PREZIDENTA UKRAÏNY No. 806/2014: Pro Den' zakhisnika Ukraïny. www.president.gov.ua/documents/8062014-17816

Porter, D. (2017). Sport and National Identity. In R. Edelman & W. Wilson (eds.), *The Oxford Handbook of Sports History* (pp. 477–486). Oxford University Press. www.oxfordhandbooks.com/view/10.1093/oxfordhb/9780199858910.001.0001/oxfordhb-9780199858910-e-33

Prestupnosti.net. (2014a, May 6). Separatist Tsarev dlia rossiiskikh SMI fantaziruet, chto Nikolaevshchina voidet v 'respubliku Novorossiia'. *News.pn*. https://news.pn/ru/criminal/103461

Prestupnosti.net. (2014b, November 30). V Slavianske naiden ubitym glavred donetskogo izdaniia —SMI. *News.pn*. https://news.pn/ru/criminal/119779

Prigodich, N. (2015, February 20). Glavnyi redaktor gazety 'Donbass' Aleksandr Brizh: 'Iz redaktsii menya vyveli pod dulom avtomata'. *Tut.by*. https://news.tut.by/society/436459.html?crnd=4043

Pro Gorod. (2014). Na sleduiushchii den' posle pogroma v redaktsii gazety 'Gorniak' g. Torez. Video. *YouTube.com*. www.youtube.com/watch?v=dOYrAp7DuuA

PRportal. (2014). Boeviki 'LNR' i mediaprostranstvo Luganshchiny. *PRportal.com.ua*. https://prportal.com.ua/Peredovitsa/boeviki-lnr-i-mediaprostranstvo-luganshchiny

Pushilin, D. (2017, July 18). Zaiavlenie Denisa Pushilina o sozdanii gosudarstva Malorossiia. *Denis-Pushilin.ru*. https://denis-pushilin.ru/news/zayavlenie-denisa-pushilina-o-sozdanii-gosudarstva-malorossiya/

Putin, V. (2022). Address by the president of the Russian Federation. *En.Kremlin.ru*. http://en.kremlin.ru/events/president/news/67843

Pyrlik, H. (2014, March 24). Napadenie na zhurnalistsa i militseiskaia proverka. Itogi mitingov v Khar'kove. *Mediaport.ua*. www.mediaport.ua/napadenie-na-zhurnalista-i-milietseyskaya-proverka-itogi-mitingov-v-harkove

Radio Maksimum. (2014, December 9). 'DNR' zobov'iazaly vsi ZMI, vkliuchaiuchy bloheriv, prokhodyty reestratsiiu. *Maximum.fm*. https://maximum.fm/dnr-zobovyazali-vsi-zmi-vklyuchayuchi-blogeriv-prohoditi-reyestraciyu_n72227

Radio Svoboda. (2014a, March 2). U Donets'ku na korespondenta Radio Svoboda skoieno napad. *Radiosvoboda.org*. www.radiosvoboda.org/a/25282589.html

Radio Svoboda. (2014b, March 10). Nevidomi ne puskali zhurnalistiv na preskonferentsiiu Klichka u Kharkovi. *Radiosvoboda.org*. www.radiosvoboda.org/a/25291674.html

Radio Svoboda. (2014c, March 10). U Luhans'ku z mitingu vyhnaly zhurnalistiv. *Radiosvoboda.org.* www.radiosvoboda.org/a/25291756.html

Radio Svoboda. (2014d, July 4). Boiovyky zakhopyly Luhans'ku teleradiokompaniiu. *Radiosvoboda.org.* www.radiosvoboda.org/a/25445970.html

Radio Svoboda. (2016, May 11). V OBSE zanepokoeni opryliudnenniam personal'-nykh danykh zhurnalistiv saitom 'Myrotvorets". *Radiosvoboda.org.* www.radiosvoboda.org/a/news/27728717.html

Radio Svoboda. (2017a, June 11). SBU podtverdila: V Donetske ischez zhurnalist Aseev (Vasin). *Svoboda.org.* www.svoboda.org/a/28540720.html

Radio Svoboda. (2017b, December 4). Pomsta za pravdu. Serbs'kii boiovyk pohrozhue zhurnalistam Radio Svoboda. *Radiosvoboda.org.* www.radiosvoboda.org/a/28892399.html

Rebrova, Li. (2014, August 17). 'LNR-TV': Chto pokazyvaiut golubye ekrany 'respubliki'? *Informator.Media.* http://informator.media/archives/171483

Respubliki, S. M. L. N. (2016, June 19). O vnesenii izmenenii v proekt Programmy sotsial'no-ekonomicheskogo razvitiia Luganskoi Narodnoi Respubliki na 2016 god. *Sovminlnr.ru.*

Reuters. (2014, May 25). Italian journalist and Russian colleague reported killed in Ukraine. *Reuters.com.* www.reuters.com/article/us-ukraine-crisis-journalist/italian-journalist-believed-killed-near-slaviansk-ukraine-idUSBREA4O03L20140525

RFE/RL. (2014). Separatists declare 'People's Republic' in Ukraine's Luhansk. *RFERL.org.* www.rferl.org/a/separatists-declare-luhansk-peoples-republic/25364894.html

RIA Novosti. (2014, August 27). Prichinoi zaderzhaniia krymskikh zhurnalistov stali foto marsha plennykh. *RIA.ru.* https://ria.ru/world/20140827/1021565716.html

RIA Novosti. (2015a, March 12). Vlasti LNR ogranichili transliatsiiu 23 ukrainskikh telekanalov i 'Dozhdia'. *RIA.ru.* https://ria.ru/world/20150312/1052149708.html

RIA Novosti. (2015b, July 31). Minister sviazi LNR: v respublike budet svoi mobil'nyi operator. *RIA.ru.* https://ria.ru/world/20150731/1155824498.html

RIA Novosti. (2016, September 10). V DNR zaiavili o podgotovke ukrainskikh diversantov pod vidom zhurnalistov. *RIA.ru.* https://ria.ru/world/20160910/1476593941.html

RIA Novosti Ukraina. (2014, September 26). V Luganske osvobozhden zhurnalist ALeksandr Belokobyl'skii. *RIAN.com.ua.* https://rian.com.ua/politics/20140926/357555429.html

Rodina. (2015a, August 7). Khartsyzsk: Operativno. *Rodina.* http://gazeta-dnr.ru//?p=809

Rodina. (2015b, August 21). Khartsyzsk: Operativno (nomer za 20–26 avgusta). *Rodina.* http://gazeta-dnr.ru//?p=2011

Rodina. (2015c, December 21). Novosti. *Rodina.* http://gazeta-dnr.ru//?p=15422

Rodnoe Priazov'e. (2015, August 5). Za lozhnyi vyzov – Pridetsia otvechat'. *Rodnoe Priazov'e.* http://gazeta-dnr.ru//?p=445

Romanyshyn, Y. (2017, February 3). UK photographer's eyes injured in mortar attack in Avdiyivka. *Kyiv Post.* www.kyivpost.com/ukraine-politics/uk-photographers-eyes-injured-mortar-attack-adviyivka.html

Romein, D. (2016, February 23). MH17: Potential suspects and witnesses from the 53rd Anti-Aircraft Missile Brigade. *Bellingcat.com.* www.bellingcat.com/news/uk-and-europe/2016/02/23/53rd-report-en/

Ronzheimer, P. (2014, May 12). Wahlbetrug in der Ukraine. *Bild.de.* www.bild.de/video/clip/wahlfaelschung/wahlbetrug-ukraine-35928762.bild.html

Roozenbeek, J. (2020a). Identity discourse in local newspapers before, during and after military conflict: A case study of Kramatorsk. *Demokratizatsiya: The Journal of Post-Soviet Democratization, 28*(3), 419–459.

Roozenbeek, J. (2020b). Media and identity in wartime Donbas, 2014–2017. PhD dissertation, University of Cambridge.

Roozenbeek, J. (2022). The failure of Russian propaganda. *Cam.ac.uk.* www.cam.ac.uk/stories/donbaspropaganda

Roozenbeek, J., & van der Linden, S. (2024). *The Psychology of Misinformation.* Cambridge University Press.

Rosbalt. (2014, May 21). V 'Luganskoi narodnoi respublike' poiavilsia ministr oborony. *Rosbalt.ru.* www.rosbalt.ru/world/2014/05/21/1271079.html

RTÉ News. (2022). Elderly Ukrainian woman berates occupying Russian soldiers. Video. *YouTube.com.* www.youtube.com/watch?v=oQFGwkOWtKo

Rudin, M. (2016, April 25). Conspiracy files: Who shot down MH17? *BBC News.* www.bbc.co.uk/news/magazine-35706048

Russkaia Vesna. (2015, February 6). DNR ob'iavila o preemstvennosti k Donetskoi Respublike, provozglashennoi v 1917 godu. *Rusvesna.su.* https://rusvesna.su/news/1423248170

Russnov.ru. (2014, May 30). Press-konferentsiia V.D. Bolotova 30.05.2014. *Rusnov.ru.* http://russnov.ru/press-konferenciya-v-d-bolotova-30-05-2014/

Sabera, I. (2016, February 22). The struggle of displaced journalists in Ukraine. *Open Society Foundations.* www.opensocietyfoundations.org/voices/struggle-displaced-journalists-ukraine

Sakwa, R. (2015a). *Frontline Ukraine: Crisis in the Borderlands.* I. B. Tauris.

Sakwa, R. (2015b). Monism vs. pluralism. *E-International Relations.* www.e-ir.info/2015/05/21/monism-vs-pluralism/

Salem, H. (2014, May 11). Eastern Ukrainians vote for a new uncertain future in rebel organized referendum. *Vice News.* https://news.vice.com/en_us/article/9kvgm8/eastern-ukrainians-vote-for-a-new-uncertain-future-in-rebel-organized-referendum

Salhani, C. (2006). Media in conflict: Inciting violence in Kosovo. *Georgetown Journal of International Affairs, 7*(1), 33–39.

Sampson, P. (2022, March 14). Acclaimed filmmaker Brent Renaud shot, killed in Ukraine. *AP News.* https://apnews.com/article/brent-renaud-obituary-russia-ukraine-bd0aa404e1b64dbdc464b6660fd280af

Sarotte, M. E. (2022). *Not One Inch: America, Russia, and the Making of Post–Cold War Stalemate.* Yale University Press.

Sasse, G., & Lackner, A. (2018). War and identity: The case of the Donbas in Ukraine. *Post-Soviet Affairs, 34*(2–3), 139–157. https://doi.org/10.1080/1060586X.2018.1452209

Sasse, G., & Lackner, A. (2019). Attitudes and identities across the Donbas front line: What has changed from 2016 to 2019? *Zentrum für Osteuropa- und*

internationale   Studien.   www.zois-berlin.de/publikationen/attitudes-and-iden
tities-across-the-donbas-front-line-what-has-changed-from-2016-to-2019

Savranskaya, S., & Blanton, T. (2017, December 12). NATO expansion: What
Gorbachev heard. *National Security Archive.* https://nsarchive.gwu.edu/briefing-
book/russia-programs/2017-12-12/nato-expansion-what-gorbachev-heard-west
ern-leaders-early

Segodnia.ua. (2014, July 16). V Donetske i okrestnostiakh otkliucheny pochti vse ukrainskie telekanaly. *Segodnya.ua.* www.segodnya.ua/regions/donetsk/v-donecke-i-okrest
nostyah-otklyucheny-pochti-vse-ukrainskie-telekanaly–537269.html

Segodnia.ua. (2017, July 19). V Donetske ischezli telekanaly boevikov. *Segodnya.ua.*
www.segodnya.ua/regions/donetsk/v-donecke-ischezli-telekanaly-boevikov-
1039606.html

Segodnya.ua. (2014a, May 22). Boeviki 'DNR' ugrozhaiut zhurnalistam 'Segodnia' v
Donetske. *Segodnya.ua.* www.segodnya.ua/regions/donetsk/boeviki-dnr-ugroz
hayut-sotrudnikam-segodnya-v-donecke-522292.html

Segodnya.ua. (2014b, May 25). V Donetske vooruzhennye liudy zakhvatili telekanal.
Segodnya.ua.   www.segodnya.ua/regions/donetsk/v-donecke-vooruzhennye-
lyudi-zahvatili-telekanal–523036.html

Semiryad, N. Y., & Voskoboinikov, S. G. (2019). The history of Donetsk-Krivoy Rog
Republic. *сборник научных статей 4-й Международной научной
конференции перспективных разработок молодых ученых.* https://elibrary
.ru/item.asp?id=41588436

Seneghini, F. (2014, May 24). Ucraina, morto Andy Rocchelli. Arriva la conferma
della Farnesina. *Corriere della Serra.* www.corriere.it/esteri/14_maggio_24/
ucraina-giornalista-italiano-ucciso-villaggio-donetsk-ac190120-e378-11e3-a0b2-
0f0bd7a1f5dc.shtml

Shandra, A. (2016, May 8). 'DNR's' propaganda apparatus exposed. Part 1:
'Russophobe, get him out of Donetsk'. *Euromaidanpress.com.* http://
euromaidanpress.com/2016/08/05/hack-reveals-how-dnr-denied-accreditation-
to-disloyal-journalists/

Shao, C., Ciampaglia, G. L., Flammini, A., & Menczer, F. (2017). The spread of fake
news by social bots. *CoRR, abs/1707.0.* http://arxiv.org/abs/1707.07592

Shaposhnikov, R. (2014, September 2). Post. *Facebook.com.* www.facebook.com/
roadcontrol.ua/posts/697462290333542

Shevel, O. (2015). The parliamentary elections in Ukraine, October 2014. *Electoral
Studies, 39,* 153–177.

Shkiriak, Z. (2016, January 23). Post. *Facebook.com.* www.facebook.com/zoryan
.zoryan/posts/1017773344950279?pnref=story

Shtal', A. (2014, May 5). V Kramatorske perestaiut vykhodit' gazety.
Kramatorskaia Pravda. http://krampravda.dn.ua/index.php?option=com_con
tent&view=category&id=1&layout=blog&limitstart=1070

Sidel'nikova, M. (2014, October 16). Uchashchiesia Kramatorskoi Ukrainskoi
Gimnazii ugoshchali soldat medom i varen'em. *Tehnopolis.com.ua.* https://
tehnopolis.com.ua/index.php?option=com_content&view=article&id=
10052:2014-10-16-08-41-18&catid=59:2011-01-11-21-18-52&Itemid=15

Sidorenko, L. (2011, October 19). Kramatorskie Kazaki otmetili praznik Pokrova. *Tehnopolis.* https://tehnopolis.com.ua/index.php?option=com_content&view=art icle&id=1574:2011-10-25-08-55-20&catid=59:2011-01-11-21-18-52&Itemid=15

Sidorenko, L. (2014, April 14). V Slavianske zaderzhan paren', kotoryi snimal shturm SBU. *Kp.ua.* https://kp.ua/politics/448304-v-slavianske-zaderzhan-paren-kotoryi-snymal-shturm-sbu

Simon'ian, M. (2014, May 9). Post. *Twitter.com.* https://twitter.com/M_Simonyan/status/464705734333440000

Sindelar, D. (2015, May 21). Out with a whimper: Novorossia, 2014–2015. *RFE/RL.* www.rferl.org/a/death-of-novorossia/27029267.html

Singh, S. V. (2019). Topic extraction with non-negative matrix factorization and latent Dirichlet allocation. *Github.com.* https://github.com/scikit-learn/scikit-learn/blob/master/examples/applications/plot_topics_extraction_with_nmf_lda.py

S.L. (1951). Soviet coal production since the war. *The World Today, 7*(12), 518–528.

Smith, A. (2016, September 25). Jeff Monson, former UFC fighter, is first American 'citizen' of Ukraine's rebel Luhansk state. *NBC News.* www.nbcnews.com/news/world/jeff-monson-former-ufc-fighter-first-american-citizen-ukraine-s-n653126

Smith, B. L. (2023). Propaganda. In *Encyclopaedia Brittanica.* www.britannica.com/topic/propaganda

Snezhnianskie Novosti. (2015a, September 25). Vsemirnyi den' bor'by s beshenstvom. Beshenstvo! Chto nuzhno znat'? *Snezhnianskie Novosti.* http://gazeta-dnr.ru//?p=4822

Snezhnianskie Novosti. (2015b, November 26). Glava DNR ob otmene v ukrainskom pasporte russkogo iazyka. *Snezhnianskie Novosti.* http://gazeta-dnr.ru//?p=11849

Snyder, T. (2010). *Bloodlands: Europe between Hitler and Stalin.* Vintage.

Sokol, S. (2015, June 22). Top rebel leader accuses Jews of masterminding Ukrainian revolution. *Jerusalem Post.* www.jpost.com/Diaspora/Top-rebel-leader-accuses-Jews-of-masterminding-Ukrainian-revolution-406729

Sovet Ministrov Donetskoi Narodnoi Respubliki. (2017, March 10). O sozdanii Gosudarstvennogo Predpriiatiia 'Respublikanskii Media kholding'. *Doc. Minsvyazdnr.ru.* https://doc.minsvyazdnr.ru/docs/o-sozdanii-gosudarstvennogo-predpriyatiya-respublikanskiy-media-holding

Spravochnik DNR. (2019a). Novaia Zhizn' (Starobeshevo). *Spravochnik.Vsednr.ru.* http://spravochnik.vsednr.ru/spr/novaya-zhizn/

Spravochnik DNR. (2019b). Novye gorizonty (Kirovskoe). *Spravochnik.Vsednr.ru.* http://spravochnik.vsednr.ru/spr/novye-gorizonty/

Spravochnik DNR. (2019c). Novyi Luch (Amvrosievskii raion). *Spravochnik.Vsednr. ru.* http://spravochnik.vsednr.ru/spr/novyj-luch/

Spravochnik DNR. (2019d). Rodina (Khartsyzsk). *Spravochnik.Vsednr.ru.* http://spravochnik.vsednr.ru/spr/rodina/

Spravochnik DNR. (2019e). Snezhianskie novosti. *Spravochnik.Vsednr.ru.* http://spravochnik.vsednr.ru/spr/snezhnyanskie-novosti/

Spravochnik DNR. (2019f). Znamia Pobedy (Shakhtersk). *Spravochnik.Vsednr.ru.* http://spravochnik.vsednr.ru/spr/znamya-pobedy/

Stadnichenko, O. (2014a, August 3). Kak DNR 'Dogovarivalas''s ATP o snizhenii tarifa. *Tehnopolis.com.ua.* https://tehnopolis.com.ua/index.php?option=com_con tent&view=article&id=8124:-lr-&catid=59:2011-01-11-21-18-52&Itemid=15

Stadnichenko, O. (2014b, September 14). V Kramatorske vo vremia veche ozvuchili protest i nedoverie (video). *Tehnopolis.com.ua.* https://tehnopolis.com.ua/index .php?option=com_content&view=article&id=9197:2014-09-14-06-07-16&catid= 59:2011-01-11-21-18-52&Itemid=15

Stadnichenko, O. (2014c, September 27). Kramatorsk otmechaet svoe 146-letie (foto). *Tehnopolis.com.ua.* https://tehnopolis.com.ua/index.php?option=com_content& view=article&id=9550:—146-&catid=59:2011-01-11-21-18-52&Itemid=15

Statista. (2023, April). Do you support Poland's NATO membership? www.statista .com/statistics/1125292/poland-attitude-towards-nato/

Stepanova, A. (2014a, April 17). Kak proshla spetsoperatsiia po osvobozhdeniiu aero-droma v Kramatorske. *Novosti Kramatorska.* https://hi.dn.ua/index.php?option= com_content&view=article&id=45931&catid=55:kramatorsk&Itemid=147

Stepanova, A. (2014b, April 22). Zhurnalist 'NK' pobyval na KPP kramatorskogo aerodroma (FOTO). *Novosti Kramatorska.* https://hi.dn.ua/index.php?option= com_content&view=article&id=46131&catid=55:kramatorsk&Itemid=147

StopFake. (2017). Time for the ninth MH17 disinformation round. *StopFake.org.* www.stopfake.org/en/time-for-the-ninth-mh17-disinformation-round/

Strelkov, I. I. (2014, July 17). Vkontakte post. *vk.com.* https://web.archive.org/web/ 20140717155720/https://vk.com/wall-57424472_7256

Suprycheva, E. (2014, April 22). Korrespondent 'KP' dvoe sutok provela v plenu v Slavianske [foto]. *Komsomol'skaia Pravda.* https://kp.ua/politics/449329-korre spondent-kp-dvoe-sutok-provela-v-slavianske

Suslov, M. (2017). The production of 'Novorossiya': A territorial brand in public debates. *Europe–Asia Studies, 69*(2), 202–221. https://doi.org/10.1080/09668136 .2017.1285009

Svetikov, A. (2015, June 16). V 'LNR' startoval chempionat po futbolu. S uchastiem . . . 'Zari'. *Segodnia v Severodonetske.* http://svsever.lg.ua/2015/06/v_lnr_startoval_ chempionat_po_futbolu._s_uchastiem. . ._zari_

Sxid.info. (2014, May 1). V Luganske na chastote 'Pervogo natsional'nogo' teper' transliruiut kanal 'Rossiia 24'. *Sxid.com.* http://cxid.info/v-luganske-na-chas tote-laquo-pervogo-nacionalnogo-raquo-teper-transliruut-kanal-laquo-rossiya- 24-raquo-n114031

Sydney Morning Herald. (2015, April 17). Ukraine journalist Oles Buzina killed by masked gunmen in Kiev —Interior ministry. *SMH.com.au.* www.smh.com.au/ world/ukraine-journalist-oles-buzina-killed-by-masked-gunmen-in-kiev-inter ior-ministry-20150416-1mmvgl.html

Szostek, J. (2017). The power and limits of Russia's strategic narrative in Ukraine: The role of linkage. *Perspectives on Politics, 15*(2), 379–395. https://doi.org/10.1017/ S153759271700007X

Tajfel, H. (1982). Social psychology of intergroup relations. *Annual Review of Psychology, 33*(1), 1–39.

Taninecz Miller, D. (2019). Topics and emotions in Russian Twitter propaganda. *First Monday, 24*(5). https://doi.org/10.5210/fm.v24i5.9638

Taras, R., FIlippova, O., & Pobeda, N. (2004). Ukraine's transnationals, far-away locals and xenophobes: The prospects for Europeanness. *Europe–Asia Studies, 56*(6), 835–856.

Taylor, A. (2014, May 8). Meet the 'nobodies' who said no to Putin. *Washington Post.* www.washingtonpost.com/news/worldviews/wp/2014/05/08/meet-the-nobodies-who-said-no-to-putin/?noredirect=on

Tehnopolis. (2013a, September 4). Kaban'ia korrida otmeniaetsia! *Tehnopolis.com.ua.* https://tehnopolis.com.ua/index.php?option=com_content&view=article&id=4579:2013-09-09-203606&catid=59:2011-01-11-21-18-52&Itemid=15

Tehnopolis. (2013b, December 2). Kramatorchane i Vseukrainskaia Aktsiia Protesta. *Tehnopolis.com.ua.* https://tehnopolis.com.ua/index.php?option=com_content&view=article&id=4989:2013-12-02-141513&catid=59:2011-01-11-21-18-52&Itemid=15

Tehnopolis. (2014, September 17). SBU obrashchaetsia k Kramatorchanam. *Tehnopolis.com.ua.* https://tehnopolis.com.ua/index.php?option=com_content&view=article&id=9277:2014-09-17-13-00-56&catid=59:2011-01-11-21-18-52&Itemid=15

Telebachennia KAPRI. (2014, February 8). Soversheno napadenie na zdanie Televideniia 'Kapri'. Donetskaia oblast'. Video. *YouTube.com.* www.youtube.com/watch?v=PomalZBsYxE

Telegraf.by. (2014, March 2). Mitingi v Donetske: Palatochnyi gorodok 'za Rossiiu' i izbitye zhurnalisty. *Telegraf.by.* https://telegraf.by/2014/03/mitingi-v-donecke-palatochnii-gorodok-za-rossiyu-i-izbitie-jurnalisti

Telekanal Iunion. (2017, March 10). Fond 'Edinyi Donbass' nachal rabotu v DNR. *Tk-Union.tv.* http://tk-union.tv/fond-«edinyij-donbass»-nachal-rabotu-v-dnr.-10.03.2017-8486.html

Telekanal LOT. (2014, March 10). Bez kupiur. Zakhvat telekanala 'IRTA'. Video. *YouTube.com.* www.youtube.com/watch?v=SNafXk-03y8

Telekanal 'Oplot TV'. (2016, October 25). Programma 'Kstati': Pochetnyi konsul DNR v Chekhii Nela Liskova. Video. *YouTube.com.* www.youtube.com/watch?v=2IACp2SUA6A

Telekrytyka. (2015, April 16). Zhurnalista Serhiia Sukhoboka po-zviriachomu vbyly v Kyevi. Proshchannia —17 kvitnia. *Telekritika.ua.* https://web.archive.org/web/20150417184214/www.telekritika.ua/profesija/2015-04-16/106121

Tolz, V., & Teper, Y. (2018). Broadcasting agitainment: A new media strategy of Putin's third presidency. *Post-Soviet Affairs, 34*(4), 213–227. https://doi.org/10.1080/1060586X.2018.1459023

Torezskii Gorniak. (2016, April 4). Predstaviteli Rossiiskoi Federatsii vruchili nagradu kollektivu Donetskoi muzdramy. *Torezskii Gorniak.* http://gazeta-dnr.ru//?p=27225

Tsenzor.net. (2014, October 2). Terroristy v Donetske zapustili v efir svoi amatorskii telekanal. *Censor.net.ua.* https://censor.net.ua/news/305286/terroristy_v_donetske_zapustili_v_efir_svoyi_amatorskiyi_telekanal

TSN Ukraina. (2014a, March 6). Prorosiis'ki aktyvisty syloiu zakhopyly teleradiokompaniiu 'Donbas'. *Tsn.ua.* https://tsn.ua/ukrayina/prorosiyski-aktivisti-siloyu-zahopili-teleradiokompaniyu-donbas-338303.html

TSN Ukraina. (2014b, April 24). Pid chas zbil'nennia zakhoplenoï mis'krady mariupolia postrazhdalo p'iatero liudei. *Tsn.ua.* https://tsn.ua/politika/pid-chas-zvilnen nya-zahoplenoyi-miskradi-mariupolya-postrazhdalo-p-yatero-lyudey-346781 .html

TSN Ukraina. (2014c, April 24). Pid chas zvil'nennia zakhoplenoï mis'krady mariupolia postrazhdalo p'iatero liudei. *Tsn.ua.* https://tsn.ua/politika/pid-chas-zvilnen nya-zahoplenoyi-miskradi-mariupolya-postrazhdalo-p-yatero-lyudey-346781 .html

TSN Ukraina. (2014d, July 10). Znimal'na hrupa '1+1' potrapyla pid obstril poblyzu Sivers'ka. *Tsn.ua.* https://tsn.ua/ukrayina/znimalna-grupa-1-1-potrapila-pid-obstril-poblizu-siverska-358552.html

Tulul, M. (2017, December 8). Beyond the scandal: What is Ukraine's new education law really about? *Opendemocracy.net.* www.opendemocracy.net/en/odr/ukraines-new-education-law/

Tymchuk, D. (2014, May 19). Post. *Facebook.com.* www.facebook.com/dmitry .tymchuk/posts/499841370144523

Ukraine News One Russian. (2014, May 16). Lanet otkliuchil ukrainskie kanaly v Severodonetske. Video. *YouTube.com.* www.youtube.com/watch?v=lXAJ-bzq8ZI

Ukraïns'ka Pravda. (2014a, March 16). Kharkivs' ki separatysty poprosyly Rosiiu vvesty myrotvorchi viis'ka. *Pravda.com.ua.* www.pravda.com.ua/news/2014/03/ 16/7019051/

Ukraïns'ka Pravda. (2014b, April 12). U Slov'ians'ku kryms'ki 'zeleni cholovichky' zakhopyly zhurnalistiv i zaboronyly pratsiuvaty. *Pravda.com.ua.* www.pravda .com.ua/news/2014/04/12/7022202/

Ukraïns'ka Pravda. (2014c, November 3). Donets'ki boiovyky za nich porakhuvaly holosy: 'peremih' Zakharchenko. *Ukraïns'ka Pravda.* www.pravda.com.ua/news/ 2014/11/3/7043027/

Ukrainska Pravda. (2021, December 9). Italiiis'kyi sud ostatochno vypravdav natsh-vardiitsia Markiva. www.pravda.com.ua/news/2021/12/9/7316860/

Ukraïns'ki Novyny. (2014, May 12). Neizvestnye otkliuchili 'Radio-Era FM' v Donetske. *Ukranews.com.* https://ukranews.com/news/245386-neyzvestnye-otk lyuchyly-radyo-ehra-fm-v-donecke

Ukrinform. (2022, April 1). Documentary photographer, photojournalist Maks Levin found dead in Kyiv region. www.ukrinform.net/rubric-ato/3446547-documen tary-photographer-photojournalist-maks-levin-found-dead-in-kyiv-region.html

Umland, A. (2019). Irregular militias and radical nationalism in post-Euromaydan Ukraine: The prehistory and emergence of the 'Azov' battalion in 2014. *Terrorism and Political Violence,* *31*(1), 105–131. https://doi.org/10.1080/ 09546553.2018.1555974

UNHCR. (2018, September 11). New hope for pensioners struggling to survive in Ukraine. *UNHCR.org.* www.unhcr.org/news/latest/2018/9/5b97bf004/new-hope-pensioners-struggling-survive-ukraine.html

UNIAN. (2017a, July 4). Amnesty International vysunula vymohy boiovykam 'DNR' shchodo znyknennia u Donets'ku zhurnalista Aseeva. *UNIAN.ua.* www.unian.ua/ society/2010796-amnesty-international-visunula-vimogi-boyovikam-dnr-schodo-zniknennya-u-donetsku-jurnalista-aseeva.html

UNIAN. (2017b, July 18). SMI uznali, byl li Kreml' v kurse bredovoi idei Zakharchenko o 'Malorossii'. *UNIAN.net*. www.unian.net/politics/2035014-smi-uznali-byil-li-kreml-v-kurse-bredovoy-idei-zaharchenko-o-malorossii.html

United Nations. (1994, December 21). Conference on disarmament. *CD/1285*. https://documents-dds-ny.un.org/doc/UNDOC/GEN/G94/652/92/PDF/G9465292.pdf?OpenElement

Upolnomochennyi po pravam cheloveka v Rossiiskoi Federatsii. (2014, May 30). Spisok narushenii prav sotrudnikov SMI na territorii Ukrainy. *Ombudsmanrf.org*. http://old.ombudsmanrf.org/component/content/article/87-внимание/7396-нарушения-прав-журналистов-на-территории-украины

URA-Inform. (2014, May 24). DNR i LNR ob'edinilis' v Novorossiiu. *Ura.dn.ua*. http://ura.dn.ua/24.05.2014/156849.html

URA-Inform.Donbass. (2014a, June 17). Zhurnalista 'URA-Inform.Donbass' uderzhivaiut v zdanii zakhvachennoi prokuratury Donetska. *Ura.dn.ua*. http://ura.dn.ua/17.06.2014/157930.html

URA-Inform.Donbass. (2014b, November 30). 'URA-Inform.Donbass' vremenno priostanavlivaet svoiu rabotu. *Ura.dn.ua*. http://ura.dn.ua/30.11.2014/164108.html

US Department of State. (2006). Letter from Boris N. Yeltsin to William J. Clinton, September 15, 1993. *National Security Archive*. https://nsarchive.gwu.edu/document/16376-document-04-retranslation-yeltsin-letter

V Makeevke – VMakeevke.com. (2014, May 22). Pavel Gubarev v Donetske vystupil na s'ezde partii 'Novorossiia'. Video. *YouTube.com*. www.youtube.com/watch?v=HAP18RkP-5U&feature=youtu.be

Vaganov, S. (2014, February 21). Bditel'nyi donchanin u OGA. Video. *YouTube.com*. www.youtube.com/watch?v=BGs-RFJPAJM&feature=youtu.be

Vatnik, Z. (2017, July 18). Viacheslav Gubin: Ob'iavlenie o sozdanii gosudarstva Malorossiia 18 07 17 Aktual'n. Video. *YouTube.com*. www.youtube.com/watch?v=zojIQPL3MHA

Vechernii Donetsk. (2014, June 26). Respubliki ob'edinilis'. 'Dolzhnost' prezidenta ne predusmotrena'. *Vecherka.Donetsk.ua*. https://web.archive.org/web/20150301000000*/http://vecherka.donetsk.ua/index.php?id=4647&show=news&newsid=107644#.W2RF_NJKhPY

Venice Commission. (2017). *Ukraine – Opinion on the Provisions of the Law on Education of 5 September 2017, Which Concern the Use of the State Language and Minority and Other Languages in Education, Adopted by the Commission at Its 113th Plenary Session (Venice, 8–9 December 2017)*. Council of Europe.

Verkhovna Rada Ukraïny. (2015, January 27). Proekte Postanovy pro tymchasove pryzupynennia akredytatsiï zhurnalistiv ta tekhnichnykh pracsivnykiv deiakykh zasobiv masovoï iinformatsiï Rosiis'koï Federatsiï pry orhanakh derzhavnoï vlady Ukraïny. *W1.C1.Rada.gov.ua*. http://w1.c1.rada.gov.ua/pls/zweb2/webproc4_2?id=&pf3516=1853&skl=9

Vetrova, M. (2017, July 22). Masterstvo perevoploshcheniia. *Novorossia*. http://novopressa.ru/articles-535.html

Vlasenko, A. (2016, October 5). 'My zhili kak v okkupatsii'. Zhurnalist s Donbassa izbezhal zastenok SBU. *Aif.ru*. www.aif.ru/society/people/my_zhili_kak_v_okkupacii_zhurnalist_s_donbassa_izbezhal_zastenok_sbu

Voigtländer, N., & Voth, H.-J. (2015). Nazi indoctrination and anti-Semitic beliefs in Germany. *Proceedings of the National Academy of Sciences, 112*(26), 7931–7936. https://doi.org/10.1073/pnas.1414822112

Volkov, D., & Kolesnikov, A. (2022). *My Country, Right or Wrong: Russian Public Opinion on Ukraine.* Carnegie Endowment for International Peace. https://carnegieendowment.org/2022/09/07/my-country-right-or-wrong-russian-public-opinion-on-ukraine-pub-87803

Von Twickel, N. (2017, July 24). Explaining the coup in Luhansk. *Open Democracy.* www.opendemocracy.net/en/odr/explaining-coup-in-luhansk/

Von Twickel, N. (2018, June 7). Russian puppet 'LNR' opens 'consulate' in Sicily and other overlooked stories from Donbas. *Euromaidan Press.* http://euromaidanpress.com/2018/07/06/zakharchenko-enhances-power-donetsk-uni-seeks-russian-accreditation-fake-lnr-consulate-in-eu/

Vremia Chitat'. (2019). Makeevskii Rabochii. *Время-Читать.Рф.* http://время-читать.рф/макеевский-рабочий-днр/

Vzgliad. (2014, July 4). Pravitel'stvo LNR otpravleno v otstavku. *Vz.ru.* https://vz.ru/news/2014/7/4/694120.html

Walker, S., & Grytsenko, O. (2015, January 21). Ukraine forces admit loss of Donetsk airport to rebels. *Guardian.* www.theguardian.com/world/2015/jan/21/russia-ukraine-war-fighting-east

Walker, S., Grytsenko, O., & Amos, H. (2014, May 12). Ukraine: pro-Russia separatists set for victory in eastern region referendum. The Guardian. www.theguardian.com/world/2014/may/11/eastern-ukraine-referendum-donetsk-luhansk

Waquet, A., & Vincent, J. (2011). Wartime rugby and football: Sports elites, French military teams and international meets during the First World War. *The International Journal of the History of Sport, 28*(3–4), 372–392.

Wikimedia. (2014a). Biulleten' referenduma Donetskoi Narodnoi Respubliki. *Wikimedia.org.* https://ru.wikipedia.org/wiki/Референдум_о_самоопределении_Донецкой_Народной_Республики#/media/Файл:Бюллетень_референдума_Донецкой_Народной_Республики_(2014).png

Wikimedia. (2014b). Biulleten' referenduma Luganskoi Narodnoi Respubliki. *Wikimedia.org.* https://upload.wikimedia.org/wikipedia/ru/f/fb/Бюллетень_референдума_Луганской_Народной_Республики_%282014%29.png

Wikimedia (2014). Flag of the Donetsk People's Republic. https://commons.wikimedia.org/wiki/File:Donetsk_People%27s_Republic_flag.png

Wikimedia (2017). Proposed flag of Malorossiia. https://en.wikipedia.org/wiki/File:Proposed_flag_of_Malorossiya.svg

Wikipedia. (2019). Provintsiia (gazeta). *Wikipedia.org.* https://ru.wikipedia.org/wiki/Провинция_(газета)

Wilson, A. (1995). The Donbas between Ukraine and Russia: The use of history in political disputes. *Journal of Contemporary History, 30*(2), 265–289. https://doi.org/10.1177/002200949503000204

Wilson, A. (1997). *Ukrainian Nationalism in the 1990s: A Minority Faith.* Cambridge University Press.

Wilson, A. (2005). *Ukraine's Orange Revolution.* Yale University Press.

Wilson, A. (2016). The Donbas in 2014: Explaining civil conflict perhaps, but not civil war. *Europe–Asia Studies*, *68*(4), 631–652. https://doi.org/10.1080/09668136.2016.1176994

Wilson, A. (2022). *The Ukrainians: The Story of How a People Became a Nation*. Yale University Press.

Xpress-Klub. (2016, May 12). Veteran prinimal pozdravleniia. *Xpress-Klub*. http://xpressclub.ru/news/page/273

Xpress-Klub. (2017, March 28). Pis'mo v nomer 'VSE DLIA FRONTA! VSE'. *Xpress-Klub*. http://xpressclub.ru/news/page/220

Xpress-Klub. (2019). 'Ekspress-klub' – Vash nadezhnyi partner v biznese! *Xpressclub.ru*. http://xpressclub.ru/about/paper/

XXI Vek. (2017a, March 28). Sinoptiki prognoziruiut 28 marta v LNR do 11 gradusov tepla, mestami dozhd' so snegom. *XXI Vek*. http://xxiveklnr.su/novosti/37-sinoptiki-prognoziruyut-28-marta-v-lnr-do-11-gradusov-tepla-mestami-dozhd-so-snegom.html

XXI Vek. (2017b, April 15). Boeviki razmestili na linii soprikosnoveniia tanki, RSZO 'Grad' i SAU. *XXI Vek*. http://xxiveklnr.su/novosti/528-boeviki-razmestili-na-linii-soprikosnoveniya-tanki-rszo-grad-i-sau.html

XXI Vek. (2017c, April 24). Deinego: Zasedanie podgruppy po bezopasnosti perenositsia iz-za podryva avtomobiliia OBSE. *XXI Vek*. http://xxiveklnr.su/novosti/669-deynego-zasedanie-podgruppy-po-bezopasnosti-perenositsya-iz-za-podryva-avtomobilya-obse.html

Yablokov, I. (2015). Conspiracy theories as a Russian public diplomacy tool: The case of Russia today (RT). *Politics*, *35*(3–4), 301–315. https://doi.org/10.1111/1467-9256.12097

Yadocent. (2014, September 3). Pravitel'stvo Luganskoi Narodnoi Respubliki. *Yadocent.Livejournal.com*. http://yadocent.livejournal.com/619501.html

Zhao, W. X., Jiang, J., Weng, J., He, J., Lim, E.-P., Yan, H., & Li, X. (2011). Comparing twitter and traditional media using topic models. *European Conference on Information Retrieval*, 338–349.

Zhurdom. (2014, June 27). DNR obiazala vse SMI na 10 dnei proiti pereregistratsiiu. *Jourdom.ru*. http://jourdom.ru/news/53300

Zhurzhenko, T. (2014). A divided nation? Reconsidering the role of identity politics in the Ukraine crisis. *Die Friedens-Warte*, *89*(1–2), 249–267.

ZIK. (2014, July 24). L'vivs'kyi zhurnalist Iurii Leliavs'kyi znovu potrapyv u polon. *Zik.ua*. https://zik.ua/news/2014/07/24/lvivskyy_zhurnalist_yuriy_lelyavskyy_znovu_potrapyv_u_polon_508678

Znamia Pobedy. (2015a, August 7). Ne zarasti travoi. *Znamia Pobedy*. http://gazeta-dnr.ru//?p=864

Znamia Pobedy. (2015b, August 7). Poluchit' professiiu, ne pokidaia gorod … *Znamia Pobedy*. http://gazeta-dnr.ru//?p=855

Znamia Pobedy. (2015c, August 7). 'Shakhterskaia-Glubokaia' – shakhta, bez kotoroi gorodu ne zhit'. *Znamia Pobedy*. http://gazeta-dnr.ru//?p=869

Znamia Pobedy. (2015d, August 21). Iz raznotsvet'ia bisera tvoriatsia chudesa. *Znamia Pobedy*. http://gazeta-dnr.ru//?p=1950

Znamia Pobedy. (2015e, August 31). Gran', cherez kotoruiu uzhe ne perestupit'. *Znamia Pobedy.* http://gazeta-dnr.ru//?p=2540

Znamia Pobedy. (2015f, August 31). Pozdravlenie Glavy DNR Aleksandra Zakharchenko. *Znamia Pobedy.* http://gazeta-dnr.ru//?p=2571

Znamia Pobedy. (2015g, September 4). Ocherednaia pobeda! *Znamia Pobedy.* http://gazeta-dnr.ru//?p=3011

Znamia Pobedy. (2015h, September 14). Pobezhdat' fashizm – U nas v krovi! *Znamia Pobedy.* http://gazeta-dnr.ru//?p=3792

Znamia Pobedy. (2015i, November 27). Chto luchshe – Dva ili odin? *Znamia Pobedy.* http://gazeta-dnr.ru//?p=12279

Zubach, N. (2016, July 20). Kurskaia zemlia kak ona est': Glazami delegatsii iz Donbassa. *Formator.Info.* http://formator.info/m_Article?id=21043&saved=1& m=yes

INDEX

For EU product safety concerns, contact us at Calle de José Abascal, 56–1°,
28003 Madrid, Spain or eugpsr@cambridge.org.

www.ingramcontent.com/pod-product-compliance
Ingram Content Group UK Ltd.
Pitfield, Milton Keynes, MK11 3LW, UK
UKHW020334150425
457198UK00019B/269

9 7 8 1 0 0 9 2 4 4 0 0 8